OZ: THE WONDERFUL WIZARD OF OZ. Contains material originally published in magazine form as THE WONDERFUL WIZARD OF OZ #1-8. Third printing 2009. ISBN# 978-0-7851-2921-9. Published by MARVEL PUBLISHING, INC., a subsidiary of MARVEL ENTERTAINMENT, INC. OFFICE OF PUBLICATION: 417 5th Avenue, New York, NY 10016. Copyright © 2008 and 2009 Marvel Characters, Inc. All rights reserved. $29.99 per copy in the U.S. (GST #R127032852); Canadian Agreement #40668537. All characters featured in this issue and the distinctive names and likenesses thereof, and all related indicia are trademarks of Marvel Characters, Inc. No similarity between any of the names, characters, persons, and/or institutions in this magazine with those of any living or dead person or institution is intended, and any such similarity which may exist is purely coincidental. **Printed in the U.S.A.** ALAN FINE, EVP - Office Of The Chief Executive Marvel Entertainment, Inc. & CMO Marvel Characters B.V.; DAN BUCKLEY, Chief Executive Officer and Publisher - Print, Animation & Digital Media; JIM SOKOLOWSKI, Chief Operating Officer; DAVID GABRIEL, SVP of Publishing Sales & Circulation; DAVID BOGART, SVP of Business Affairs & Talent Management; MICHAEL PASCIULLO, VP Merchandising & Communications; JIM O'KEEFE, VP of Operations & Logistics; DAN CARR, Executive Director of Publishing Technology; JUSTIN F. GABRIE, Director of Publishing & Editorial Operations; SUSAN CRESPI, Editorial Operations Manager; ALEX MORALES, Publishing Operations Manager; STAN LEE, Chairman Emeritus. For information regarding advertising in Marvel Comics or on Marvel.com, please contact Mitch Dane, Advertising Director, at mdane@marvel.com. For Marvel subscription inquiries, please call 800-217-9158. **Manufactured between 11/16/09 and 12/16/09 by R.R. DONNELLEY, INC., SALEM, VA, USA.**

10 9 8 7 6 5 4 3

THE WONDERFUL WIZARD OF OZ

ADAPTED FROM THE NOVEL BY L. FRANK BAUM

Writer: ERIC SHANOWER
Artist: SKOTTIE YOUNG
Colorist: JEAN-FRANCOIS BEAULIEU
Letterer: JEFF ECKLEBERRY

Assistant Editors: LAUREN SANKOVITCH & LAUREN HENRY
Associate Editor: NATE COSBY
Senior Editor: RALPH MACCHIO

Special Thanks to Chris Allo, Rich Ginter, Jeff Suter & Jim Nausedas

Collection Editor: MARK D. BEAZLEY
Assistant Editors: JOHN DENNING & ALEX STARBUCK
Editor, Special Projects: JENNIFER GRÜNWALD
Senior Editor, Special Projects: JEFF YOUNGQUIST
Senior Vice President of Sales: DAVID GABRIEL
Production: JERRY KALINOWSKI
Book Design: SPRING HOTELING
Sketchbook Design: ROMMEL ALAMA & SPRING HOTELING

Editor in Chief: JOE QUESADA
Publisher: DAN BUCKLEY
Executive Producer: ALAN FINE

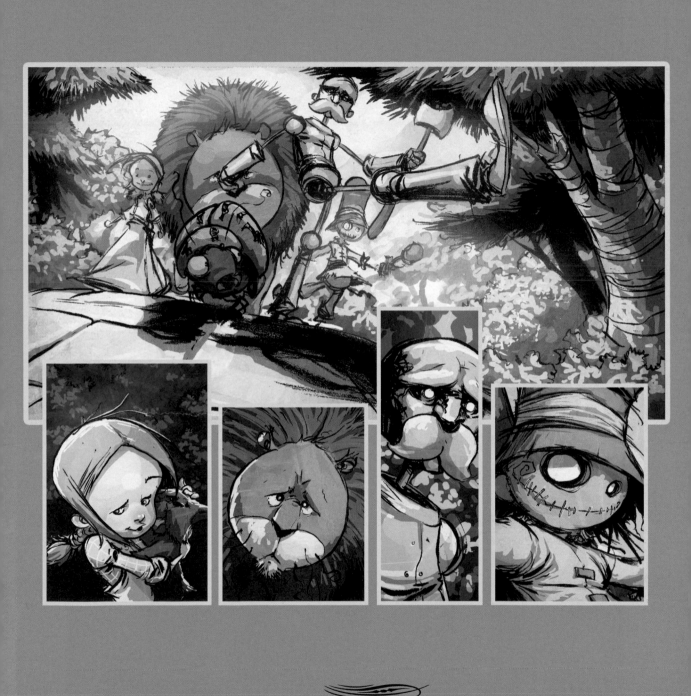

BLAME IT ON TOTO

If Dorothy Gale's dog hadn't scrambled under the bed to escape a cyclone, then Dorothy would have found safety in the cyclone cellar. Her adventures in the Land of Oz would never have occurred. Dorothy would have emerged from the cellar and life would have gone on much as before, as she lived through gray days on the Kansas prairies. Dorothy would never know how huge a gap had been left in her life.

If Toto hadn't scrambled under the bed, Dorothy's life isn't the only one that would have been left with a huge gap. Consider the author of *The Wonderful Wizard of Oz*, L. Frank Baum.

He was born Lyman Frank Baum in Chittenango, New York, in 1856. He didn't like the name Lyman, so settled for being called Frank, shortening his first name to its initial. Baum tried many professions before he became primarily a writer of children's books. Biographers seem fond of reducing his life story to a string of professional failures before he hit it big with *The Wonderful Wizard of Oz*. But that version is oversimplified. He didn't fail at everything. Before Oz he was a breeder of fancy chickens (successful), an oil salesman (unsuccessful), a playwright (successful), an actor (successful), a theater director (successful), a manager of a dry goods store (unsuccessful), a newspaper editor (unsuccessful), a journalist (successful), a crockery salesman (he missed his wife and children, so he gave it up), and an author (successful).

Baum's personal life before Oz had as many successes as his professional life. He was born on a large estate to rich parents who educated their children well and even indulged young Frank with a small printing press on which he published a family newspaper. In 1882, Baum married Maud Gage. Their marriage was a happy partnership, and they eventually had four sons. Maud was the daughter of Matilda Joslyn Gage, a prominent figure in the movement to obtain women the right to vote. Matilda encouraged her son-in-law to write down and publish the stories he invented for his sons and their friends.

The publication in 1900 of *The Wonderful Wizard of Oz* was a turning point for Baum. The book's popularity propelled the already best-selling writer into the top rank of children's authors. Baum, ever with an eye on theater, began a stage adaptation of the book. The result reached Broadway in 1903, running and touring for years, making stars of its lead actors, and prompting Baum to write more Oz books and more Oz theatricals (both on stage and on film). Oz's success led Baum to write books of many types, to travel, and to live the life of a wealthy man. The Oz books became so popular that when Baum tried to quit the series, he couldn't afford to. Oz had entered not only Baum's life and the lives of his family, but the lives of publishers, illustrators, actors, producers, and the lives of every child who read an Oz book and every adult who went to the theater to see the antics of the Scarecrow and Tin Woodman.

L. Frank Baum died in 1919, but Oz lived on. Other writers continued the Oz books through 1963 and forty volumes in the "official" series. Oz theatrical adaptations reached a peak in 1939 when MGM studios filmed the story with Judy Garland in the role of Dorothy. For many people, that film's version of Oz, ingrained into the American consciousness through annual television airings, eclipses all other versions, including Baum's original book. But Oz books and Oz movies have never stopped.

My own exposure to Oz probably began with a television broadcast of the MGM movie. Then one day in a bookstore, I found, next to a copy of *The Wizard of Oz*, three more Oz books by L. Frank Baum.

I chose one of them, *The Road to Oz*, and my fate was sealed. I wanted to read *all* the Oz books and decided that when I grew up, I'd write and illustrate new Oz books for the world to read. But why wait till I grew up? I began to write Oz stories and draw Oz illustrations. I constructed Oz pop-ups, directed and acted in Oz plays with my sister and neighborhood friends, and joined The International Wizard of Oz Club (www.ozclub.org).

I finally did grow up—more or less—and began to publish my own Oz books. Only these books weren't quite the same sort I'd envisioned as a child. They were comics. For many years I'd loved comics as much as I loved Oz. And now I was joining these two passions of my life.

But it didn't stop with comics. I've continued with other Oz projects, writing and illustrating more traditional Oz books, co-founding a publishing house—Hungry Tiger Press—devoted to Oz and the works of L. Frank Baum, writing reviews and articles, attending Oz conventions, even choreographing and performing in an Oz ballet. The impact of Oz on my life—the people I've met, the places I've gone, the things I've learned and seen and read and absorbed—is impossible to detail.

Needless to state, not everyone is influenced by Oz so strongly. But Oz pervades American culture to such an extent that few people don't recognize some version of Dorothy, the Scarecrow, the Wicked Witch of the West, and the story's other prominent characters. And beyond America, *The Wizard of Oz* is translated into many languages, inspiring further variations—including a completely different series of books in Russia, which has gone on to spawn its own movies, comics, and more.

If Toto hadn't scrambled under the bed to escape the cyclone, there's no telling how huge a gap would have been left—not only in Dorothy's life, not only in L. Frank Baum's life, not only in my life, but in the life of the entire world.

The fact that Marvel Comics chose to publish this version of *The Wonderful Wizard of Oz* as one of their comics adaptations of classic literature is yet another indication of the story's import. Baum's book is now a classic. That this comics adaptation goes back to that book as its source is one of the aspects that drew me to this project. *The Wonderful Wizard of Oz* has been told again and again in so many different versions and permutations that many of the original's details have been obscured or forgotten. But they haven't been lost. Here they are again, those wonderful Baum touches—the green spectacles, the Good Witch of the North's kiss, and—one of my favorites—the way the Soldier with the Green Whiskers makes Dorothy and her friends wipe their feet before they enter the Wizard's palace. It's all here, brought to life anew by the lively art of Skottie Young and the vibrant color of Jean-François Beaulieu.

I hope you enjoy it. It was created, as Baum himself said in his introduction to the original book, "to pleasure the children of today"—whether those children are actually young or simply young-at-heart.

And if you do enjoy it, you might take a moment to murmur a word of thanks to Toto.

ERIC SHANOWER
SAN DIEGO, JULY 2009

Folklore, legends, myths and fairy tales have followed childhood through the ages, for every healthy youngster has a wholesome and instinctive love for stories fantastic, marvelous and manifestly unreal.

The story of "The Wonderful Wizard of Oz" was written solely to please children of today. It aspires to being a modernized fairy tale, in which the wonderment and joy are retained and the heartaches and nightmares are left out.

L. FRANK BAUM CHICAGO, APRIL, 1900.

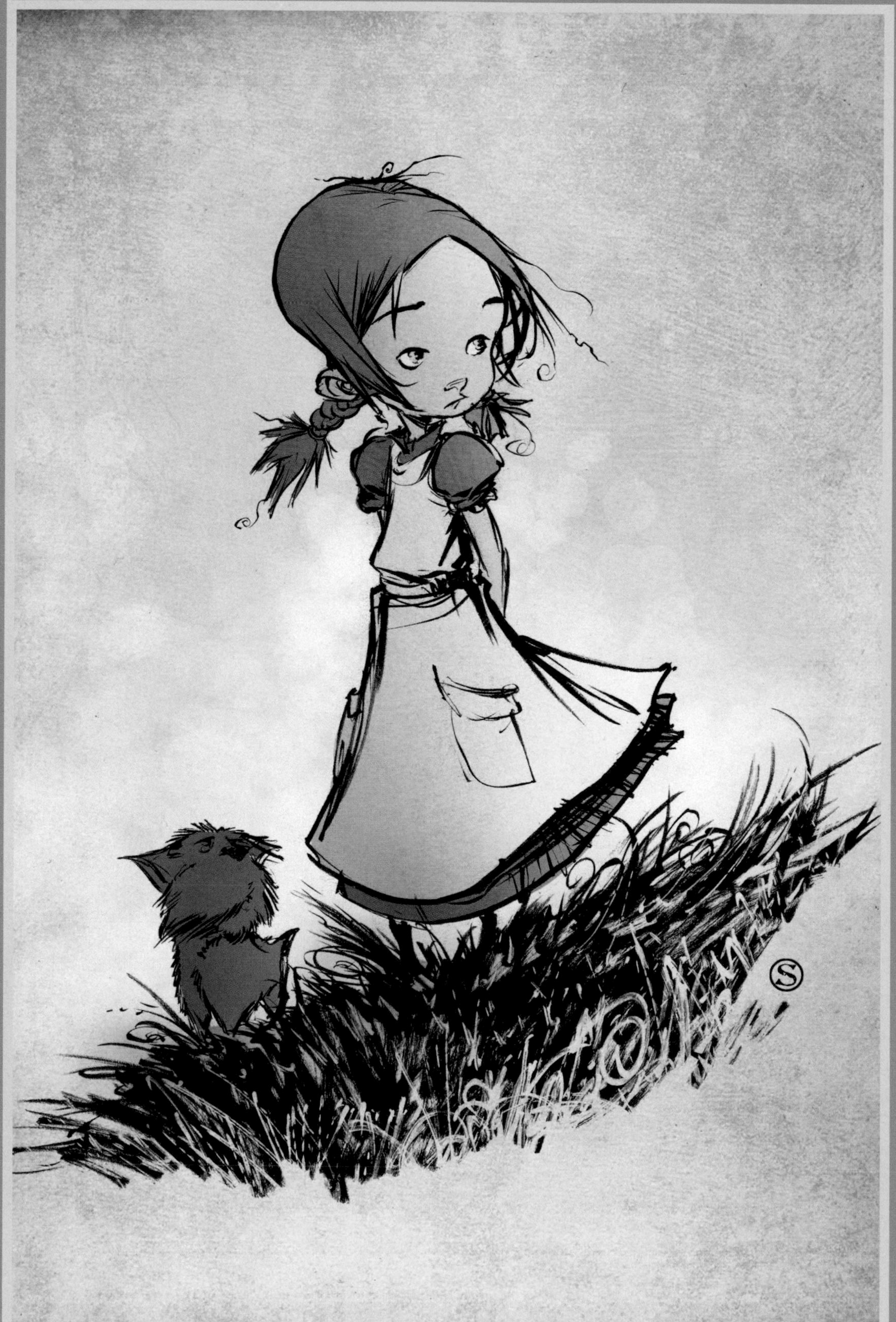

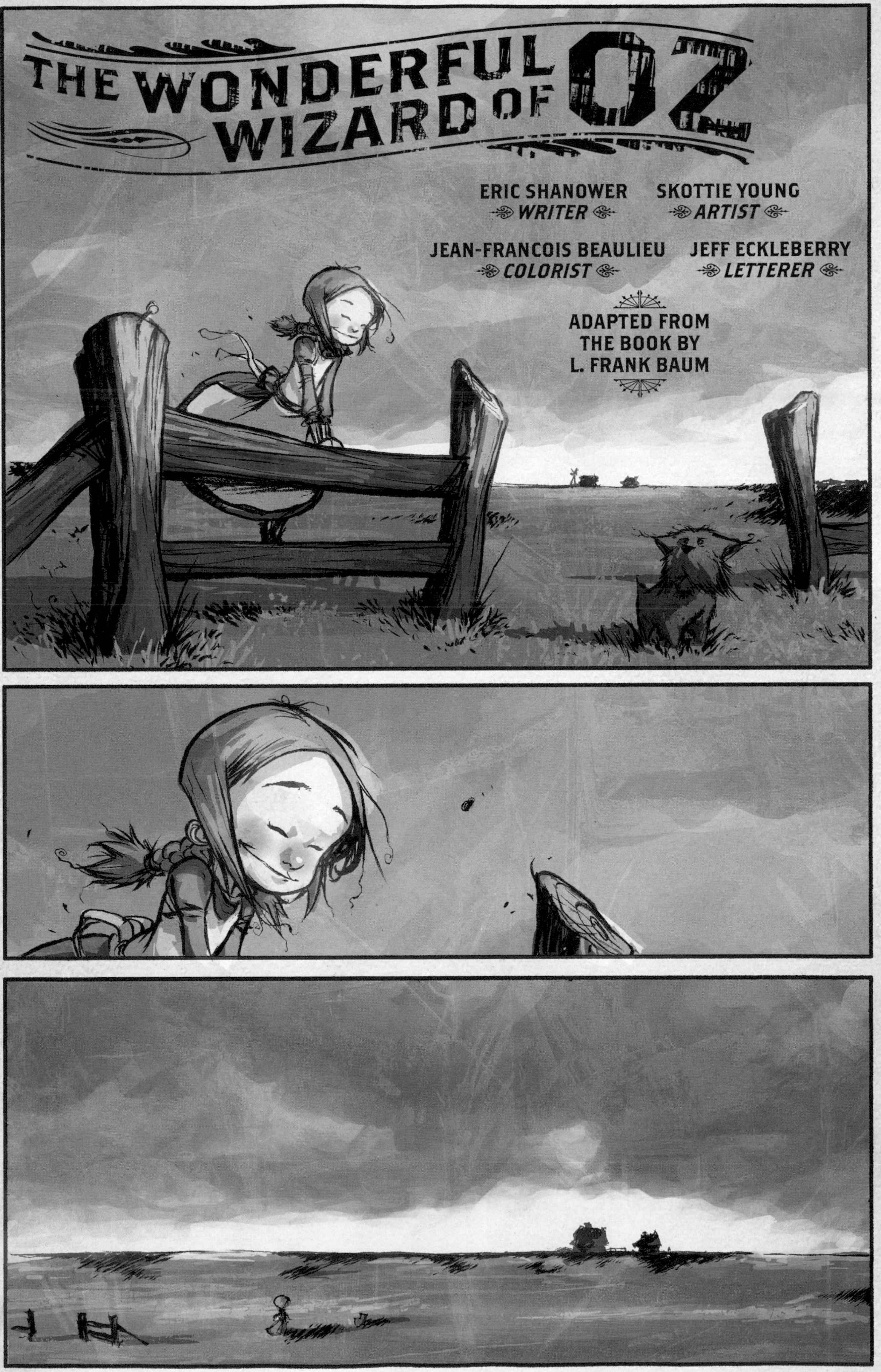
THE WONDERFUL WIZARD OF OZ
ERIC SHANOWER
WRITER
SKOTTIE YOUNG
ARTIST
JEAN-FRANCOIS BEAULIEU
COLORIST
JEFF ECKLEBERRY
LETTERER
ADAPTED FROM THE BOOK BY L. FRANK BAUM

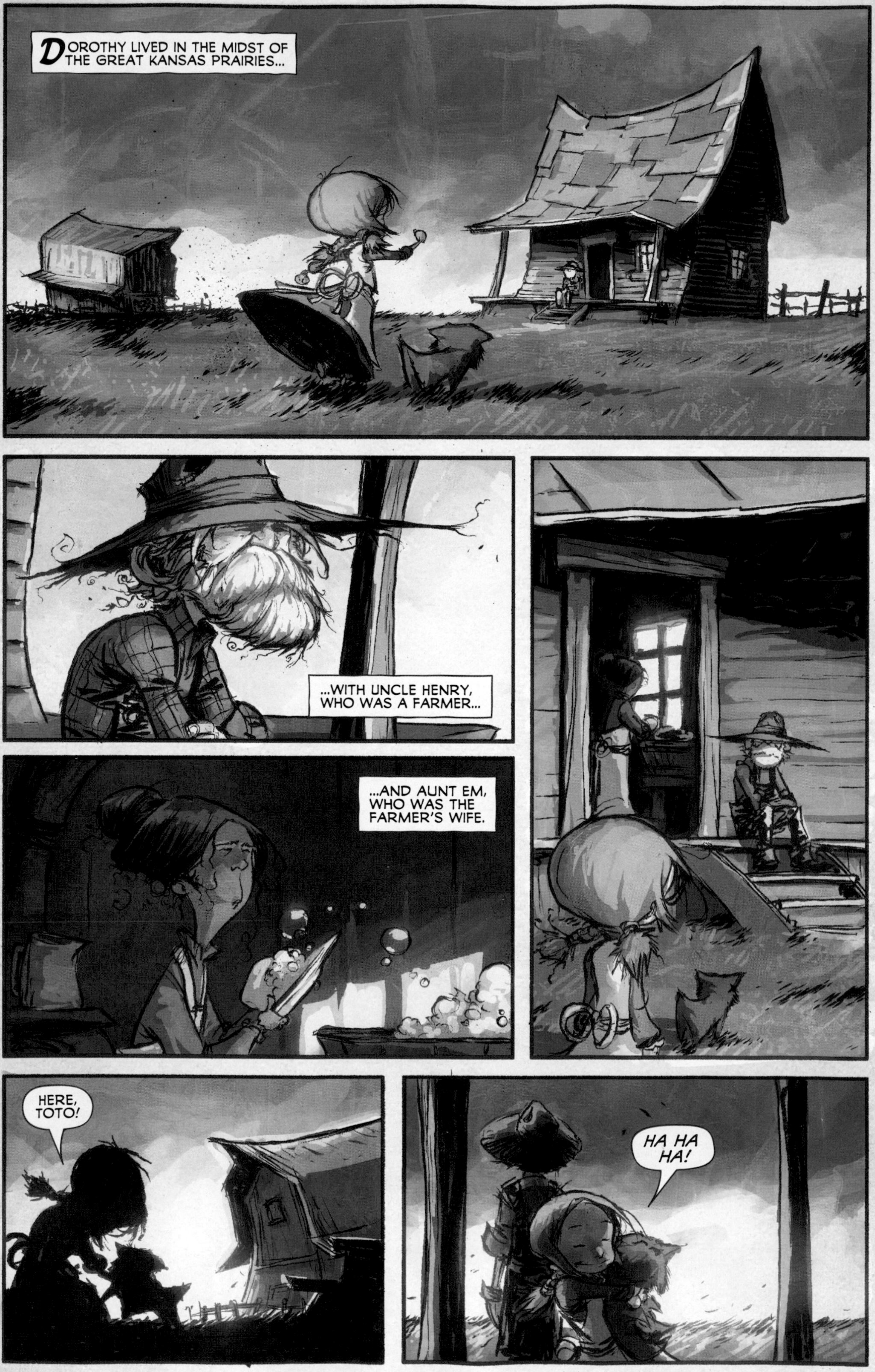
DOROTHY LIVED IN THE MIDST OF THE GREAT KANSAS PRAIRIES...
...WITH UNCLE HENRY, WHO WAS A FARMER...
...AND AUNT EM, WHO WAS THE FARMER'S WIFE.
HERE, TOTO!
HA HA HA!

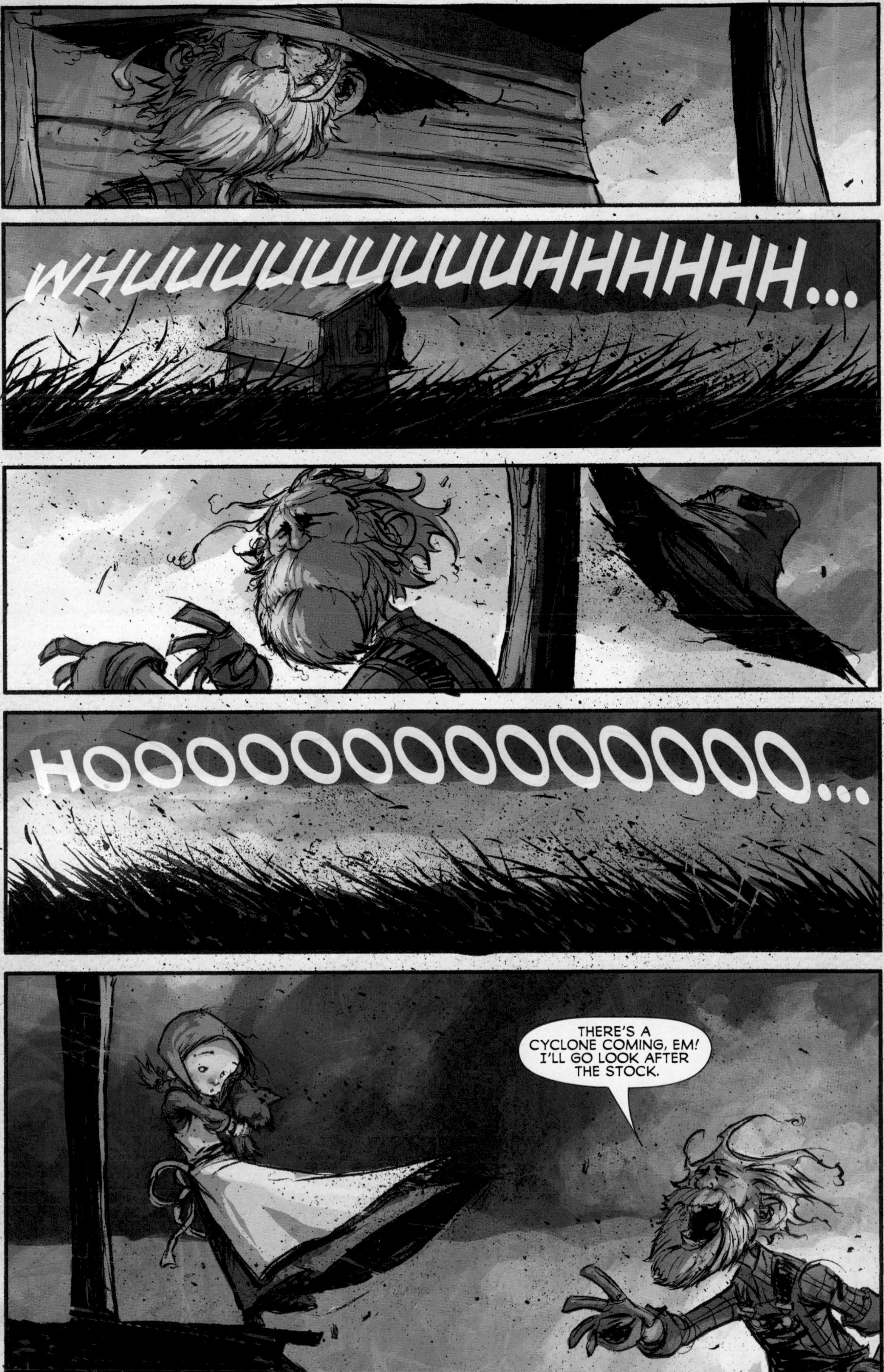
WHUUUUUUUUUUUHHHHHH...
HOOOOOOOOOOOOOO...
THERE'S A CYCLONE COMING, EM! I'LL GO LOOK AFTER THE STOCK.

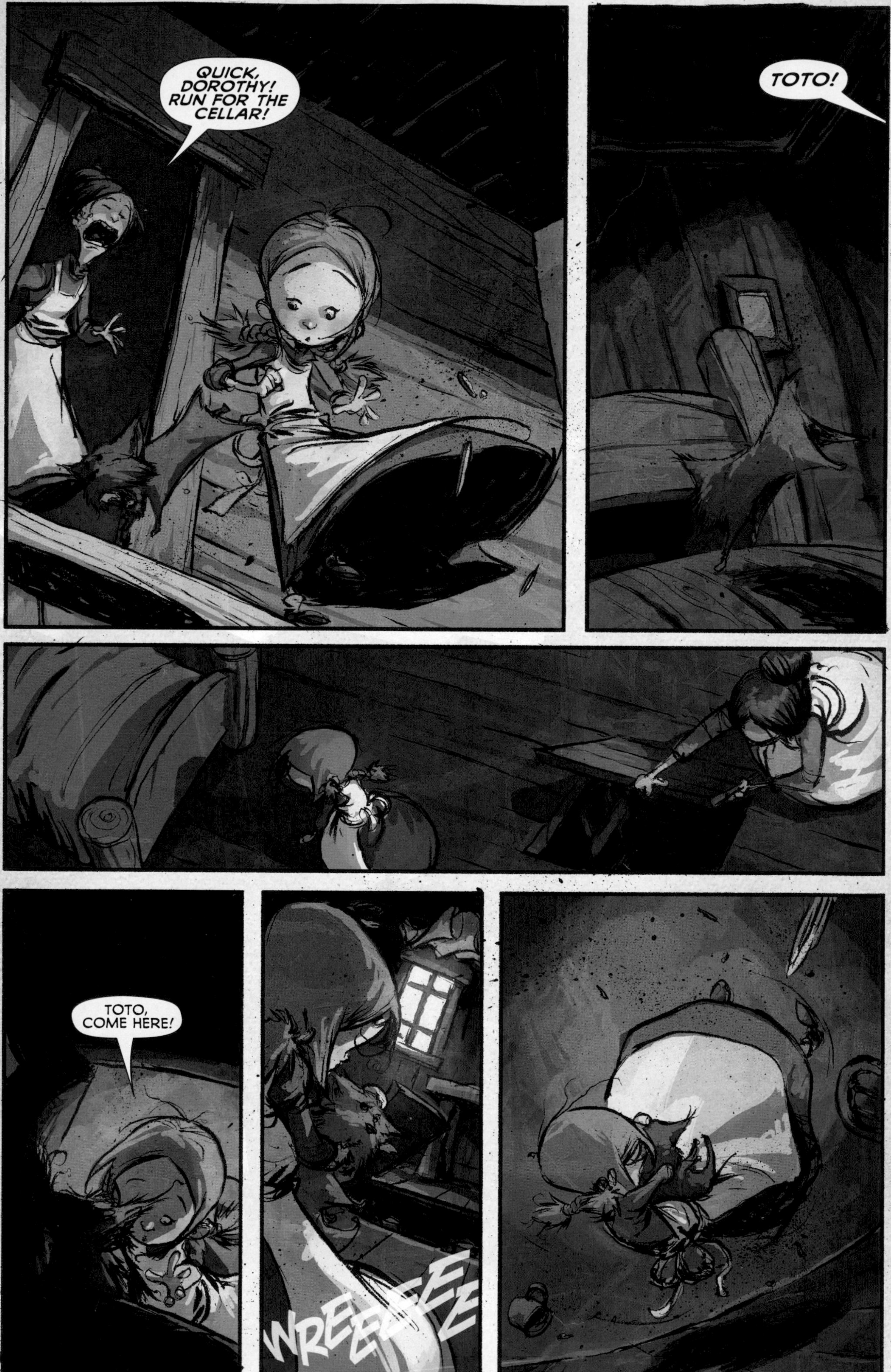
QUICK, DOROTHY! RUN FOR THE CELLAR!
TOTO!
TOTO, COME HERE!
WREEEEEE

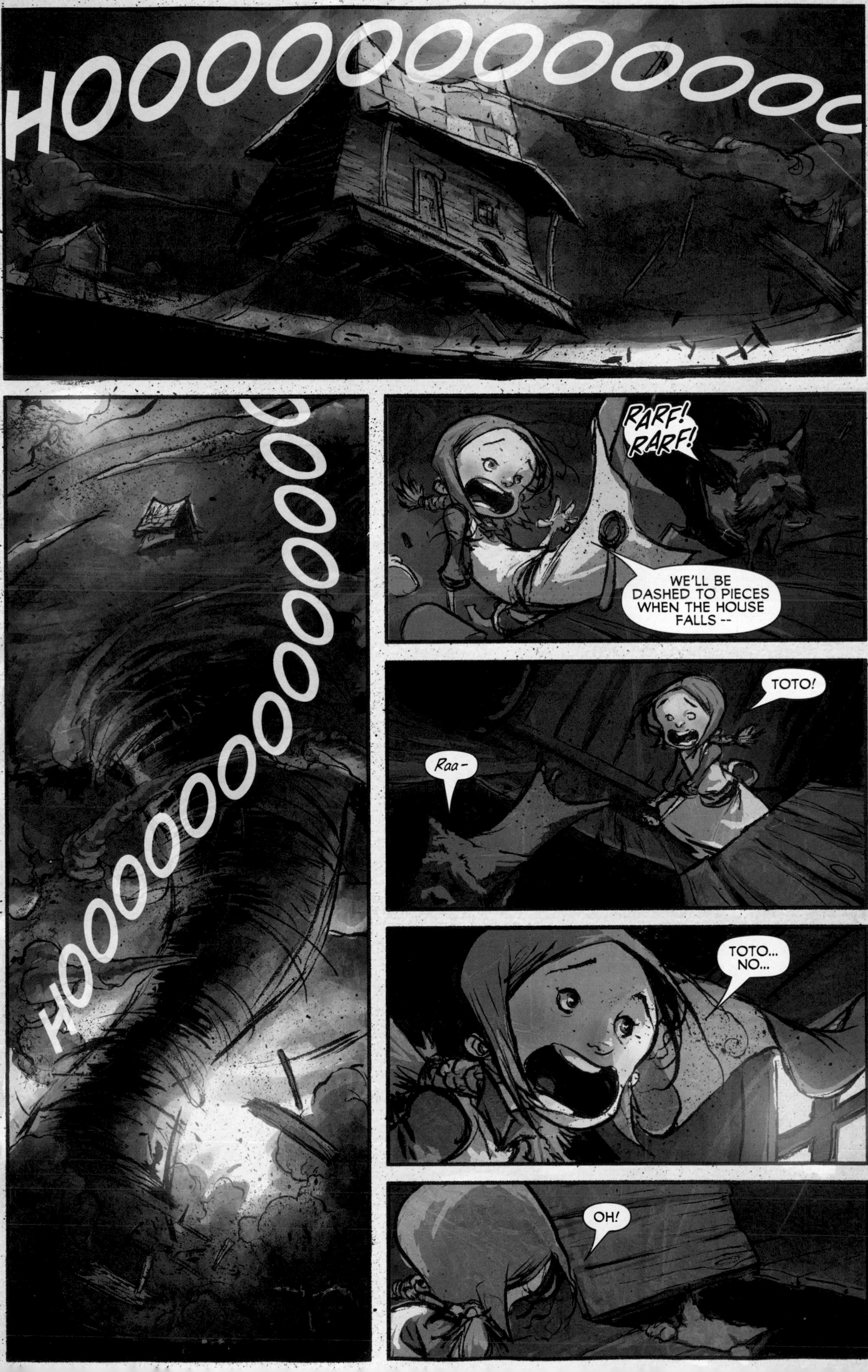

HOOOOOOOOOOOO
HOOOOOOOOOOOOOOO
RARF! RARF!
WE'LL BE DASHED TO PIECES WHEN THE HOUSE FALLS --
TOTO!
Raa-
TOTO... NO...
OH!

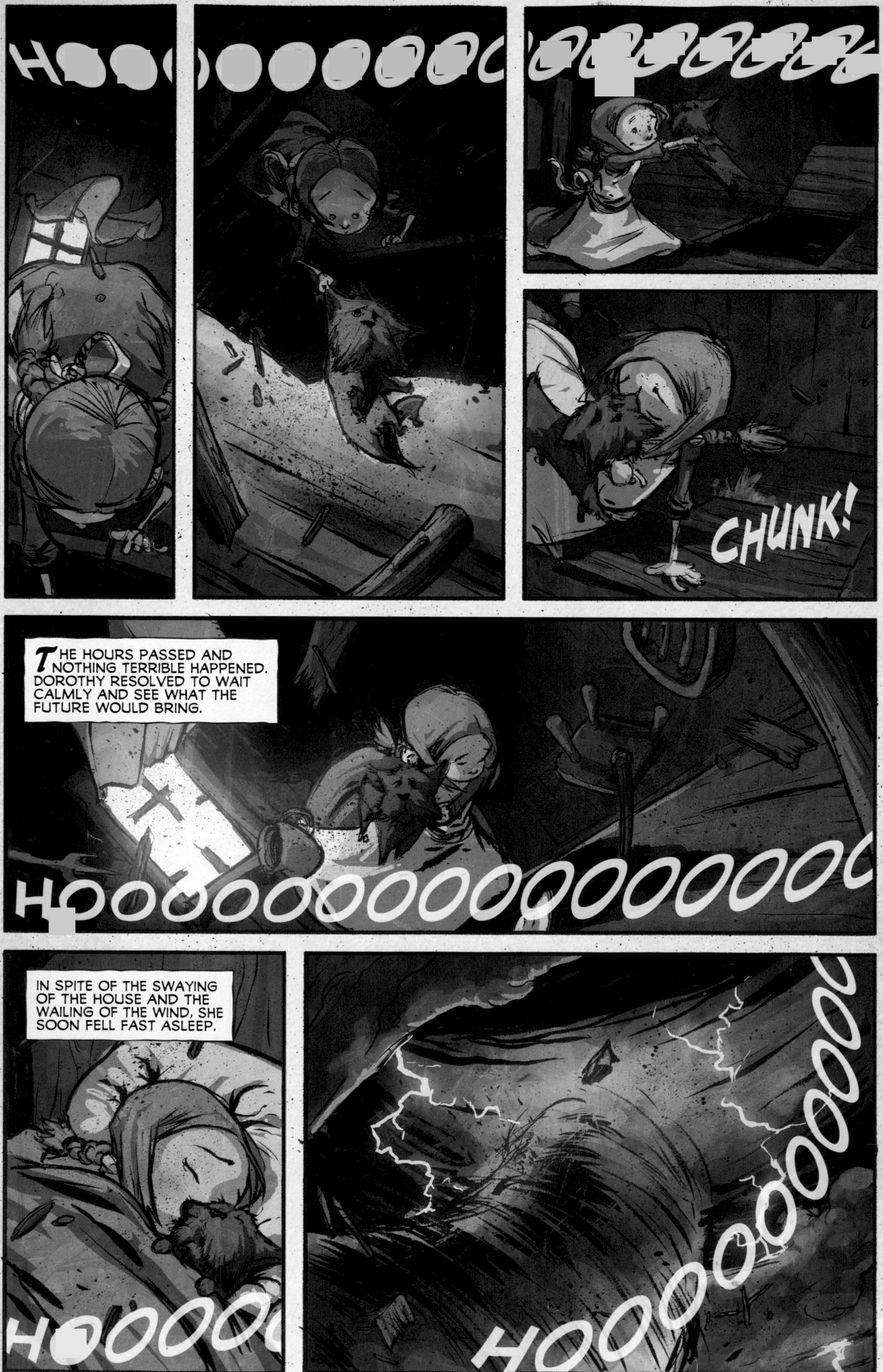
HOOOOOOOOOOOOOOOOOOOOOO
CHUNK!
THE HOURS PASSED AND NOTHING TERRIBLE HAPPENED. DOROTHY RESOLVED TO WAIT CALMLY AND SEE WHAT THE FUTURE WOULD BRING.
HOOOOOOOOOOOOOOOOO
IN SPITE OF THE SWAYING OF THE HOUSE AND THE WAILING OF THE WIND, SHE SOON FELL FAST ASLEEP.
HOOOOO
HOOOOOOOOOOOOOO

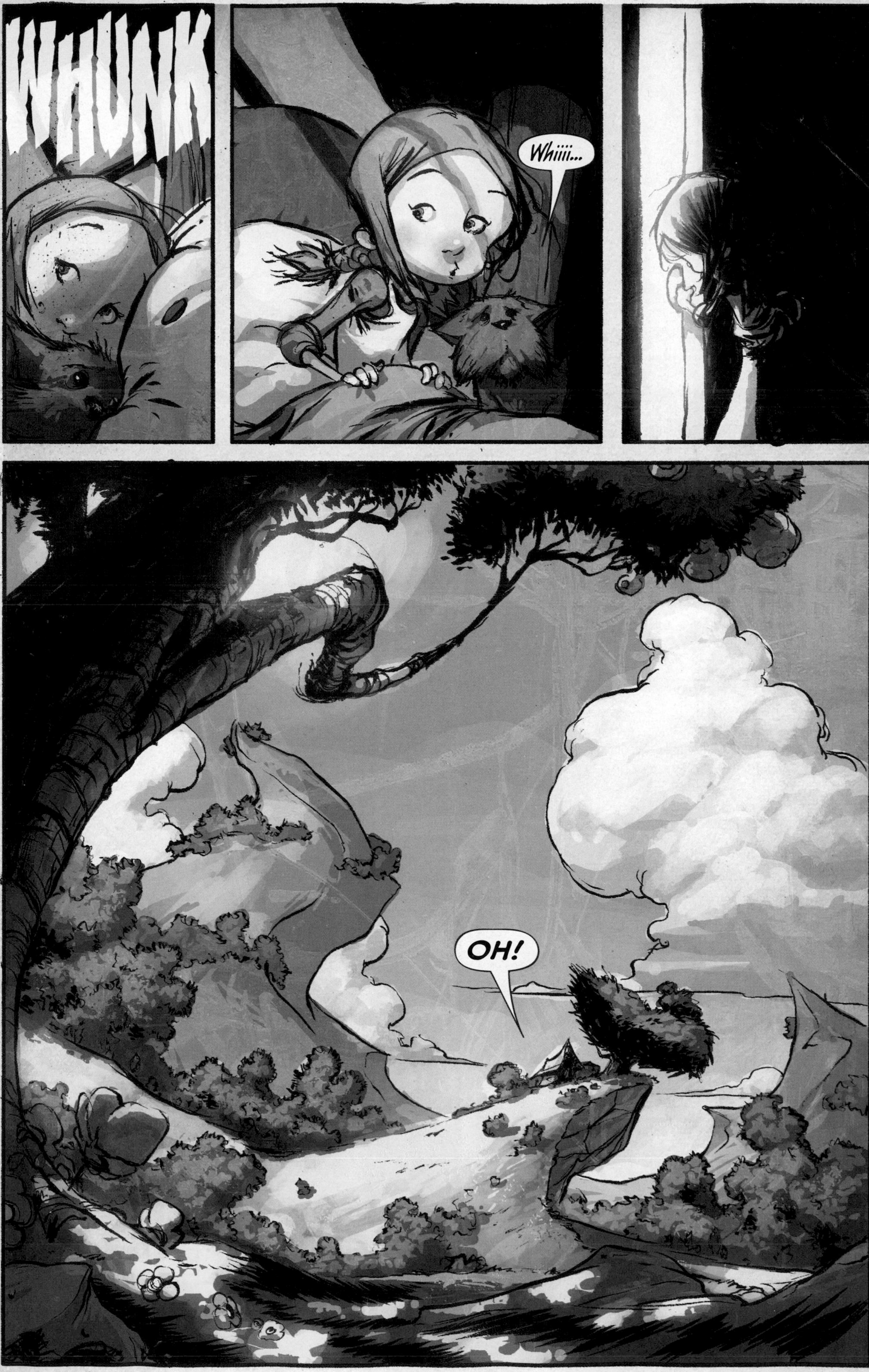
WHUNK
Whiiii...
OH!

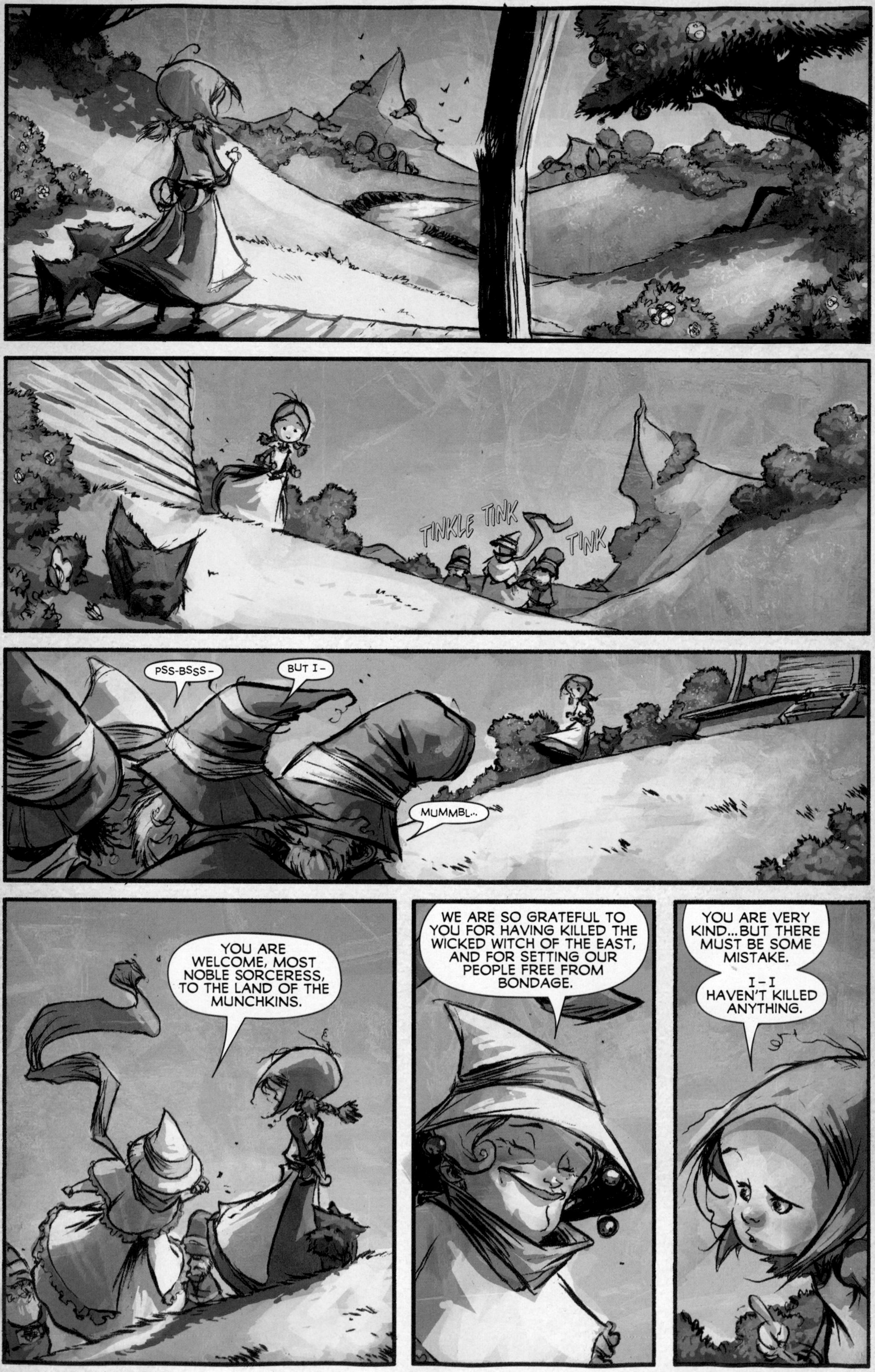
TINKLE TINK
TINK
PSS-BSSS-
BUT I-
MUMMBL...
YOU ARE WELCOME, MOST NOBLE SORCERESS, TO THE LAND OF THE MUNCHKINS.
WE ARE SO GRATEFUL TO YOU FOR HAVING KILLED THE WICKED WITCH OF THE EAST, AND FOR SETTING OUR PEOPLE FREE FROM BONDAGE.
YOU ARE VERY KIND...BUT THERE MUST BE SOME MISTAKE.
I-I HAVEN'T KILLED ANYTHING.

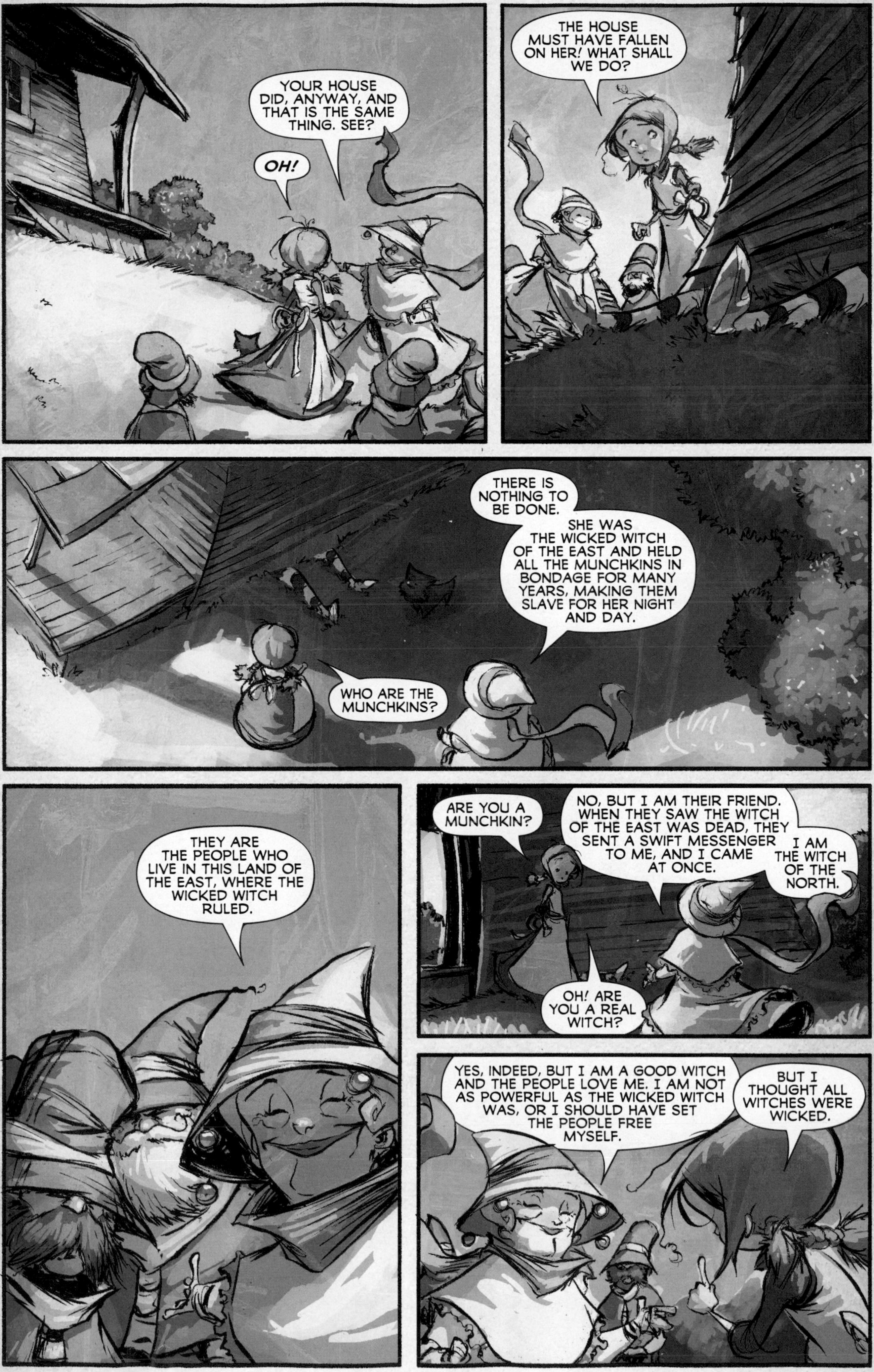
YOUR HOUSE DID, ANYWAY, AND THAT IS THE SAME THING. SEE?
OH!
THE HOUSE MUST HAVE FALLEN ON HER! WHAT SHALL WE DO?
THERE IS NOTHING TO BE DONE.
SHE WAS THE WICKED WITCH OF THE EAST AND HELD ALL THE MUNCHKINS IN BONDAGE FOR MANY YEARS, MAKING THEM SLAVE FOR HER NIGHT AND DAY.
WHO ARE THE MUNCHKINS?
THEY ARE THE PEOPLE WHO LIVE IN THIS LAND OF THE EAST, WHERE THE WICKED WITCH RULED.
ARE YOU A MUNCHKIN?
NO, BUT I AM THEIR FRIEND. WHEN THEY SAW THE WITCH OF THE EAST WAS DEAD, THEY SENT A SWIFT MESSENGER TO ME, AND I CAME AT ONCE.
I AM THE WITCH OF THE NORTH.
OH! ARE YOU A REAL WITCH?
YES, INDEED, BUT I AM A GOOD WITCH AND THE PEOPLE LOVE ME. I AM NOT AS POWERFUL AS THE WICKED WITCH WAS, OR I SHOULD HAVE SET THE PEOPLE FREE MYSELF.
BUT I THOUGHT ALL WITCHES WERE WICKED.

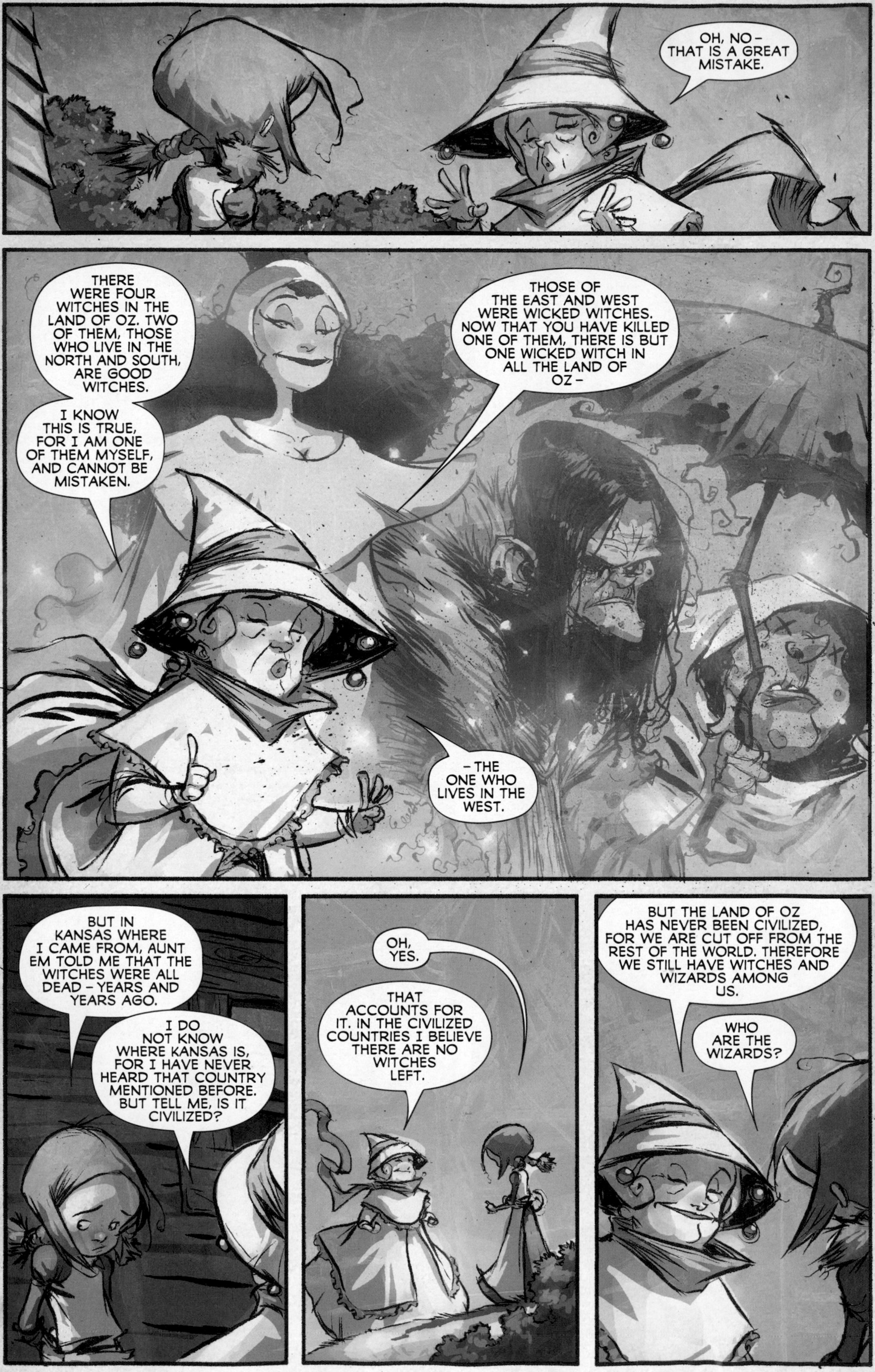
OH, NO– THAT IS A GREAT MISTAKE.
THERE WERE FOUR WITCHES IN THE LAND OF OZ. TWO OF THEM, THOSE WHO LIVE IN THE NORTH AND SOUTH, ARE GOOD WITCHES.
I KNOW THIS IS TRUE, FOR I AM ONE OF THEM MYSELF, AND CANNOT BE MISTAKEN.
THOSE OF THE EAST AND WEST WERE WICKED WITCHES. NOW THAT YOU HAVE KILLED ONE OF THEM, THERE IS BUT ONE WICKED WITCH IN ALL THE LAND OF OZ–
–THE ONE WHO LIVES IN THE WEST.
BUT IN KANSAS WHERE I CAME FROM, AUNT EM TOLD ME THAT THE WITCHES WERE ALL DEAD–YEARS AND YEARS AGO.
I DO NOT KNOW WHERE KANSAS IS, FOR I HAVE NEVER HEARD THAT COUNTRY MENTIONED BEFORE. BUT TELL ME, IS IT CIVILIZED?
OH, YES.
THAT ACCOUNTS FOR IT. IN THE CIVILIZED COUNTRIES I BELIEVE THERE ARE NO WITCHES LEFT.
BUT THE LAND OF OZ HAS NEVER BEEN CIVILIZED, FOR WE ARE CUT OFF FROM THE REST OF THE WORLD. THEREFORE WE STILL HAVE WITCHES AND WIZARDS AMONG US.
WHO ARE THE WIZARDS?

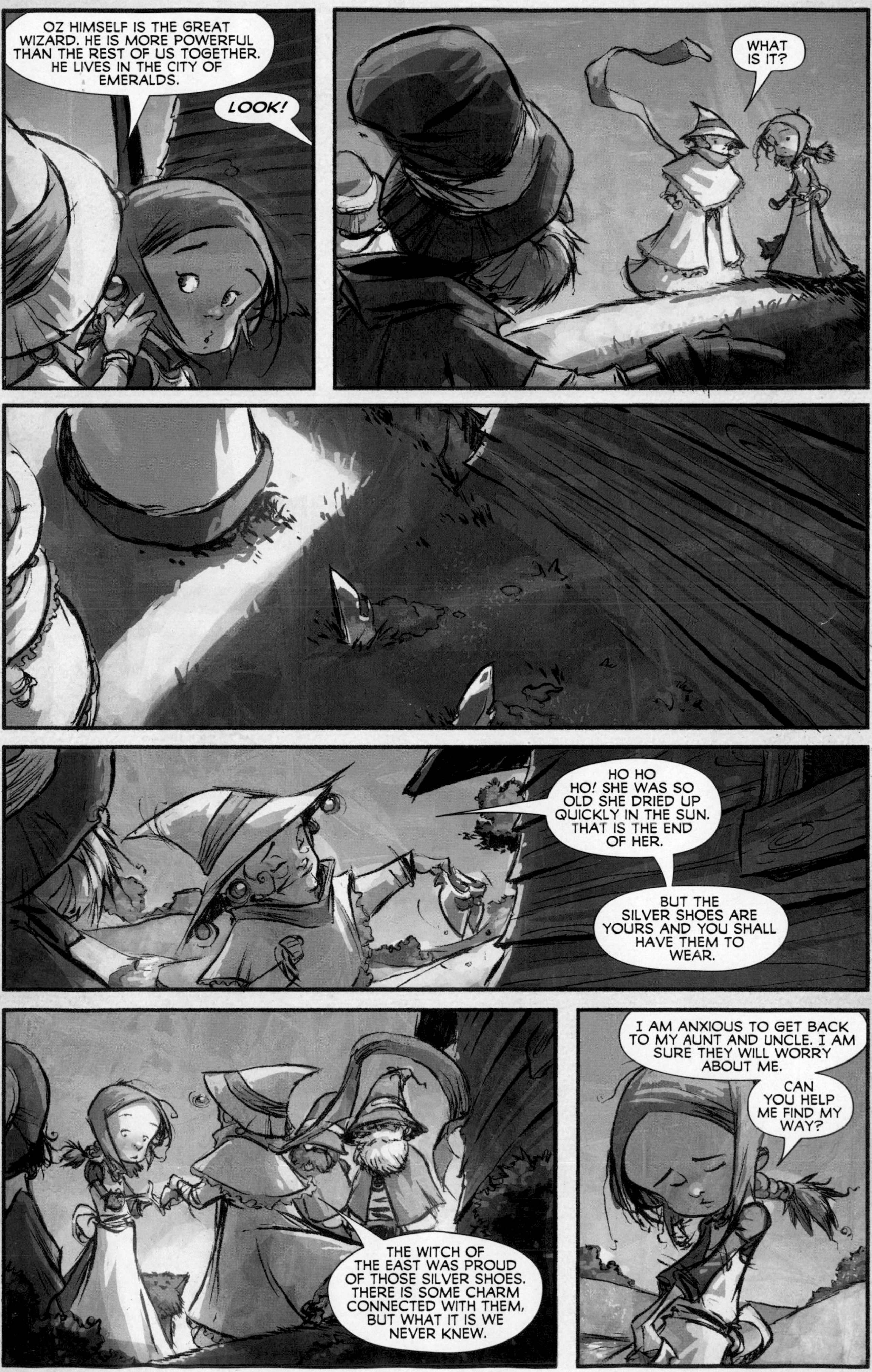
OZ HIMSELF IS THE GREAT WIZARD. HE IS MORE POWERFUL THAN THE REST OF US TOGETHER. HE LIVES IN THE CITY OF EMERALDS.
LOOK!
WHAT IS IT?
HO HO HO! SHE WAS SO OLD SHE DRIED UP QUICKLY IN THE SUN. THAT IS THE END OF HER.
BUT THE SILVER SHOES ARE YOURS AND YOU SHALL HAVE THEM TO WEAR.
THE WITCH OF THE EAST WAS PROUD OF THOSE SILVER SHOES. THERE IS SOME CHARM CONNECTED WITH THEM, BUT WHAT IT IS WE NEVER KNEW.
I AM ANXIOUS TO GET BACK TO MY AUNT AND UNCLE. I AM SURE THEY WILL WORRY ABOUT ME.
CAN YOU HELP ME FIND MY WAY?

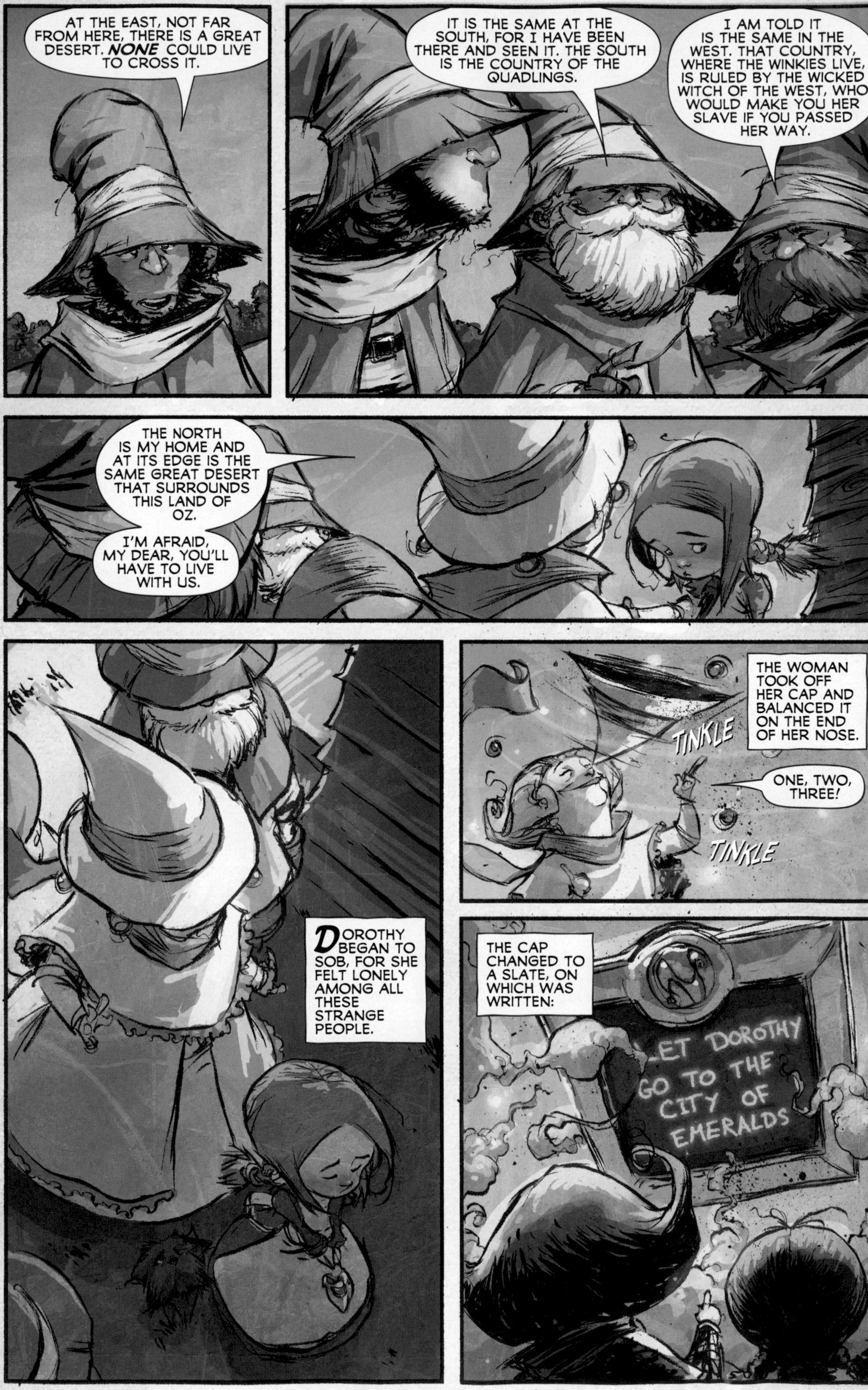

AT THE EAST, NOT FAR FROM HERE, THERE IS A GREAT DESERT. *NONE* COULD LIVE TO CROSS IT.
IT IS THE SAME AT THE SOUTH, FOR I HAVE BEEN THERE AND SEEN IT. THE SOUTH IS THE COUNTRY OF THE QUADLINGS.
I AM TOLD IT IS THE SAME IN THE WEST. THAT COUNTRY, WHERE THE WINKIES LIVE, IS RULED BY THE WICKED WITCH OF THE WEST, WHO WOULD MAKE YOU HER SLAVE IF YOU PASSED HER WAY.
THE NORTH IS MY HOME AND AT ITS EDGE IS THE SAME GREAT DESERT THAT SURROUNDS THIS LAND OF OZ.
I'M AFRAID, MY DEAR, YOU'LL HAVE TO LIVE WITH US.
DOROTHY BEGAN TO SOB, FOR SHE FELT LONELY AMONG ALL THESE STRANGE PEOPLE.
THE WOMAN TOOK OFF HER CAP AND BALANCED IT ON THE END OF HER NOSE.
TINKLE
ONE, TWO, THREE!
TINKLE
THE CAP CHANGED TO A SLATE, ON WHICH WAS WRITTEN:
LET DOROTHY GO TO THE CITY OF EMERALDS

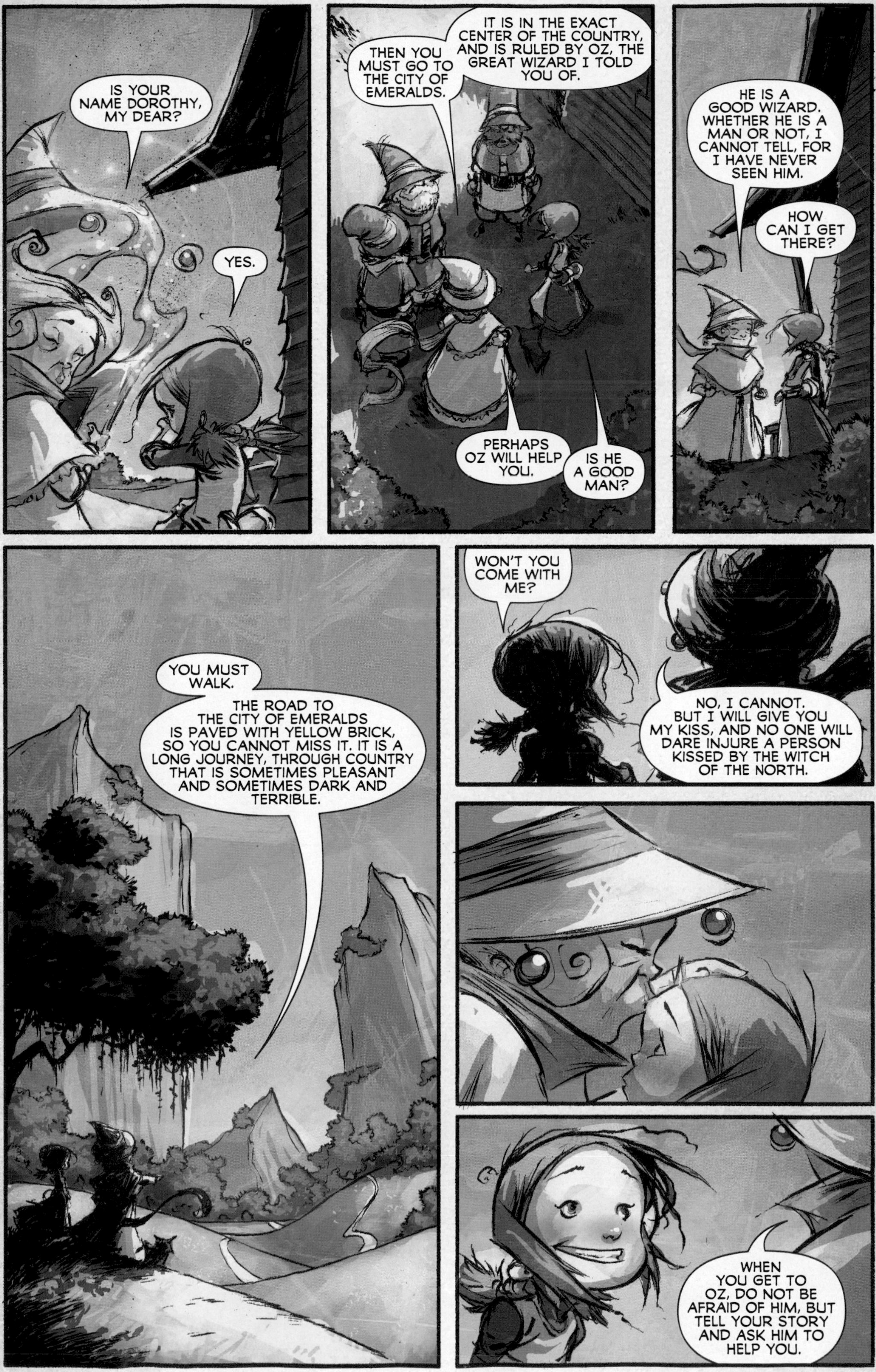
IS YOUR NAME DOROTHY, MY DEAR?
YES.
THEN YOU MUST GO TO THE CITY OF EMERALDS.
IT IS IN THE EXACT CENTER OF THE COUNTRY, AND IS RULED BY OZ, THE GREAT WIZARD I TOLD YOU OF.
PERHAPS OZ WILL HELP YOU.
IS HE A GOOD MAN?
HE IS A GOOD WIZARD. WHETHER HE IS A MAN OR NOT, I CANNOT TELL, FOR I HAVE NEVER SEEN HIM.
HOW CAN I GET THERE?
YOU MUST WALK.
THE ROAD TO THE CITY OF EMERALDS IS PAVED WITH YELLOW BRICK, SO YOU CANNOT MISS IT. IT IS A LONG JOURNEY, THROUGH COUNTRY THAT IS SOMETIMES PLEASANT AND SOMETIMES DARK AND TERRIBLE.
WON'T YOU COME WITH ME?
NO, I CANNOT. BUT I WILL GIVE YOU MY KISS, AND NO ONE WILL DARE INJURE A PERSON KISSED BY THE WITCH OF THE NORTH.
WHEN YOU GET TO OZ, DO NOT BE AFRAID OF HIM, BUT TELL YOUR STORY AND ASK HIM TO HELP YOU.

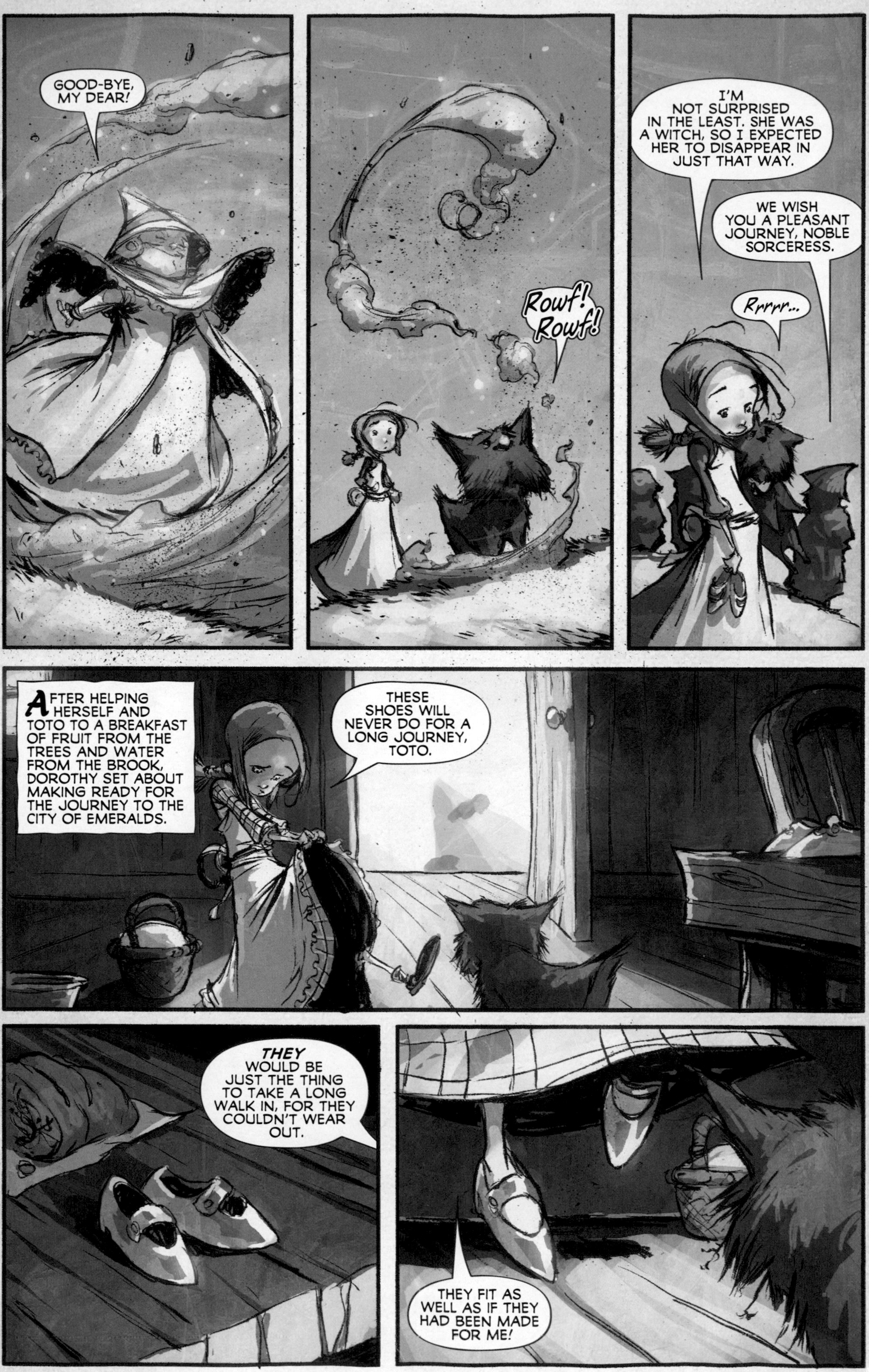
GOOD-BYE, MY DEAR!
Rowf! Rowf!
I'M NOT SURPRISED IN THE LEAST. SHE WAS A WITCH, SO I EXPECTED HER TO DISAPPEAR IN JUST THAT WAY.
WE WISH YOU A PLEASANT JOURNEY, NOBLE SORCERESS.
Rrrrr...
AFTER HELPING HERSELF AND TOTO TO A BREAKFAST OF FRUIT FROM THE TREES AND WATER FROM THE BROOK, DOROTHY SET ABOUT MAKING READY FOR THE JOURNEY TO THE CITY OF EMERALDS.
THESE SHOES WILL NEVER DO FOR A LONG JOURNEY, TOTO.
THEY WOULD BE JUST THE THING TO TAKE A LONG WALK IN, FOR THEY COULDN'T WEAR OUT.
THEY FIT AS WELL AS IF THEY HAD BEEN MADE FOR ME!

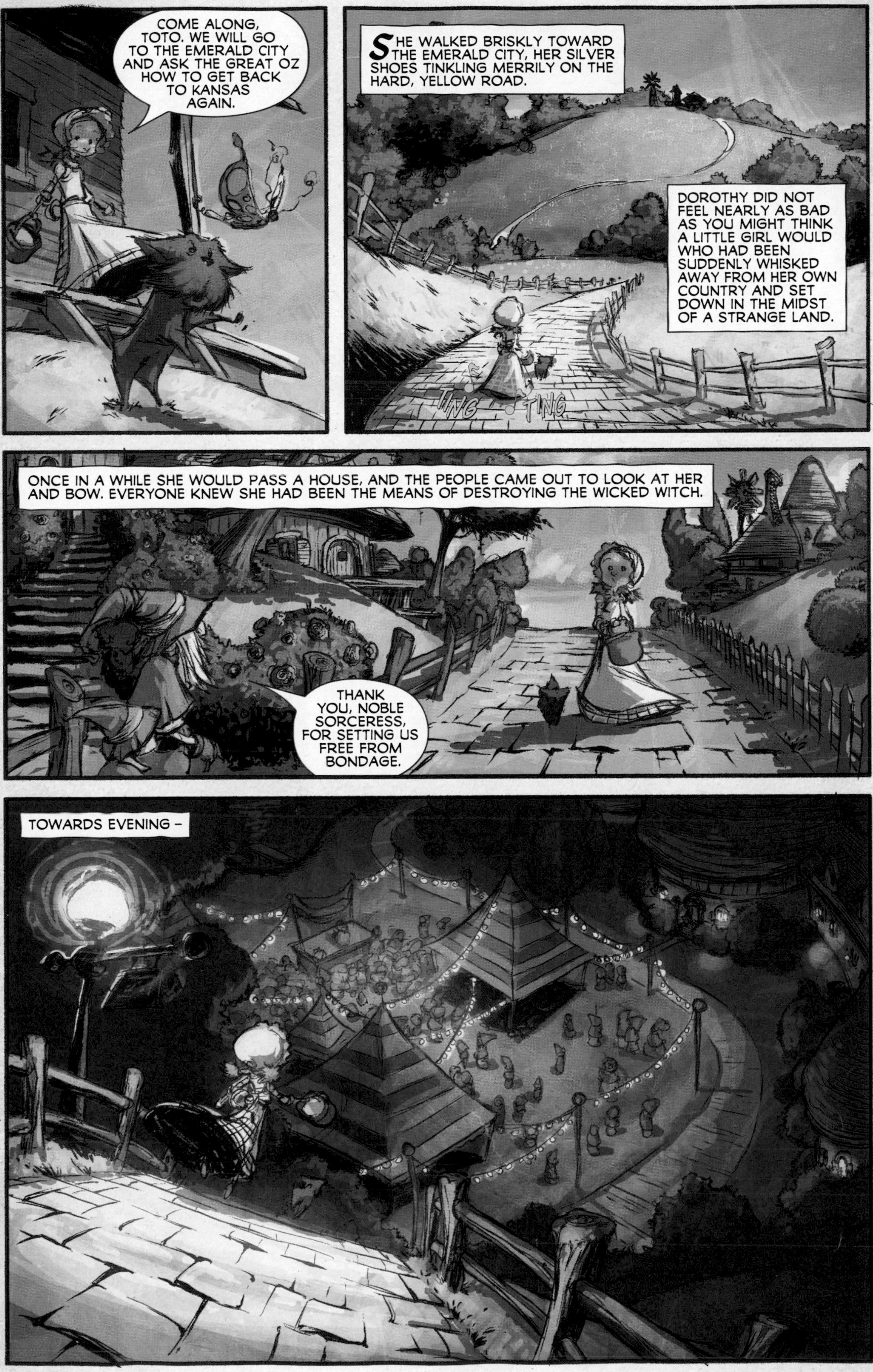
COME ALONG, TOTO. WE WILL GO TO THE EMERALD CITY AND ASK THE GREAT OZ HOW TO GET BACK TO KANSAS AGAIN.
SHE WALKED BRISKLY TOWARD THE EMERALD CITY, HER SILVER SHOES TINKLING MERRILY ON THE HARD, YELLOW ROAD.
DOROTHY DID NOT FEEL NEARLY AS BAD AS YOU MIGHT THINK A LITTLE GIRL WOULD WHO HAD BEEN SUDDENLY WHISKED AWAY FROM HER OWN COUNTRY AND SET DOWN IN THE MIDST OF A STRANGE LAND.
TING
TING
ONCE IN A WHILE SHE WOULD PASS A HOUSE, AND THE PEOPLE CAME OUT TO LOOK AT HER AND BOW. EVERYONE KNEW SHE HAD BEEN THE MEANS OF DESTROYING THE WICKED WITCH.
THANK YOU, NOBLE SORCERESS, FOR SETTING US FREE FROM BONDAGE.
TOWARDS EVENING –

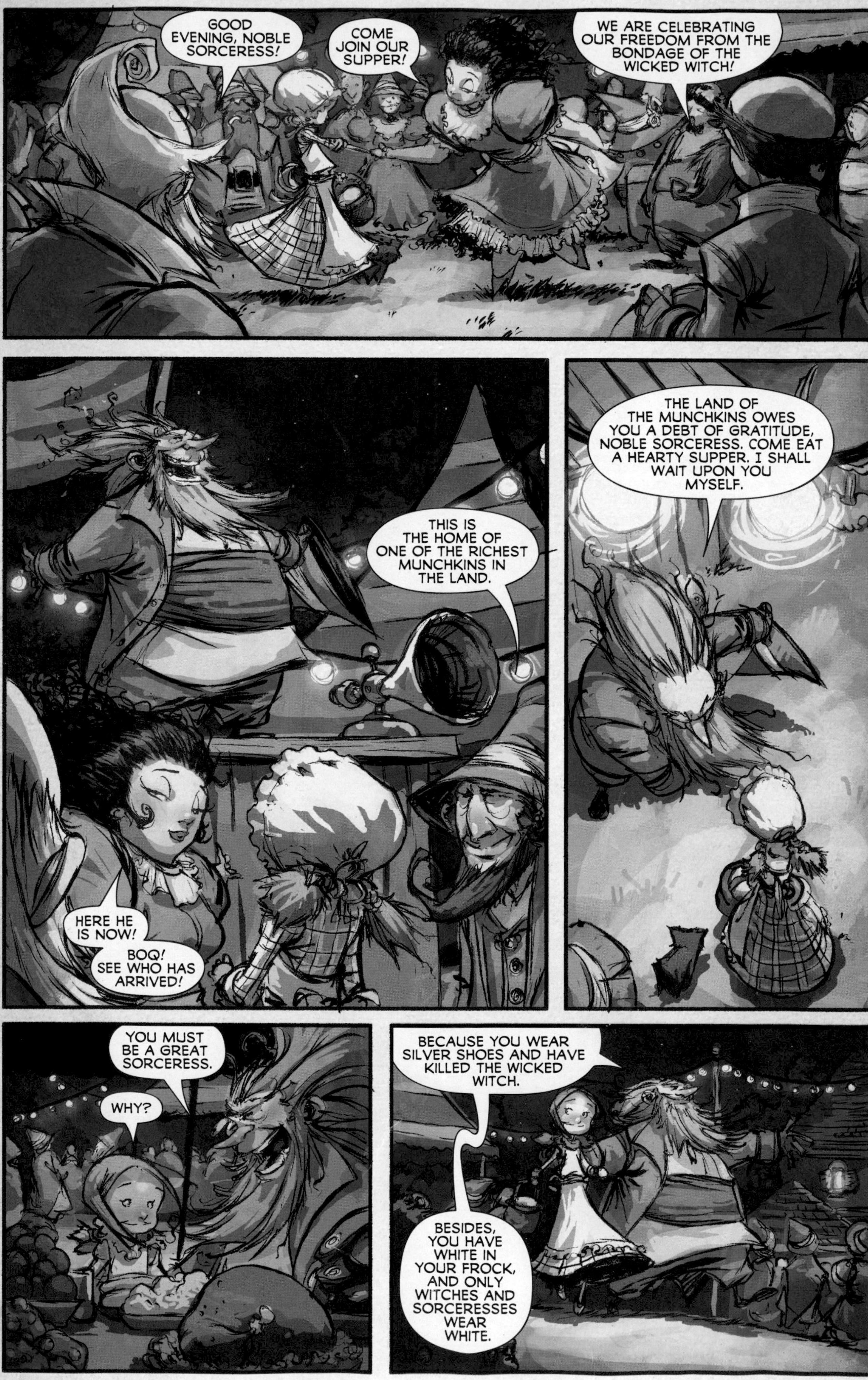
GOOD EVENING, NOBLE SORCERESS!
COME JOIN OUR SUPPER!
WE ARE CELEBRATING OUR FREEDOM FROM THE BONDAGE OF THE WICKED WITCH!
THIS IS THE HOME OF ONE OF THE RICHEST MUNCHKINS IN THE LAND.
HERE HE IS NOW!
BOQ! SEE WHO HAS ARRIVED!
THE LAND OF THE MUNCHKINS OWES YOU A DEBT OF GRATITUDE, NOBLE SORCERESS. COME EAT A HEARTY SUPPER. I SHALL WAIT UPON YOU MYSELF.
YOU MUST BE A GREAT SORCERESS.
WHY?
BECAUSE YOU WEAR SILVER SHOES AND HAVE KILLED THE WICKED WITCH.
BESIDES, YOU HAVE WHITE IN YOUR FROCK, AND ONLY WITCHES AND SORCERESSES WEAR WHITE.

MY DRESS IS BLUE AND WHITE CHECKED.

IT IS KIND OF YOU TO WEAR THAT.

BLUE IS THE COLOR OF THE MUNCHKINS, AND WHITE IS THE WITCH COLOR. SO WE KNOW YOU ARE A FRIENDLY WITCH.

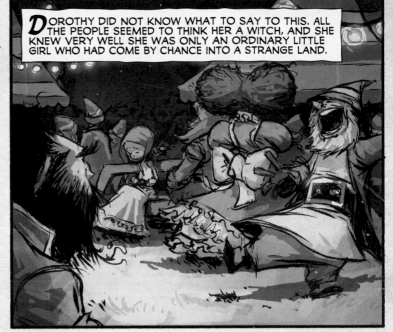

DOROTHY DID NOT KNOW WHAT TO SAY TO THIS. ALL THE PEOPLE SEEMED TO THINK HER A WITCH, AND SHE KNEW VERY WELL SHE WAS ONLY AN ORDINARY LITTLE GIRL WHO HAD COME BY CHANCE INTO A STRANGE LAND.

WHEN SHE HAD TIRED OF WATCHING THE DANCING, BOQ LED HER TO A ROOM WITH A PRETTY BED.

IN THE MORNING —

HEEEEE!

HA HA HA!

TOTO IS A FINE CURIOSITY TO ALL OF US. WE'VE NEVER SEEN A DOG BEFORE.

HOW FAR IS IT TO THE EMERALD CITY?

I DO NOT KNOW, FOR I HAVE NEVER BEEN THERE.

IT IS BETTER FOR PEOPLE TO KEEP AWAY FROM OZ, UNLESS THEY HAVE BUSINESS WITH HIM.

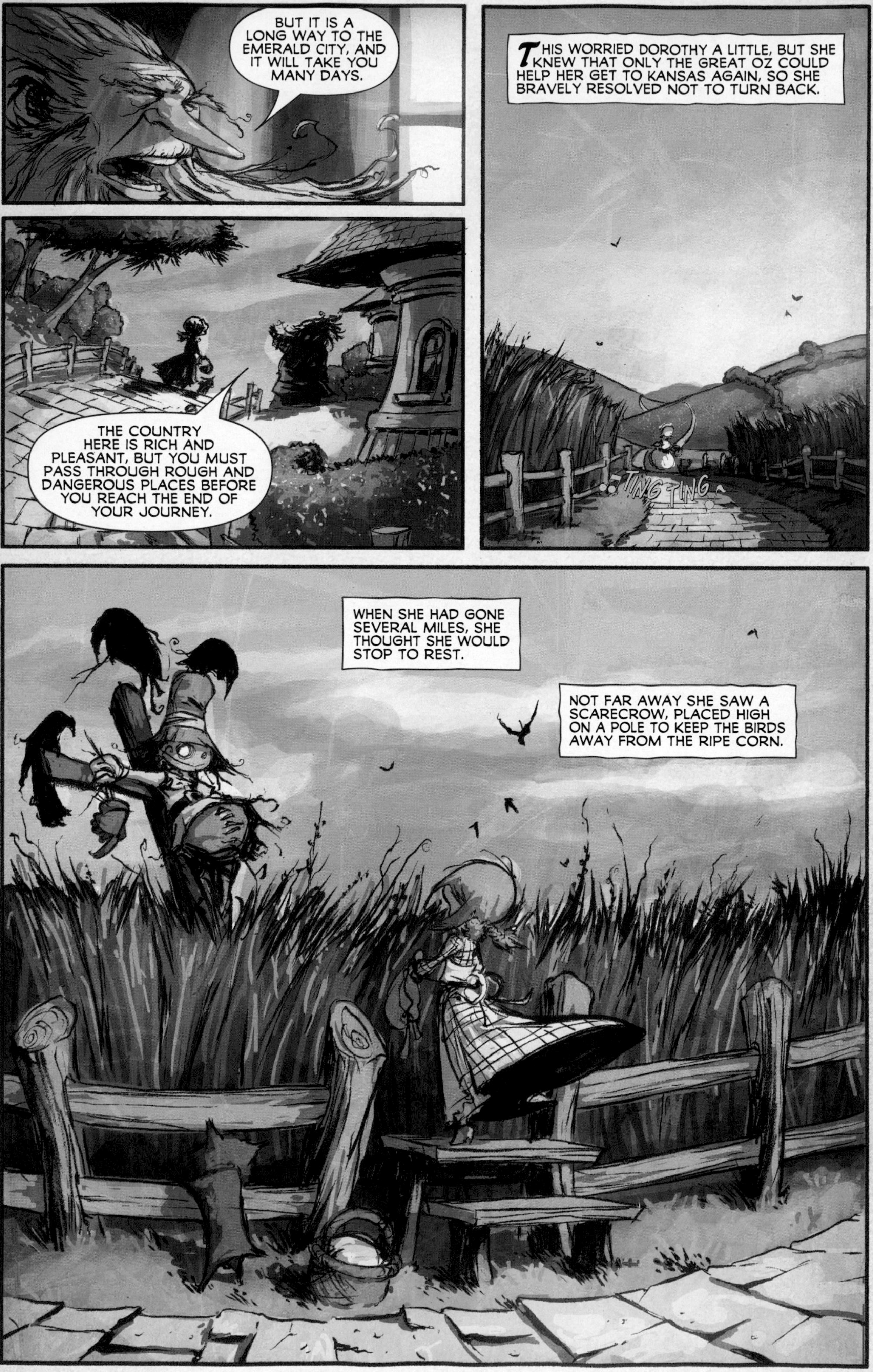
BUT IT IS A LONG WAY TO THE EMERALD CITY, AND IT WILL TAKE YOU MANY DAYS.
THE COUNTRY HERE IS RICH AND PLEASANT, BUT YOU MUST PASS THROUGH ROUGH AND DANGEROUS PLACES BEFORE YOU REACH THE END OF YOUR JOURNEY.
THIS WORRIED DOROTHY A LITTLE, BUT SHE KNEW THAT ONLY THE GREAT OZ COULD HELP HER GET TO KANSAS AGAIN, SO SHE BRAVELY RESOLVED NOT TO TURN BACK.
TING TING
WHEN SHE HAD GONE SEVERAL MILES, SHE THOUGHT SHE WOULD STOP TO REST.
NOT FAR AWAY SHE SAW A SCARECROW, PLACED HIGH ON A POLE TO KEEP THE BIRDS AWAY FROM THE RIPE CORN.

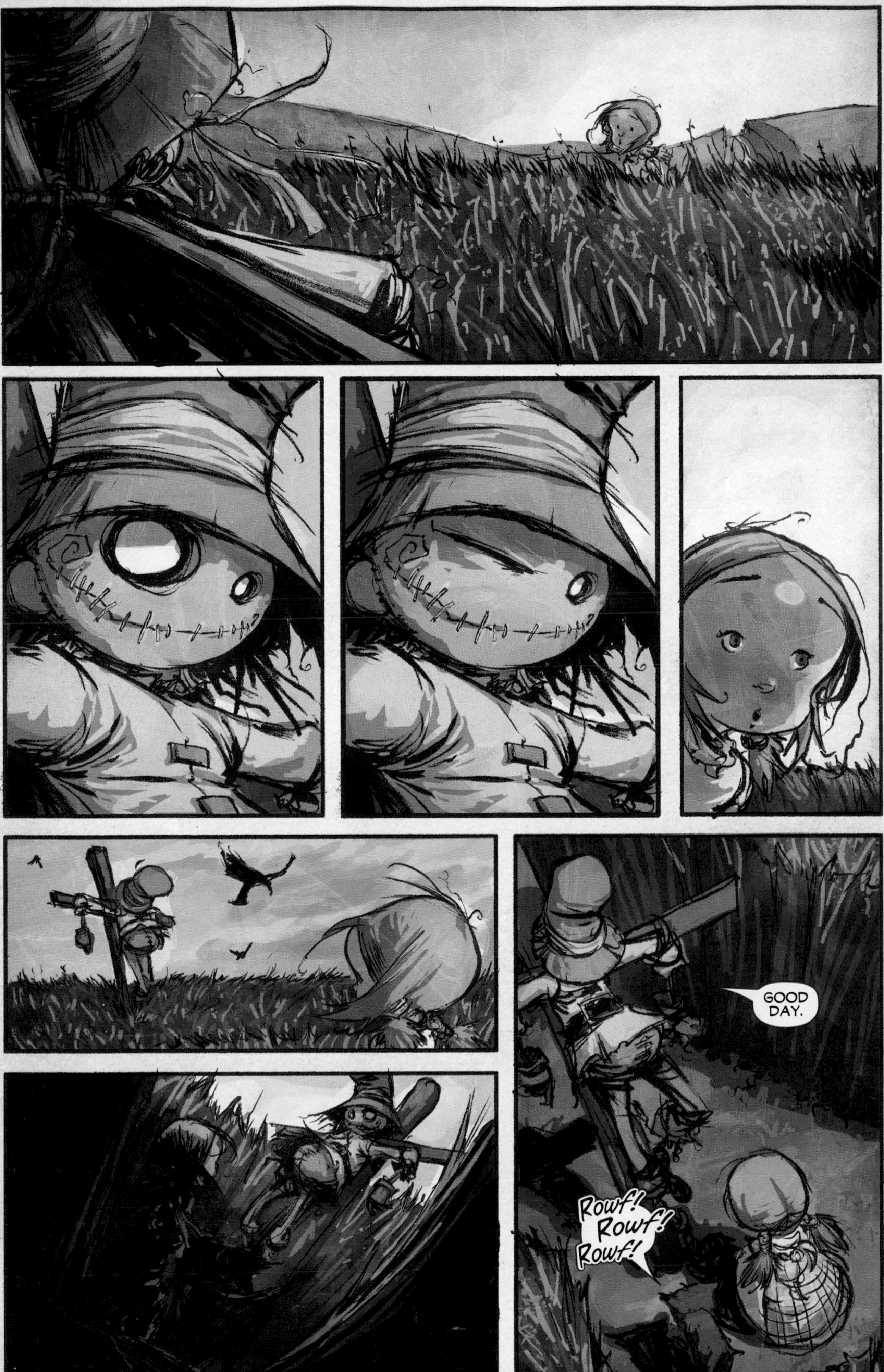
GOOD DAY.
Rowf! Rowf! Rowf!

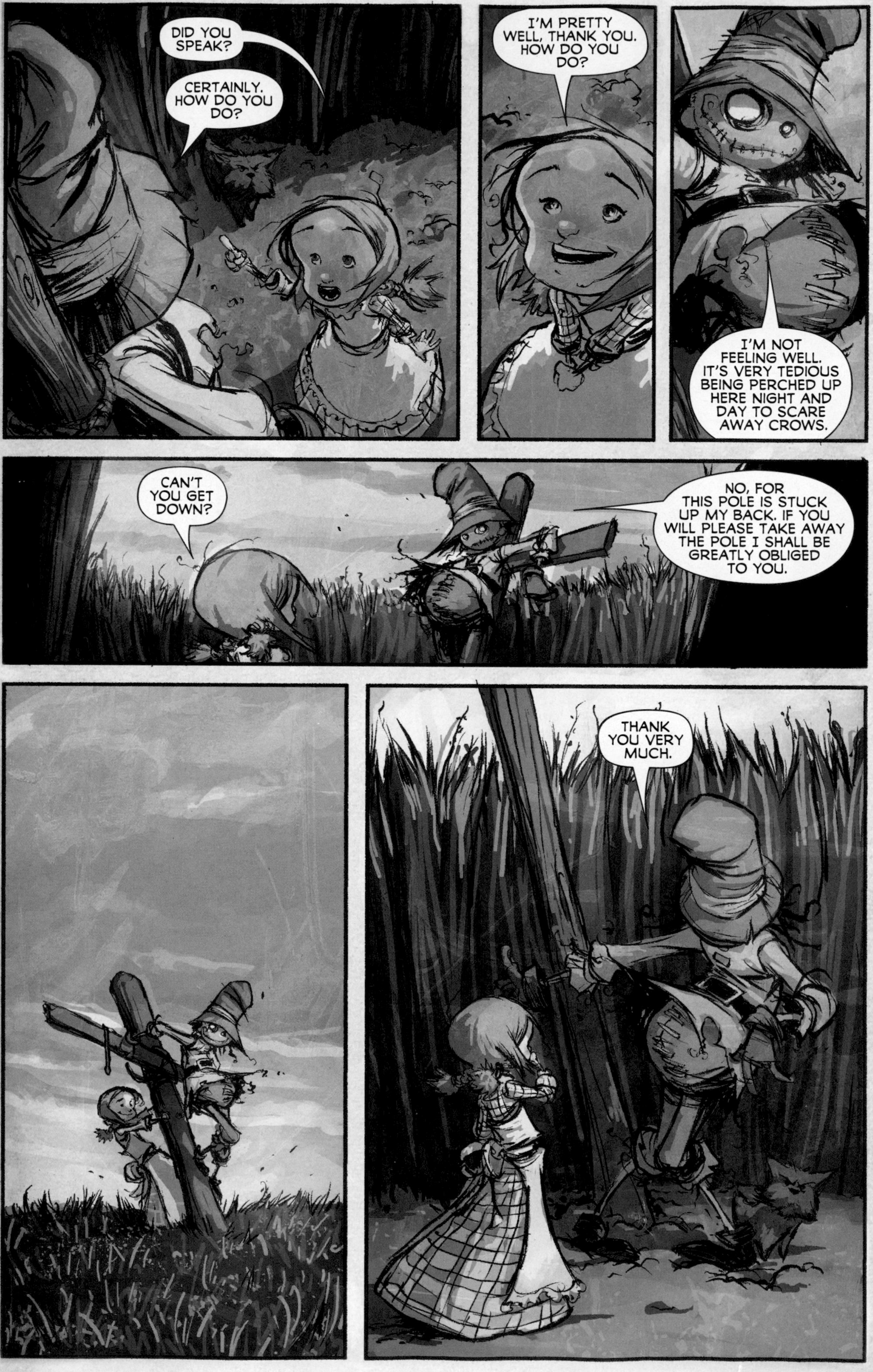
DID YOU SPEAK?
CERTAINLY. HOW DO YOU DO?
I'M PRETTY WELL, THANK YOU. HOW DO YOU DO?
I'M NOT FEELING WELL. IT'S VERY TEDIOUS BEING PERCHED UP HERE NIGHT AND DAY TO SCARE AWAY CROWS.
CAN'T YOU GET DOWN?
NO, FOR THIS POLE IS STUCK UP MY BACK. IF YOU WILL PLEASE TAKE AWAY THE POLE I SHALL BE GREATLY OBLIGED TO YOU.
THANK YOU VERY MUCH.

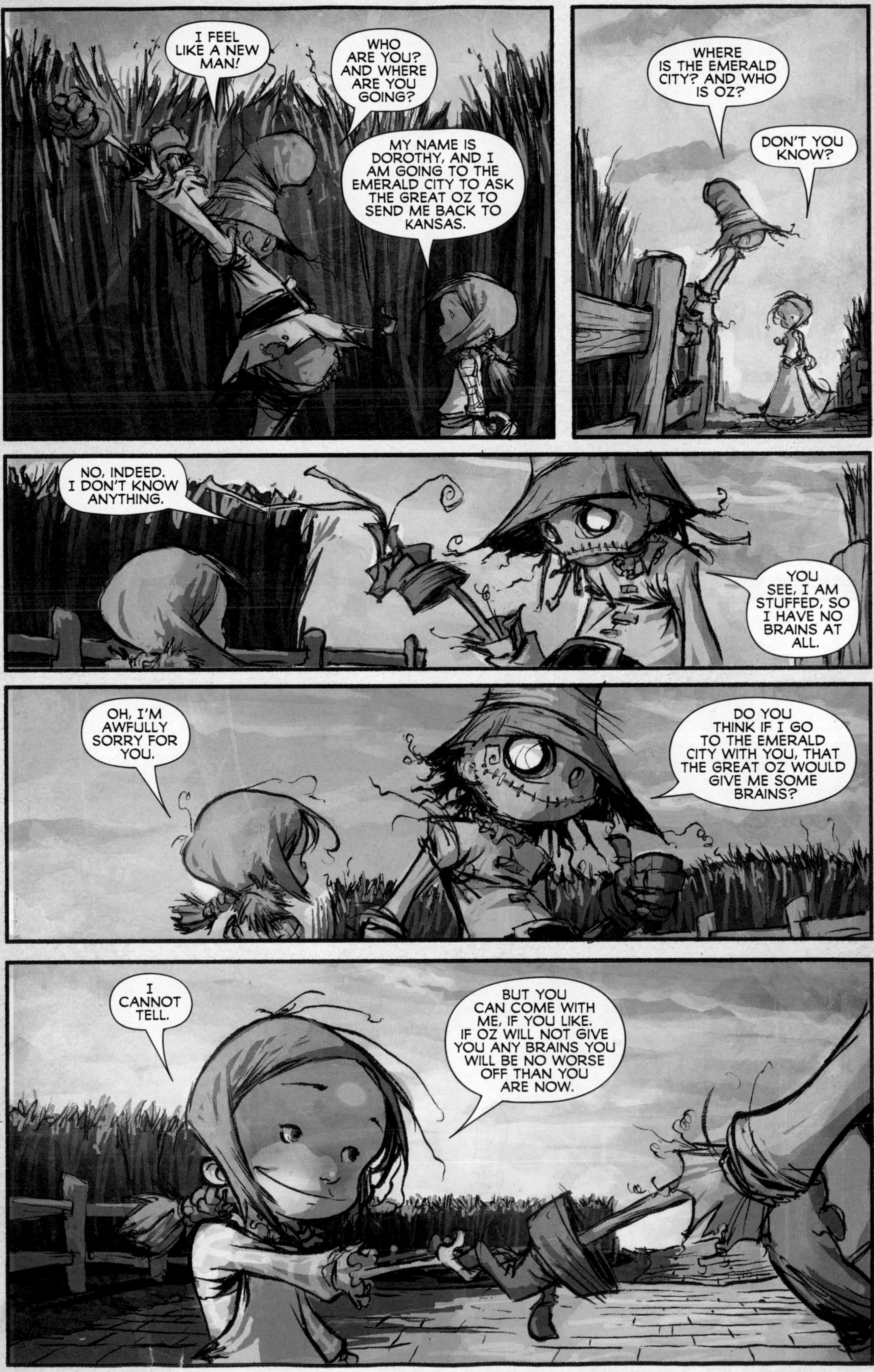

I FEEL LIKE A NEW MAN!
WHO ARE YOU? AND WHERE ARE YOU GOING?
MY NAME IS DOROTHY, AND I AM GOING TO THE EMERALD CITY TO ASK THE GREAT OZ TO SEND ME BACK TO KANSAS.
WHERE IS THE EMERALD CITY? AND WHO IS OZ?
DON'T YOU KNOW?
NO, INDEED. I DON'T KNOW ANYTHING.
YOU SEE, I AM STUFFED, SO I HAVE NO BRAINS AT ALL.
OH, I'M AWFULLY SORRY FOR YOU.
DO YOU THINK IF I GO TO THE EMERALD CITY WITH YOU, THAT THE GREAT OZ WOULD GIVE ME SOME BRAINS?
I CANNOT TELL.
BUT YOU CAN COME WITH ME, IF YOU LIKE. IF OZ WILL NOT GIVE YOU ANY BRAINS YOU WILL BE NO WORSE OFF THAN YOU ARE NOW.

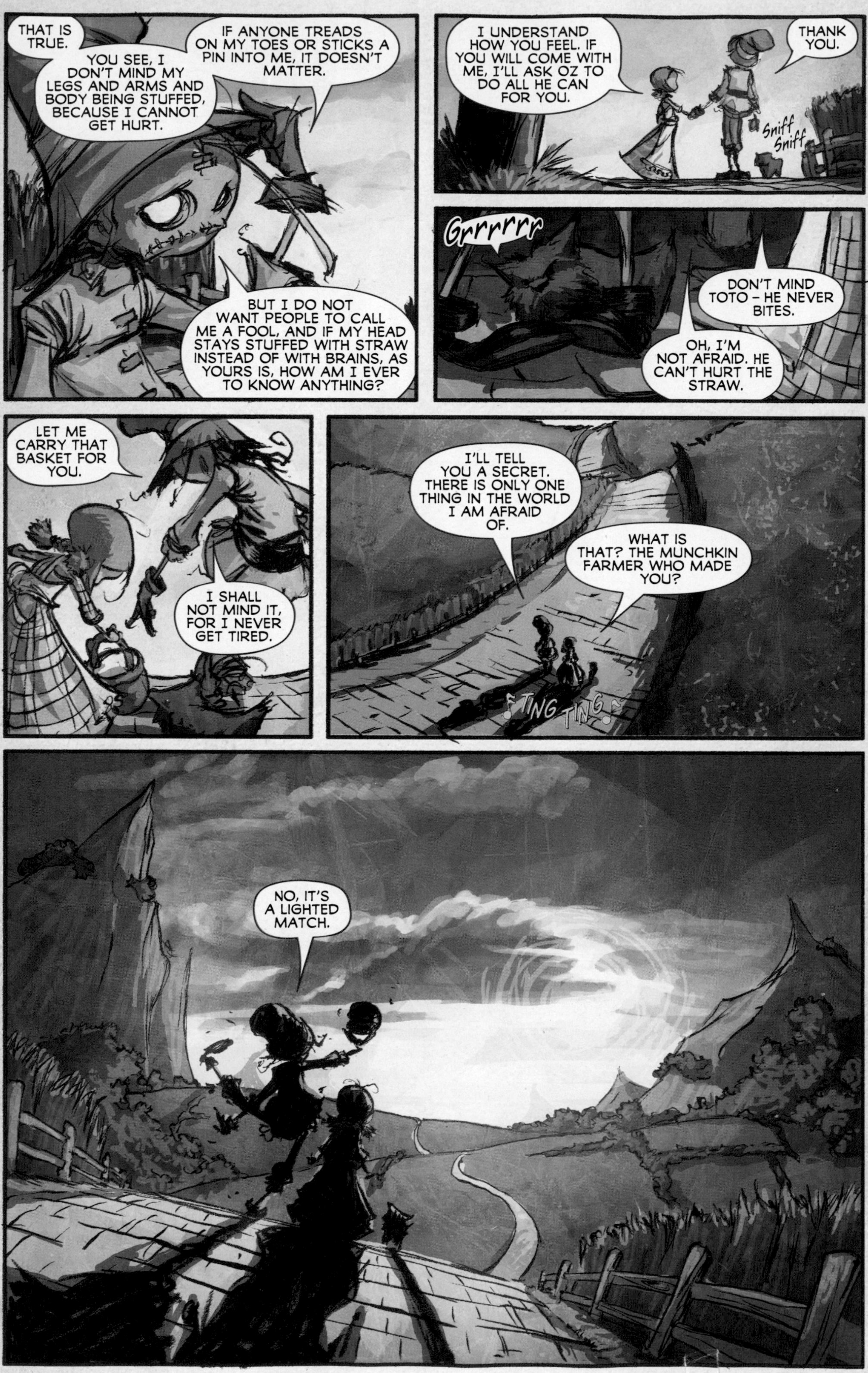
THAT IS TRUE.
YOU SEE, I DON'T MIND MY LEGS AND ARMS AND BODY BEING STUFFED, BECAUSE I CANNOT GET HURT.
IF ANYONE TREADS ON MY TOES OR STICKS A PIN INTO ME, IT DOESN'T MATTER.
BUT I DO NOT WANT PEOPLE TO CALL ME A FOOL, AND IF MY HEAD STAYS STUFFED WITH STRAW INSTEAD OF WITH BRAINS, AS YOURS IS, HOW AM I EVER TO KNOW ANYTHING?
I UNDERSTAND HOW YOU FEEL. IF YOU WILL COME WITH ME, I'LL ASK OZ TO DO ALL HE CAN FOR YOU.
THANK YOU.
Sniff Sniff
Grrrrrr
DON'T MIND TOTO – HE NEVER BITES.
OH, I'M NOT AFRAID. HE CAN'T HURT THE STRAW.
LET ME CARRY THAT BASKET FOR YOU.
I SHALL NOT MIND IT, FOR I NEVER GET TIRED.
I'LL TELL YOU A SECRET. THERE IS ONLY ONE THING IN THE WORLD I AM AFRAID OF.
WHAT IS THAT? THE MUNCHKIN FARMER WHO MADE YOU?
TING TING
NO, IT'S A LIGHTED MATCH.

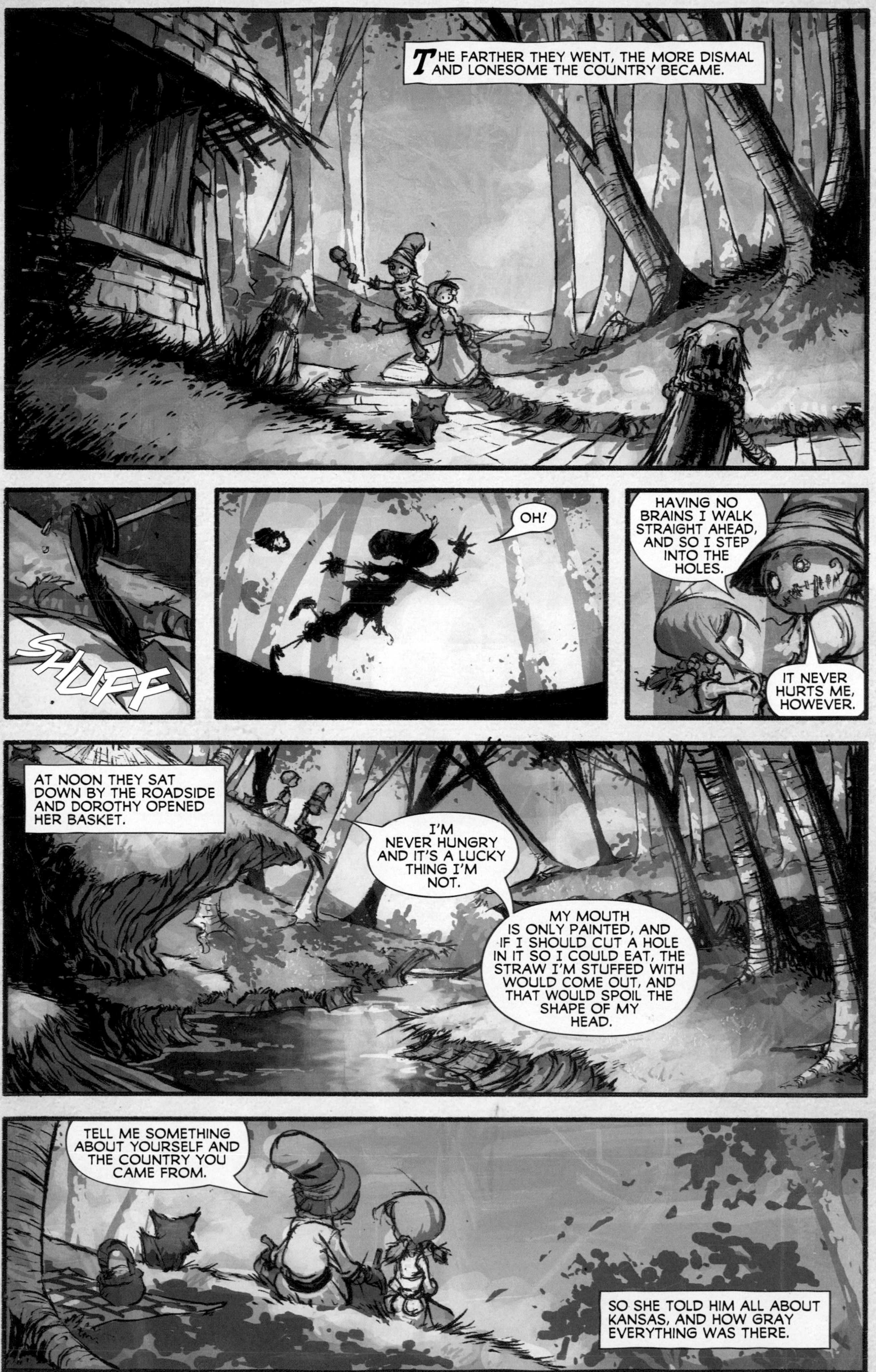
THE FARTHER THEY WENT, THE MORE DISMAL AND LONESOME THE COUNTRY BECAME.
SHUFF
OH!
HAVING NO BRAINS I WALK STRAIGHT AHEAD, AND SO I STEP INTO THE HOLES.
IT NEVER HURTS ME, HOWEVER.
AT NOON THEY SAT DOWN BY THE ROADSIDE AND DOROTHY OPENED HER BASKET.
I'M NEVER HUNGRY AND IT'S A LUCKY THING I'M NOT.
MY MOUTH IS ONLY PAINTED, AND IF I SHOULD CUT A HOLE IN IT SO I COULD EAT, THE STRAW I'M STUFFED WITH WOULD COME OUT, AND THAT WOULD SPOIL THE SHAPE OF MY HEAD.
TELL ME SOMETHING ABOUT YOURSELF AND THE COUNTRY YOU CAME FROM.
SO SHE TOLD HIM ALL ABOUT KANSAS, AND HOW GRAY EVERYTHING WAS THERE.

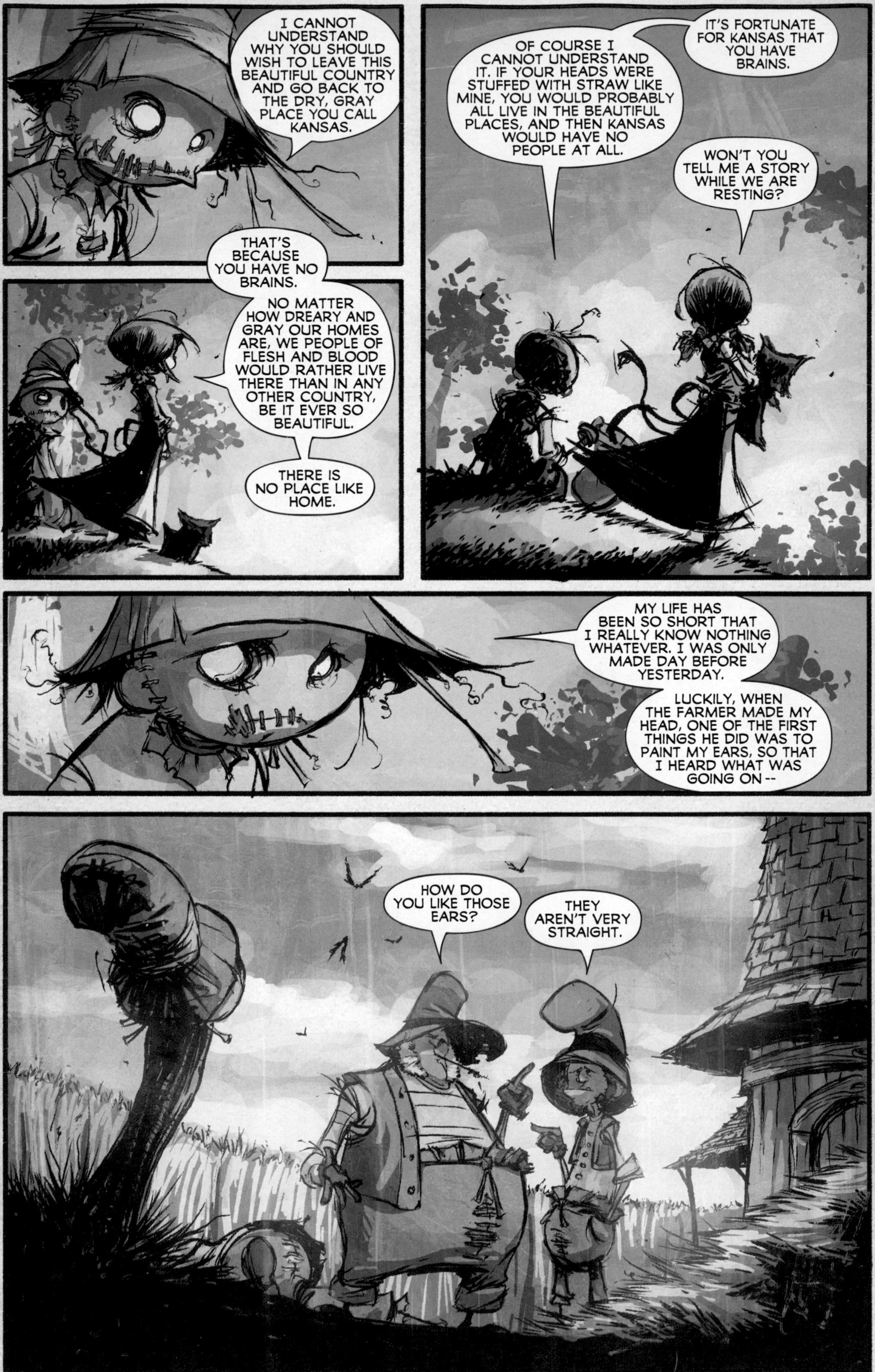
I CANNOT UNDERSTAND WHY YOU SHOULD WISH TO LEAVE THIS BEAUTIFUL COUNTRY AND GO BACK TO THE DRY, GRAY PLACE YOU CALL KANSAS.
THAT'S BECAUSE YOU HAVE NO BRAINS.
NO MATTER HOW DREARY AND GRAY OUR HOMES ARE, WE PEOPLE OF FLESH AND BLOOD WOULD RATHER LIVE THERE THAN IN ANY OTHER COUNTRY, BE IT EVER SO BEAUTIFUL.
THERE IS NO PLACE LIKE HOME.
OF COURSE I CANNOT UNDERSTAND IT. IF YOUR HEADS WERE STUFFED WITH STRAW LIKE MINE, YOU WOULD PROBABLY ALL LIVE IN THE BEAUTIFUL PLACES, AND THEN KANSAS WOULD HAVE NO PEOPLE AT ALL.
IT'S FORTUNATE FOR KANSAS THAT YOU HAVE BRAINS.
WON'T YOU TELL ME A STORY WHILE WE ARE RESTING?
MY LIFE HAS BEEN SO SHORT THAT I REALLY KNOW NOTHING WHATEVER. I WAS ONLY MADE DAY BEFORE YESTERDAY.
LUCKILY, WHEN THE FARMER MADE MY HEAD, ONE OF THE FIRST THINGS HE DID WAS TO PAINT MY EARS, SO THAT I HEARD WHAT WAS GOING ON --
HOW DO YOU LIKE THOSE EARS?
THEY AREN'T VERY STRAIGHT.

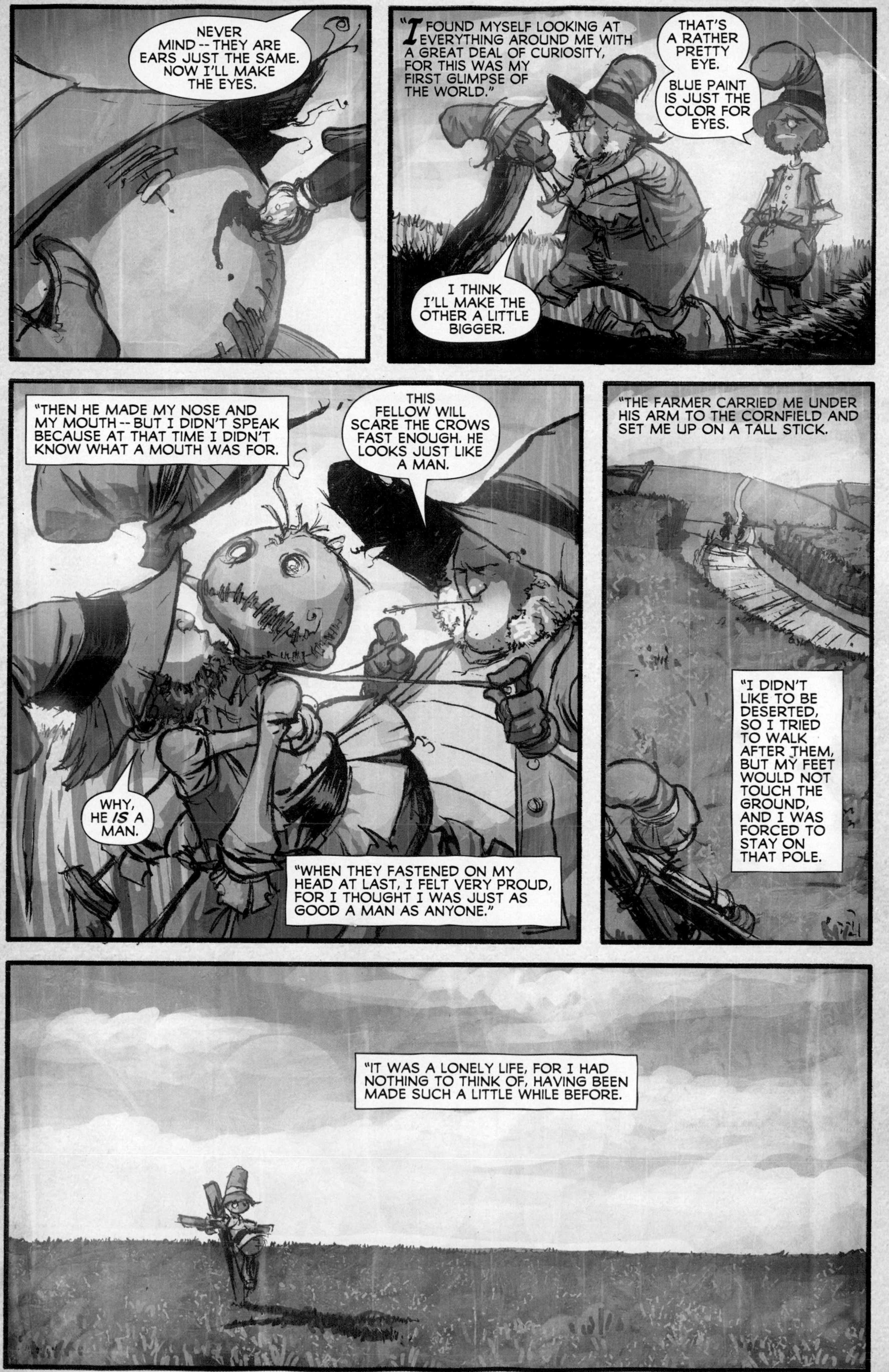
NEVER MIND -- THEY ARE EARS JUST THE SAME. NOW I'LL MAKE THE EYES.
"I FOUND MYSELF LOOKING AT EVERYTHING AROUND ME WITH A GREAT DEAL OF CURIOSITY, FOR THIS WAS MY FIRST GLIMPSE OF THE WORLD."
THAT'S A RATHER PRETTY EYE.
BLUE PAINT IS JUST THE COLOR FOR EYES.
I THINK I'LL MAKE THE OTHER A LITTLE BIGGER.
"THEN HE MADE MY NOSE AND MY MOUTH -- BUT I DIDN'T SPEAK BECAUSE AT THAT TIME I DIDN'T KNOW WHAT A MOUTH WAS FOR.
THIS FELLOW WILL SCARE THE CROWS FAST ENOUGH. HE LOOKS JUST LIKE A MAN.
WHY, HE *IS* A MAN.
"WHEN THEY FASTENED ON MY HEAD AT LAST, I FELT VERY PROUD, FOR I THOUGHT I WAS JUST AS GOOD A MAN AS ANYONE."
"THE FARMER CARRIED ME UNDER HIS ARM TO THE CORNFIELD AND SET ME UP ON A TALL STICK.
"I DIDN'T LIKE TO BE DESERTED, SO I TRIED TO WALK AFTER THEM, BUT MY FEET WOULD NOT TOUCH THE GROUND, AND I WAS FORCED TO STAY ON THAT POLE.
"IT WAS A LONELY LIFE, FOR I HAD NOTHING TO THINK OF, HAVING BEEN MADE SUCH A LITTLE WHILE BEFORE.

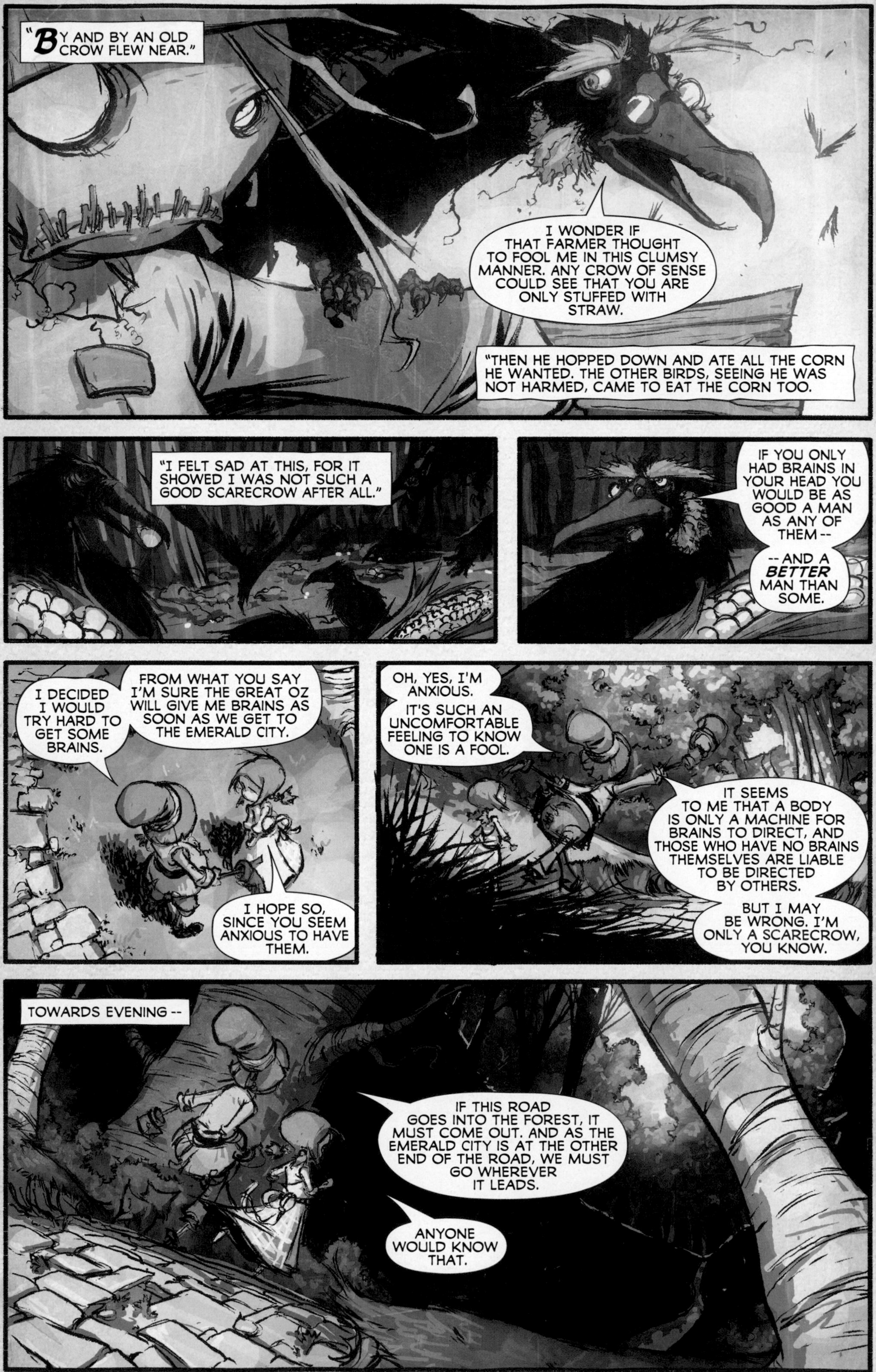
"BY AND BY AN OLD CROW FLEW NEAR."
I WONDER IF THAT FARMER THOUGHT TO FOOL ME IN THIS CLUMSY MANNER. ANY CROW OF SENSE COULD SEE THAT YOU ARE ONLY STUFFED WITH STRAW.
"THEN HE HOPPED DOWN AND ATE ALL THE CORN HE WANTED. THE OTHER BIRDS, SEEING HE WAS NOT HARMED, CAME TO EAT THE CORN TOO.
"I FELT SAD AT THIS, FOR IT SHOWED I WAS NOT SUCH A GOOD SCARECROW AFTER ALL."
IF YOU ONLY HAD BRAINS IN YOUR HEAD YOU WOULD BE AS GOOD A MAN AS ANY OF THEM --
-- AND A ***BETTER*** MAN THAN SOME.
I DECIDED I WOULD TRY HARD TO GET SOME BRAINS.
FROM WHAT YOU SAY I'M SURE THE GREAT OZ WILL GIVE ME BRAINS AS SOON AS WE GET TO THE EMERALD CITY.
I HOPE SO, SINCE YOU SEEM ANXIOUS TO HAVE THEM.
OH, YES, I'M ANXIOUS.
IT'S SUCH AN UNCOMFORTABLE FEELING TO KNOW ONE IS A FOOL.
IT SEEMS TO ME THAT A BODY IS ONLY A MACHINE FOR BRAINS TO DIRECT, AND THOSE WHO HAVE NO BRAINS THEMSELVES ARE LIABLE TO BE DIRECTED BY OTHERS.
BUT I MAY BE WRONG. I'M ONLY A SCARECROW, YOU KNOW.
TOWARDS EVENING --
IF THIS ROAD GOES INTO THE FOREST, IT MUST COME OUT. AND AS THE EMERALD CITY IS AT THE OTHER END OF THE ROAD, WE MUST GO WHEREVER IT LEADS.
ANYONE WOULD KNOW THAT.

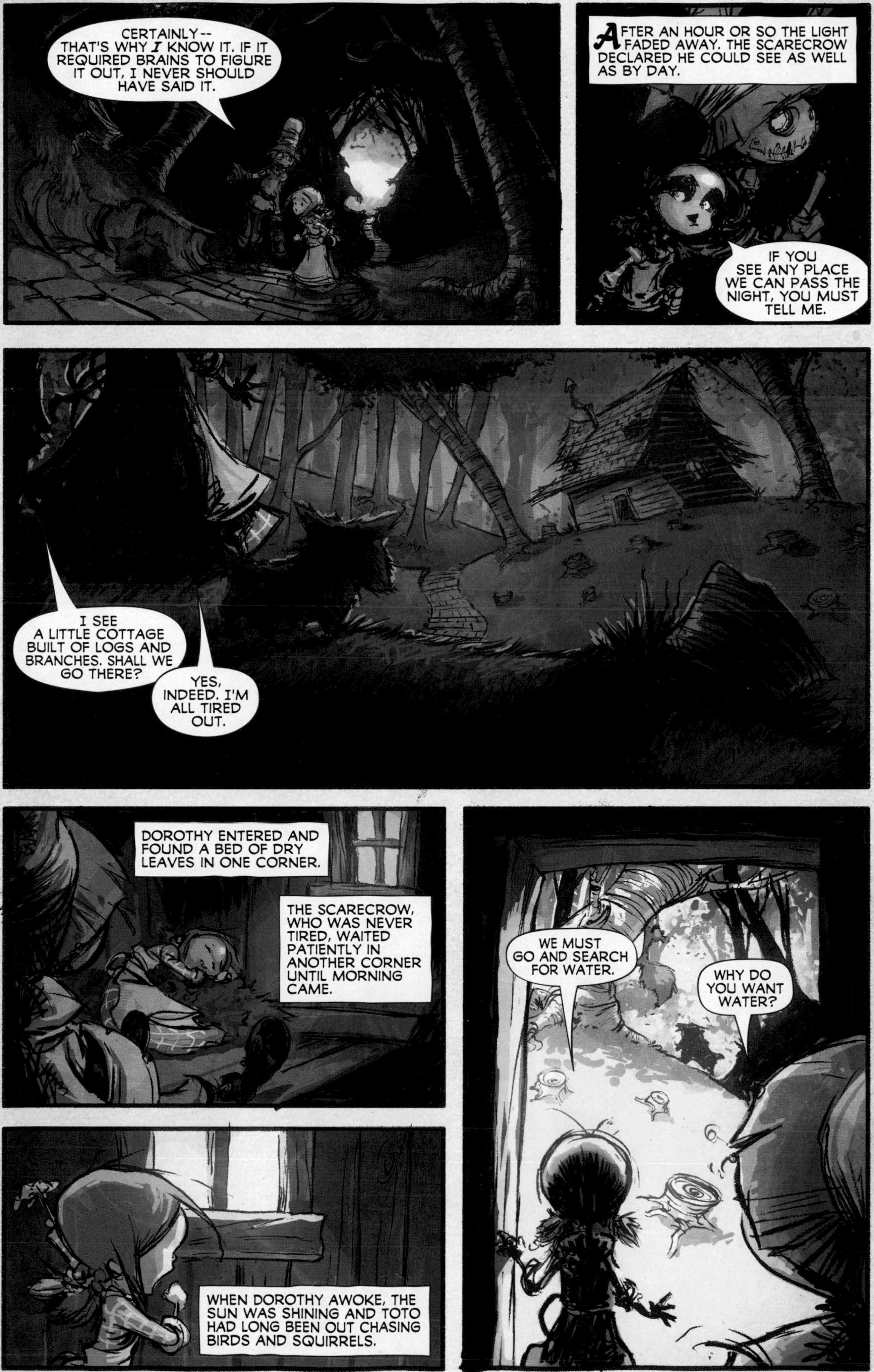
CERTAINLY-- THAT'S WHY I KNOW IT. IF IT REQUIRED BRAINS TO FIGURE IT OUT, I NEVER SHOULD HAVE SAID IT.
AFTER AN HOUR OR SO THE LIGHT FADED AWAY. THE SCARECROW DECLARED HE COULD SEE AS WELL AS BY DAY.
IF YOU SEE ANY PLACE WE CAN PASS THE NIGHT, YOU MUST TELL ME.
I SEE A LITTLE COTTAGE BUILT OF LOGS AND BRANCHES. SHALL WE GO THERE?
YES, INDEED. I'M ALL TIRED OUT.
DOROTHY ENTERED AND FOUND A BED OF DRY LEAVES IN ONE CORNER.
THE SCARECROW, WHO WAS NEVER TIRED, WAITED PATIENTLY IN ANOTHER CORNER UNTIL MORNING CAME.
WHEN DOROTHY AWOKE, THE SUN WAS SHINING AND TOTO HAD LONG BEEN OUT CHASING BIRDS AND SQUIRRELS.
WE MUST GO AND SEARCH FOR WATER.
WHY DO YOU WANT WATER?

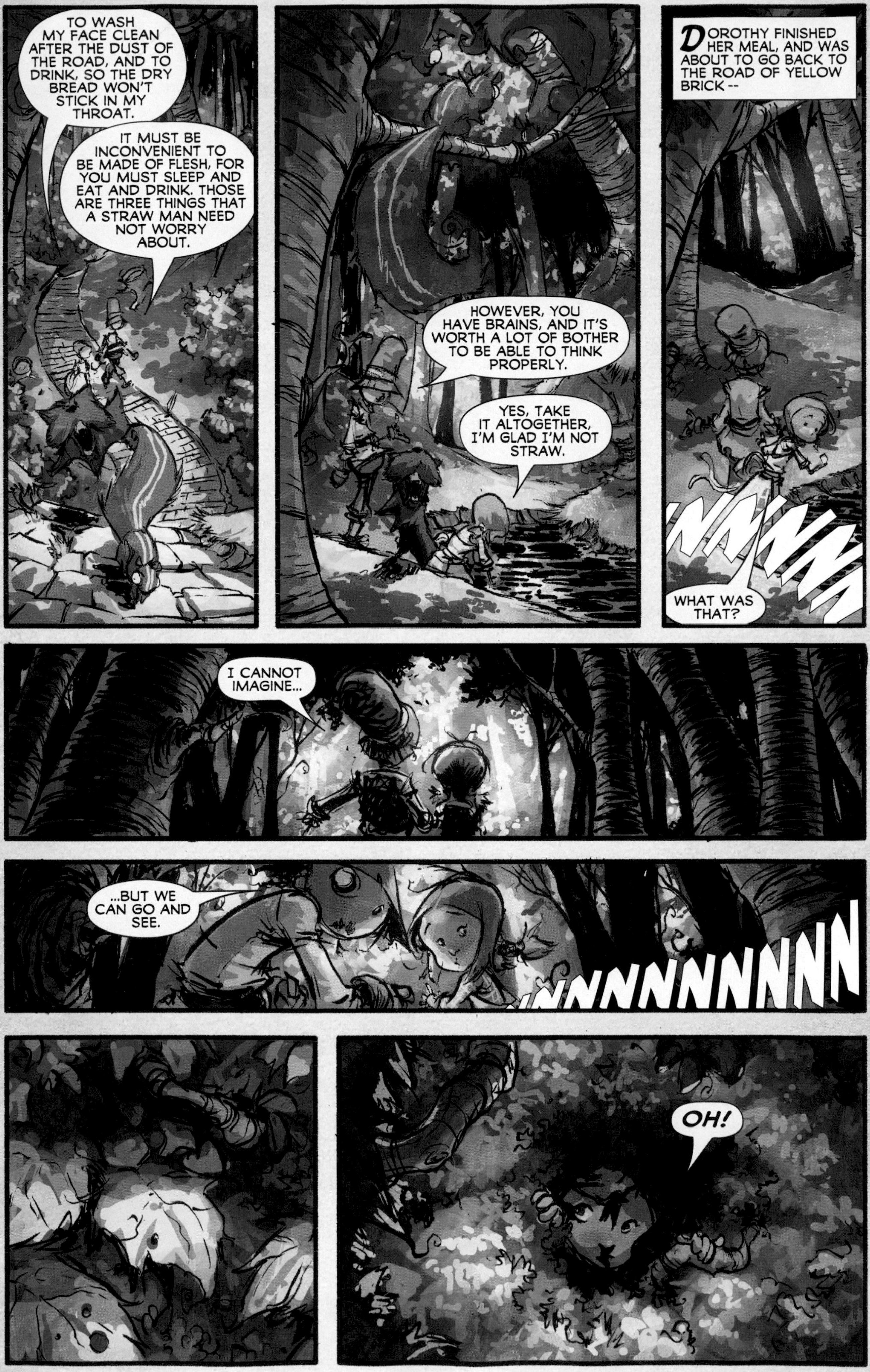
TO WASH MY FACE CLEAN AFTER THE DUST OF THE ROAD, AND TO DRINK, SO THE DRY BREAD WON'T STICK IN MY THROAT.
IT MUST BE INCONVENIENT TO BE MADE OF FLESH, FOR YOU MUST SLEEP AND EAT AND DRINK. THOSE ARE THREE THINGS THAT A STRAW MAN NEED NOT WORRY ABOUT.
HOWEVER, YOU HAVE BRAINS, AND IT'S WORTH A LOT OF BOTHER TO BE ABLE TO THINK PROPERLY.
YES, TAKE IT ALTOGETHER, I'M GLAD I'M NOT STRAW.
DOROTHY FINISHED HER MEAL, AND WAS ABOUT TO GO BACK TO THE ROAD OF YELLOW BRICK --
NNNNNN
WHAT WAS THAT?
I CANNOT IMAGINE...
...BUT WE CAN GO AND SEE.
NNNNNNNNNNNN
OH!

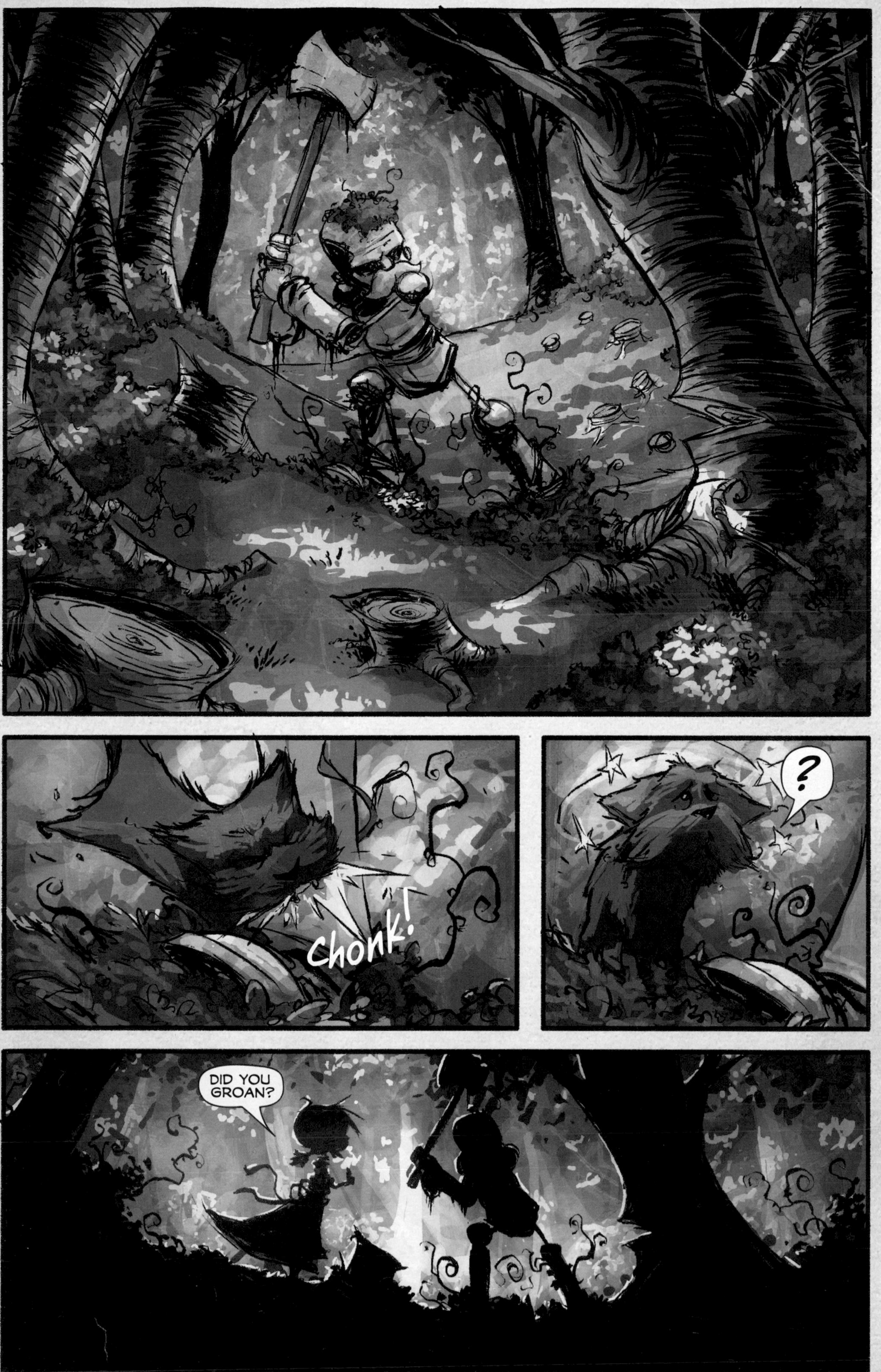
Chonk!
?
DID YOU GROAN?

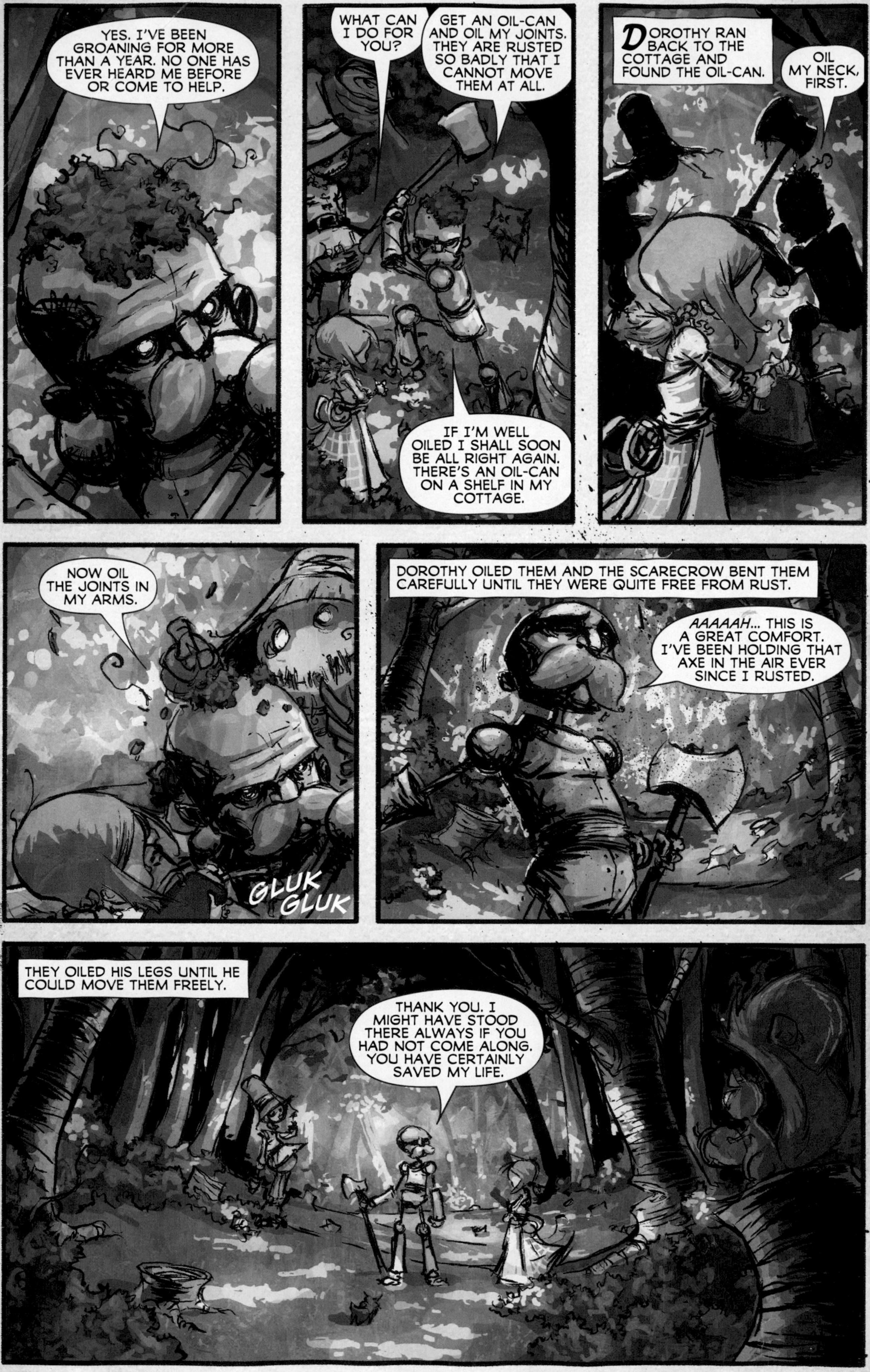
YES. I'VE BEEN GROANING FOR MORE THAN A YEAR. NO ONE HAS EVER HEARD ME BEFORE OR COME TO HELP.
WHAT CAN I DO FOR YOU?
GET AN OIL-CAN AND OIL MY JOINTS. THEY ARE RUSTED SO BADLY THAT I CANNOT MOVE THEM AT ALL.
IF I'M WELL OILED I SHALL SOON BE ALL RIGHT AGAIN. THERE'S AN OIL-CAN ON A SHELF IN MY COTTAGE.
DOROTHY RAN BACK TO THE COTTAGE AND FOUND THE OIL-CAN.
OIL MY NECK, FIRST.
NOW OIL THE JOINTS IN MY ARMS.
GLUK GLUK
DOROTHY OILED THEM AND THE SCARECROW BENT THEM CAREFULLY UNTIL THEY WERE QUITE FREE FROM RUST.
AAAAAH... THIS IS A GREAT COMFORT. I'VE BEEN HOLDING THAT AXE IN THE AIR EVER SINCE I RUSTED.
THEY OILED HIS LEGS UNTIL HE COULD MOVE THEM FREELY.
THANK YOU. I MIGHT HAVE STOOD THERE ALWAYS IF YOU HAD NOT COME ALONG. YOU HAVE CERTAINLY SAVED MY LIFE.

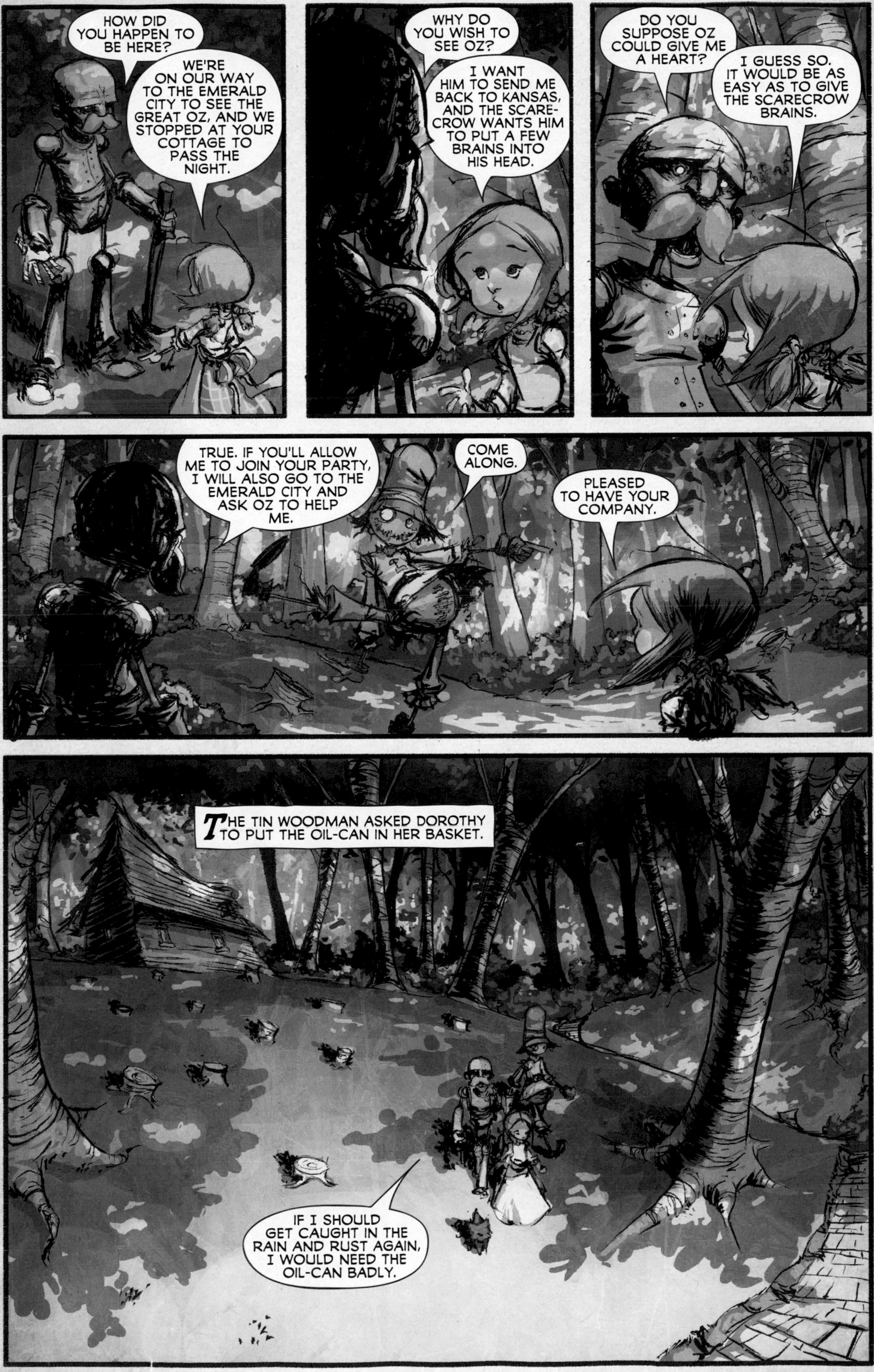
HOW DID YOU HAPPEN TO BE HERE?
WE'RE ON OUR WAY TO THE EMERALD CITY TO SEE THE GREAT OZ, AND WE STOPPED AT YOUR COTTAGE TO PASS THE NIGHT.
WHY DO YOU WISH TO SEE OZ?
I WANT HIM TO SEND ME BACK TO KANSAS, AND THE SCARE-CROW WANTS HIM TO PUT A FEW BRAINS INTO HIS HEAD.
DO YOU SUPPOSE OZ COULD GIVE ME A HEART?
I GUESS SO. IT WOULD BE AS EASY AS TO GIVE THE SCARECROW BRAINS.
TRUE. IF YOU'LL ALLOW ME TO JOIN YOUR PARTY, I WILL ALSO GO TO THE EMERALD CITY AND ASK OZ TO HELP ME.
COME ALONG.
PLEASED TO HAVE YOUR COMPANY.
THE TIN WOODMAN ASKED DOROTHY TO PUT THE OIL-CAN IN HER BASKET.
IF I SHOULD GET CAUGHT IN THE RAIN AND RUST AGAIN, I WOULD NEED THE OIL-CAN BADLY.

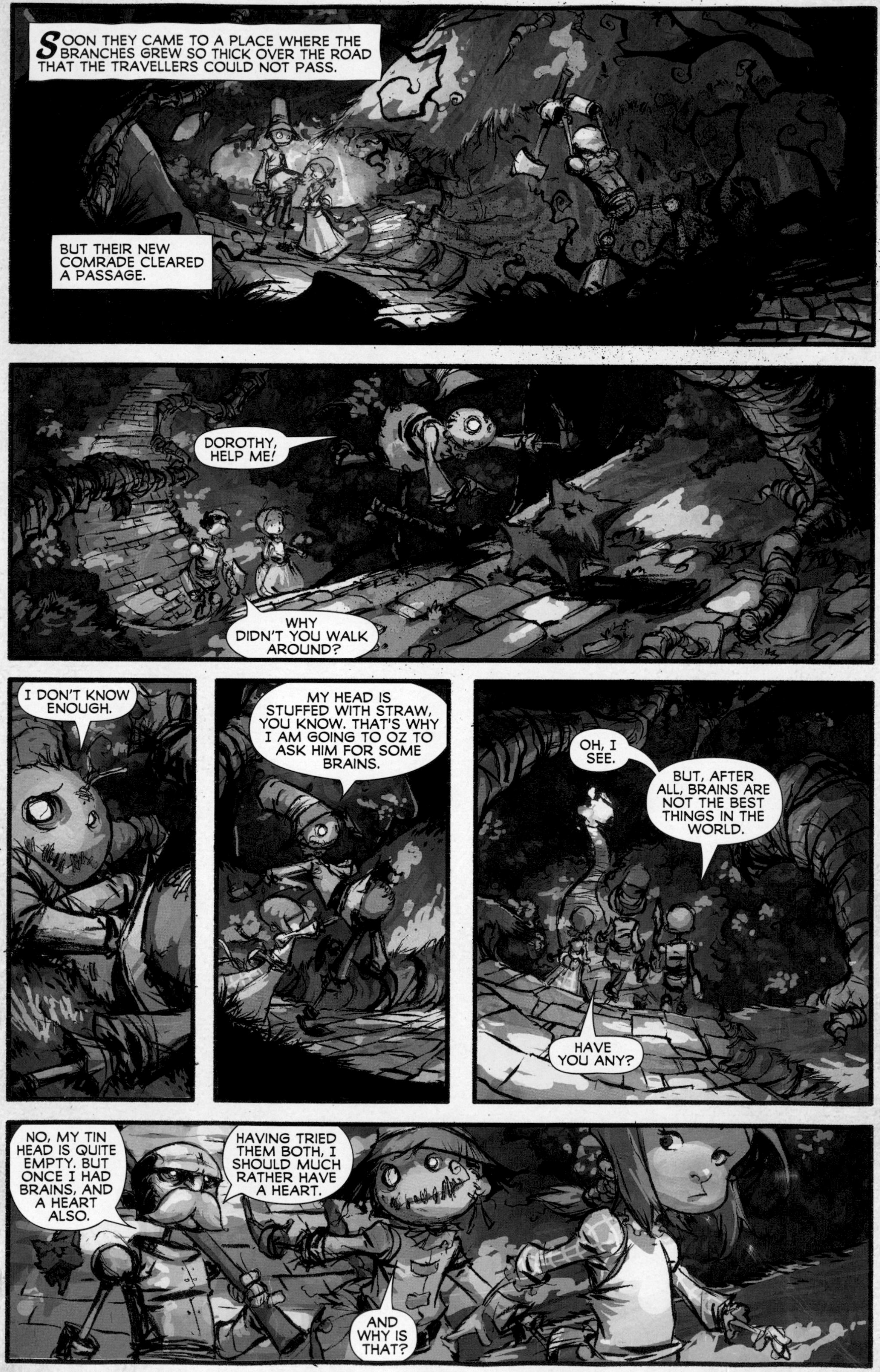
SOON THEY CAME TO A PLACE WHERE THE BRANCHES GREW SO THICK OVER THE ROAD THAT THE TRAVELLERS COULD NOT PASS.
BUT THEIR NEW COMRADE CLEARED A PASSAGE.
DOROTHY, HELP ME!
WHY DIDN'T YOU WALK AROUND?
I DON'T KNOW ENOUGH.
MY HEAD IS STUFFED WITH STRAW, YOU KNOW. THAT'S WHY I AM GOING TO OZ TO ASK HIM FOR SOME BRAINS.
OH, I SEE.
BUT, AFTER ALL, BRAINS ARE NOT THE BEST THINGS IN THE WORLD.
HAVE YOU ANY?
NO, MY TIN HEAD IS QUITE EMPTY. BUT ONCE I HAD BRAINS, AND A HEART ALSO.
HAVING TRIED THEM BOTH, I SHOULD MUCH RATHER HAVE A HEART.
AND WHY IS THAT?

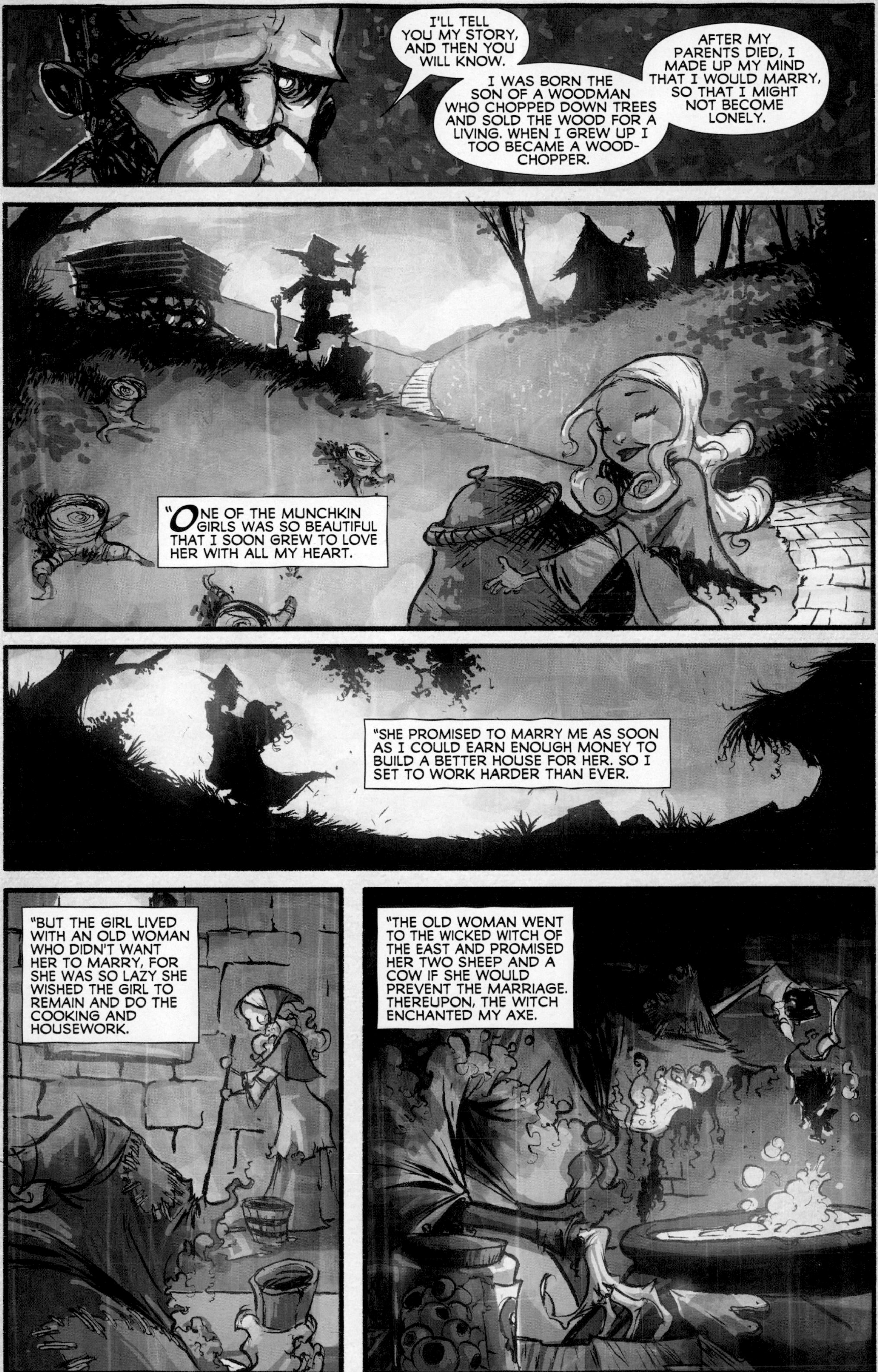
I'LL TELL YOU MY STORY, AND THEN YOU WILL KNOW.
I WAS BORN THE SON OF A WOODMAN WHO CHOPPED DOWN TREES AND SOLD THE WOOD FOR A LIVING. WHEN I GREW UP I TOO BECAME A WOOD-CHOPPER.
AFTER MY PARENTS DIED, I MADE UP MY MIND THAT I WOULD MARRY, SO THAT I MIGHT NOT BECOME LONELY.
"ONE OF THE MUNCHKIN GIRLS WAS SO BEAUTIFUL THAT I SOON GREW TO LOVE HER WITH ALL MY HEART.
"SHE PROMISED TO MARRY ME AS SOON AS I COULD EARN ENOUGH MONEY TO BUILD A BETTER HOUSE FOR HER. SO I SET TO WORK HARDER THAN EVER.
"BUT THE GIRL LIVED WITH AN OLD WOMAN WHO DIDN'T WANT HER TO MARRY, FOR SHE WAS SO LAZY SHE WISHED THE GIRL TO REMAIN AND DO THE COOKING AND HOUSEWORK.
"THE OLD WOMAN WENT TO THE WICKED WITCH OF THE EAST AND PROMISED HER TWO SHEEP AND A COW IF SHE WOULD PREVENT THE MARRIAGE. THEREUPON, THE WITCH ENCHANTED MY AXE.

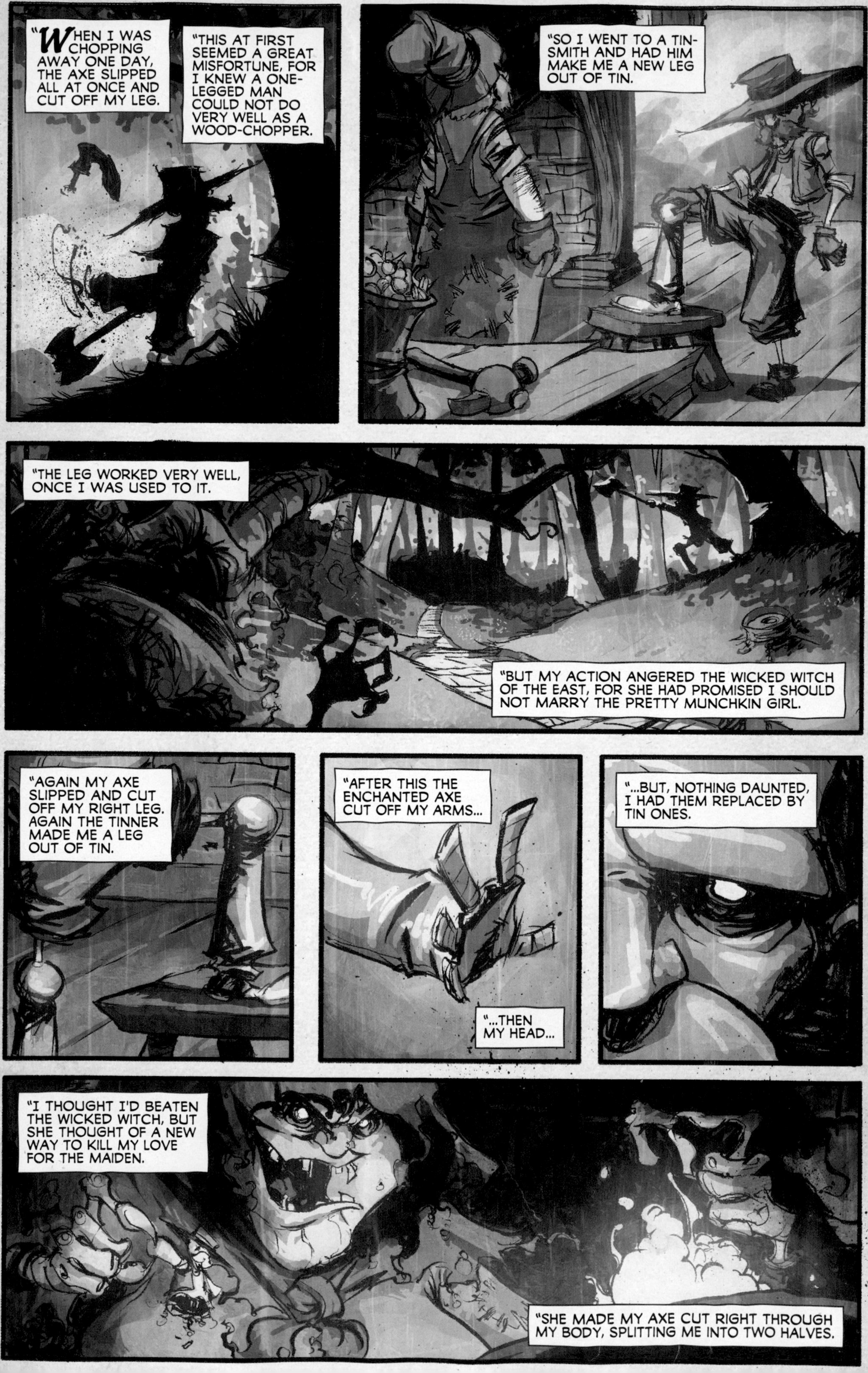
"WHEN I WAS CHOPPING AWAY ONE DAY, THE AXE SLIPPED ALL AT ONCE AND CUT OFF MY LEG.
"THIS AT FIRST SEEMED A GREAT MISFORTUNE, FOR I KNEW A ONE-LEGGED MAN COULD NOT DO VERY WELL AS A WOOD-CHOPPER.
"SO I WENT TO A TIN-SMITH AND HAD HIM MAKE ME A NEW LEG OUT OF TIN.
"THE LEG WORKED VERY WELL, ONCE I WAS USED TO IT.
"BUT MY ACTION ANGERED THE WICKED WITCH OF THE EAST, FOR SHE HAD PROMISED I SHOULD NOT MARRY THE PRETTY MUNCHKIN GIRL.
"AGAIN MY AXE SLIPPED AND CUT OFF MY RIGHT LEG. AGAIN THE TINNER MADE ME A LEG OUT OF TIN.
"AFTER THIS THE ENCHANTED AXE CUT OFF MY ARMS...
"...THEN MY HEAD...
"...BUT, NOTHING DAUNTED, I HAD THEM REPLACED BY TIN ONES.
"I THOUGHT I'D BEATEN THE WICKED WITCH, BUT SHE THOUGHT OF A NEW WAY TO KILL MY LOVE FOR THE MAIDEN.
"SHE MADE MY AXE CUT RIGHT THROUGH MY BODY, SPLITTING ME INTO TWO HALVES.

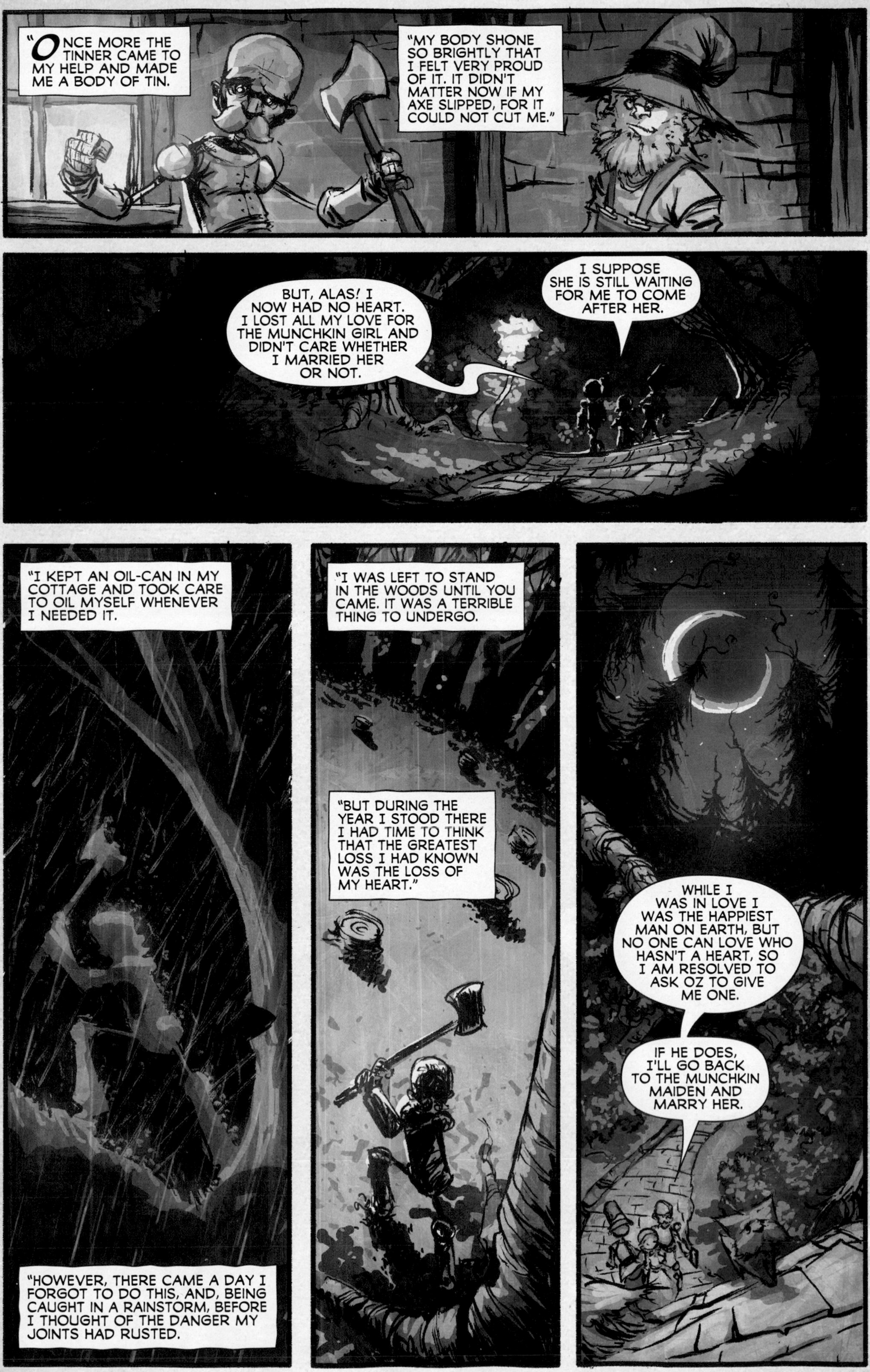
"ONCE MORE THE TINNER CAME TO MY HELP AND MADE ME A BODY OF TIN.
"MY BODY SHONE SO BRIGHTLY THAT I FELT VERY PROUD OF IT. IT DIDN'T MATTER NOW IF MY AXE SLIPPED, FOR IT COULD NOT CUT ME."
BUT, ALAS! I NOW HAD NO HEART. I LOST ALL MY LOVE FOR THE MUNCHKIN GIRL AND DIDN'T CARE WHETHER I MARRIED HER OR NOT.
I SUPPOSE SHE IS STILL WAITING FOR ME TO COME AFTER HER.
"I KEPT AN OIL-CAN IN MY COTTAGE AND TOOK CARE TO OIL MYSELF WHENEVER I NEEDED IT.
"HOWEVER, THERE CAME A DAY I FORGOT TO DO THIS, AND, BEING CAUGHT IN A RAINSTORM, BEFORE I THOUGHT OF THE DANGER MY JOINTS HAD RUSTED.
"I WAS LEFT TO STAND IN THE WOODS UNTIL YOU CAME. IT WAS A TERRIBLE THING TO UNDERGO.
"BUT DURING THE YEAR I STOOD THERE I HAD TIME TO THINK THAT THE GREATEST LOSS I HAD KNOWN WAS THE LOSS OF MY HEART."
WHILE I WAS IN LOVE I WAS THE HAPPIEST MAN ON EARTH, BUT NO ONE CAN LOVE WHO HASN'T A HEART, SO I AM RESOLVED TO ASK OZ TO GIVE ME ONE.
IF HE DOES, I'LL GO BACK TO THE MUNCHKIN MAIDEN AND MARRY HER.

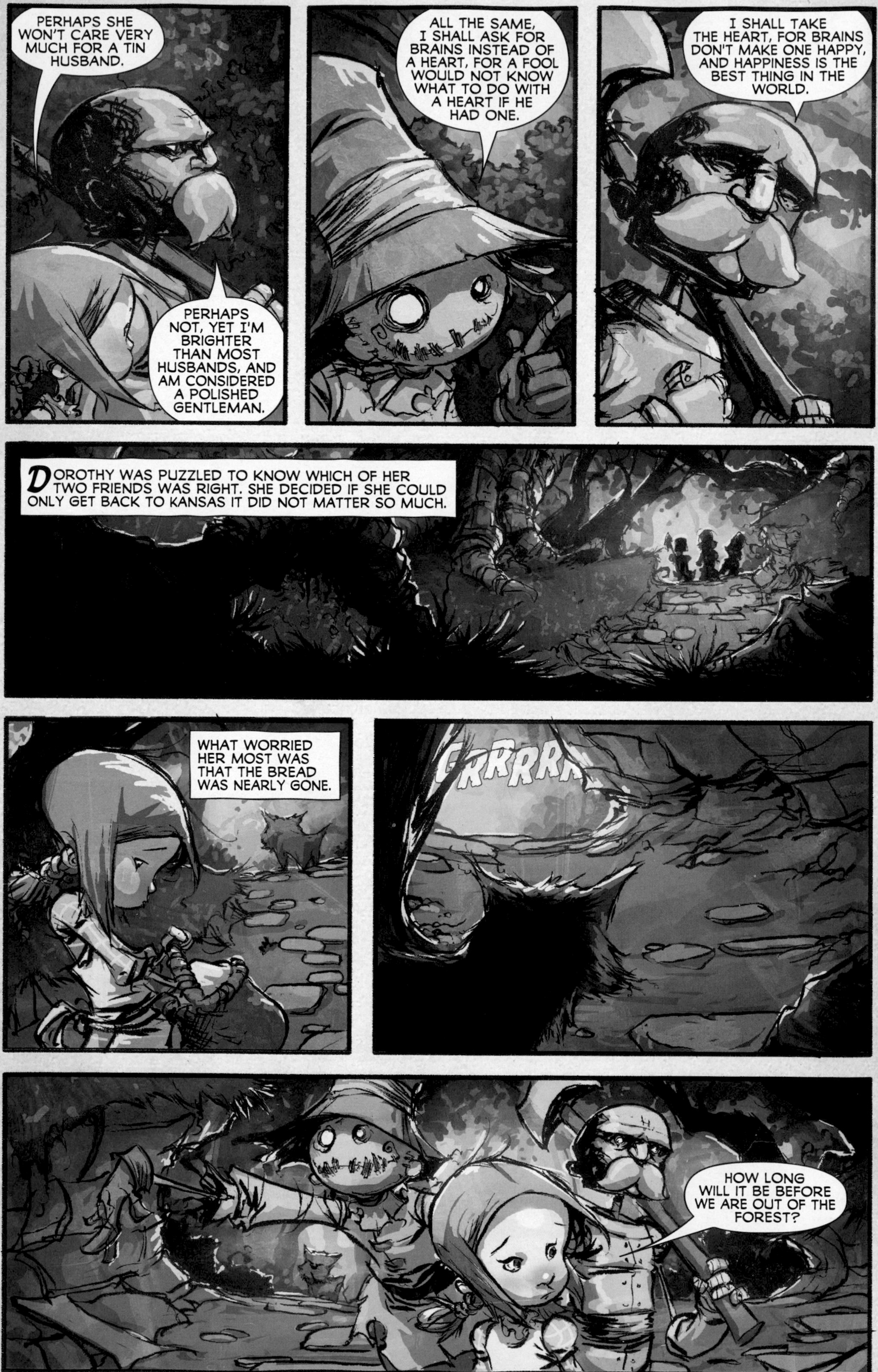
PERHAPS SHE WON'T CARE VERY MUCH FOR A TIN HUSBAND.
PERHAPS NOT, YET I'M BRIGHTER THAN MOST HUSBANDS, AND AM CONSIDERED A POLISHED GENTLEMAN.
ALL THE SAME, I SHALL ASK FOR BRAINS INSTEAD OF A HEART, FOR A FOOL WOULD NOT KNOW WHAT TO DO WITH A HEART IF HE HAD ONE.
I SHALL TAKE THE HEART, FOR BRAINS DON'T MAKE ONE HAPPY, AND HAPPINESS IS THE BEST THING IN THE WORLD.
DOROTHY WAS PUZZLED TO KNOW WHICH OF HER TWO FRIENDS WAS RIGHT. SHE DECIDED IF SHE COULD ONLY GET BACK TO KANSAS IT DID NOT MATTER SO MUCH.
WHAT WORRIED HER MOST WAS THAT THE BREAD WAS NEARLY GONE.
GRRRRR
HOW LONG WILL IT BE BEFORE WE ARE OUT OF THE FOREST?

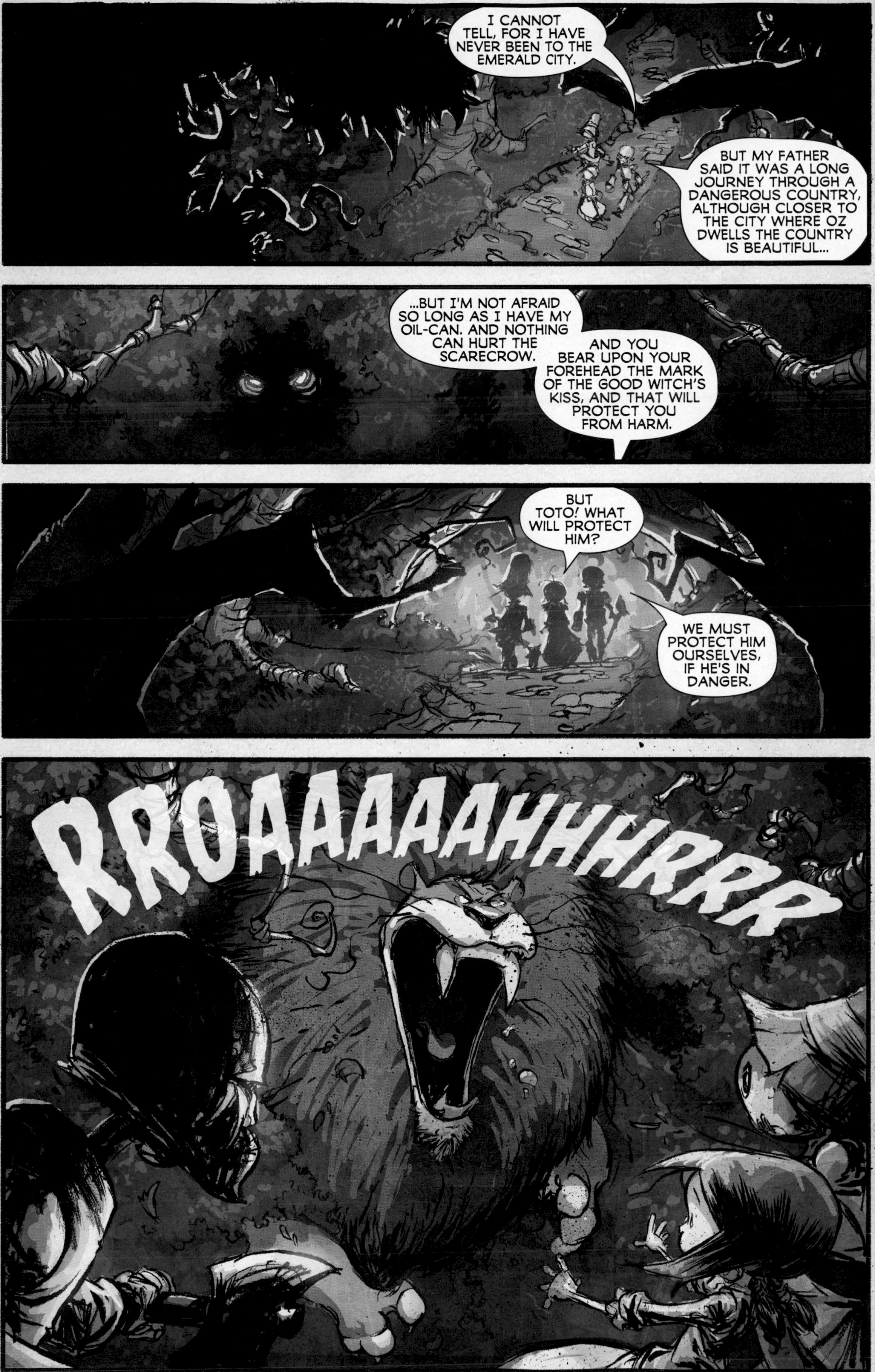
I CANNOT TELL, FOR I HAVE NEVER BEEN TO THE EMERALD CITY.
BUT MY FATHER SAID IT WAS A LONG JOURNEY THROUGH A DANGEROUS COUNTRY, ALTHOUGH CLOSER TO THE CITY WHERE OZ DWELLS THE COUNTRY IS BEAUTIFUL...
...BUT I'M NOT AFRAID SO LONG AS I HAVE MY OIL-CAN. AND NOTHING CAN HURT THE SCARECROW.
AND YOU BEAR UPON YOUR FOREHEAD THE MARK OF THE GOOD WITCH'S KISS, AND THAT WILL PROTECT YOU FROM HARM.
BUT TOTO! WHAT WILL PROTECT HIM?
WE MUST PROTECT HIM OURSELVES, IF HE'S IN DANGER.
RROAAAAAAHHHRRR

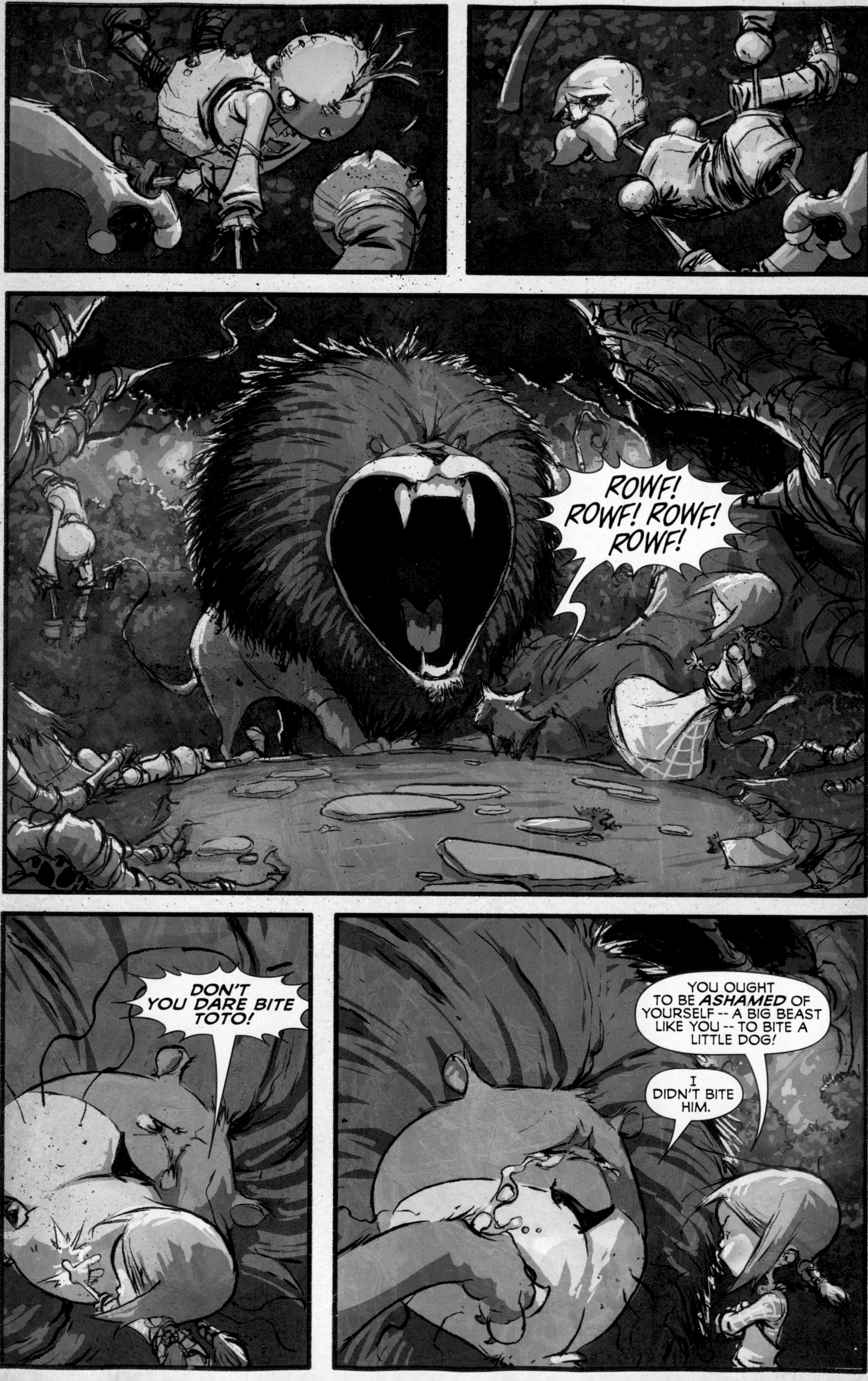
ROWF! ROWF! ROWF! ROWF!
DON'T YOU DARE BITE TOTO!
YOU OUGHT TO BE ASHAMED OF YOURSELF -- A BIG BEAST LIKE YOU -- TO BITE A LITTLE DOG!
I DIDN'T BITE HIM.

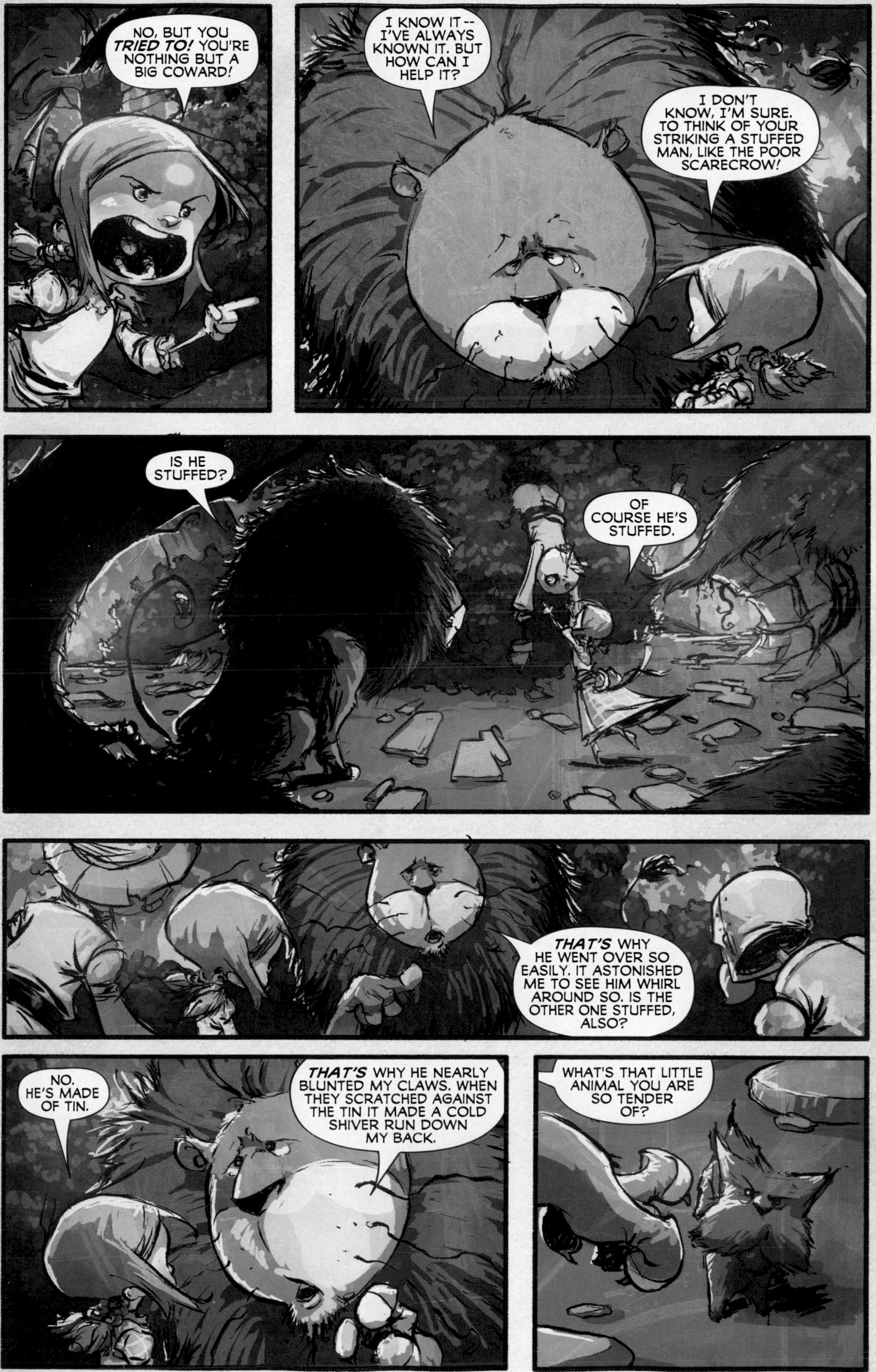
NO, BUT YOU *TRIED TO!* YOU'RE NOTHING BUT A BIG COWARD!
I KNOW IT -- I'VE ALWAYS KNOWN IT. BUT HOW CAN I HELP IT?
I DON'T KNOW, I'M SURE. TO THINK OF YOUR STRIKING A STUFFED MAN, LIKE THE POOR SCARECROW!
IS HE STUFFED?
OF COURSE HE'S STUFFED.
THAT'S WHY HE WENT OVER SO EASILY. IT ASTONISHED ME TO SEE HIM WHIRL AROUND SO. IS THE OTHER ONE STUFFED, ALSO?
NO. HE'S MADE OF TIN.
THAT'S WHY HE NEARLY BLUNTED MY CLAWS. WHEN THEY SCRATCHED AGAINST THE TIN IT MADE A COLD SHIVER RUN DOWN MY BACK.
WHAT'S THAT LITTLE ANIMAL YOU ARE SO TENDER OF?

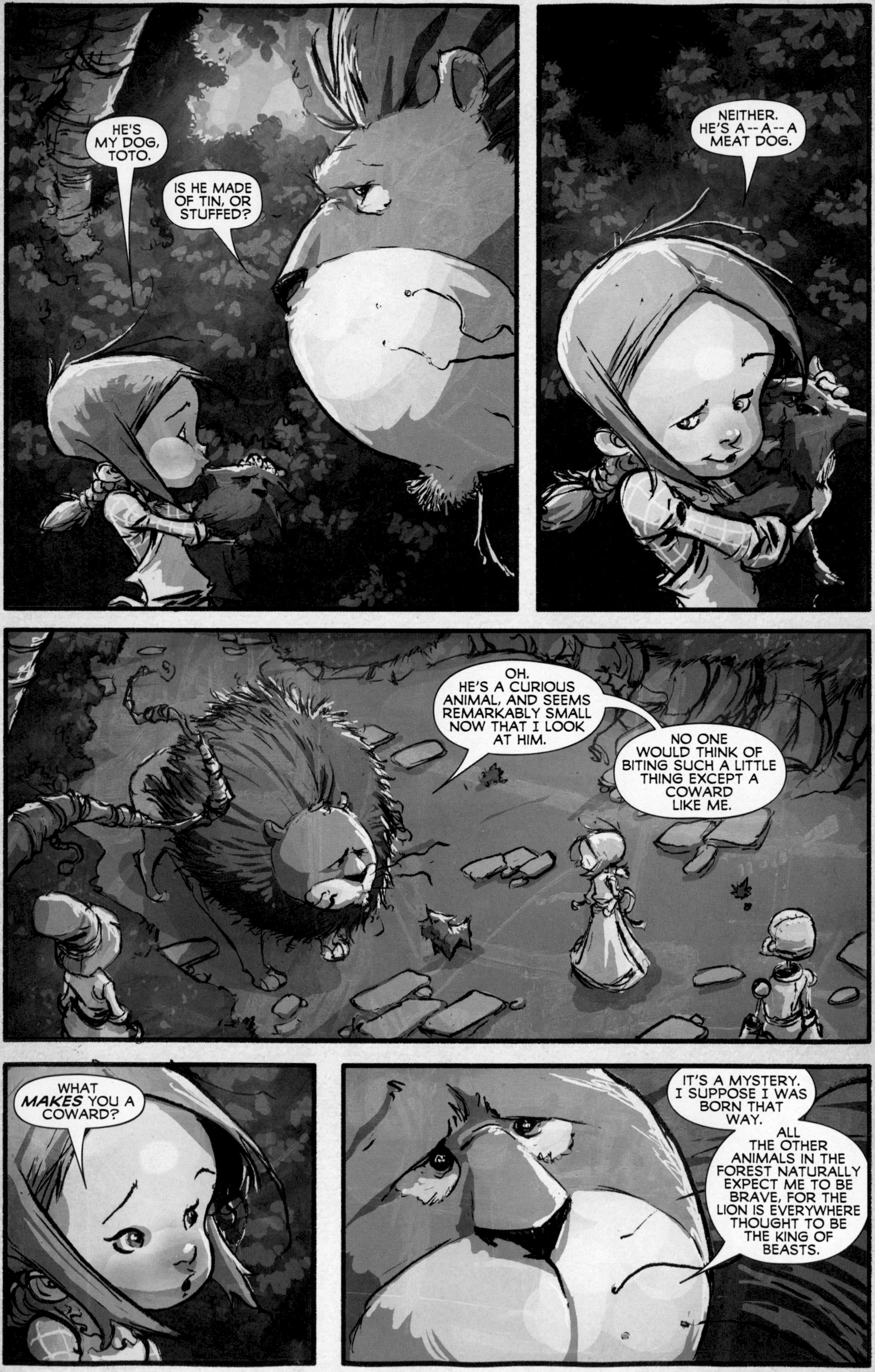

HE'S MY DOG, TOTO.
IS HE MADE OF TIN, OR STUFFED?
NEITHER. HE'S A--A--A MEAT DOG.
OH. HE'S A CURIOUS ANIMAL, AND SEEMS REMARKABLY SMALL NOW THAT I LOOK AT HIM.
NO ONE WOULD THINK OF BITING SUCH A LITTLE THING EXCEPT A COWARD LIKE ME.
WHAT *MAKES* YOU A COWARD?
IT'S A MYSTERY. I SUPPOSE I WAS BORN THAT WAY.
ALL THE OTHER ANIMALS IN THE FOREST NATURALLY EXPECT ME TO BE BRAVE, FOR THE LION IS EVERYWHERE THOUGHT TO BE THE KING OF BEASTS.

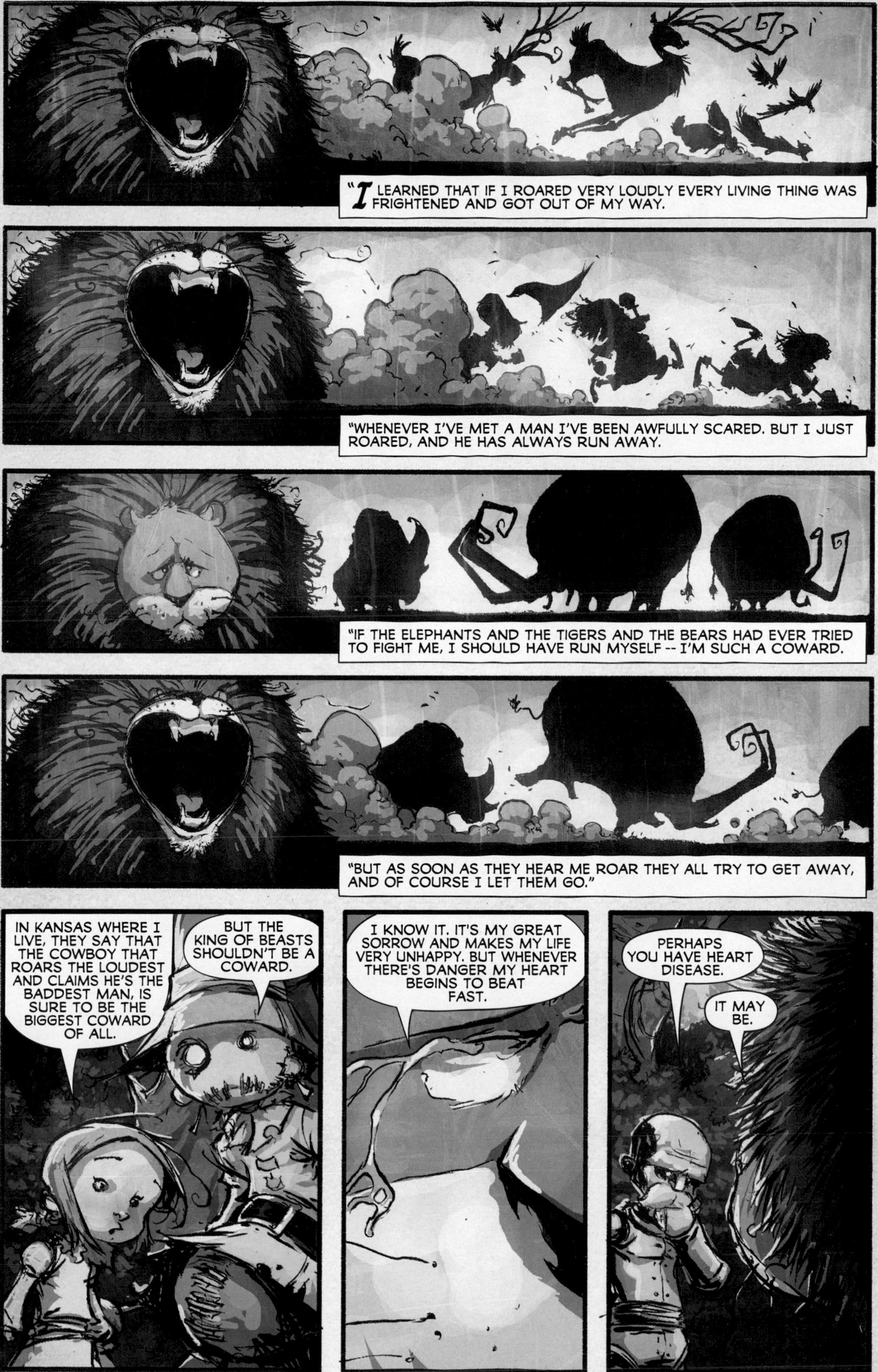
"I LEARNED THAT IF I ROARED VERY LOUDLY EVERY LIVING THING WAS FRIGHTENED AND GOT OUT OF MY WAY.
"WHENEVER I'VE MET A MAN I'VE BEEN AWFULLY SCARED. BUT I JUST ROARED, AND HE HAS ALWAYS RUN AWAY.
"IF THE ELEPHANTS AND THE TIGERS AND THE BEARS HAD EVER TRIED TO FIGHT ME, I SHOULD HAVE RUN MYSELF -- I'M SUCH A COWARD.
"BUT AS SOON AS THEY HEAR ME ROAR THEY ALL TRY TO GET AWAY, AND OF COURSE I LET THEM GO."
IN KANSAS WHERE I LIVE, THEY SAY THAT THE COWBOY THAT ROARS THE LOUDEST AND CLAIMS HE'S THE BADDEST MAN, IS SURE TO BE THE BIGGEST COWARD OF ALL.
BUT THE KING OF BEASTS SHOULDN'T BE A COWARD.
I KNOW IT. IT'S MY GREAT SORROW AND MAKES MY LIFE VERY UNHAPPY. BUT WHENEVER THERE'S DANGER MY HEART BEGINS TO BEAT FAST.
PERHAPS YOU HAVE HEART DISEASE.
IT MAY BE.

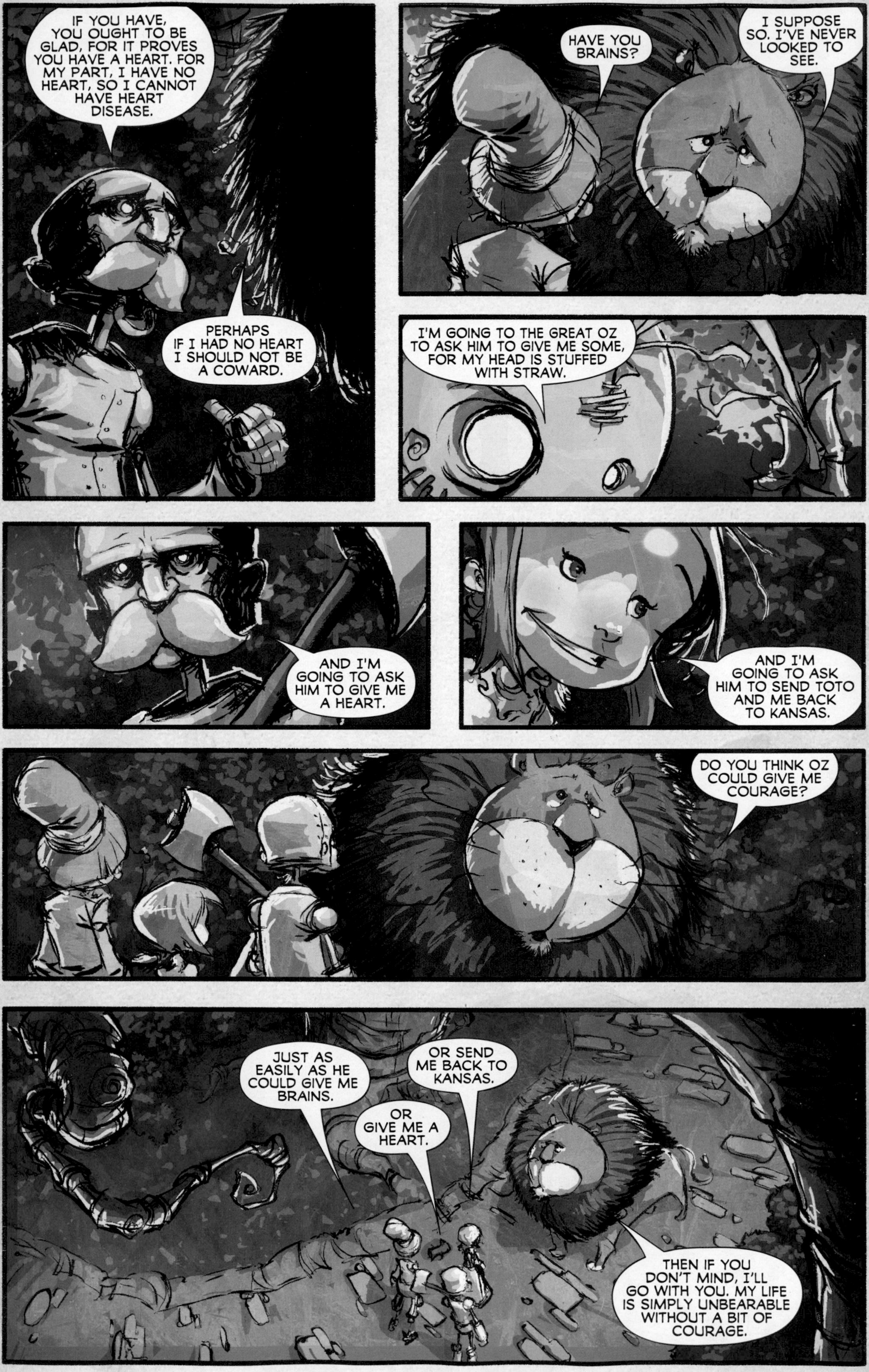
IF YOU HAVE, YOU OUGHT TO BE GLAD, FOR IT PROVES YOU HAVE A HEART. FOR MY PART, I HAVE NO HEART, SO I CANNOT HAVE HEART DISEASE.
PERHAPS IF I HAD NO HEART I SHOULD NOT BE A COWARD.
HAVE YOU BRAINS?
I SUPPOSE SO. I'VE NEVER LOOKED TO SEE.
I'M GOING TO THE GREAT OZ TO ASK HIM TO GIVE ME SOME, FOR MY HEAD IS STUFFED WITH STRAW.
AND I'M GOING TO ASK HIM TO GIVE ME A HEART.
AND I'M GOING TO ASK HIM TO SEND TOTO AND ME BACK TO KANSAS.
DO YOU THINK OZ COULD GIVE ME COURAGE?
JUST AS EASILY AS HE COULD GIVE ME BRAINS.
OR SEND ME BACK TO KANSAS.
OR GIVE ME A HEART.
THEN IF YOU DON'T MIND, I'LL GO WITH YOU. MY LIFE IS SIMPLY UNBEARABLE WITHOUT A BIT OF COURAGE.

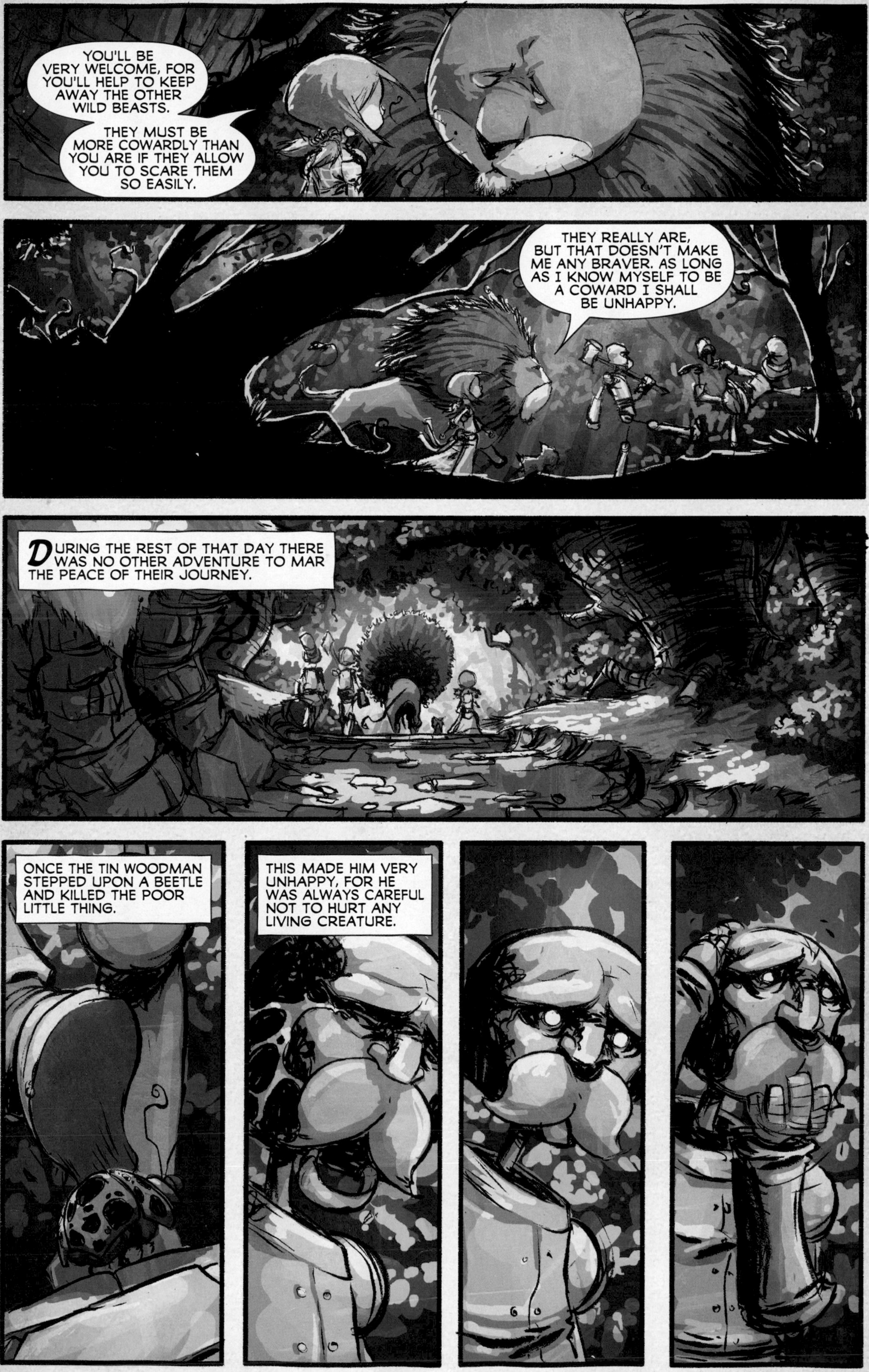
YOU'LL BE VERY WELCOME, FOR YOU'LL HELP TO KEEP AWAY THE OTHER WILD BEASTS.
THEY MUST BE MORE COWARDLY THAN YOU ARE IF THEY ALLOW YOU TO SCARE THEM SO EASILY.
THEY REALLY ARE, BUT THAT DOESN'T MAKE ME ANY BRAVER. AS LONG AS I KNOW MYSELF TO BE A COWARD I SHALL BE UNHAPPY.
DURING THE REST OF THAT DAY THERE WAS NO OTHER ADVENTURE TO MAR THE PEACE OF THEIR JOURNEY.
ONCE THE TIN WOODMAN STEPPED UPON A BEETLE AND KILLED THE POOR LITTLE THING.
THIS MADE HIM VERY UNHAPPY, FOR HE WAS ALWAYS CAREFUL NOT TO HURT ANY LIVING CREATURE.

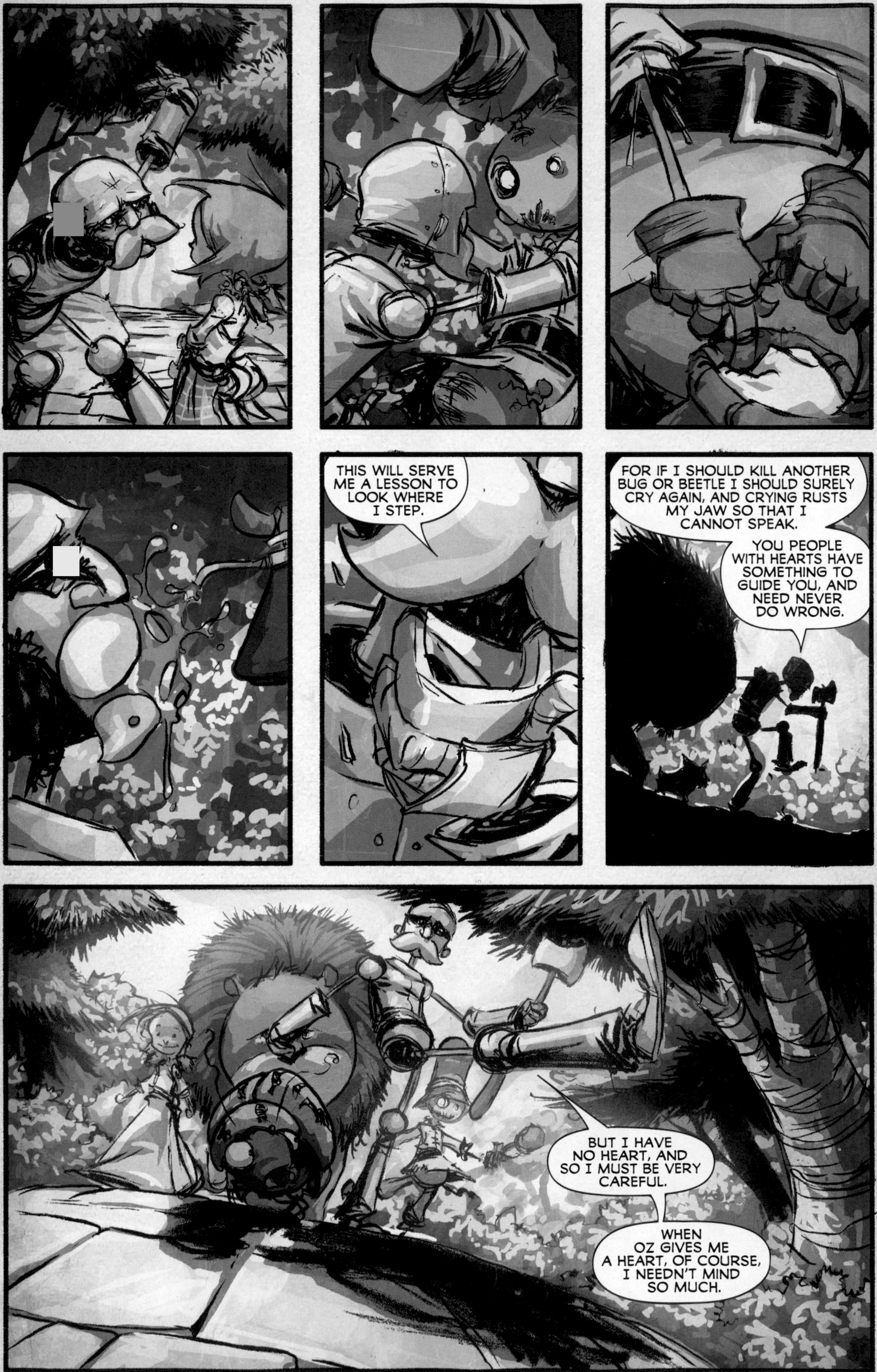
THIS WILL SERVE ME A LESSON TO LOOK WHERE I STEP.
FOR IF I SHOULD KILL ANOTHER BUG OR BEETLE I SHOULD SURELY CRY AGAIN, AND CRYING RUSTS MY JAW SO THAT I CANNOT SPEAK.
YOU PEOPLE WITH HEARTS HAVE SOMETHING TO GUIDE YOU, AND NEED NEVER DO WRONG.
BUT I HAVE NO HEART, AND SO I MUST BE VERY CAREFUL.
WHEN OZ GIVES ME A HEART, OF COURSE, I NEEDN'T MIND SO MUCH.

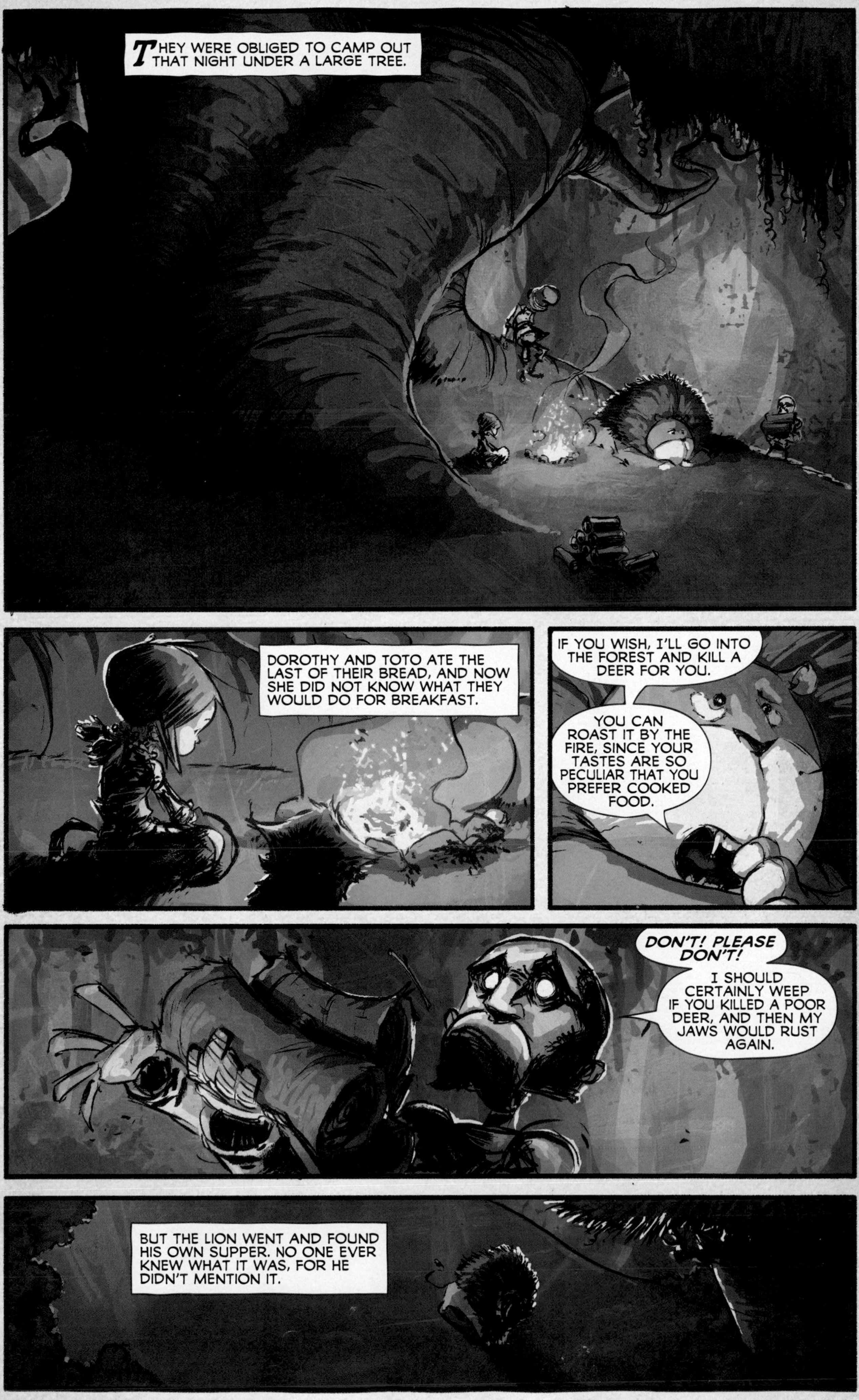
THEY WERE OBLIGED TO CAMP OUT THAT NIGHT UNDER A LARGE TREE.
DOROTHY AND TOTO ATE THE LAST OF THEIR BREAD, AND NOW SHE DID NOT KNOW WHAT THEY WOULD DO FOR BREAKFAST.
IF YOU WISH, I'LL GO INTO THE FOREST AND KILL A DEER FOR YOU.
YOU CAN ROAST IT BY THE FIRE, SINCE YOUR TASTES ARE SO PECULIAR THAT YOU PREFER COOKED FOOD.
DON'T! PLEASE DON'T!
I SHOULD CERTAINLY WEEP IF YOU KILLED A POOR DEER, AND THEN MY JAWS WOULD RUST AGAIN.
BUT THE LION WENT AND FOUND HIS OWN SUPPER. NO ONE EVER KNEW WHAT IT WAS, FOR HE DIDN'T MENTION IT.

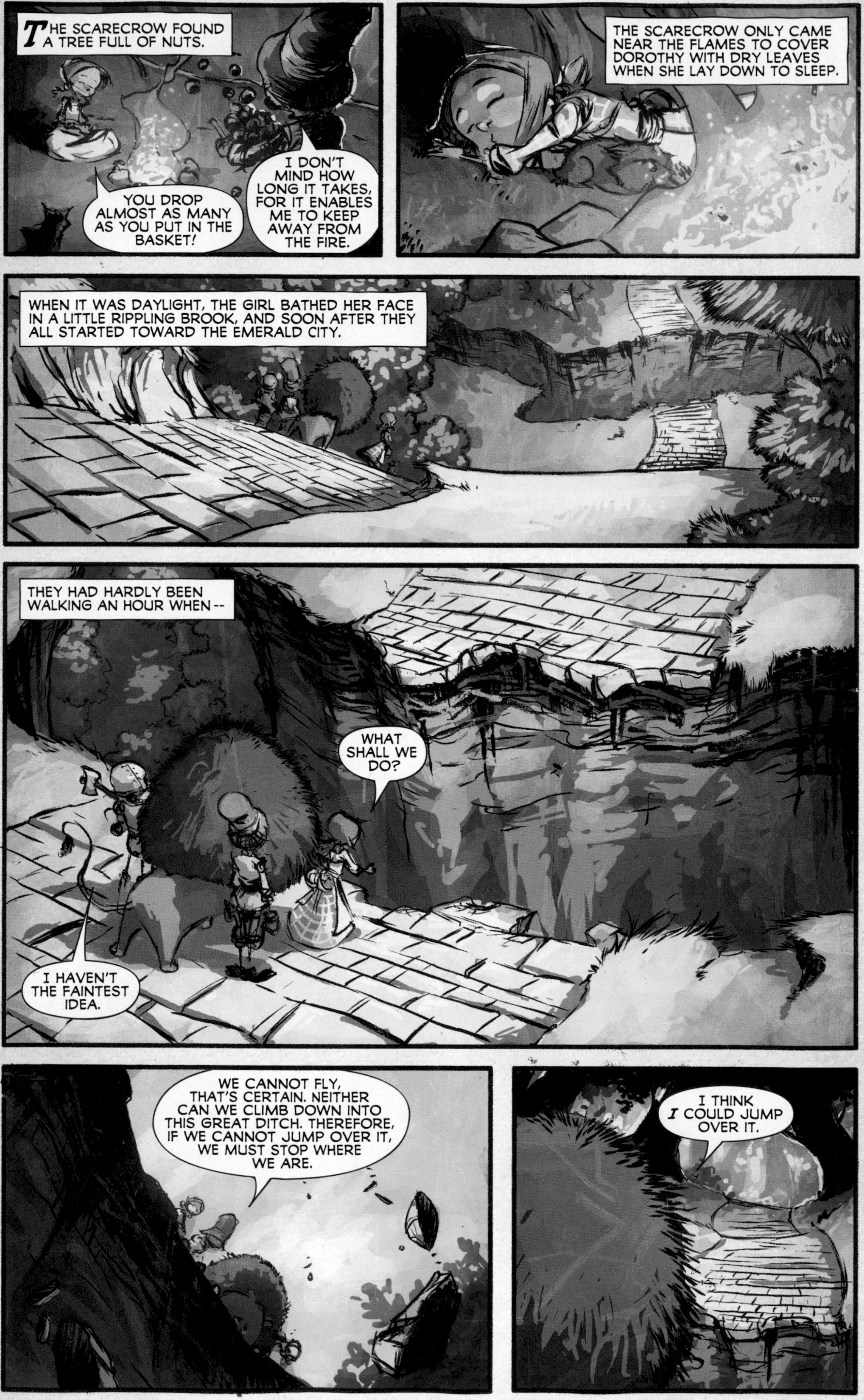
THE SCARECROW FOUND A TREE FULL OF NUTS.
YOU DROP ALMOST AS MANY AS YOU PUT IN THE BASKET!
I DON'T MIND HOW LONG IT TAKES, FOR IT ENABLES ME TO KEEP AWAY FROM THE FIRE.
THE SCARECROW ONLY CAME NEAR THE FLAMES TO COVER DOROTHY WITH DRY LEAVES WHEN SHE LAY DOWN TO SLEEP.
WHEN IT WAS DAYLIGHT, THE GIRL BATHED HER FACE IN A LITTLE RIPPLING BROOK, AND SOON AFTER THEY ALL STARTED TOWARD THE EMERALD CITY.
THEY HAD HARDLY BEEN WALKING AN HOUR WHEN--
WHAT SHALL WE DO?
I HAVEN'T THE FAINTEST IDEA.
WE CANNOT FLY, THAT'S CERTAIN. NEITHER CAN WE CLIMB DOWN INTO THIS GREAT DITCH. THEREFORE, IF WE CANNOT JUMP OVER IT, WE MUST STOP WHERE WE ARE.
I THINK *I* COULD JUMP OVER IT.

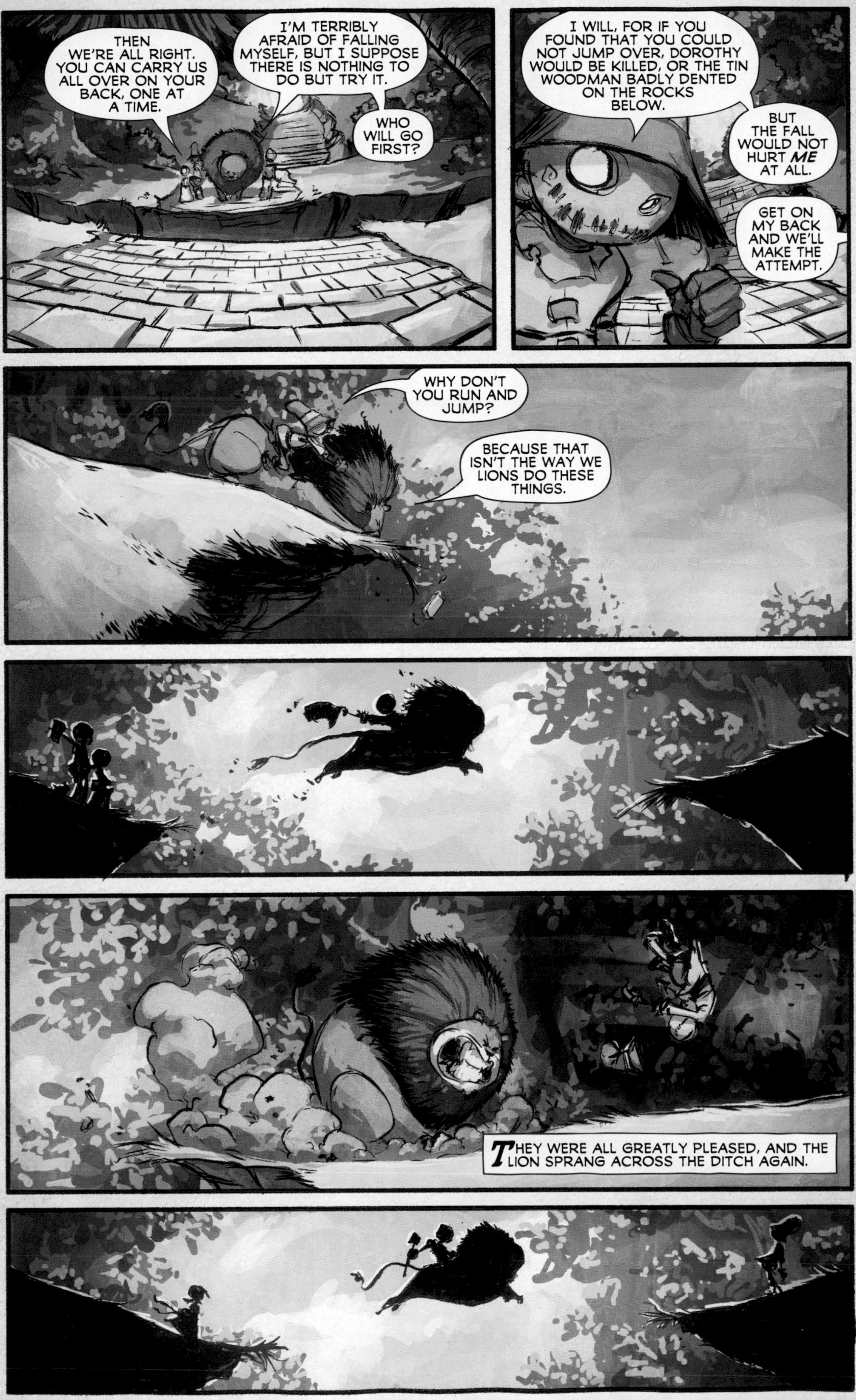
THEN WE'RE ALL RIGHT. YOU CAN CARRY US ALL OVER ON YOUR BACK, ONE AT A TIME.
I'M TERRIBLY AFRAID OF FALLING MYSELF, BUT I SUPPOSE THERE IS NOTHING TO DO BUT TRY IT.
WHO WILL GO FIRST?
I WILL, FOR IF YOU FOUND THAT YOU COULD NOT JUMP OVER, DOROTHY WOULD BE KILLED, OR THE TIN WOODMAN BADLY DENTED ON THE ROCKS BELOW.
BUT THE FALL WOULD NOT HURT *ME* AT ALL.
GET ON MY BACK AND WE'LL MAKE THE ATTEMPT.
WHY DON'T YOU RUN AND JUMP?
BECAUSE THAT ISN'T THE WAY WE LIONS DO THESE THINGS.
THEY WERE ALL GREATLY PLEASED, AND THE LION SPRANG ACROSS THE DITCH AGAIN.

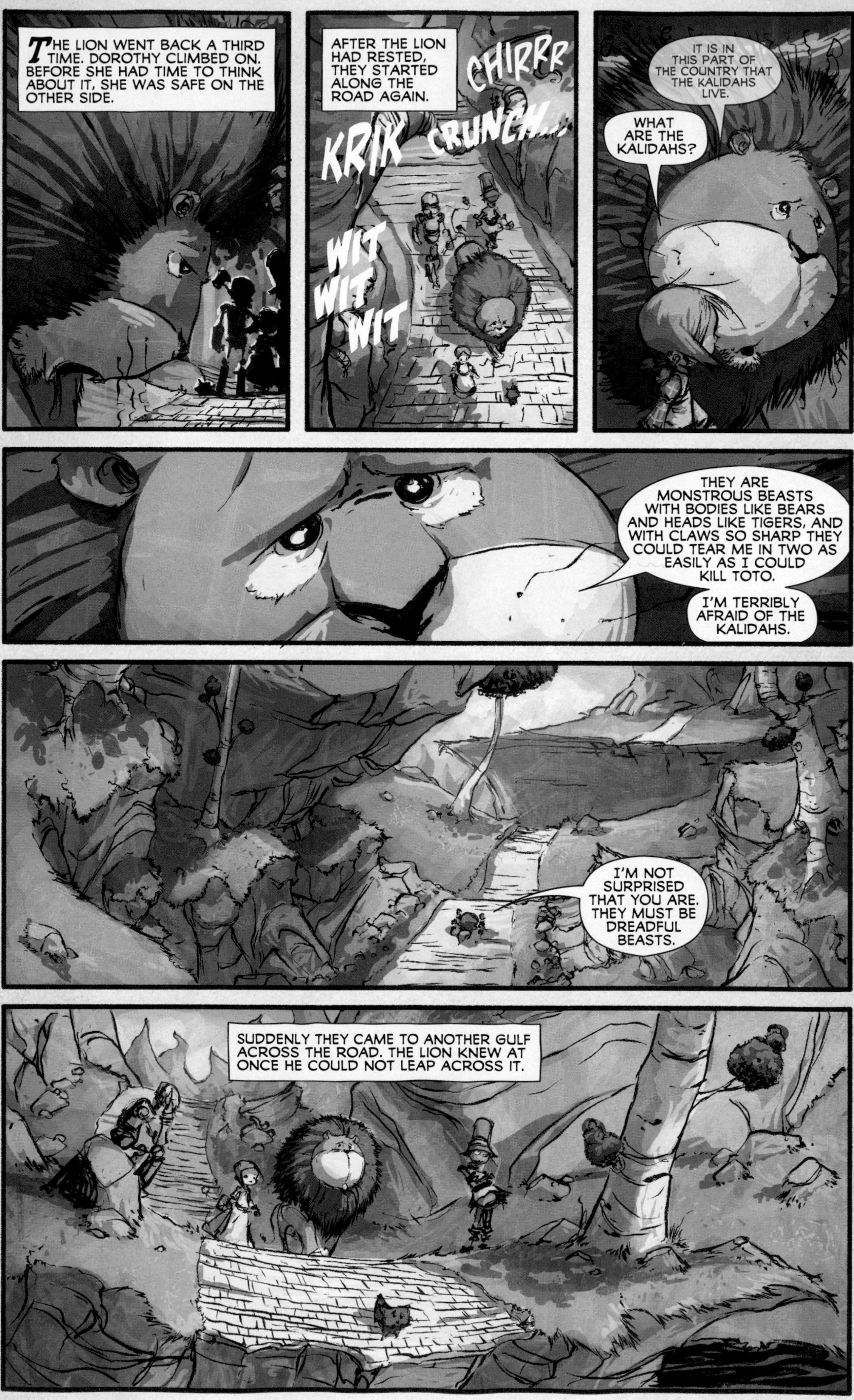

THE LION WENT BACK A THIRD TIME. DOROTHY CLIMBED ON. BEFORE SHE HAD TIME TO THINK ABOUT IT, SHE WAS SAFE ON THE OTHER SIDE.
AFTER THE LION HAD RESTED, THEY STARTED ALONG THE ROAD AGAIN.
CHIRRR
KRIK
CRUNCH...
WIT WIT WIT
IT IS IN THIS PART OF THE COUNTRY THAT THE KALIDAHS LIVE.
WHAT ARE THE KALIDAHS?
THEY ARE MONSTROUS BEASTS WITH BODIES LIKE BEARS AND HEADS LIKE TIGERS, AND WITH CLAWS SO SHARP THEY COULD TEAR ME IN TWO AS EASILY AS I COULD KILL TOTO.
I'M TERRIBLY AFRAID OF THE KALIDAHS.
I'M NOT SURPRISED THAT YOU ARE. THEY MUST BE DREADFUL BEASTS.
SUDDENLY THEY CAME TO ANOTHER GULF ACROSS THE ROAD. THE LION KNEW AT ONCE HE COULD NOT LEAP ACROSS IT.

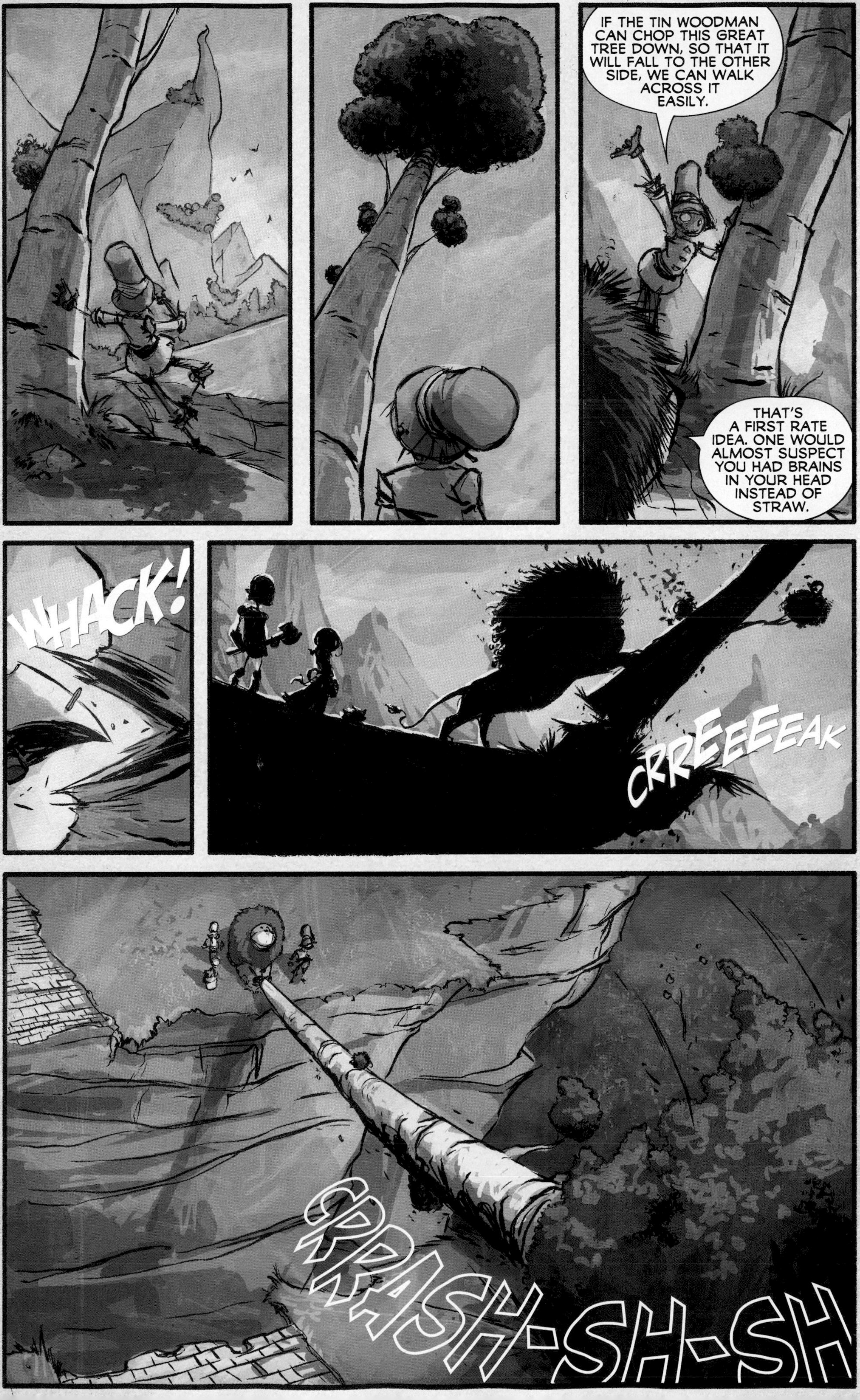
IF THE TIN WOODMAN CAN CHOP THIS GREAT TREE DOWN, SO THAT IT WILL FALL TO THE OTHER SIDE, WE CAN WALK ACROSS IT EASILY.
THAT'S A FIRST RATE IDEA. ONE WOULD ALMOST SUSPECT YOU HAD BRAINS IN YOUR HEAD INSTEAD OF STRAW.
WHACK!
CRREEEEAK
CRASH-SH-SH

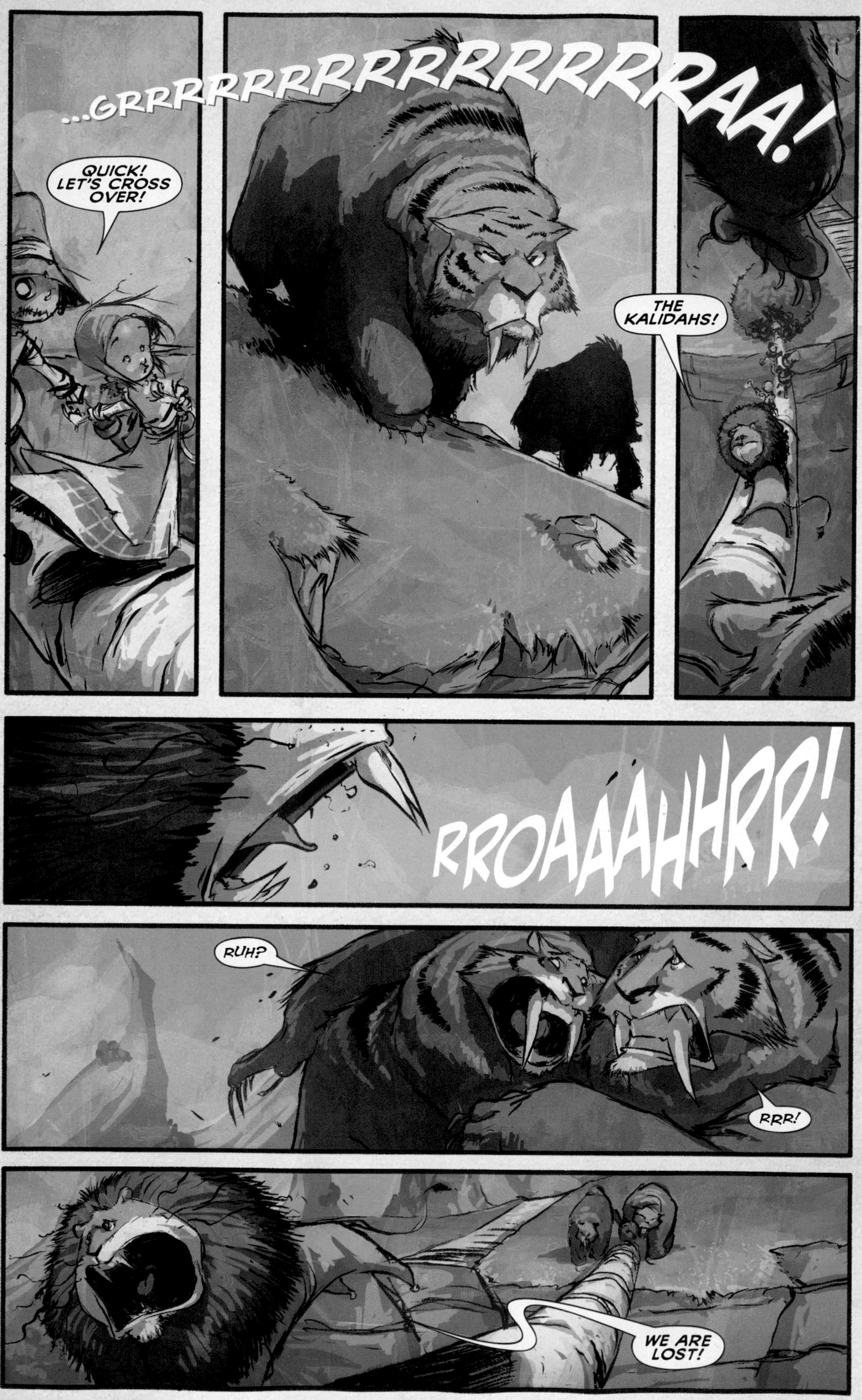
...GRRRRRRRRRRRRRRRRAA!
QUICK! LET'S CROSS OVER!
THE KALIDAHS!
RROAAAAHHRR!
RUH?
RRR!
WE ARE LOST!

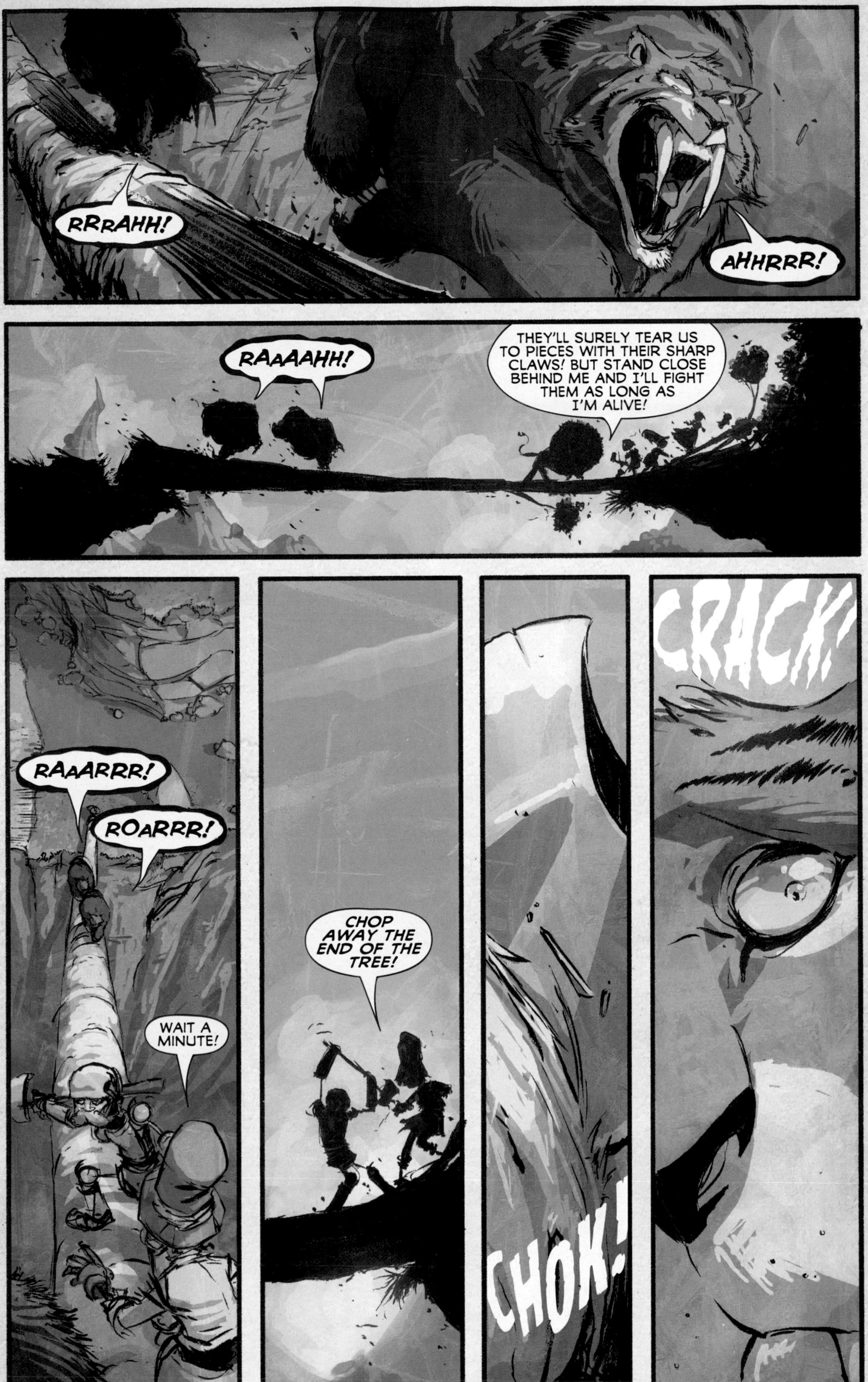
RRRAHH!
AHHRRR!
RAAAAHH!
THEY'LL SURELY TEAR US TO PIECES WITH THEIR SHARP CLAWS! BUT STAND CLOSE BEHIND ME AND I'LL FIGHT THEM AS LONG AS I'M ALIVE!
RAAARRR!
ROARRR!
WAIT A MINUTE!
CHOP AWAY THE END OF THE TREE!
CHOK!
CRACK!

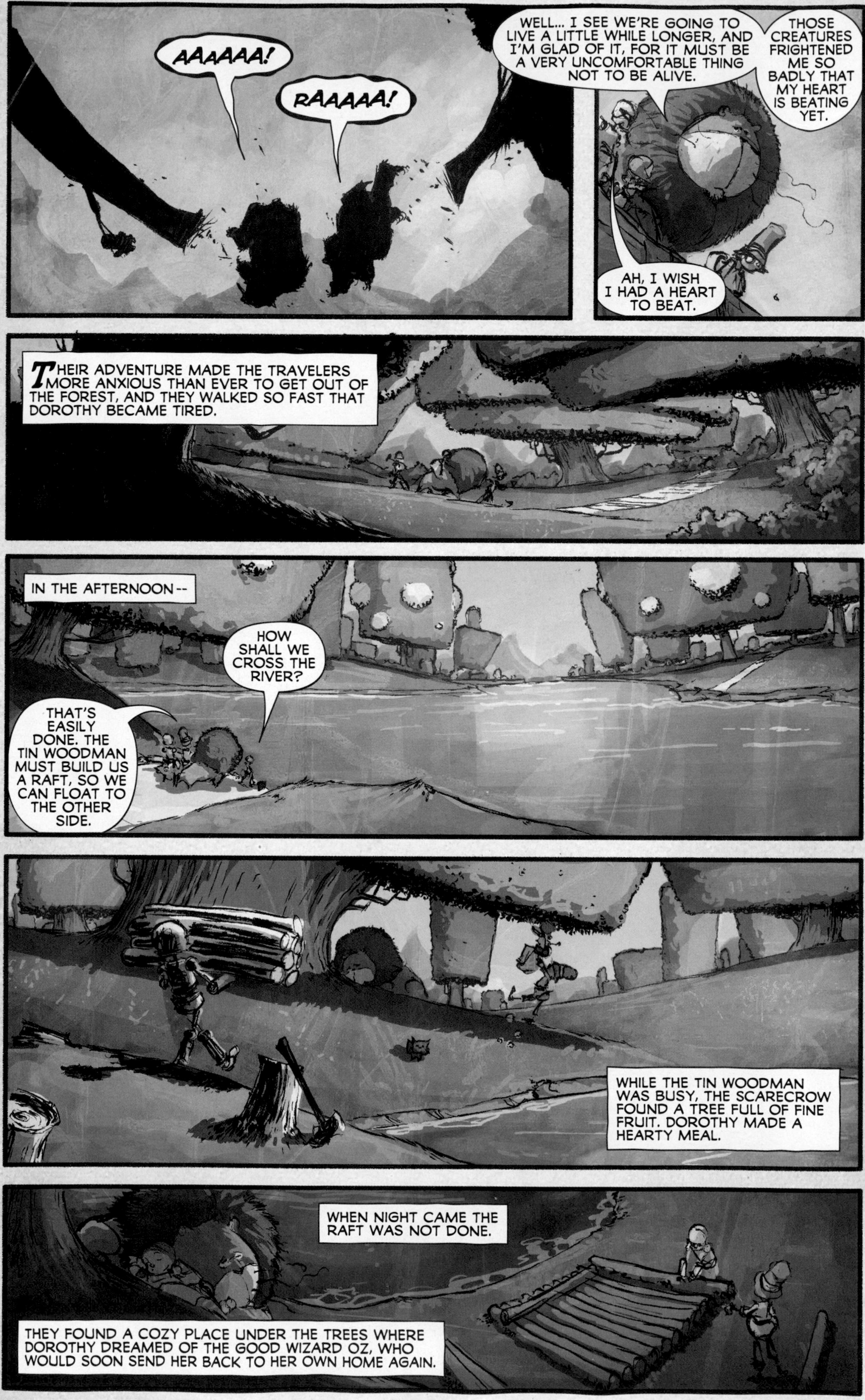
AAAAAA!
RAAAAA!
WELL... I SEE WE'RE GOING TO LIVE A LITTLE WHILE LONGER, AND I'M GLAD OF IT, FOR IT MUST BE A VERY UNCOMFORTABLE THING NOT TO BE ALIVE.
THOSE CREATURES FRIGHTENED ME SO BADLY THAT MY HEART IS BEATING YET.
AH, I WISH I HAD A HEART TO BEAT.
THEIR ADVENTURE MADE THE TRAVELERS MORE ANXIOUS THAN EVER TO GET OUT OF THE FOREST, AND THEY WALKED SO FAST THAT DOROTHY BECAME TIRED.
IN THE AFTERNOON--
HOW SHALL WE CROSS THE RIVER?
THAT'S EASILY DONE. THE TIN WOODMAN MUST BUILD US A RAFT, SO WE CAN FLOAT TO THE OTHER SIDE.
WHILE THE TIN WOODMAN WAS BUSY, THE SCARECROW FOUND A TREE FULL OF FINE FRUIT. DOROTHY MADE A HEARTY MEAL.
WHEN NIGHT CAME THE RAFT WAS NOT DONE.
THEY FOUND A COZY PLACE UNDER THE TREES WHERE DOROTHY DREAMED OF THE GOOD WIZARD OZ, WHO WOULD SOON SEND HER BACK TO HER OWN HOME AGAIN.

NEXT MORNING THEY AWAKENED REFRESHED AND FULL OF HOPE. ONLY THE RIVER NOW CUT THEM OFF FROM THE LOVELY, SUNNY COUNTRY THAT SEEMED TO BECKON THEM ON TO THE EMERALD CITY.

THEY GOT ALONG QUITE WELL AT FIRST...

...BUT WHEN THEY REACHED THE MIDDLE OF THE RIVER THE CURRENT SWEPT THE RAFT FARTHER AND FARTHER AWAY FROM THE ROAD OF YELLOW BRICK.

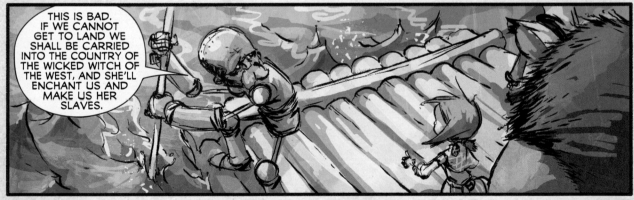

THIS IS BAD. IF WE CANNOT GET TO LAND WE SHALL BE CARRIED INTO THE COUNTRY OF THE WICKED WITCH OF THE WEST, AND SHE'LL ENCHANT US AND MAKE US HER SLAVES.

AND THEN I SHOULD GET NO BRAINS.

AND I SHOULD GET NO COURAGE.

AND I SHOULD GET NO HEART.

AND I SHOULD NEVER GET BACK TO KANSAS.

WE MUST CERTAINLY GET TO THE EMERALD CITY IF WE CAN!

OOOH --

GOOD-BYE!

SCARECROW!

*T*HE SCARECROW'S FRIENDS WERE VERY SORRY TO LEAVE HIM.

THE TIN WOODMAN BEGAN TO CRY, BUT REMEMBERED THAT HE MIGHT RUST, SO DRIED HIS TEARS ON DOROTHY'S APRON.

I'M NOW WORSE OFF THAN WHEN I FIRST MET DOROTHY.

THEN I WAS STUCK ON A POLE IN A CORNFIELD -- WHERE I COULD MAKE-BELIEVE SCARE THE CROWS, AT ANY RATE.

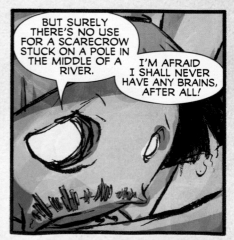

BUT SURELY THERE'S NO USE FOR A SCARECROW STUCK ON A POLE IN THE MIDDLE OF A RIVER.

I'M AFRAID I SHALL NEVER HAVE ANY BRAINS, AFTER ALL!

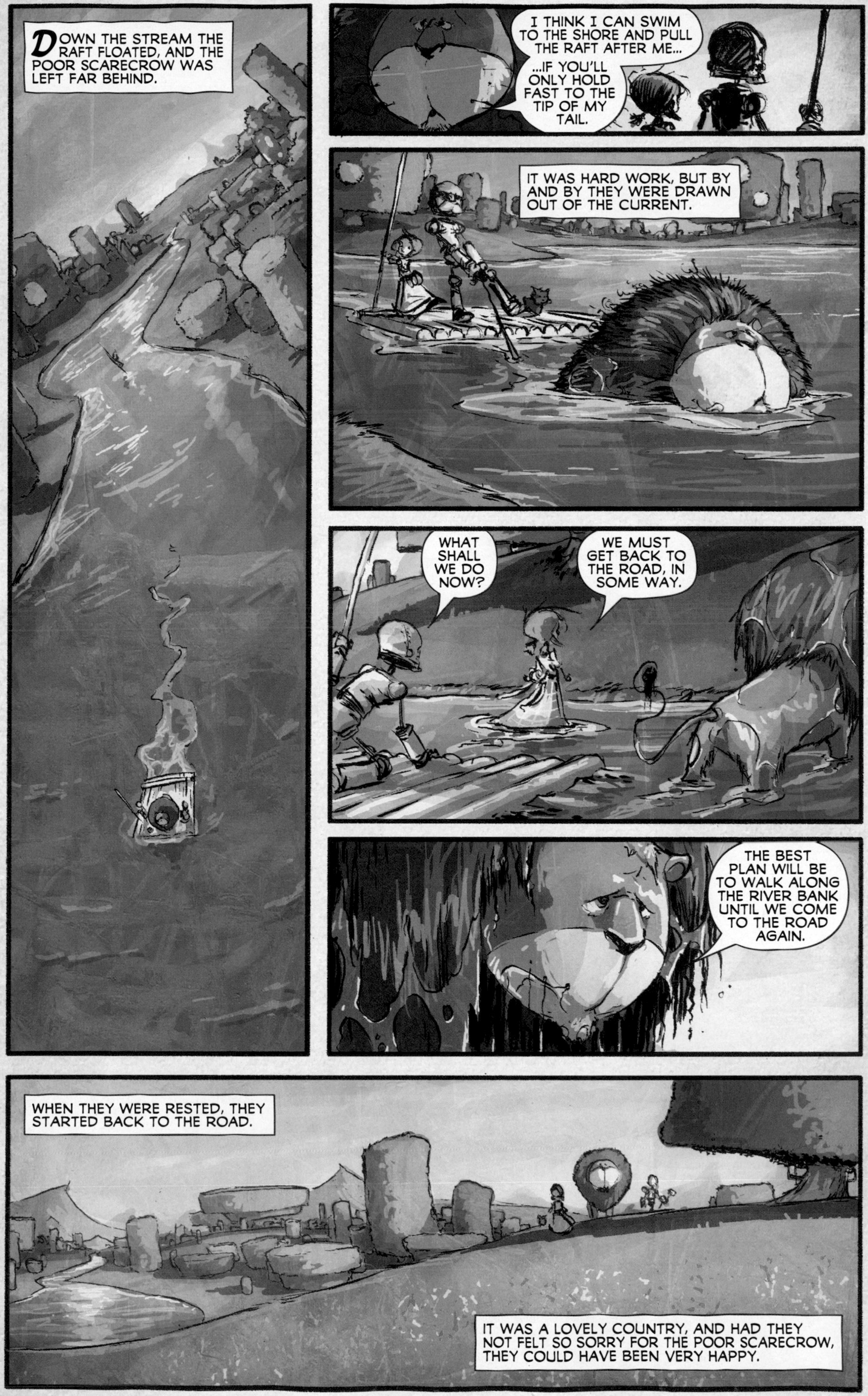

DOWN THE STREAM THE RAFT FLOATED, AND THE POOR SCARECROW WAS LEFT FAR BEHIND.
I THINK I CAN SWIM TO THE SHORE AND PULL THE RAFT AFTER ME...
...IF YOU'LL ONLY HOLD FAST TO THE TIP OF MY TAIL.
IT WAS HARD WORK, BUT BY AND BY THEY WERE DRAWN OUT OF THE CURRENT.
WHAT SHALL WE DO NOW?
WE MUST GET BACK TO THE ROAD, IN SOME WAY.
THE BEST PLAN WILL BE TO WALK ALONG THE RIVER BANK UNTIL WE COME TO THE ROAD AGAIN.
WHEN THEY WERE RESTED, THEY STARTED BACK TO THE ROAD.
IT WAS A LOVELY COUNTRY, AND HAD THEY NOT FELT SO SORRY FOR THE POOR SCARECROW, THEY COULD HAVE BEEN VERY HAPPY.

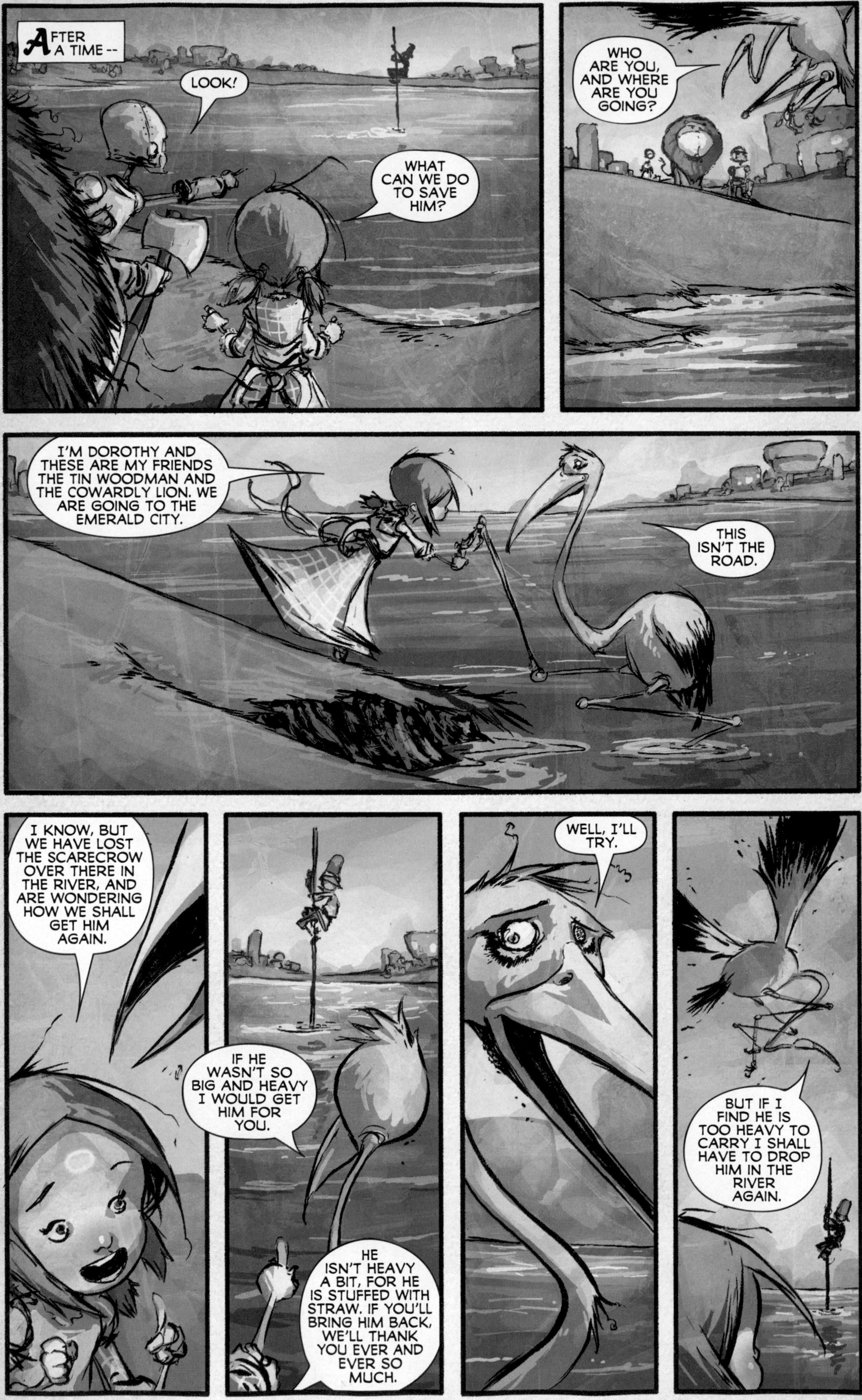
AFTER A TIME --
LOOK!
WHAT CAN WE DO TO SAVE HIM?
WHO ARE YOU, AND WHERE ARE YOU GOING?
I'M DOROTHY AND THESE ARE MY FRIENDS THE TIN WOODMAN AND THE COWARDLY LION. WE ARE GOING TO THE EMERALD CITY.
THIS ISN'T THE ROAD.
I KNOW, BUT WE HAVE LOST THE SCARECROW OVER THERE IN THE RIVER, AND ARE WONDERING HOW WE SHALL GET HIM AGAIN.
IF HE WASN'T SO BIG AND HEAVY I WOULD GET HIM FOR YOU.
HE ISN'T HEAVY A BIT, FOR HE IS STUFFED WITH STRAW. IF YOU'LL BRING HIM BACK, WE'LL THANK YOU EVER AND EVER SO MUCH.
WELL, I'LL TRY.
BUT IF I FIND HE IS TOO HEAVY TO CARRY I SHALL HAVE TO DROP HIM IN THE RIVER AGAIN.

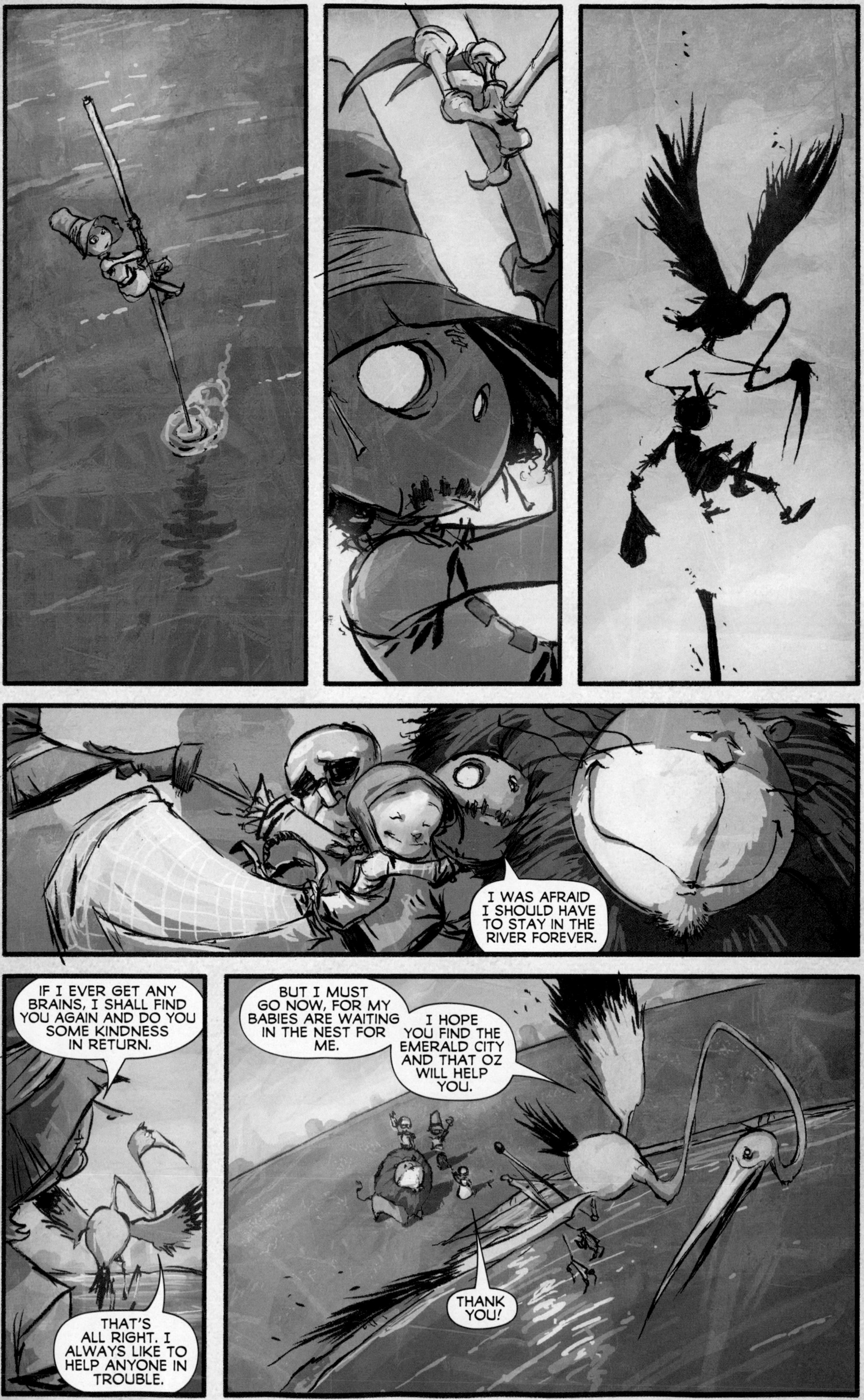
I WAS AFRAID I SHOULD HAVE TO STAY IN THE RIVER FOREVER.
IF I EVER GET ANY BRAINS, I SHALL FIND YOU AGAIN AND DO YOU SOME KINDNESS IN RETURN.
THAT'S ALL RIGHT. I ALWAYS LIKE TO HELP ANYONE IN TROUBLE.
BUT I MUST GO NOW, FOR MY BABIES ARE WAITING IN THE NEST FOR ME.
I HOPE YOU FIND THE EMERALD CITY AND THAT OZ WILL HELP YOU.
THANK YOU!

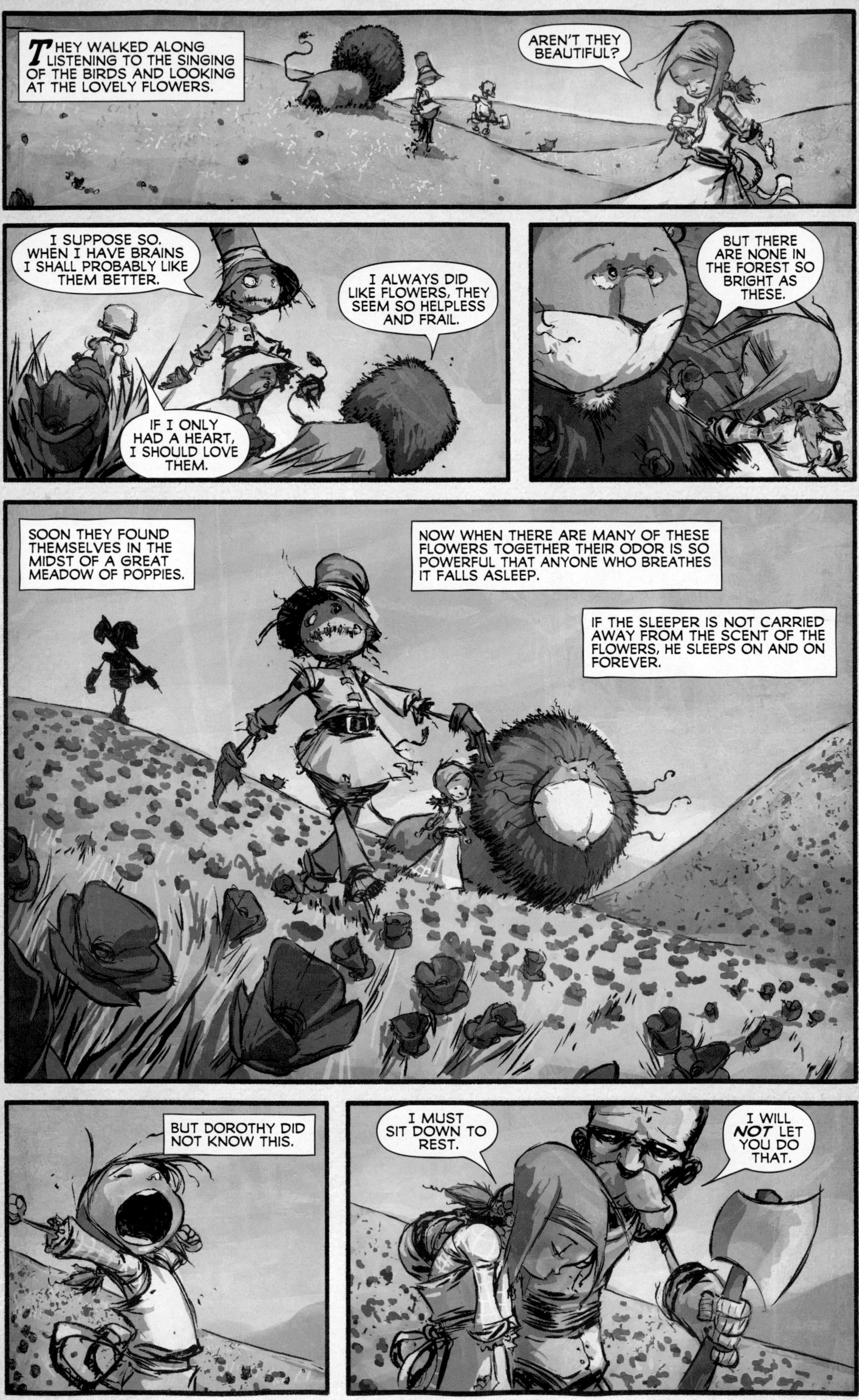
THEY WALKED ALONG LISTENING TO THE SINGING OF THE BIRDS AND LOOKING AT THE LOVELY FLOWERS.
AREN'T THEY BEAUTIFUL?
I SUPPOSE SO. WHEN I HAVE BRAINS I SHALL PROBABLY LIKE THEM BETTER.
IF I ONLY HAD A HEART, I SHOULD LOVE THEM.
I ALWAYS DID LIKE FLOWERS, THEY SEEM SO HELPLESS AND FRAIL.
BUT THERE ARE NONE IN THE FOREST SO BRIGHT AS THESE.
SOON THEY FOUND THEMSELVES IN THE MIDST OF A GREAT MEADOW OF POPPIES.
NOW WHEN THERE ARE MANY OF THESE FLOWERS TOGETHER THEIR ODOR IS SO POWERFUL THAT ANYONE WHO BREATHES IT FALLS ASLEEP.
IF THE SLEEPER IS NOT CARRIED AWAY FROM THE SCENT OF THE FLOWERS, HE SLEEPS ON AND ON FOREVER.
BUT DOROTHY DID NOT KNOW THIS.
I MUST SIT DOWN TO REST.
I WILL NOT LET YOU DO THAT.

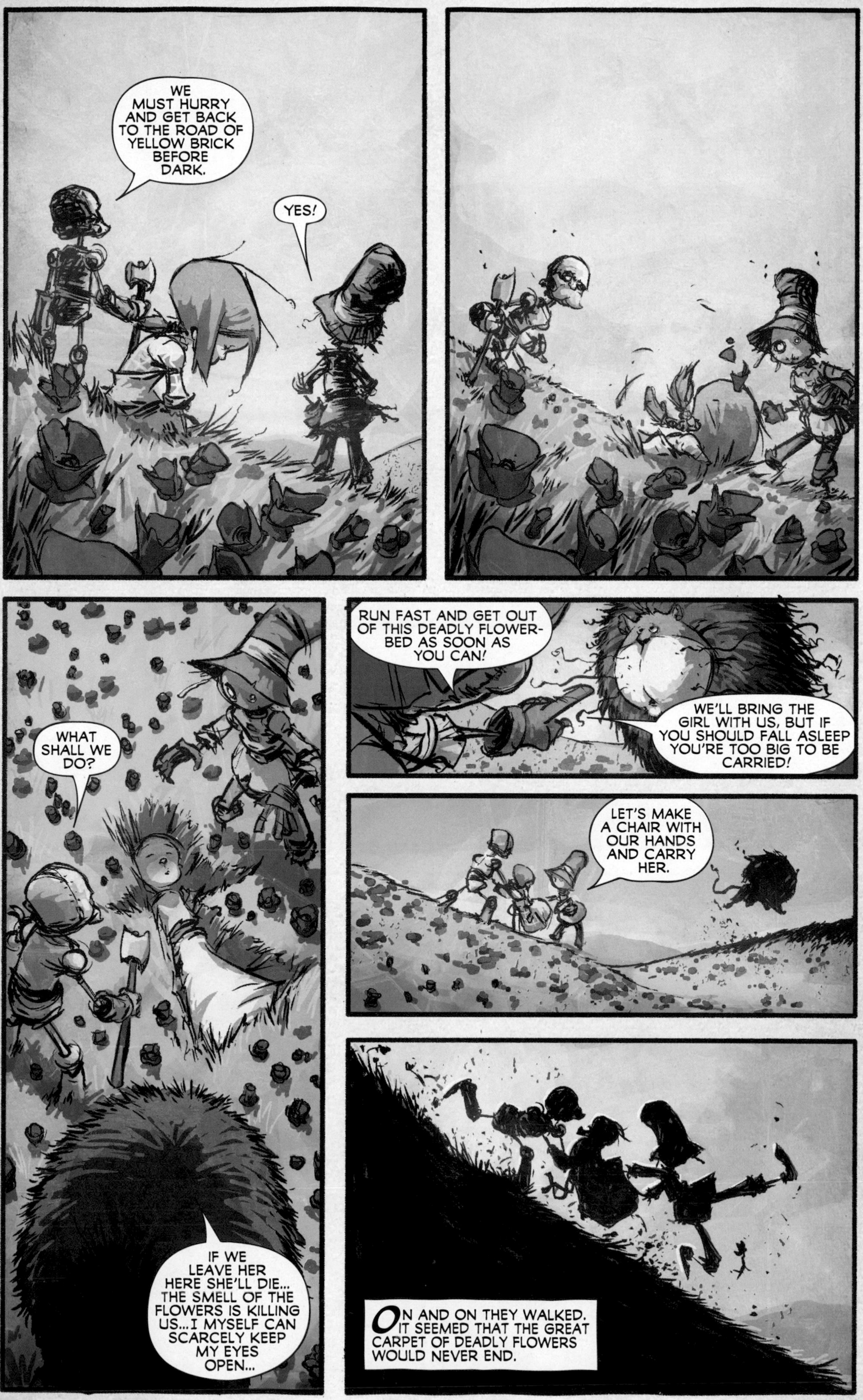
WE MUST HURRY AND GET BACK TO THE ROAD OF YELLOW BRICK BEFORE DARK.
YES!
WHAT SHALL WE DO?
IF WE LEAVE HER HERE SHE'LL DIE... THE SMELL OF THE FLOWERS IS KILLING US...I MYSELF CAN SCARCELY KEEP MY EYES OPEN...
RUN FAST AND GET OUT OF THIS DEADLY FLOWER-BED AS SOON AS YOU CAN!
WE'LL BRING THE GIRL WITH US, BUT IF YOU SHOULD FALL ASLEEP YOU'RE TOO BIG TO BE CARRIED!
LET'S MAKE A CHAIR WITH OUR HANDS AND CARRY HER.
ON AND ON THEY WALKED. IT SEEMED THAT THE GREAT CARPET OF DEADLY FLOWERS WOULD NEVER END.

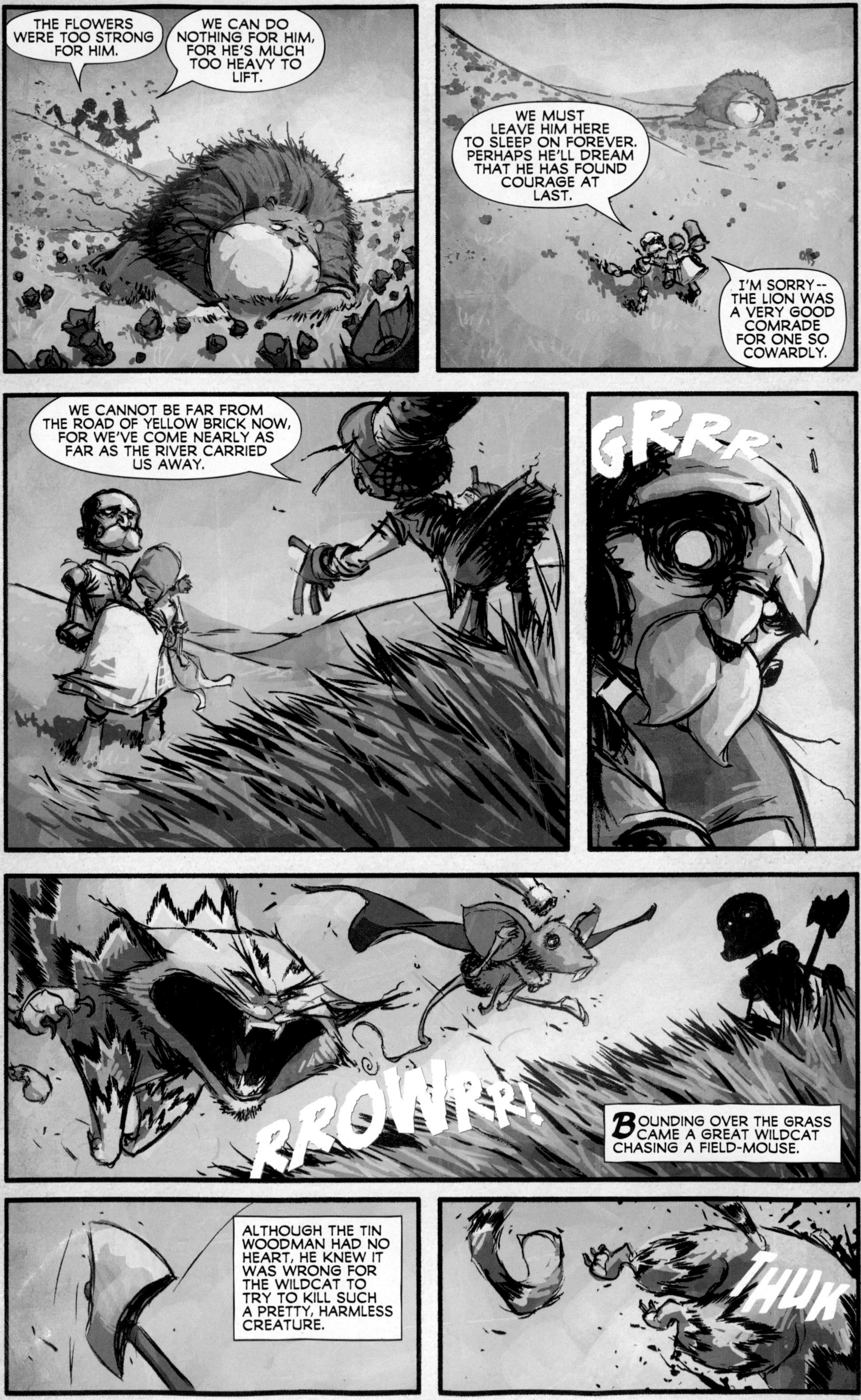
THE FLOWERS WERE TOO STRONG FOR HIM.
WE CAN DO NOTHING FOR HIM, FOR HE'S MUCH TOO HEAVY TO LIFT.
WE MUST LEAVE HIM HERE TO SLEEP ON FOREVER. PERHAPS HE'LL DREAM THAT HE HAS FOUND COURAGE AT LAST.
I'M SORRY-- THE LION WAS A VERY GOOD COMRADE FOR ONE SO COWARDLY.
WE CANNOT BE FAR FROM THE ROAD OF YELLOW BRICK NOW, FOR WE'VE COME NEARLY AS FAR AS THE RIVER CARRIED US AWAY.
GRRR
RROWRR!
BOUNDING OVER THE GRASS CAME A GREAT WILDCAT CHASING A FIELD-MOUSE.
ALTHOUGH THE TIN WOODMAN HAD NO HEART, HE KNEW IT WAS WRONG FOR THE WILDCAT TO TRY TO KILL SUCH A PRETTY, HARMLESS CREATURE.
THUK

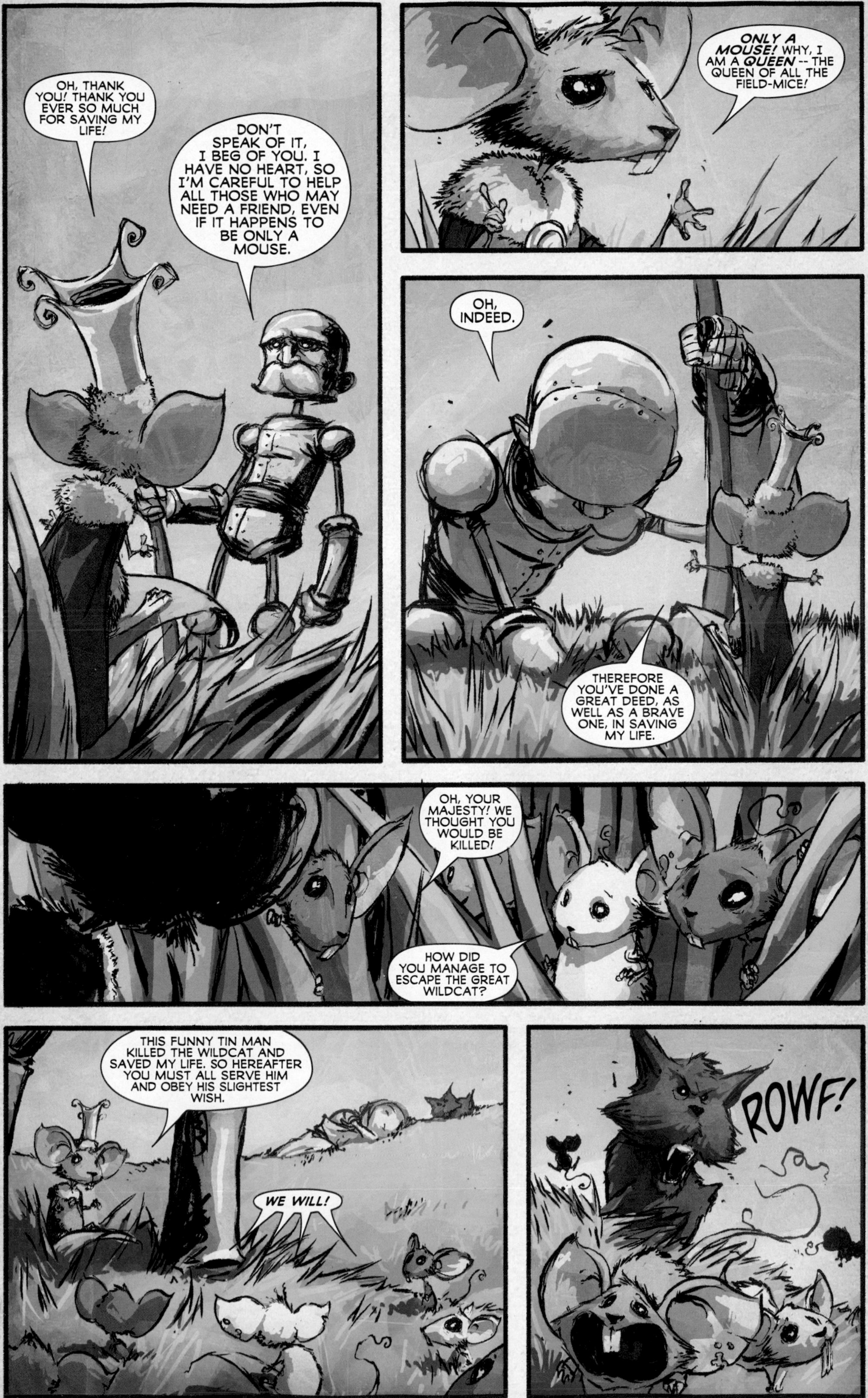
OH, THANK YOU! THANK YOU EVER SO MUCH FOR SAVING MY LIFE!
DON'T SPEAK OF IT, I BEG OF YOU. I HAVE NO HEART, SO I'M CAREFUL TO HELP ALL THOSE WHO MAY NEED A FRIEND, EVEN IF IT HAPPENS TO BE ONLY A MOUSE.
ONLY A MOUSE! WHY, I AM A QUEEN -- THE QUEEN OF ALL THE FIELD-MICE!
OH, INDEED.
THEREFORE YOU'VE DONE A GREAT DEED, AS WELL AS A BRAVE ONE, IN SAVING MY LIFE.
OH, YOUR MAJESTY! WE THOUGHT YOU WOULD BE KILLED!
HOW DID YOU MANAGE TO ESCAPE THE GREAT WILDCAT?
THIS FUNNY TIN MAN KILLED THE WILDCAT AND SAVED MY LIFE. SO HEREAFTER YOU MUST ALL SERVE HIM AND OBEY HIS SLIGHTEST WISH.
WE WILL!
ROWF!

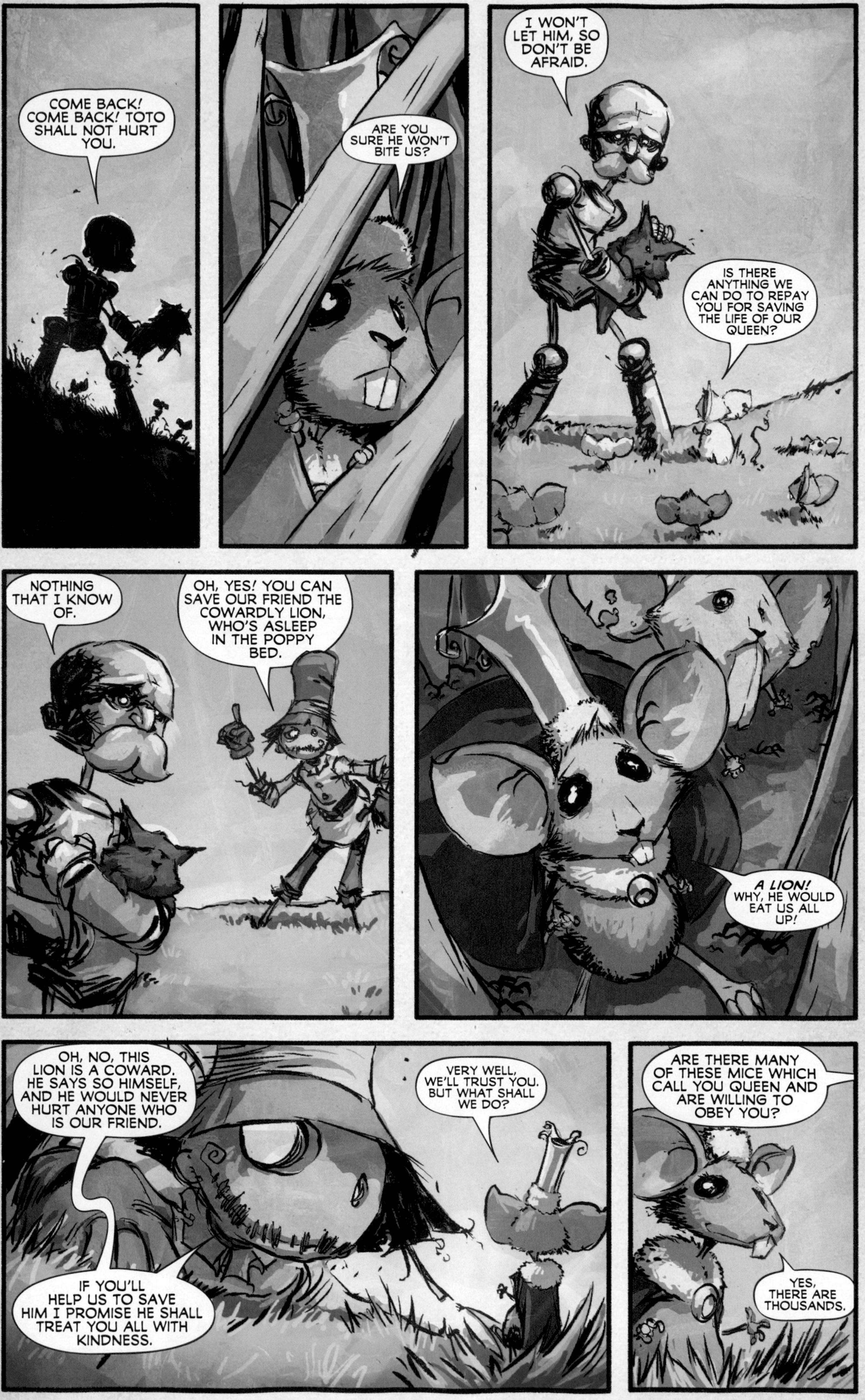
COME BACK! COME BACK! TOTO SHALL NOT HURT YOU.
ARE YOU SURE HE WON'T BITE US?
I WON'T LET HIM, SO DON'T BE AFRAID.
IS THERE ANYTHING WE CAN DO TO REPAY YOU FOR SAVING THE LIFE OF OUR QUEEN?
NOTHING THAT I KNOW OF.
OH, YES! YOU CAN SAVE OUR FRIEND THE COWARDLY LION, WHO'S ASLEEP IN THE POPPY BED.
A LION! WHY, HE WOULD EAT US ALL UP!
OH, NO, THIS LION IS A COWARD. HE SAYS SO HIMSELF, AND HE WOULD NEVER HURT ANYONE WHO IS OUR FRIEND.
IF YOU'LL HELP US TO SAVE HIM I PROMISE HE SHALL TREAT YOU ALL WITH KINDNESS.
VERY WELL, WE'LL TRUST YOU. BUT WHAT SHALL WE DO?
ARE THERE MANY OF THESE MICE WHICH CALL YOU QUEEN AND ARE WILLING TO OBEY YOU?
YES, THERE ARE THOUSANDS.

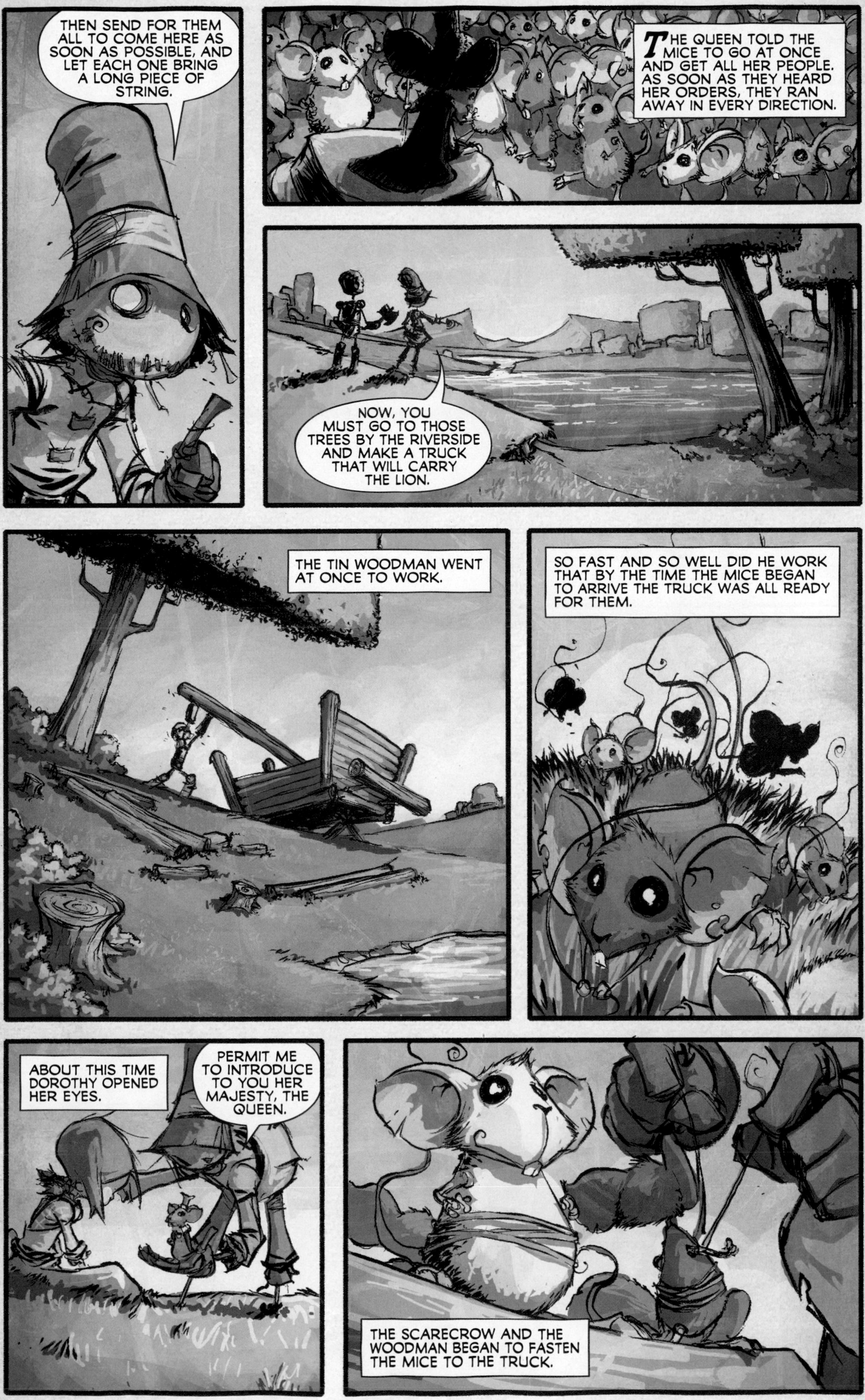
THEN SEND FOR THEM ALL TO COME HERE AS SOON AS POSSIBLE, AND LET EACH ONE BRING A LONG PIECE OF STRING.
THE QUEEN TOLD THE MICE TO GO AT ONCE AND GET ALL HER PEOPLE. AS SOON AS THEY HEARD HER ORDERS, THEY RAN AWAY IN EVERY DIRECTION.
NOW, YOU MUST GO TO THOSE TREES BY THE RIVERSIDE AND MAKE A TRUCK THAT WILL CARRY THE LION.
THE TIN WOODMAN WENT AT ONCE TO WORK.
SO FAST AND SO WELL DID HE WORK THAT BY THE TIME THE MICE BEGAN TO ARRIVE THE TRUCK WAS ALL READY FOR THEM.
ABOUT THIS TIME DOROTHY OPENED HER EYES.
PERMIT ME TO INTRODUCE TO YOU HER MAJESTY, THE QUEEN.
THE SCARECROW AND THE WOODMAN BEGAN TO FASTEN THE MICE TO THE TRUCK.

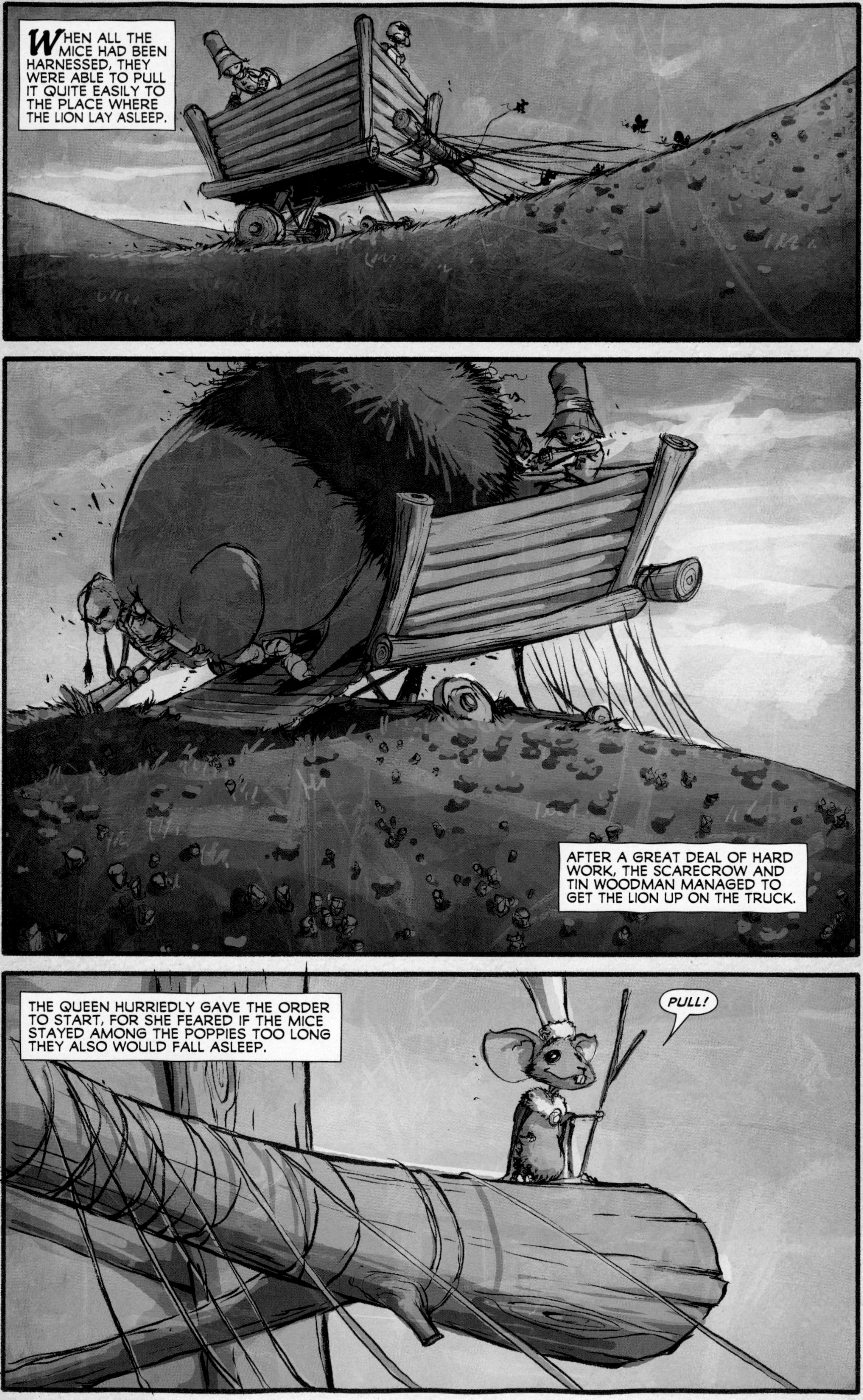
WHEN ALL THE MICE HAD BEEN HARNESSED, THEY WERE ABLE TO PULL IT QUITE EASILY TO THE PLACE WHERE THE LION LAY ASLEEP.
AFTER A GREAT DEAL OF HARD WORK, THE SCARECROW AND TIN WOODMAN MANAGED TO GET THE LION UP ON THE TRUCK.
THE QUEEN HURRIEDLY GAVE THE ORDER TO START, FOR SHE FEARED IF THE MICE STAYED AMONG THE POPPIES TOO LONG THEY ALSO WOULD FALL ASLEEP.
PULL!

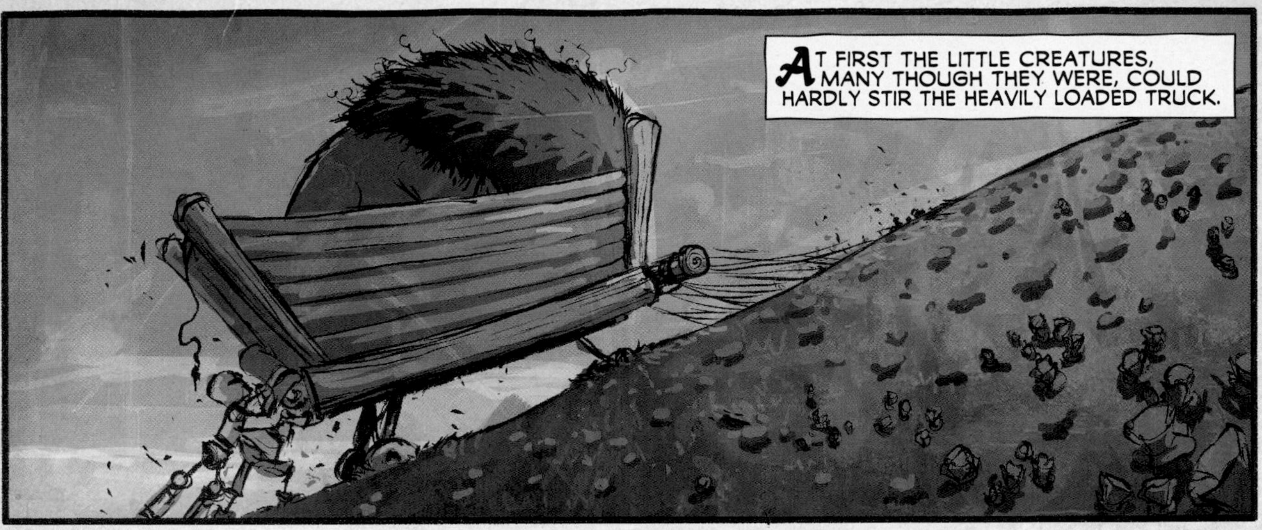
AT FIRST THE LITTLE CREATURES, MANY THOUGH THEY WERE, COULD HARDLY STIR THE HEAVILY LOADED TRUCK.

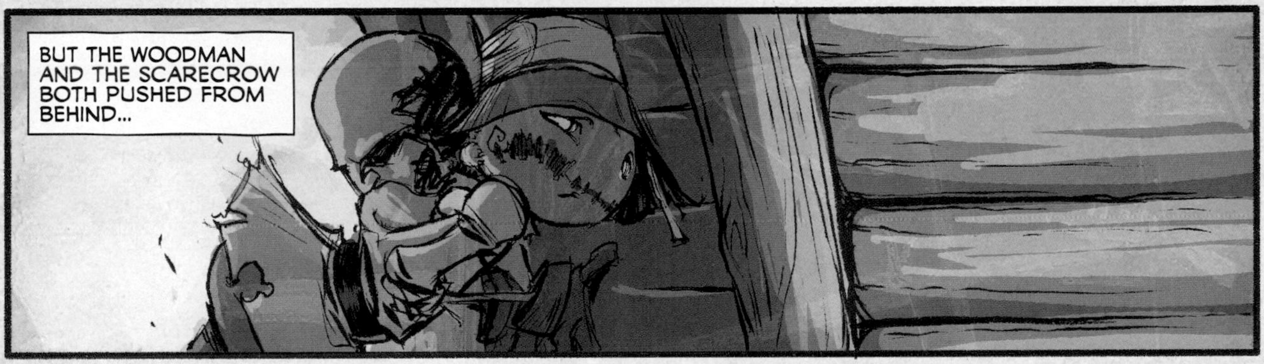
BUT THE WOODMAN AND THE SCARECROW BOTH PUSHED FROM BEHIND...

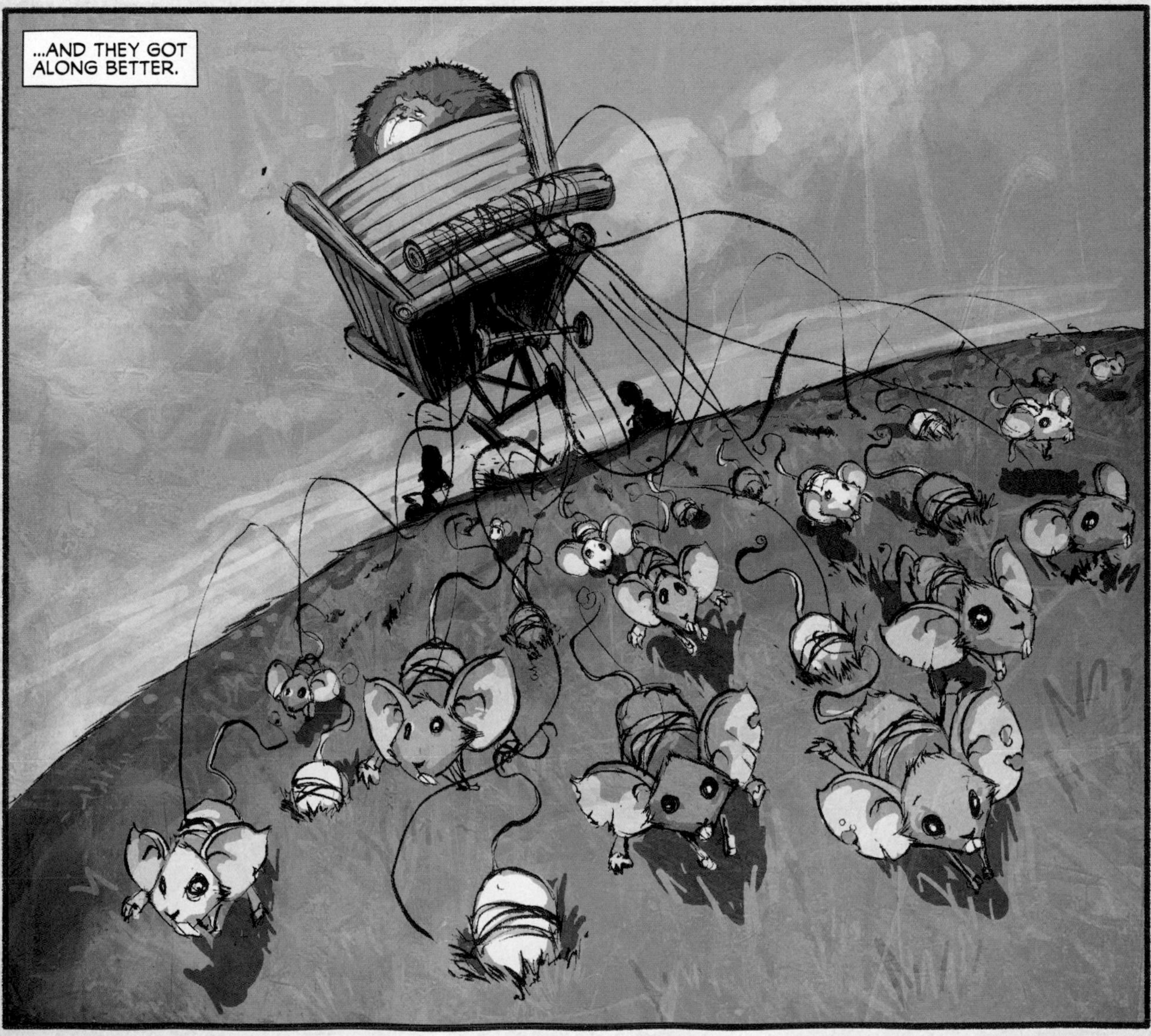
...AND THEY GOT ALONG BETTER.

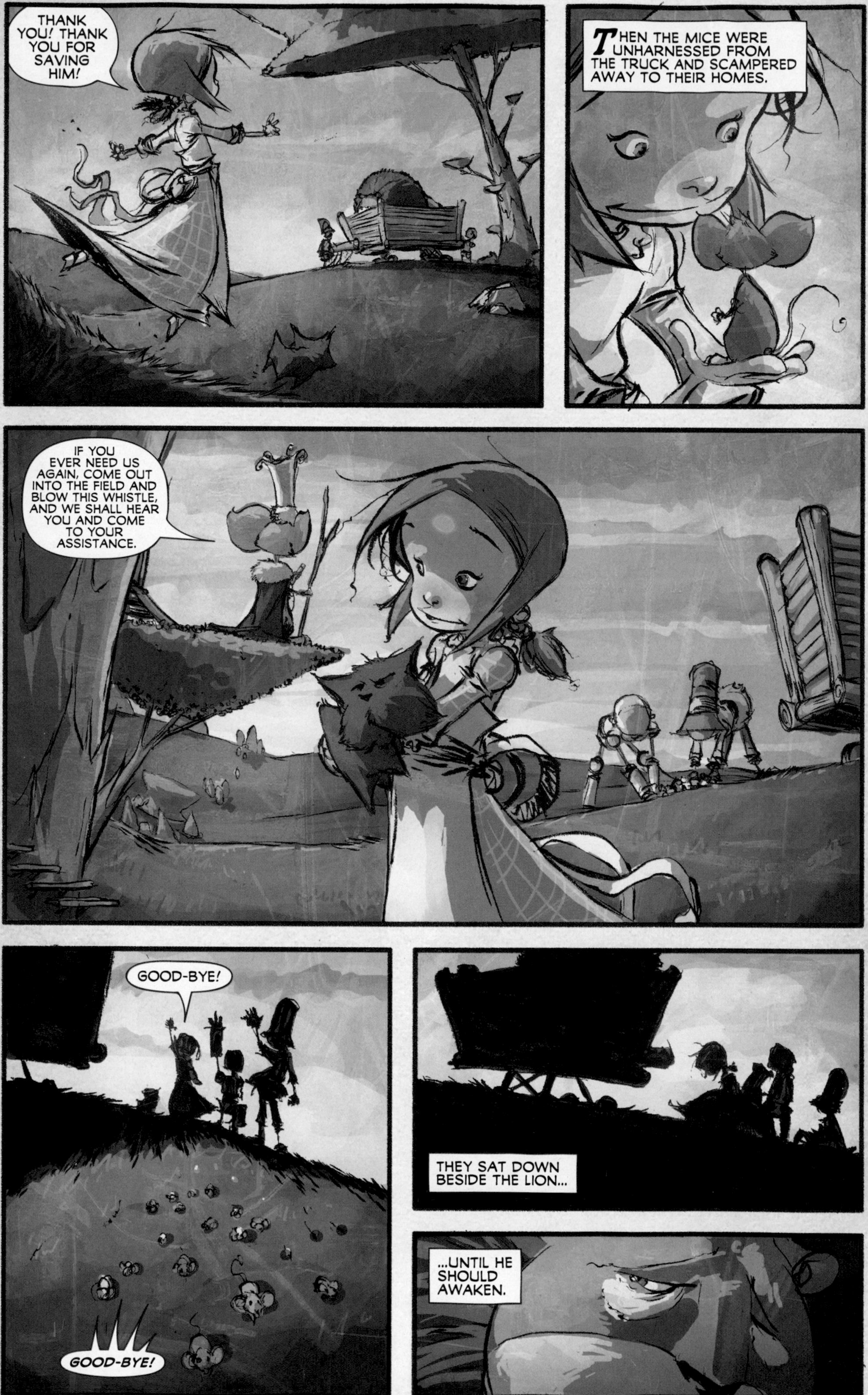
THANK YOU! THANK YOU FOR SAVING HIM!
THEN THE MICE WERE UNHARNESSED FROM THE TRUCK AND SCAMPERED AWAY TO THEIR HOMES.
IF YOU EVER NEED US AGAIN, COME OUT INTO THE FIELD AND BLOW THIS WHISTLE, AND WE SHALL HEAR YOU AND COME TO YOUR ASSISTANCE.
GOOD-BYE!
GOOD-BYE!
THEY SAT DOWN BESIDE THE LION...
...UNTIL HE SHOULD AWAKEN.

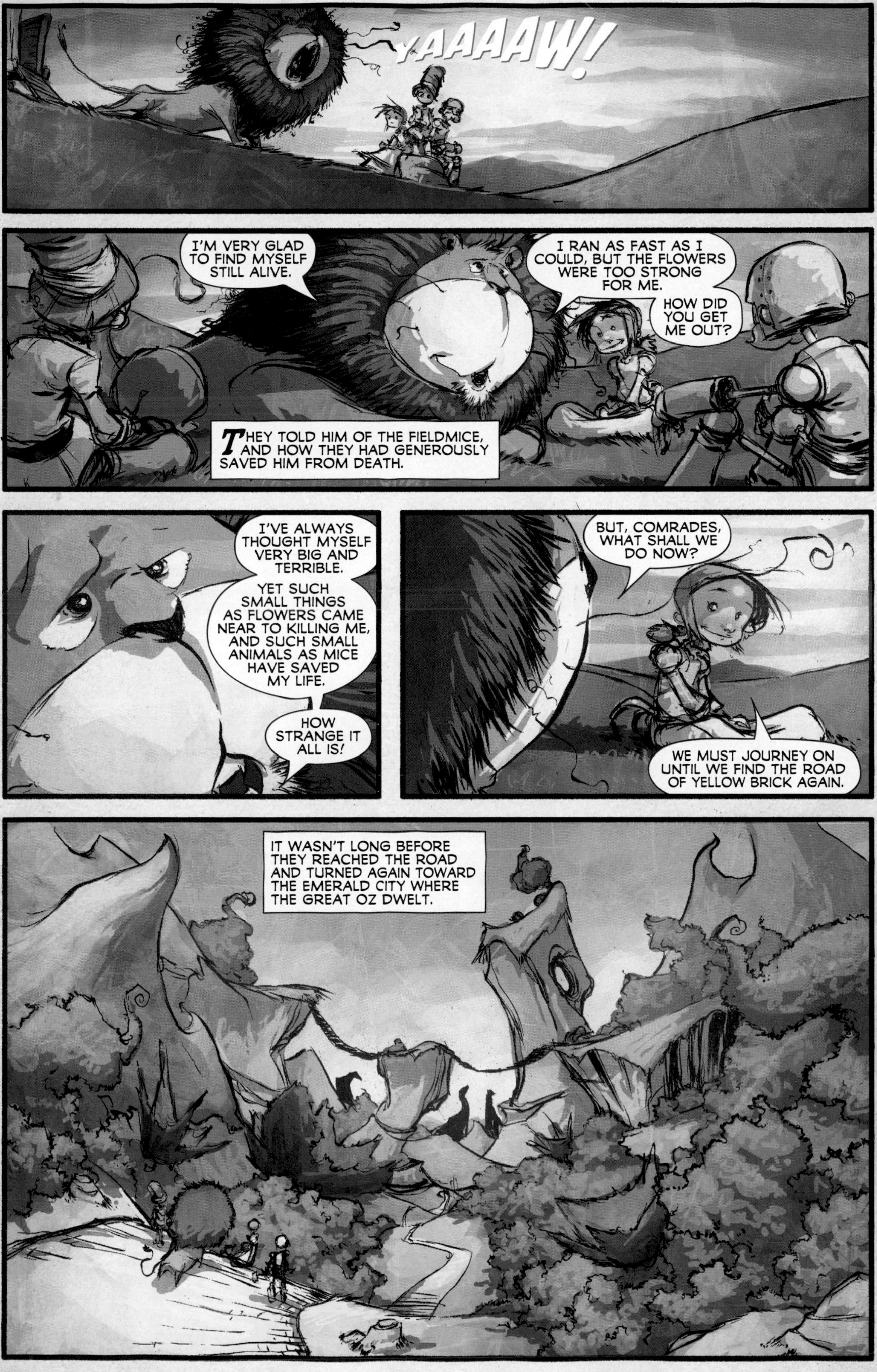
YAAAAW!
I'M VERY GLAD TO FIND MYSELF STILL ALIVE.
I RAN AS FAST AS I COULD, BUT THE FLOWERS WERE TOO STRONG FOR ME.
HOW DID YOU GET ME OUT?
THEY TOLD HIM OF THE FIELDMICE, AND HOW THEY HAD GENEROUSLY SAVED HIM FROM DEATH.
I'VE ALWAYS THOUGHT MYSELF VERY BIG AND TERRIBLE.
YET SUCH SMALL THINGS AS FLOWERS CAME NEAR TO KILLING ME, AND SUCH SMALL ANIMALS AS MICE HAVE SAVED MY LIFE.
HOW STRANGE IT ALL IS!
BUT, COMRADES, WHAT SHALL WE DO NOW?
WE MUST JOURNEY ON UNTIL WE FIND THE ROAD OF YELLOW BRICK AGAIN.
IT WASN'T LONG BEFORE THEY REACHED THE ROAD AND TURNED AGAIN TOWARD THE EMERALD CITY WHERE THE GREAT OZ DWELT.

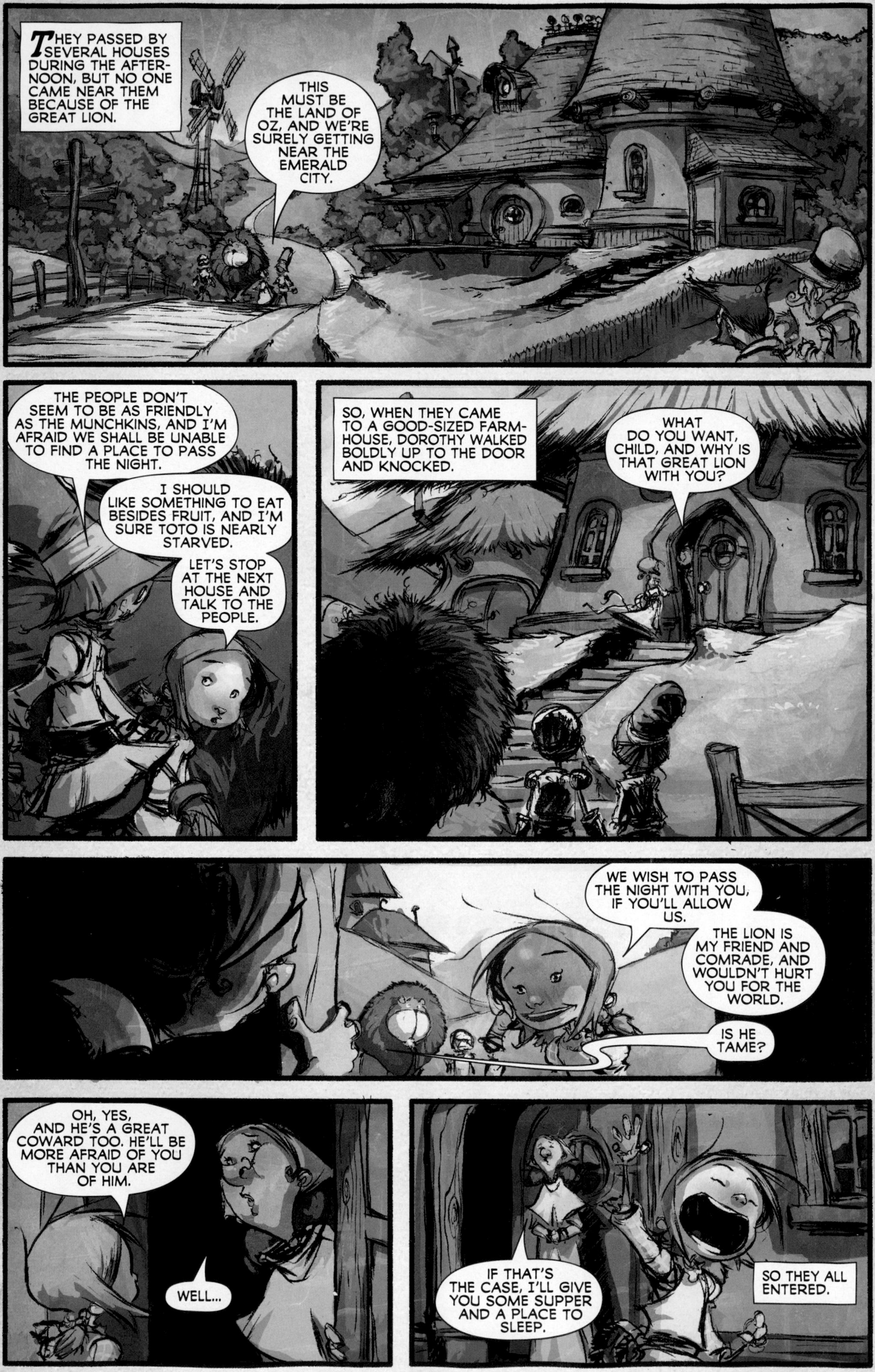
THEY PASSED BY SEVERAL HOUSES DURING THE AFTERNOON, BUT NO ONE CAME NEAR THEM BECAUSE OF THE GREAT LION.
THIS MUST BE THE LAND OF OZ, AND WE'RE SURELY GETTING NEAR THE EMERALD CITY.
THE PEOPLE DON'T SEEM TO BE AS FRIENDLY AS THE MUNCHKINS, AND I'M AFRAID WE SHALL BE UNABLE TO FIND A PLACE TO PASS THE NIGHT.
I SHOULD LIKE SOMETHING TO EAT BESIDES FRUIT, AND I'M SURE TOTO IS NEARLY STARVED.
LET'S STOP AT THE NEXT HOUSE AND TALK TO THE PEOPLE.
SO, WHEN THEY CAME TO A GOOD-SIZED FARMHOUSE, DOROTHY WALKED BOLDLY UP TO THE DOOR AND KNOCKED.
WHAT DO YOU WANT, CHILD, AND WHY IS THAT GREAT LION WITH YOU?
WE WISH TO PASS THE NIGHT WITH YOU, IF YOU'LL ALLOW US.
THE LION IS MY FRIEND AND COMRADE, AND WOULDN'T HURT YOU FOR THE WORLD.
IS HE TAME?
OH, YES, AND HE'S A GREAT COWARD TOO. HE'LL BE MORE AFRAID OF YOU THAN YOU ARE OF HIM.
WELL...
IF THAT'S THE CASE, I'LL GIVE YOU SOME SUPPER AND A PLACE TO SLEEP.
SO THEY ALL ENTERED.

WHILE THE WOMAN WAS BUSY LAYING THE TABLE --

WHERE ARE YOU ALL GOING?

TO THE EMERALD CITY TO SEE THE GREAT OZ.

OH, INDEED! ARE YOU SURE THAT OZ WILL SEE YOU?

WHY NOT?

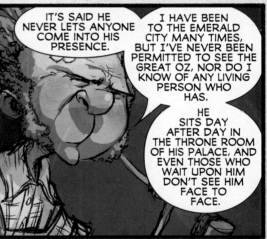

IT'S SAID HE NEVER LETS ANYONE COME INTO HIS PRESENCE.

I HAVE BEEN TO THE EMERALD CITY MANY TIMES, BUT I'VE NEVER BEEN PERMITTED TO SEE THE GREAT OZ, NOR DO I KNOW OF ANY LIVING PERSON WHO HAS.

HE SITS DAY AFTER DAY IN THE THRONE ROOM OF HIS PALACE, AND EVEN THOSE WHO WAIT UPON HIM DON'T SEE HIM FACE TO FACE.

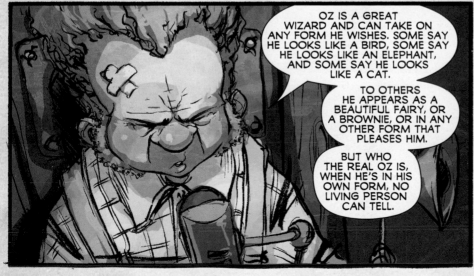

OZ IS A GREAT WIZARD AND CAN TAKE ON ANY FORM HE WISHES. SOME SAY HE LOOKS LIKE A BIRD, SOME SAY HE LOOKS LIKE AN ELEPHANT, AND SOME SAY HE LOOKS LIKE A CAT.

TO OTHERS HE APPEARS AS A BEAUTIFUL FAIRY, OR A BROWNIE, OR IN ANY OTHER FORM THAT PLEASES HIM.

BUT WHO THE REAL OZ IS, WHEN HE'S IN HIS OWN FORM, NO LIVING PERSON CAN TELL.

THAT'S VERY STRANGE. BUT WE MUST TRY TO SEE HIM, OR WE SHALL HAVE MADE OUR JOURNEY FOR NOTHING.

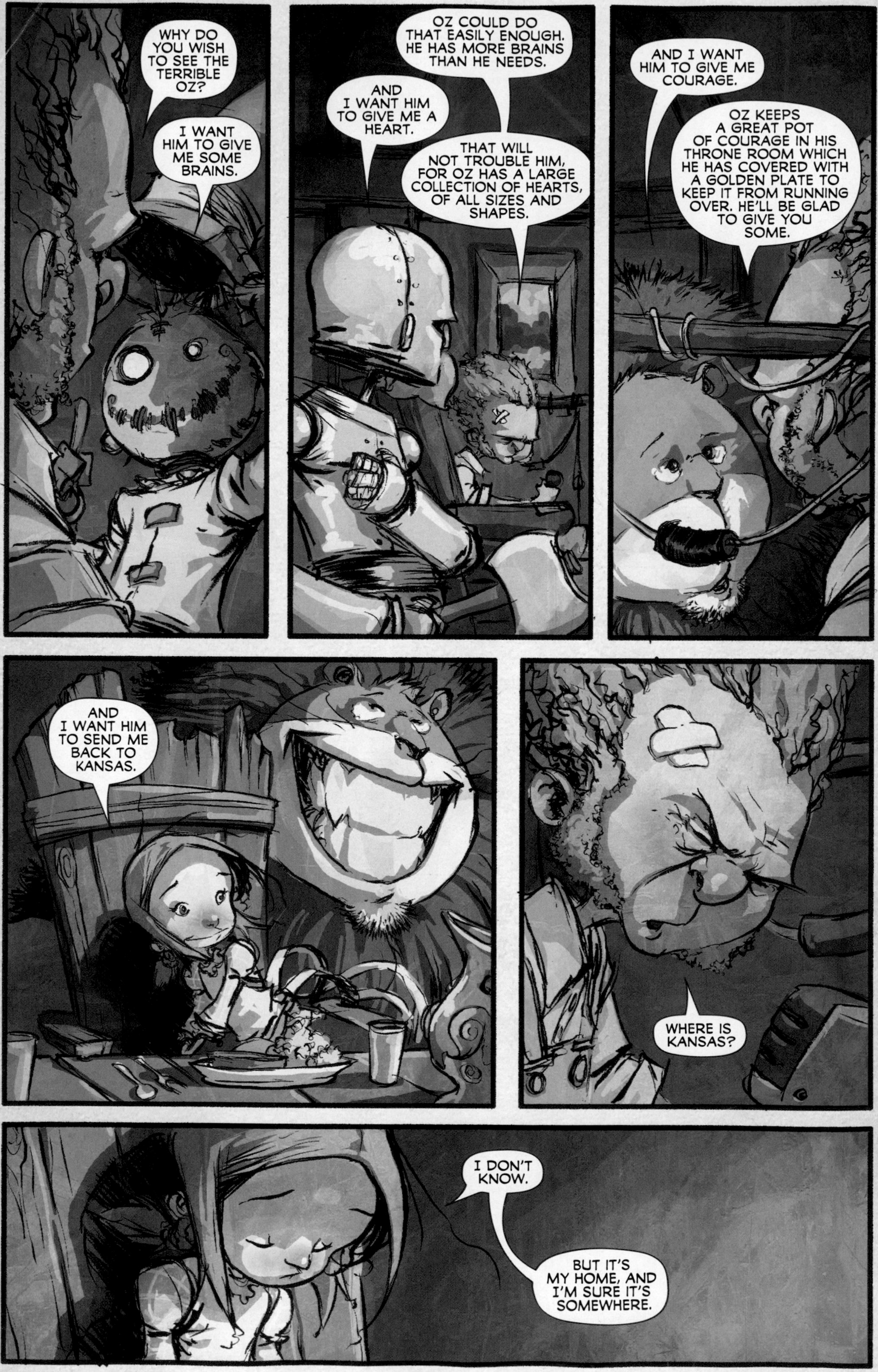
WHY DO YOU WISH TO SEE THE TERRIBLE OZ?
I WANT HIM TO GIVE ME SOME BRAINS.
OZ COULD DO THAT EASILY ENOUGH. HE HAS MORE BRAINS THAN HE NEEDS.
AND I WANT HIM TO GIVE ME A HEART.
THAT WILL NOT TROUBLE HIM, FOR OZ HAS A LARGE COLLECTION OF HEARTS, OF ALL SIZES AND SHAPES.
AND I WANT HIM TO GIVE ME COURAGE.
OZ KEEPS A GREAT POT OF COURAGE IN HIS THRONE ROOM WHICH HE HAS COVERED WITH A GOLDEN PLATE TO KEEP IT FROM RUNNING OVER. HE'LL BE GLAD TO GIVE YOU SOME.
AND I WANT HIM TO SEND ME BACK TO KANSAS.
WHERE IS KANSAS?
I DON'T KNOW.
BUT IT'S MY HOME, AND I'M SURE IT'S SOMEWHERE.

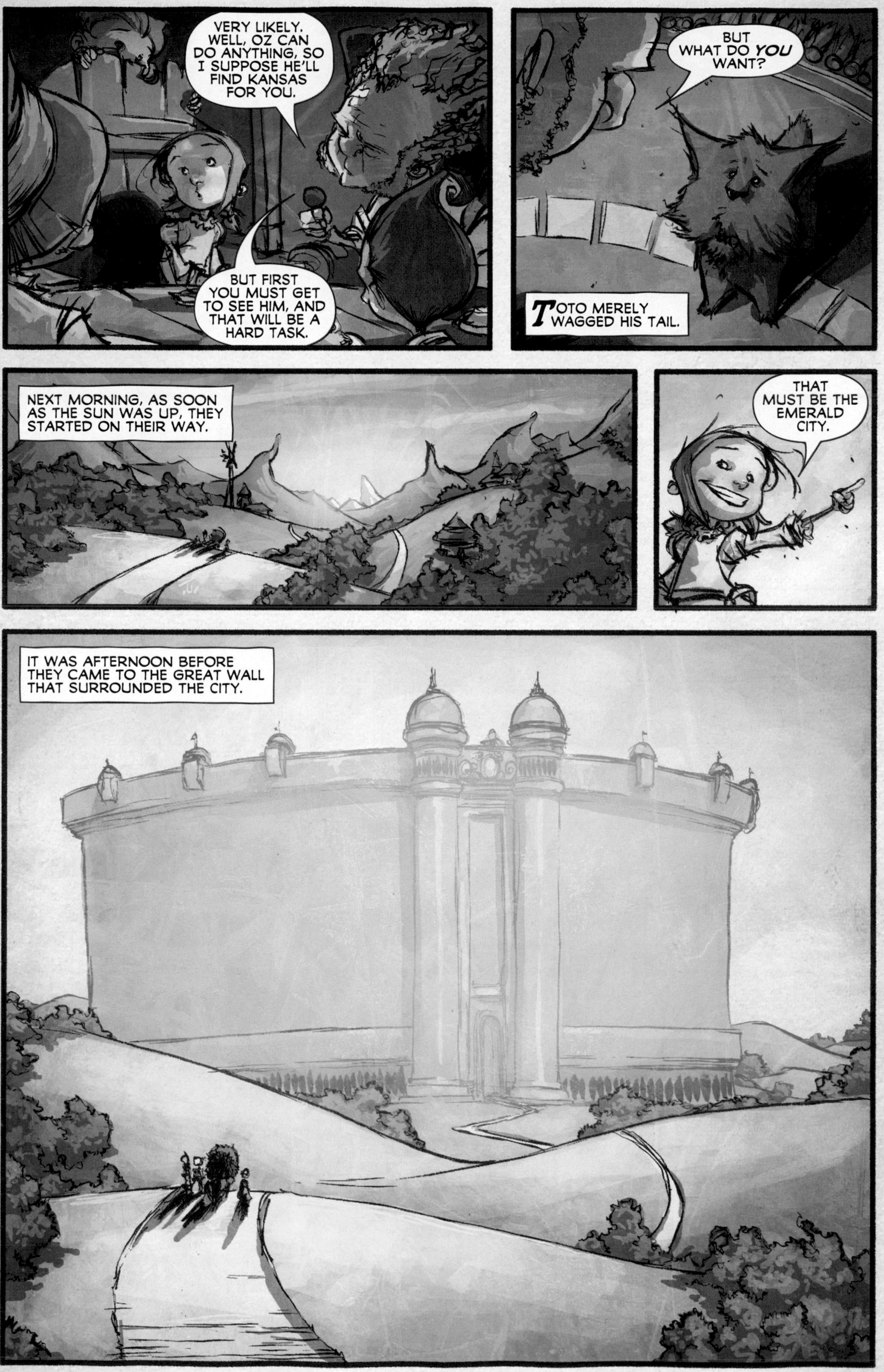
VERY LIKELY. WELL, OZ CAN DO ANYTHING, SO I SUPPOSE HE'LL FIND KANSAS FOR YOU.
BUT FIRST YOU MUST GET TO SEE HIM, AND THAT WILL BE A HARD TASK.
BUT WHAT DO *YOU* WANT?
TOTO MERELY WAGGED HIS TAIL.
NEXT MORNING, AS SOON AS THE SUN WAS UP, THEY STARTED ON THEIR WAY.
THAT MUST BE THE EMERALD CITY.
IT WAS AFTERNOON BEFORE THEY CAME TO THE GREAT WALL THAT SURROUNDED THE CITY.

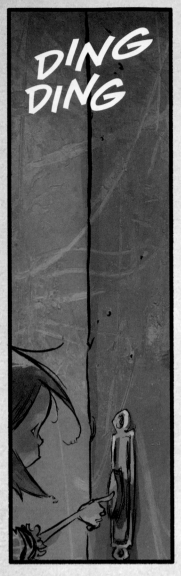

DING DING

WHAT DO YOU WISH IN THE EMERALD CITY?

WE CAME HERE TO SEE THE GREAT OZ.

IT HAS BEEN MANY YEARS SINCE ANYONE ASKED ME TO SEE OZ.

HE'S POWERFUL AND TERRIBLE. IF YOU COME ON AN IDLE OR FOOLISH ERRAND TO BOTHER THE WISE REFLECTIONS OF THE GREAT WIZARD, HE MIGHT BE ANGRY AND DESTROY YOU ALL IN AN INSTANT.

IT'S NOT A FOOLISH ERRAND, NOR AN IDLE ONE. IT'S IMPORTANT, AND WE'VE BEEN TOLD THAT OZ IS A GOOD WIZARD.

SO HE IS, AND HE RULES THE EMERALD CITY WISELY AND WELL.

BUT TO THOSE WHO ARE NOT HONEST, OR WHO APPROACH HIM FROM CURIOSITY, HE'S MOST TERRIBLE.

FEW HAVE EVER DARED ASK TO SEE HIS FACE.

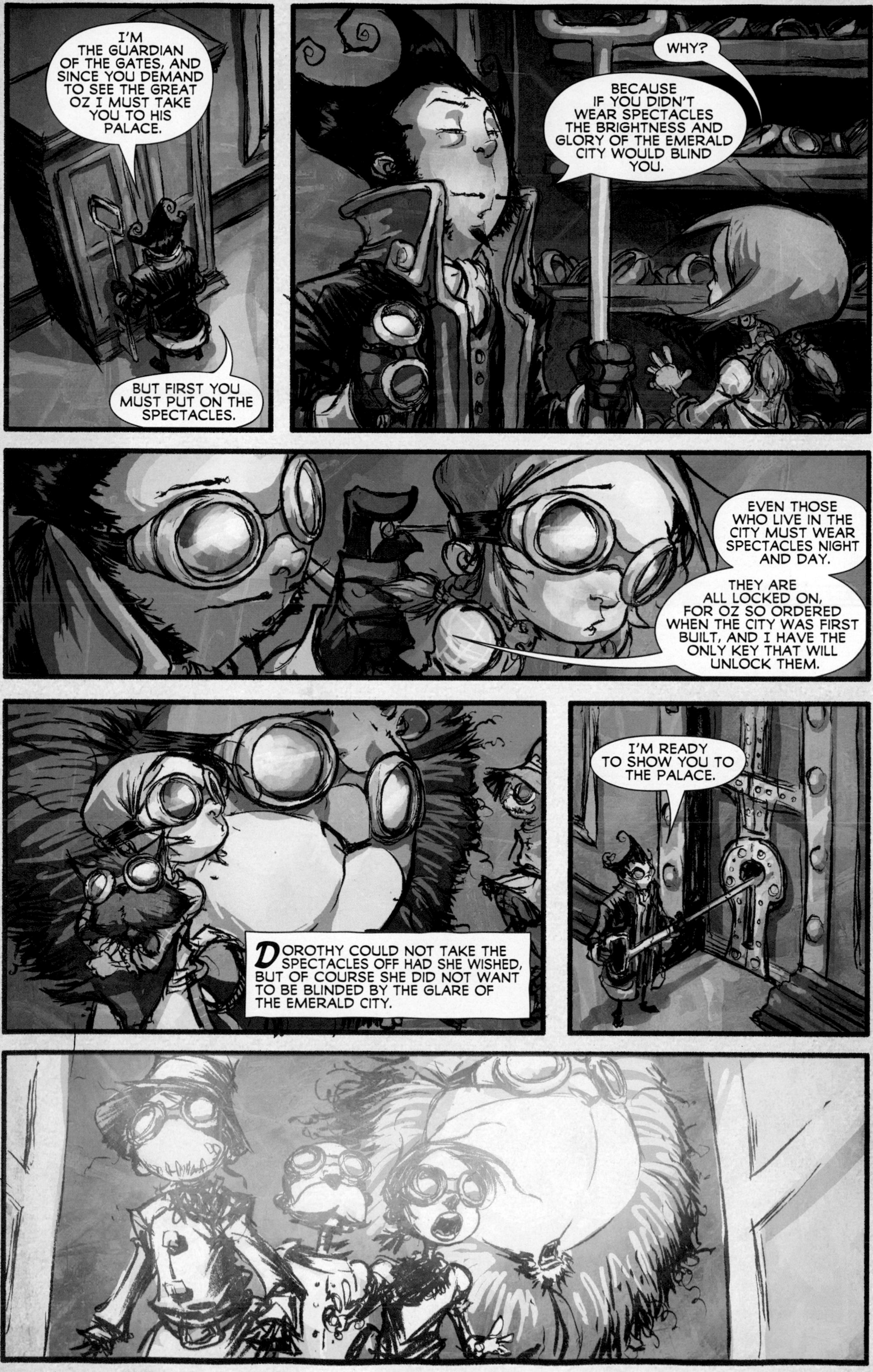
I'M THE GUARDIAN OF THE GATES, AND SINCE YOU DEMAND TO SEE THE GREAT OZ I MUST TAKE YOU TO HIS PALACE.
BUT FIRST YOU MUST PUT ON THE SPECTACLES.
WHY?
BECAUSE IF YOU DIDN'T WEAR SPECTACLES THE BRIGHTNESS AND GLORY OF THE EMERALD CITY WOULD BLIND YOU.
EVEN THOSE WHO LIVE IN THE CITY MUST WEAR SPECTACLES NIGHT AND DAY.
THEY ARE ALL LOCKED ON, FOR OZ SO ORDERED WHEN THE CITY WAS FIRST BUILT, AND I HAVE THE ONLY KEY THAT WILL UNLOCK THEM.
DOROTHY COULD NOT TAKE THE SPECTACLES OFF HAD SHE WISHED, BUT OF COURSE SHE DID NOT WANT TO BE BLINDED BY THE GLARE OF THE EMERALD CITY.
I'M READY TO SHOW YOU TO THE PALACE.

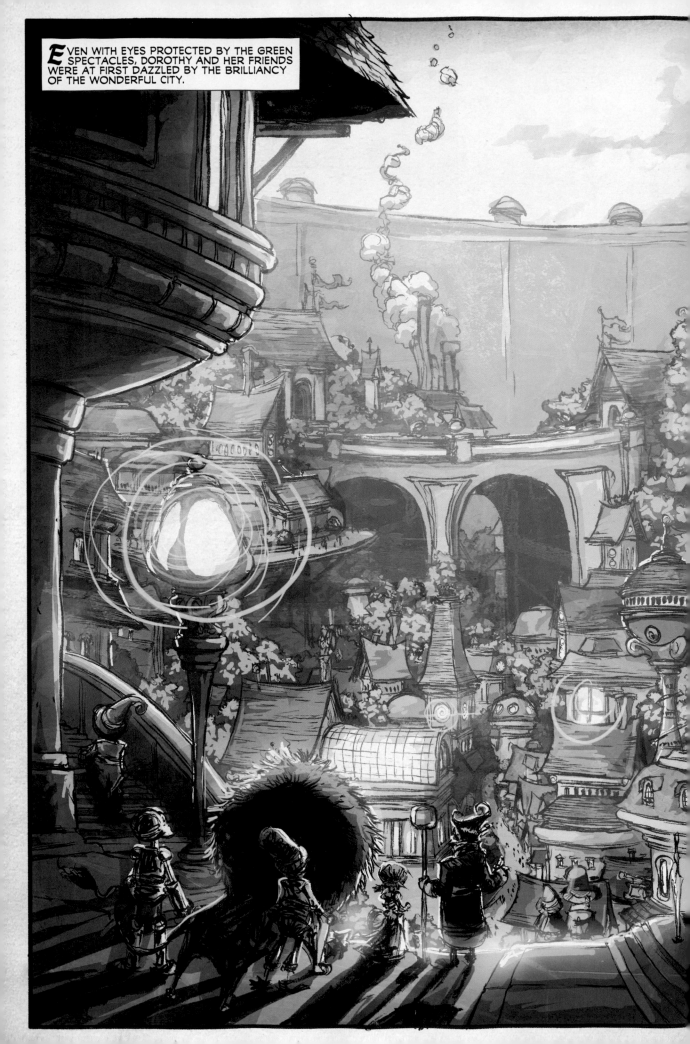

EVEN WITH EYES PROTECTED BY THE GREEN SPECTACLES, DOROTHY AND HER FRIENDS WERE AT FIRST DAZZLED BY THE BRILLIANCY OF THE WONDERFUL CITY.

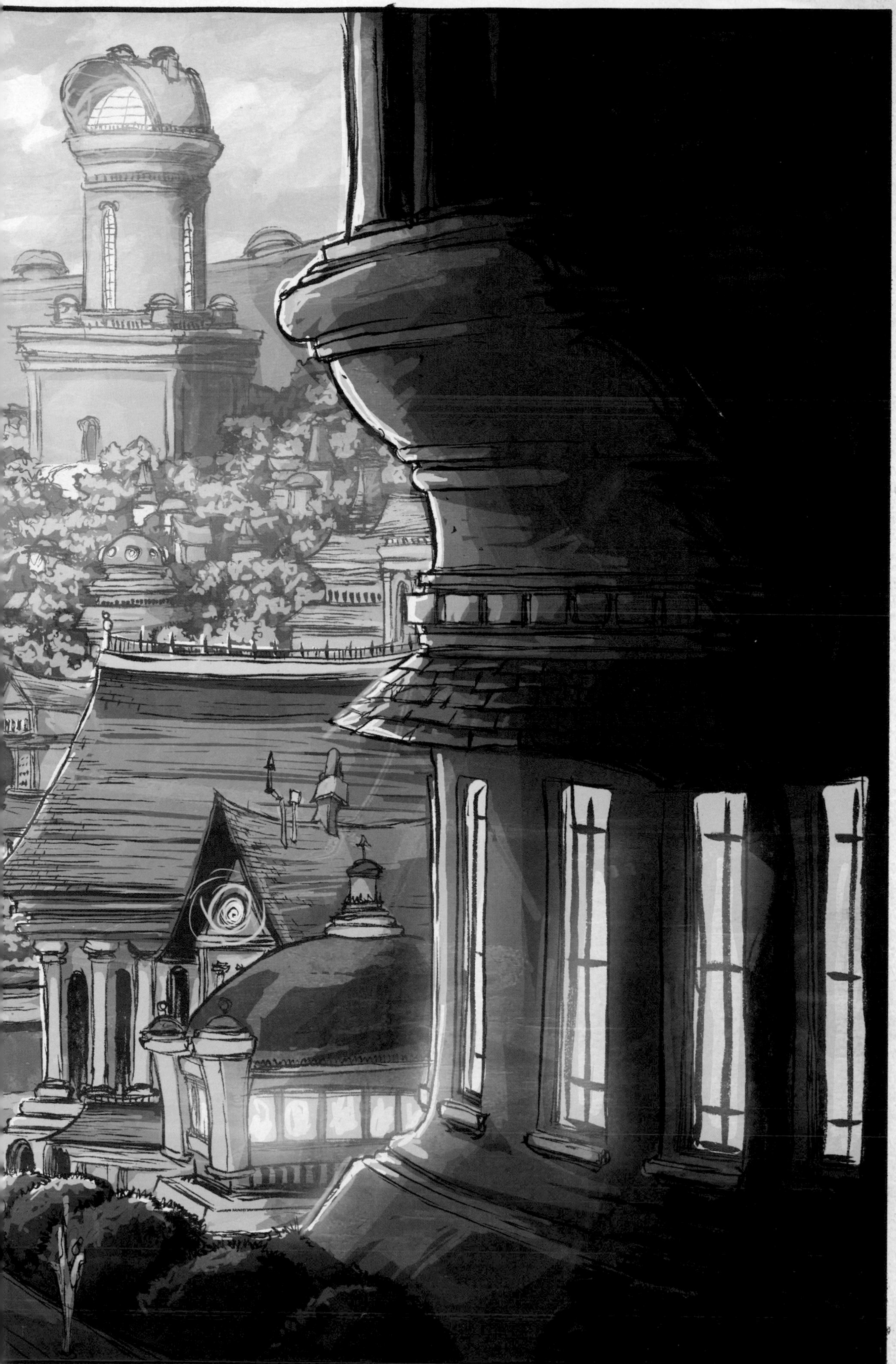

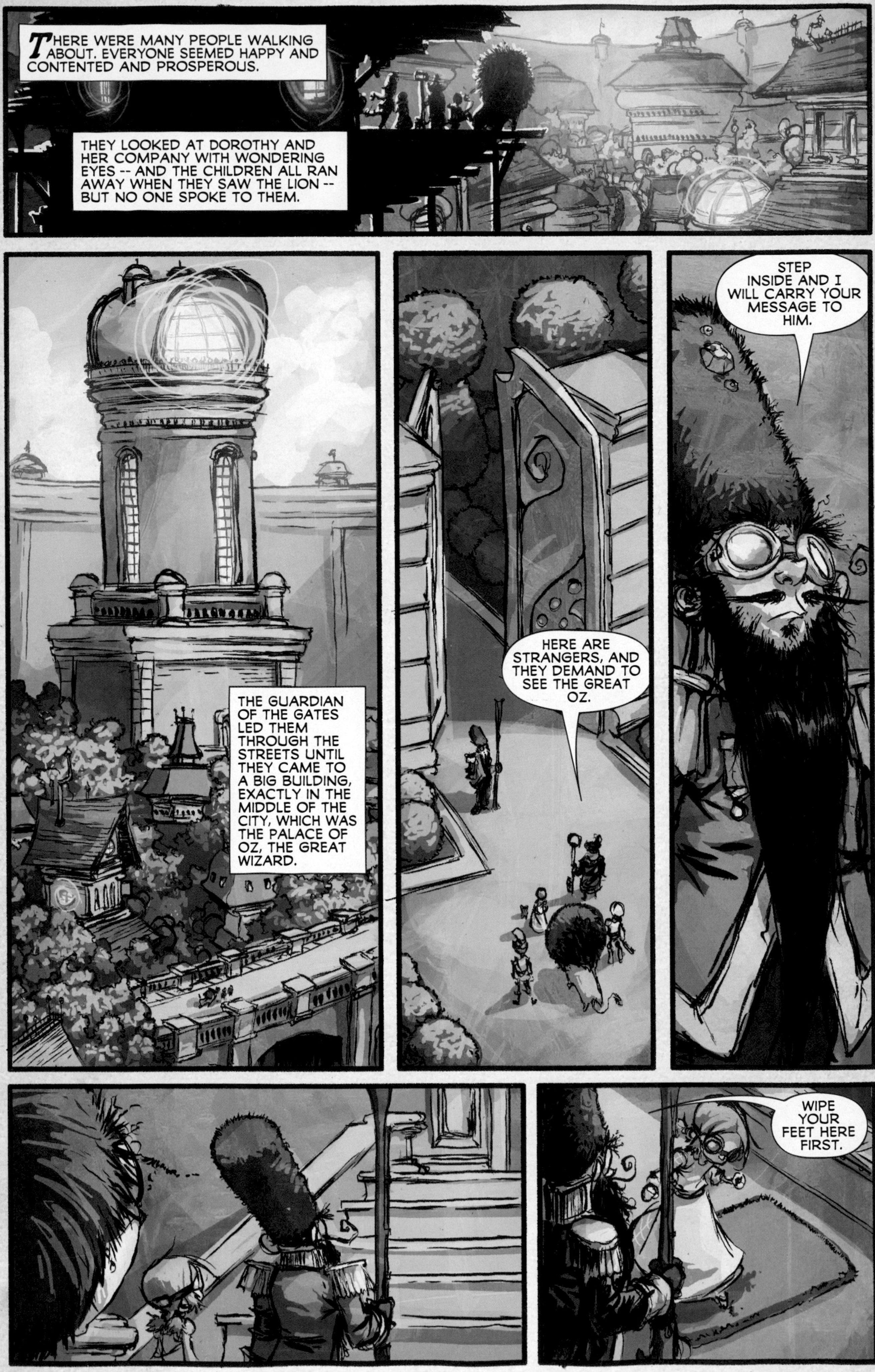
THERE WERE MANY PEOPLE WALKING ABOUT. EVERYONE SEEMED HAPPY AND CONTENTED AND PROSPEROUS.
THEY LOOKED AT DOROTHY AND HER COMPANY WITH WONDERING EYES -- AND THE CHILDREN ALL RAN AWAY WHEN THEY SAW THE LION -- BUT NO ONE SPOKE TO THEM.
THE GUARDIAN OF THE GATES LED THEM THROUGH THE STREETS UNTIL THEY CAME TO A BIG BUILDING, EXACTLY IN THE MIDDLE OF THE CITY, WHICH WAS THE PALACE OF OZ, THE GREAT WIZARD.
HERE ARE STRANGERS, AND THEY DEMAND TO SEE THE GREAT OZ.
STEP INSIDE AND I WILL CARRY YOUR MESSAGE TO HIM.
WIPE YOUR FEET HERE FIRST.

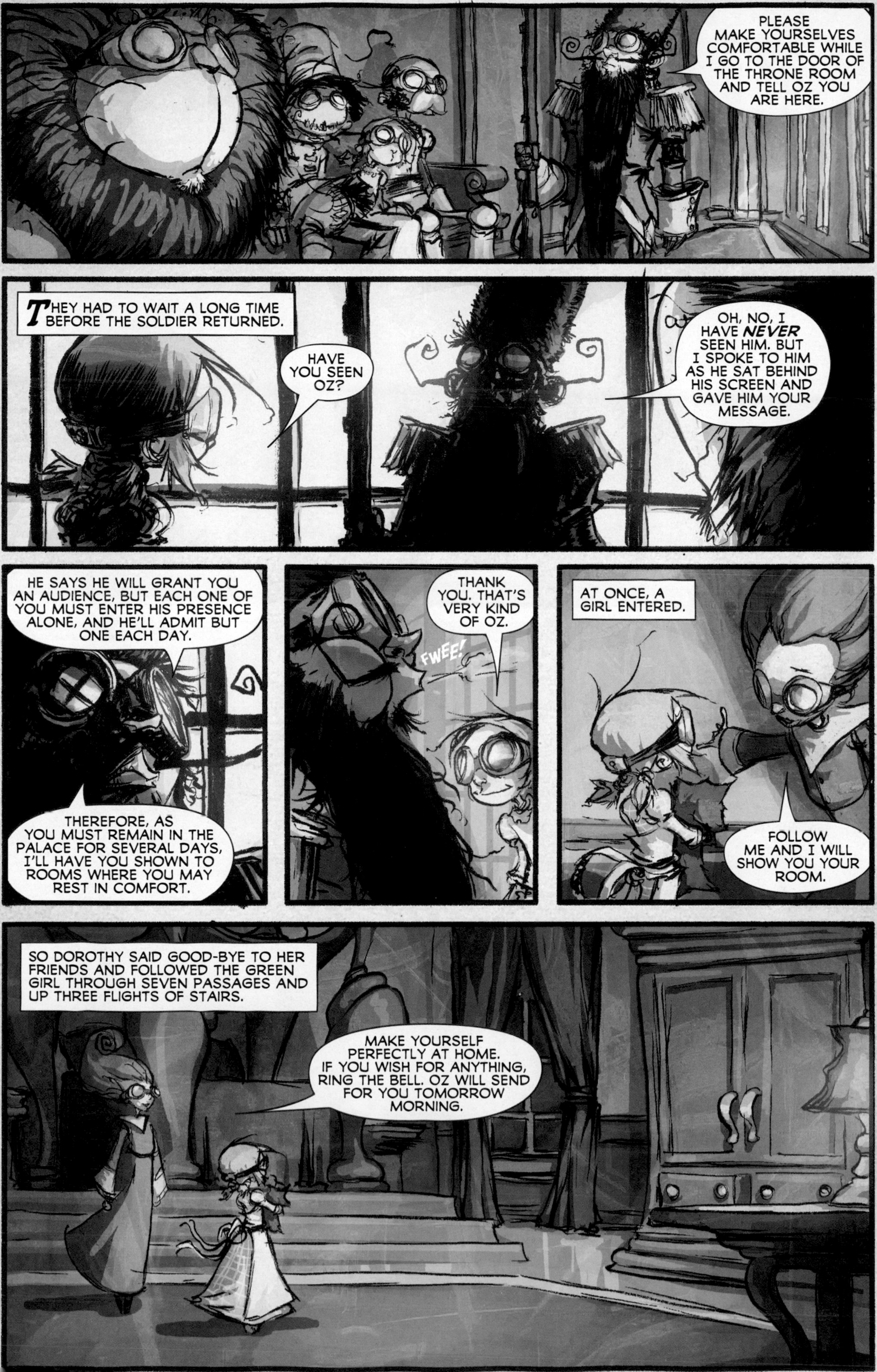
PLEASE MAKE YOURSELVES COMFORTABLE WHILE I GO TO THE DOOR OF THE THRONE ROOM AND TELL OZ YOU ARE HERE.
THEY HAD TO WAIT A LONG TIME BEFORE THE SOLDIER RETURNED.
HAVE YOU SEEN OZ?
OH, NO, I HAVE NEVER SEEN HIM. BUT I SPOKE TO HIM AS HE SAT BEHIND HIS SCREEN AND GAVE HIM YOUR MESSAGE.
HE SAYS HE WILL GRANT YOU AN AUDIENCE, BUT EACH ONE OF YOU MUST ENTER HIS PRESENCE ALONE, AND HE'LL ADMIT BUT ONE EACH DAY.
THEREFORE, AS YOU MUST REMAIN IN THE PALACE FOR SEVERAL DAYS, I'LL HAVE YOU SHOWN TO ROOMS WHERE YOU MAY REST IN COMFORT.
THANK YOU. THAT'S VERY KIND OF OZ.
FWEE!
AT ONCE, A GIRL ENTERED.
FOLLOW ME AND I WILL SHOW YOU YOUR ROOM.
SO DOROTHY SAID GOOD-BYE TO HER FRIENDS AND FOLLOWED THE GREEN GIRL THROUGH SEVEN PASSAGES AND UP THREE FLIGHTS OF STAIRS.
MAKE YOURSELF PERFECTLY AT HOME. IF YOU WISH FOR ANYTHING, RING THE BELL. OZ WILL SEND FOR YOU TOMORROW MORNING.

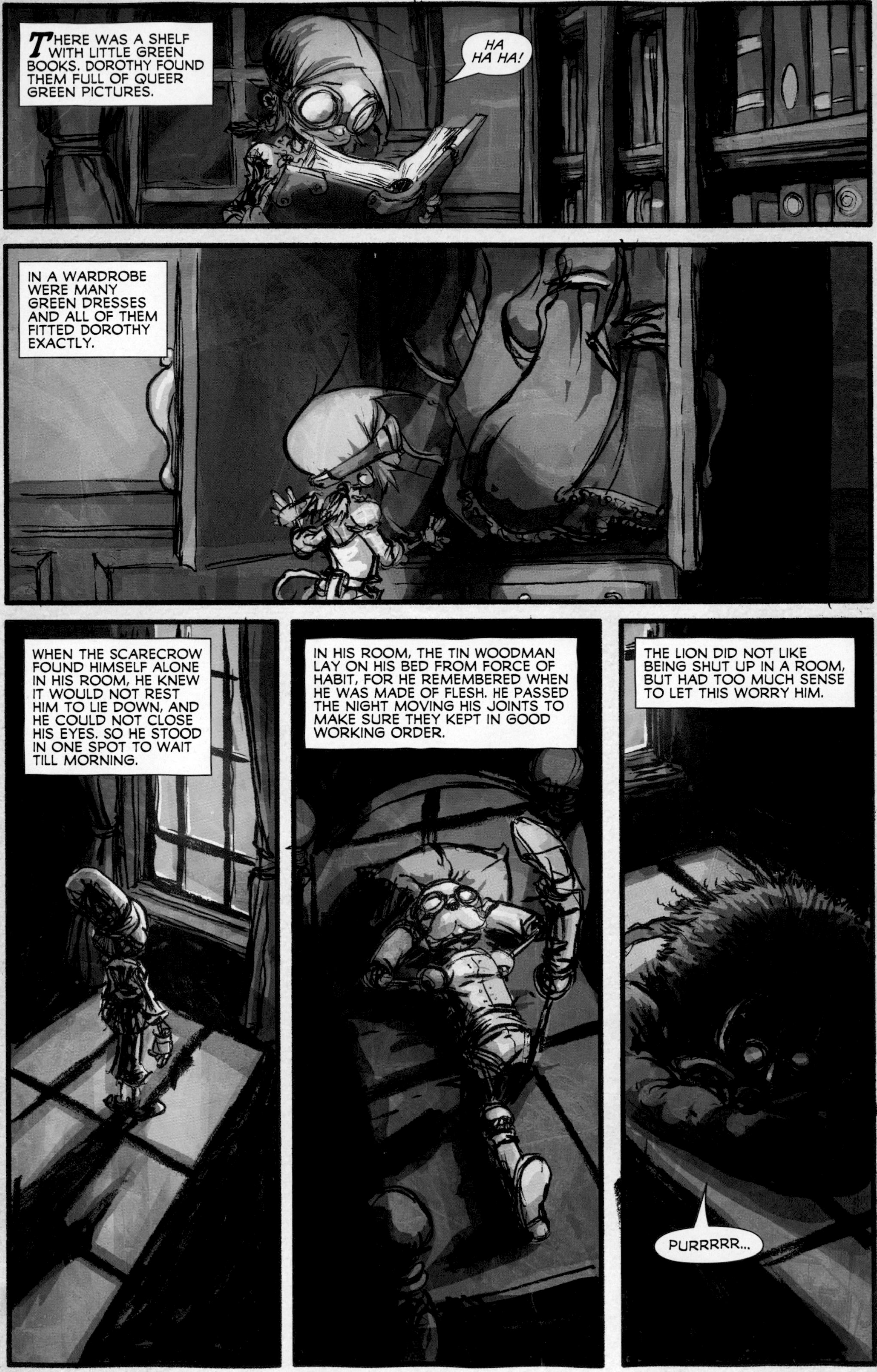
THERE WAS A SHELF WITH LITTLE GREEN BOOKS. DOROTHY FOUND THEM FULL OF QUEER GREEN PICTURES.
HA HA HA!
IN A WARDROBE WERE MANY GREEN DRESSES AND ALL OF THEM FITTED DOROTHY EXACTLY.
WHEN THE SCARECROW FOUND HIMSELF ALONE IN HIS ROOM, HE KNEW IT WOULD NOT REST HIM TO LIE DOWN, AND HE COULD NOT CLOSE HIS EYES. SO HE STOOD IN ONE SPOT TO WAIT TILL MORNING.
IN HIS ROOM, THE TIN WOODMAN LAY ON HIS BED FROM FORCE OF HABIT, FOR HE REMEMBERED WHEN HE WAS MADE OF FLESH. HE PASSED THE NIGHT MOVING HIS JOINTS TO MAKE SURE THEY KEPT IN GOOD WORKING ORDER.
THE LION DID NOT LIKE BEING SHUT UP IN A ROOM, BUT HAD TOO MUCH SENSE TO LET THIS WORRY HIM.
PURRRRR...

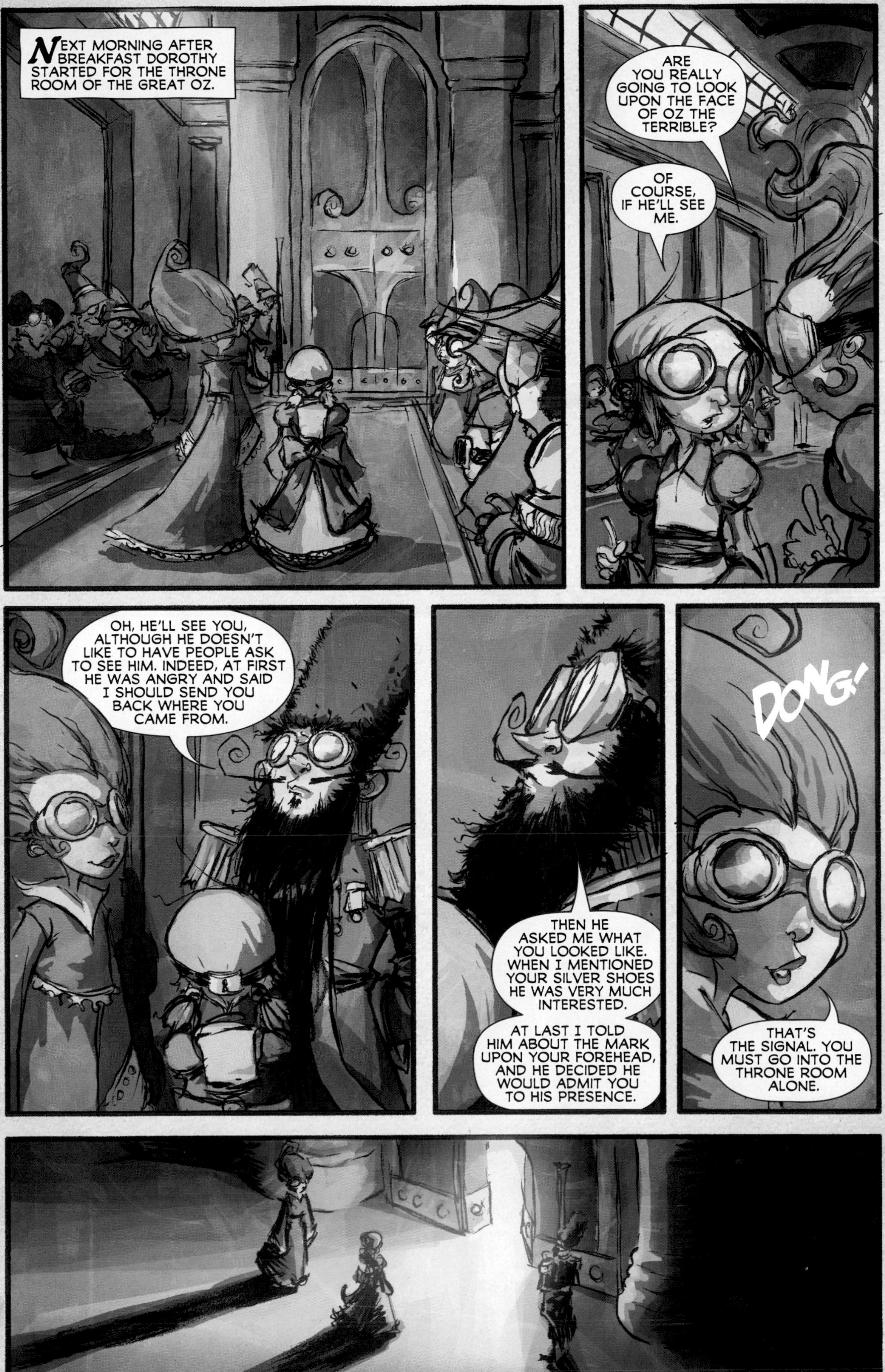
NEXT MORNING AFTER BREAKFAST DOROTHY STARTED FOR THE THRONE ROOM OF THE GREAT OZ.
ARE YOU REALLY GOING TO LOOK UPON THE FACE OF OZ THE TERRIBLE?
OF COURSE, IF HE'LL SEE ME.
OH, HE'LL SEE YOU, ALTHOUGH HE DOESN'T LIKE TO HAVE PEOPLE ASK TO SEE HIM. INDEED, AT FIRST HE WAS ANGRY AND SAID I SHOULD SEND YOU BACK WHERE YOU CAME FROM.
THEN HE ASKED ME WHAT YOU LOOKED LIKE. WHEN I MENTIONED YOUR SILVER SHOES HE WAS VERY MUCH INTERESTED.
AT LAST I TOLD HIM ABOUT THE MARK UPON YOUR FOREHEAD, AND HE DECIDED HE WOULD ADMIT YOU TO HIS PRESENCE.
DONG!
THAT'S THE SIGNAL. YOU MUST GO INTO THE THRONE ROOM ALONE.

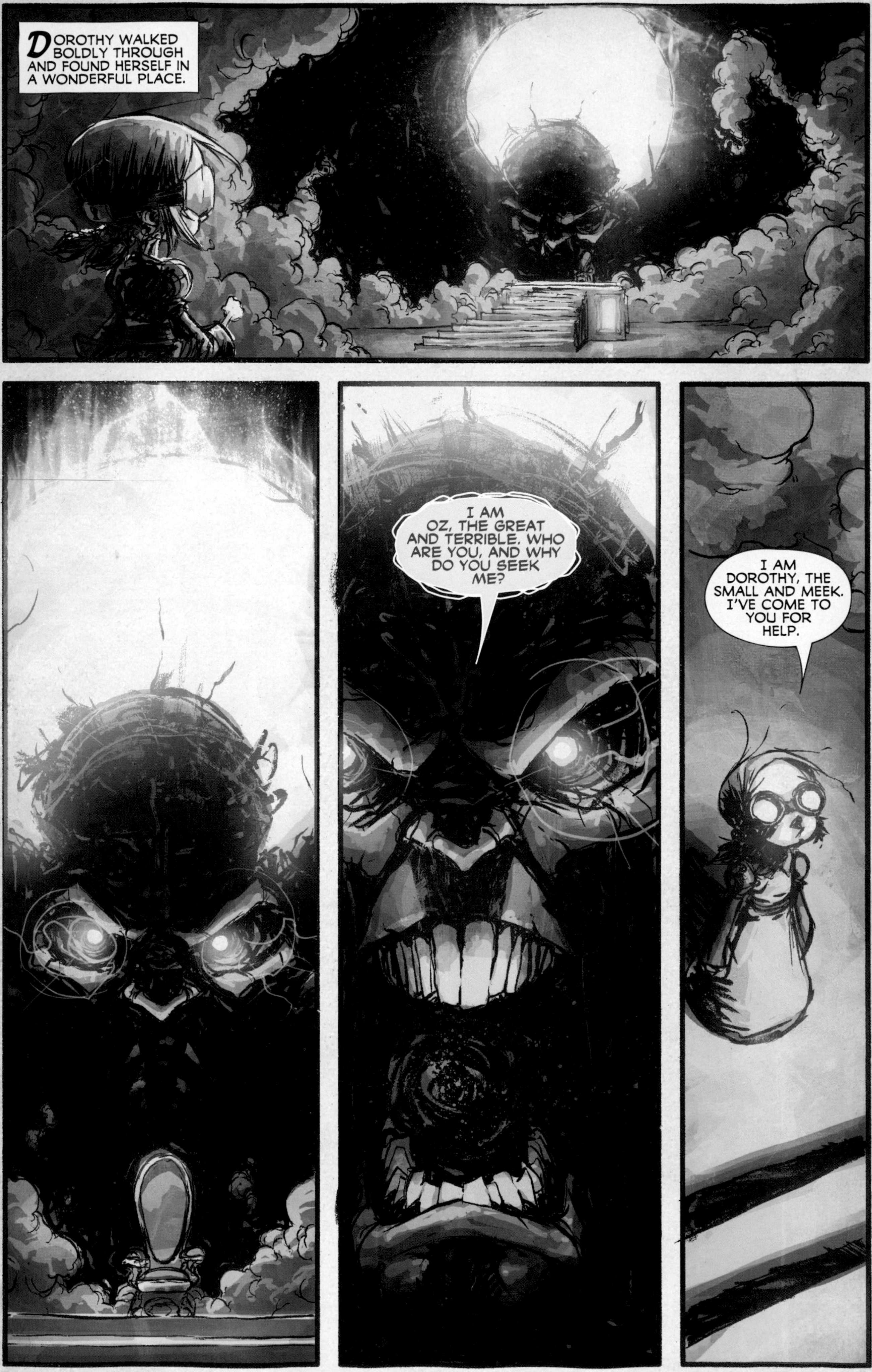
DOROTHY WALKED BOLDLY THROUGH AND FOUND HERSELF IN A WONDERFUL PLACE.
I AM OZ, THE GREAT AND TERRIBLE. WHO ARE YOU, AND WHY DO YOU SEEK ME?
I AM DOROTHY, THE SMALL AND MEEK. I'VE COME TO YOU FOR HELP.

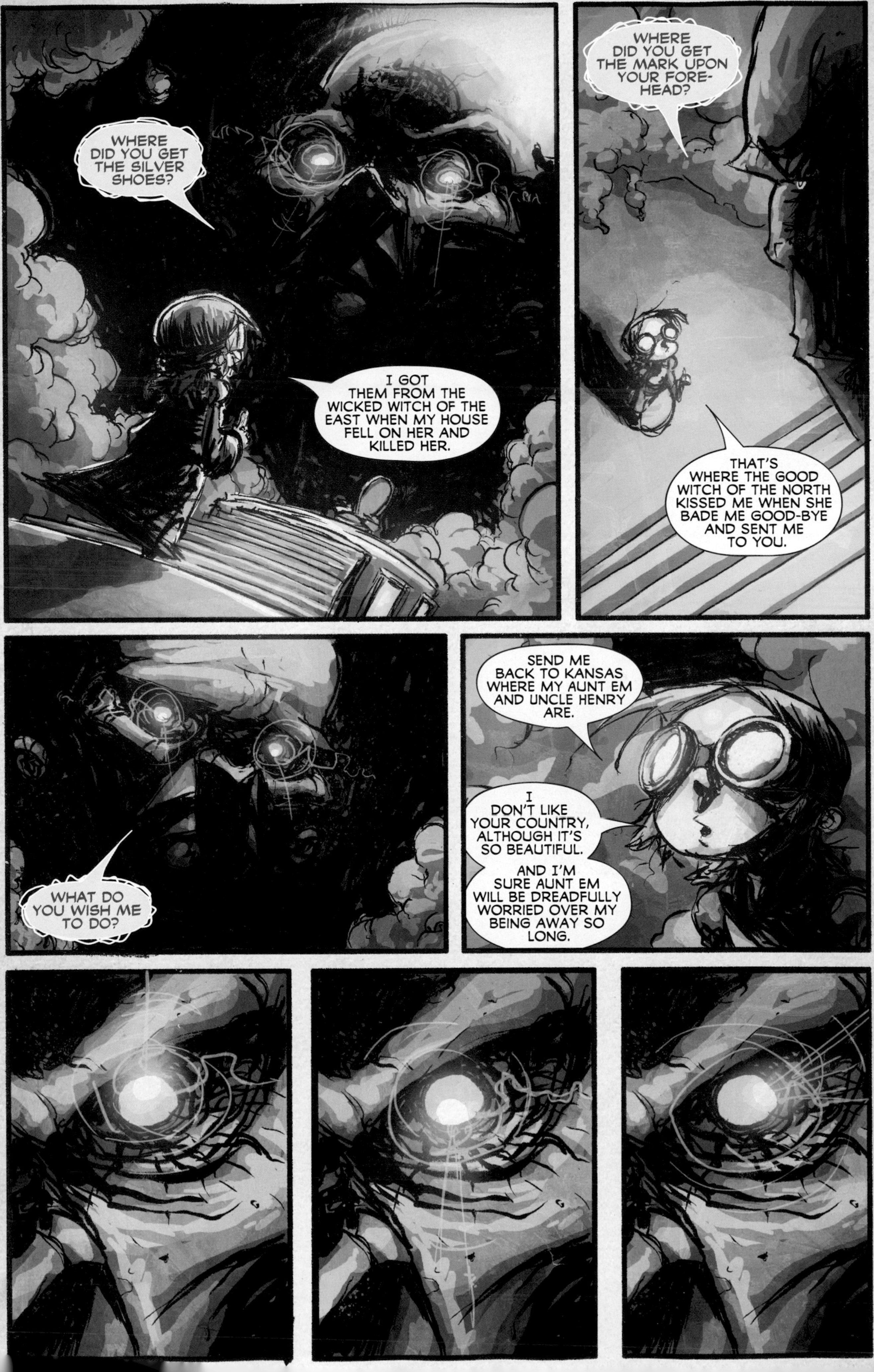
WHERE DID YOU GET THE SILVER SHOES?
I GOT THEM FROM THE WICKED WITCH OF THE EAST WHEN MY HOUSE FELL ON HER AND KILLED HER.
WHERE DID YOU GET THE MARK UPON YOUR FORE-HEAD?
THAT'S WHERE THE GOOD WITCH OF THE NORTH KISSED ME WHEN SHE BADE ME GOOD-BYE AND SENT ME TO YOU.
WHAT DO YOU WISH ME TO DO?
SEND ME BACK TO KANSAS WHERE MY AUNT EM AND UNCLE HENRY ARE.
I DON'T LIKE YOUR COUNTRY, ALTHOUGH IT'S SO BEAUTIFUL.
AND I'M SURE AUNT EM WILL BE DREADFULLY WORRIED OVER MY BEING AWAY SO LONG.

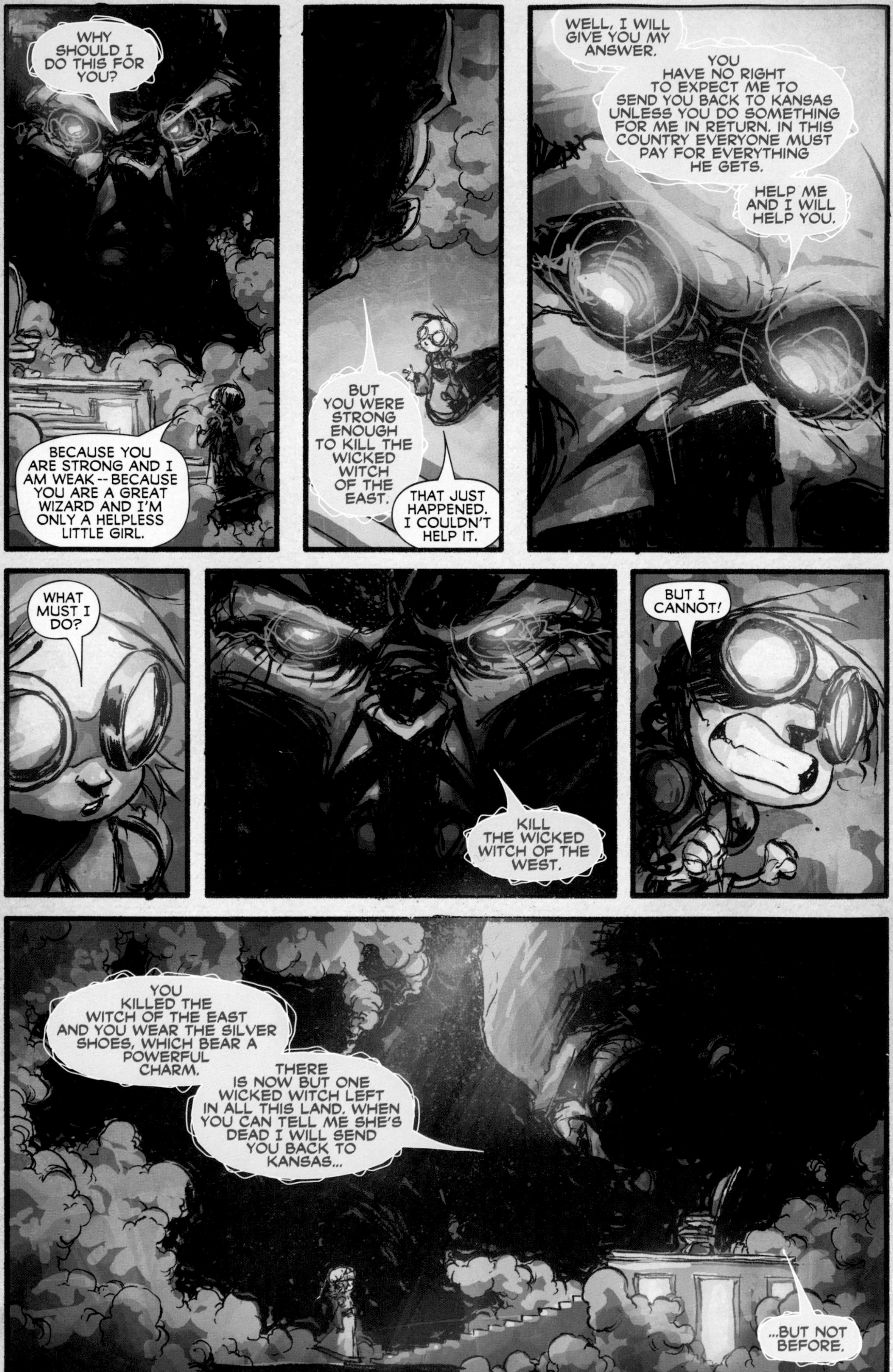
WHY SHOULD I DO THIS FOR YOU?
BECAUSE YOU ARE STRONG AND I AM WEAK -- BECAUSE YOU ARE A GREAT WIZARD AND I'M ONLY A HELPLESS LITTLE GIRL.
BUT YOU WERE STRONG ENOUGH TO KILL THE WICKED WITCH OF THE EAST.
THAT JUST HAPPENED. I COULDN'T HELP IT.
WELL, I WILL GIVE YOU MY ANSWER.
YOU HAVE NO RIGHT TO EXPECT ME TO SEND YOU BACK TO KANSAS UNLESS YOU DO SOMETHING FOR ME IN RETURN. IN THIS COUNTRY EVERYONE MUST PAY FOR EVERYTHING HE GETS.
HELP ME AND I WILL HELP YOU.
WHAT MUST I DO?
KILL THE WICKED WITCH OF THE WEST.
BUT I CANNOT!
YOU KILLED THE WITCH OF THE EAST AND YOU WEAR THE SILVER SHOES, WHICH BEAR A POWERFUL CHARM.
THERE IS NOW BUT ONE WICKED WITCH LEFT IN ALL THIS LAND. WHEN YOU CAN TELL ME SHE'S DEAD I WILL SEND YOU BACK TO KANSAS...
...BUT NOT BEFORE.

I NEVER KILLED ANYTHING WILLINGLY, AND EVEN IF I WANTED TO, HOW COULD I KILL THE WICKED WITCH?

IF YOU, WHO ARE GREAT AND TERRIBLE, CANNOT KILL HER YOURSELF, HOW DO YOU EXPECT ME TO DO IT?

I DO NOT KNOW, BUT THAT IS MY ANSWER. UNTIL THE WICKED WITCH DIES YOU WILL NOT SEE YOUR UNCLE AND AUNT AGAIN.

REMEMBER THAT THE WITCH IS WICKED-- TERRIBLY WICKED--AND OUGHT TO BE KILLED.

NOW GO, AND DON'T ASK TO SEE ME AGAIN UNTIL YOU HAVE DONE YOUR TASK.

OZ WON'T SEND ME HOME UNTIL I'VE KILLED THE WICKED WITCH OF THE WEST.

THAT I CAN NEVER DO.

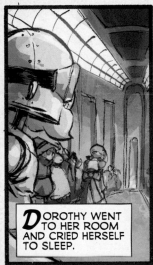

DOROTHY WENT TO HER ROOM AND CRIED HERSELF TO SLEEP.

THE NEXT MORNING --

OZ HAS SENT FOR YOU.

I am Oz, the Great and Terrible. Who are you, and why do you seek me?

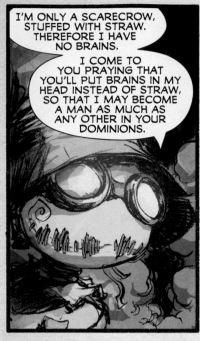

I'M ONLY A SCARECROW, STUFFED WITH STRAW. THEREFORE I HAVE NO BRAINS.

I COME TO YOU PRAYING THAT YOU'LL PUT BRAINS IN MY HEAD INSTEAD OF STRAW, SO THAT I MAY BECOME A MAN AS MUCH AS ANY OTHER IN YOUR DOMINIONS.

WHY SHOULD I DO THIS FOR YOU?

BECAUSE YOU'RE WISE AND POWERFUL, AND NO ONE ELSE CAN HELP ME.

I NEVER GRANT FAVORS WITHOUT SOME RETURN, BUT THIS MUCH I WILL PROMISE.

IF YOU WILL KILL THE WICKED WITCH OF THE WEST I'LL BESTOW UPON YOU A GREAT MANY BRAINS, AND SUCH GOOD BRAINS THAT YOU'LL BE THE WISEST MAN IN ALL THE LAND OF OZ.

I THOUGHT YOU ASKED DOROTHY TO KILL THE WITCH.

SO I DID. I DON'T CARE WHO KILLS HER. BUT UNTIL SHE'S DEAD I WILL NOT GRANT YOUR WISH.

NOW, GO, AND DO NOT SEEK ME AGAIN UNTIL YOU HAVE EARNED THE BRAINS YOU SO GREATLY DESIRE.

*T*HE SCARECROW WENT SORROWFULLY BACK TO HIS FRIENDS.

I'M SURPRISED TO FIND THAT THE WIZARD WAS NOT A GREAT HEAD, BUT A LOVELY LADY.

ALL THE SAME, SHE NEEDS A HEART AS MUCH AS THE TIN WOODMAN.

THE NEXT MORNING --

OZ HAS SENT FOR YOU. FOLLOW ME.

IF OZ IS THE HEAD, I'M SURE I SHALL NOT BE GIVEN A HEART, SINCE A HEAD HAS NO HEART OF ITS OWN AND THEREFORE CANNOT FEEL FOR ME.

BUT IF OZ IS THE LOVELY LADY, I SHALL BEG HARD FOR A HEART, FOR ALL LADIES ARE THEMSELVES SAID TO BE KINDLY HEARTED.

I AM OZ, THE GREAT AND TERRIBLE. WHO ARE YOU, AND WHY DO YOU SEEK ME?

I'M A WOODMAN AND MADE OF TIN. THEREFORE I HAVE NO HEART AND CANNOT LOVE.

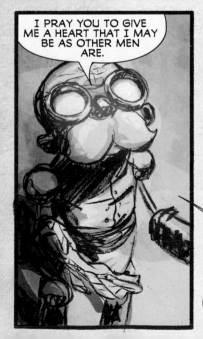

I PRAY YOU TO GIVE ME A HEART THAT I MAY BE AS OTHER MEN ARE.

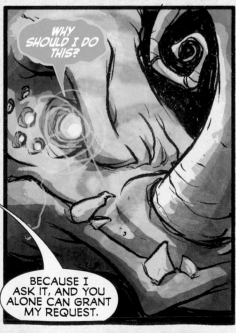

WHY SHOULD I DO THIS?

BECAUSE I ASK IT, AND YOU ALONE CAN GRANT MY REQUEST.

GRRRR..

IF YOU INDEED DESIRE A HEART, YOU MUST EARN IT.

HOW?

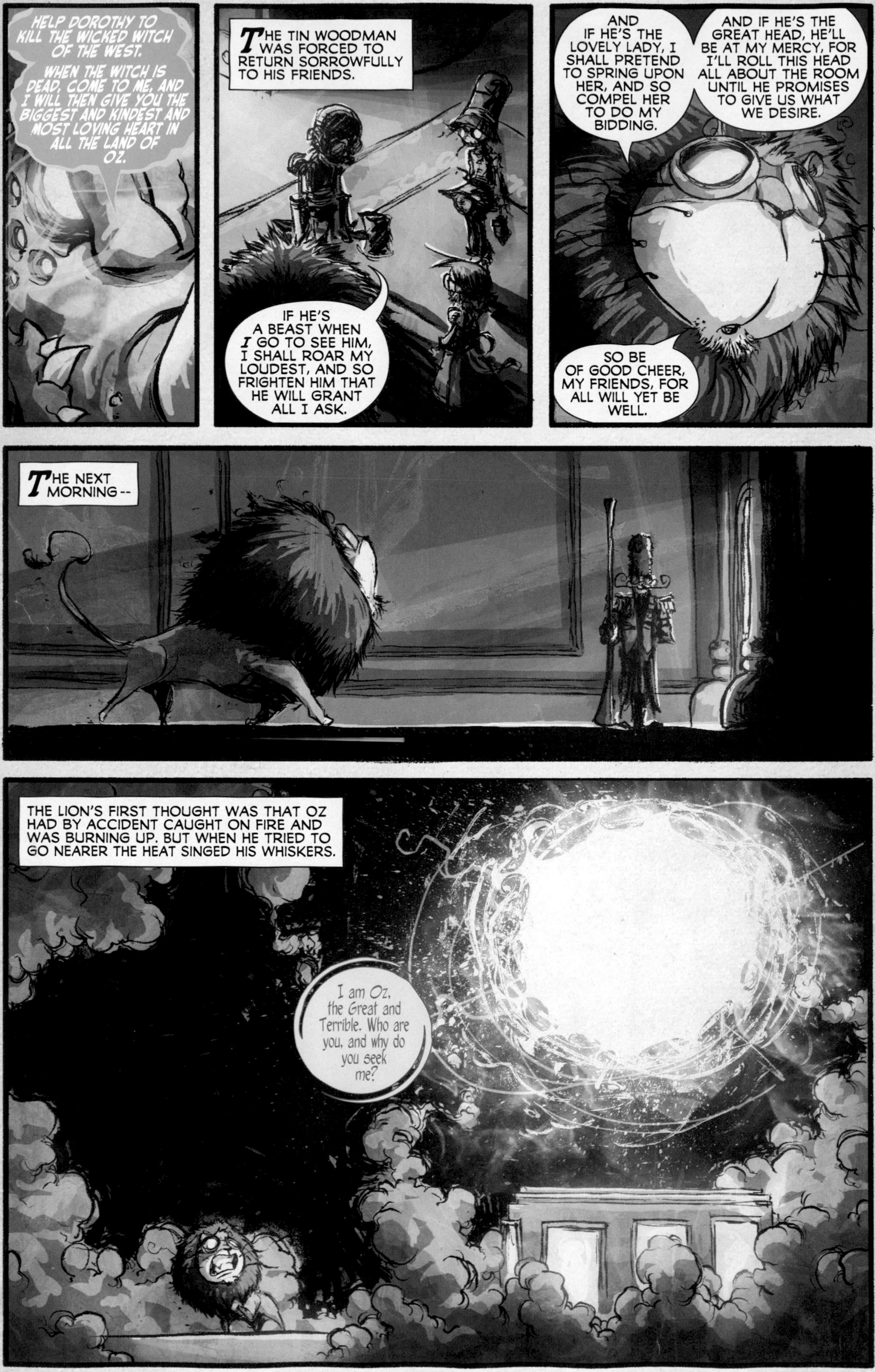
HELP DOROTHY TO KILL THE WICKED WITCH OF THE WEST.
WHEN THE WITCH IS DEAD, COME TO ME, AND I WILL THEN GIVE YOU THE BIGGEST AND KINDEST AND MOST LOVING HEART IN ALL THE LAND OF OZ.
THE TIN WOODMAN WAS FORCED TO RETURN SORROWFULLY TO HIS FRIENDS.
IF HE'S A BEAST WHEN I GO TO SEE HIM, I SHALL ROAR MY LOUDEST, AND SO FRIGHTEN HIM THAT HE WILL GRANT ALL I ASK.
AND IF HE'S THE LOVELY LADY, I SHALL PRETEND TO SPRING UPON HER, AND SO COMPEL HER TO DO MY BIDDING.
AND IF HE'S THE GREAT HEAD, HE'LL BE AT MY MERCY, FOR I'LL ROLL THIS HEAD ALL ABOUT THE ROOM UNTIL HE PROMISES TO GIVE US WHAT WE DESIRE.
SO BE OF GOOD CHEER, MY FRIENDS, FOR ALL WILL YET BE WELL.
THE NEXT MORNING --
THE LION'S FIRST THOUGHT WAS THAT OZ HAD BY ACCIDENT CAUGHT ON FIRE AND WAS BURNING UP. BUT WHEN HE TRIED TO GO NEARER THE HEAT SINGED HIS WHISKERS.
I am Oz, the Great and Terrible. Who are you, and why do you seek me?

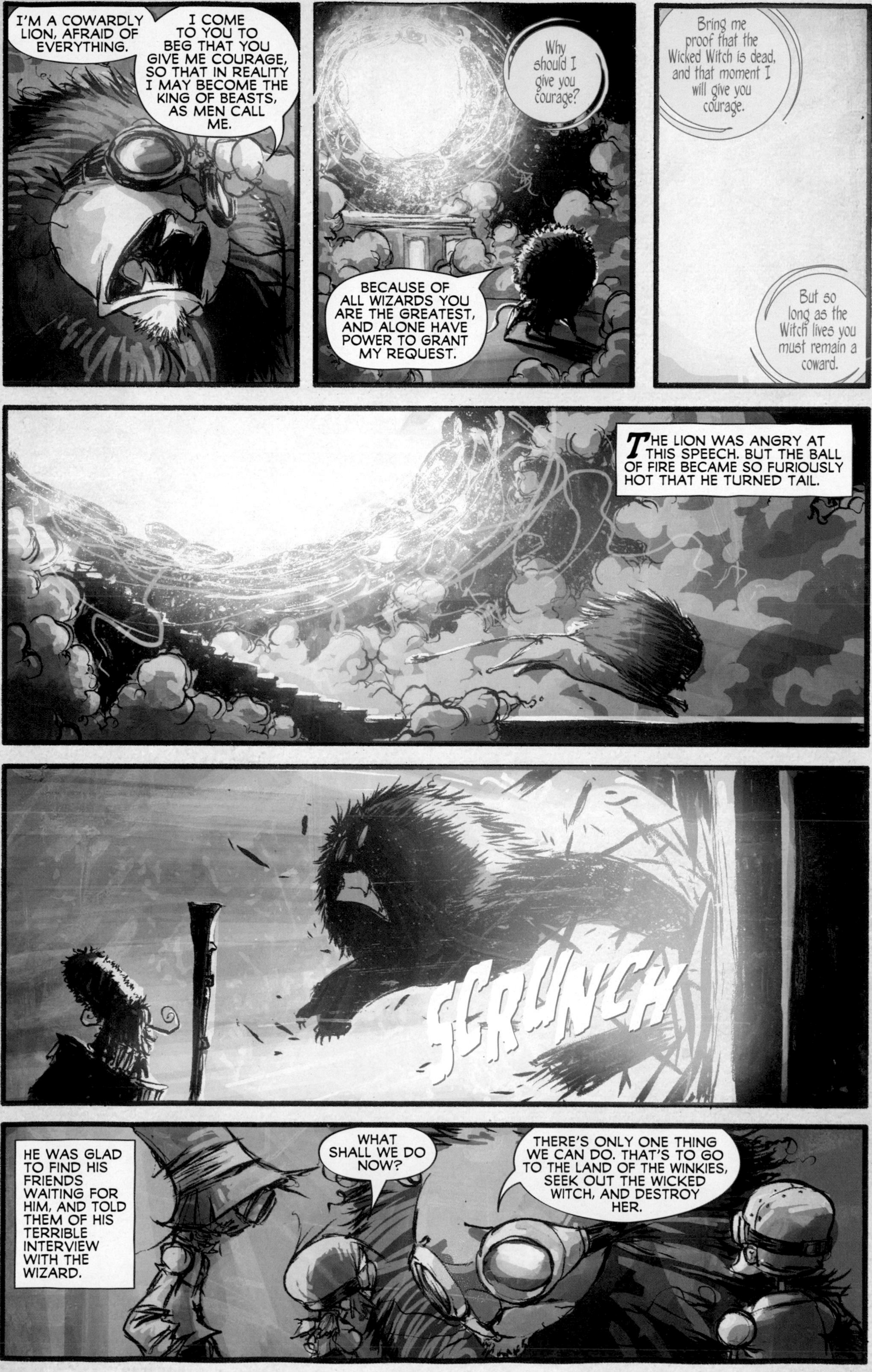

I'M A COWARDLY LION, AFRAID OF EVERYTHING.
I COME TO YOU TO BEG THAT YOU GIVE ME COURAGE, SO THAT IN REALITY I MAY BECOME THE KING OF BEASTS, AS MEN CALL ME.
Why should I give you courage?
BECAUSE OF ALL WIZARDS YOU ARE THE GREATEST, AND ALONE HAVE POWER TO GRANT MY REQUEST.
Bring me proof that the Wicked Witch is dead, and that moment I will give you courage.
But so long as the Witch lives you must remain a coward.
THE LION WAS ANGRY AT THIS SPEECH. BUT THE BALL OF FIRE BECAME SO FURIOUSLY HOT THAT HE TURNED TAIL.
SCRUNCH
HE WAS GLAD TO FIND HIS FRIENDS WAITING FOR HIM, AND TOLD THEM OF HIS TERRIBLE INTERVIEW WITH THE WIZARD.
WHAT SHALL WE DO NOW?
THERE'S ONLY ONE THING WE CAN DO. THAT'S TO GO TO THE LAND OF THE WINKIES, SEEK OUT THE WICKED WITCH, AND DESTROY HER.

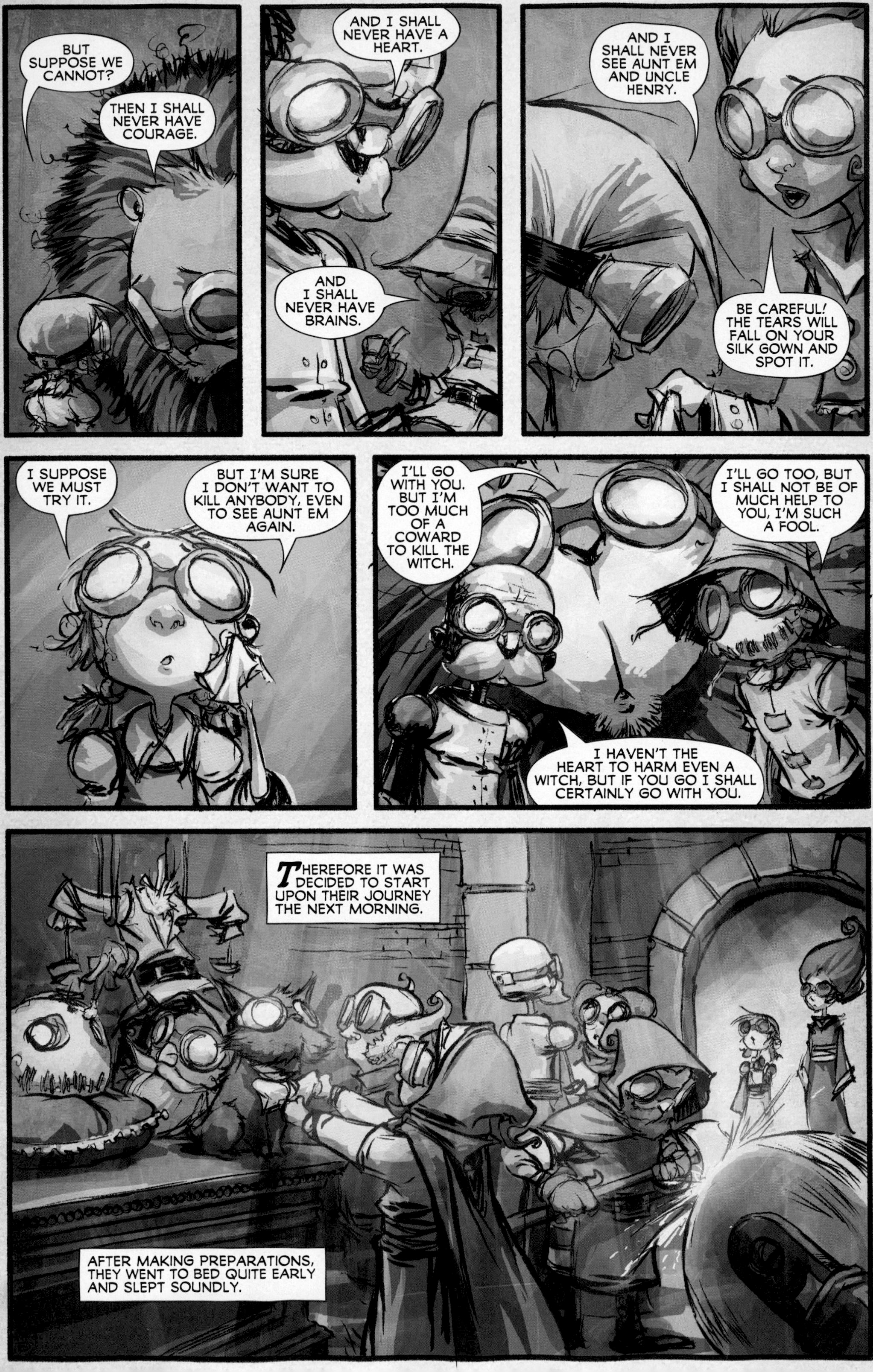
BUT SUPPOSE WE CANNOT?
THEN I SHALL NEVER HAVE COURAGE.
AND I SHALL NEVER HAVE A HEART.
AND I SHALL NEVER HAVE BRAINS.
AND I SHALL NEVER SEE AUNT EM AND UNCLE HENRY.
BE CAREFUL! THE TEARS WILL FALL ON YOUR SILK GOWN AND SPOT IT.
I SUPPOSE WE MUST TRY IT.
BUT I'M SURE I DON'T WANT TO KILL ANYBODY, EVEN TO SEE AUNT EM AGAIN.
I'LL GO WITH YOU. BUT I'M TOO MUCH OF A COWARD TO KILL THE WITCH.
I'LL GO TOO, BUT I SHALL NOT BE OF MUCH HELP TO YOU, I'M SUCH A FOOL.
I HAVEN'T THE HEART TO HARM EVEN A WITCH, BUT IF YOU GO I SHALL CERTAINLY GO WITH YOU.
THEREFORE IT WAS DECIDED TO START UPON THEIR JOURNEY THE NEXT MORNING.
AFTER MAKING PREPARATIONS, THEY WENT TO BED QUITE EARLY AND SLEPT SOUNDLY.

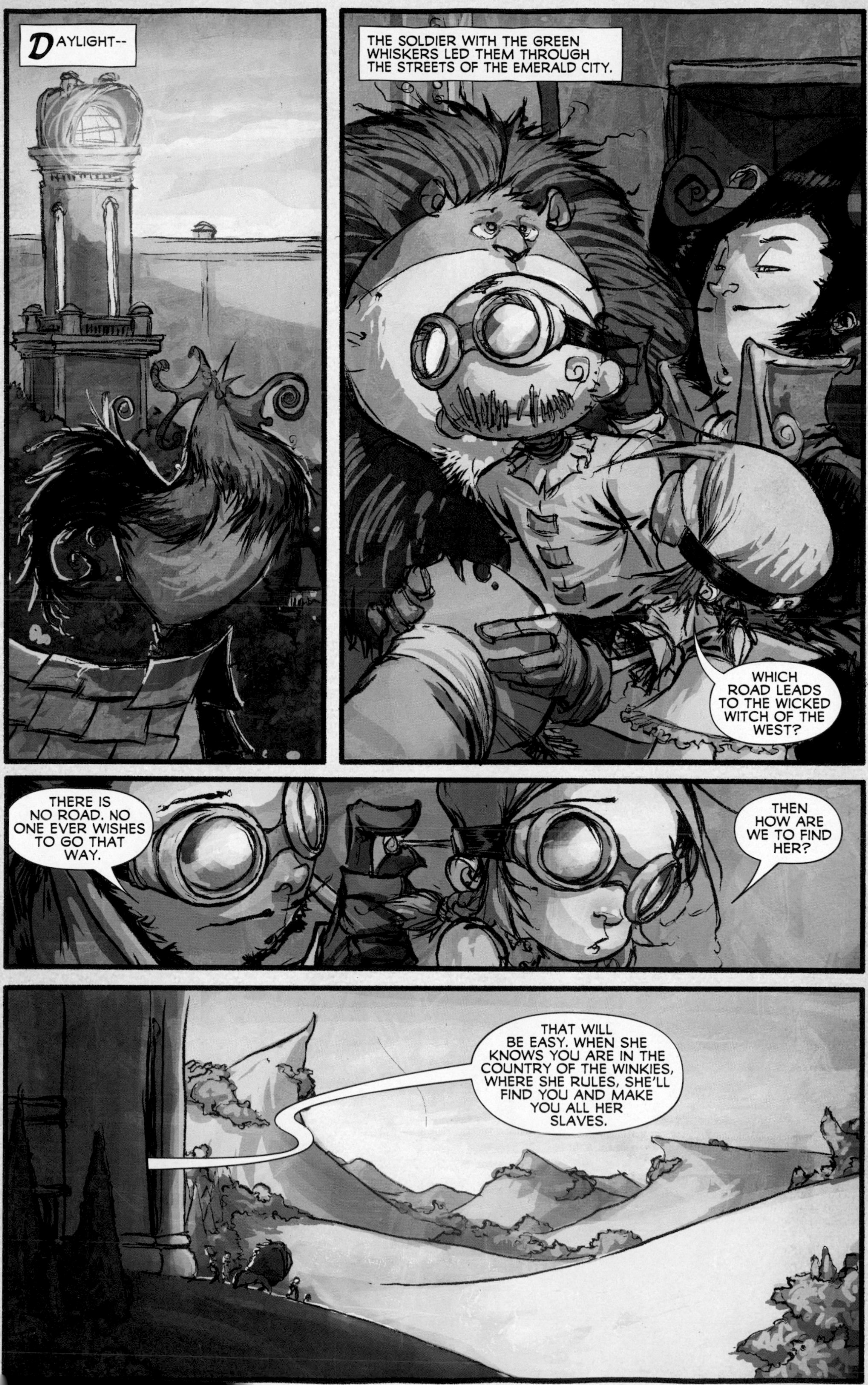
DAYLIGHT--
THE SOLDIER WITH THE GREEN WHISKERS LED THEM THROUGH THE STREETS OF THE EMERALD CITY.
WHICH ROAD LEADS TO THE WICKED WITCH OF THE WEST?
THERE IS NO ROAD. NO ONE EVER WISHES TO GO THAT WAY.
THEN HOW ARE WE TO FIND HER?
THAT WILL BE EASY. WHEN SHE KNOWS YOU ARE IN THE COUNTRY OF THE WINKIES, WHERE SHE RULES, SHE'LL FIND YOU AND MAKE YOU ALL HER SLAVES.

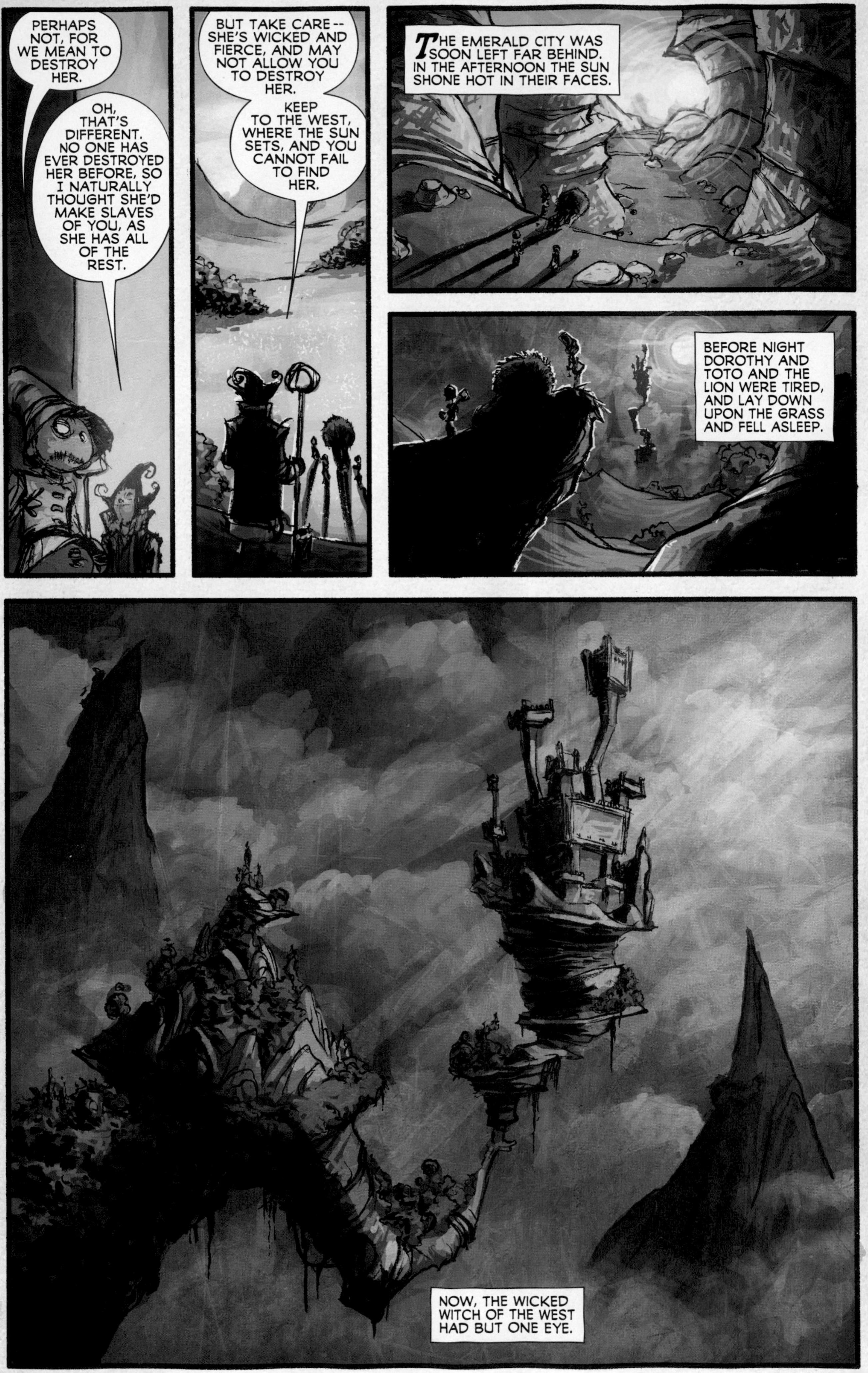
PERHAPS NOT, FOR WE MEAN TO DESTROY HER.
OH, THAT'S DIFFERENT. NO ONE HAS EVER DESTROYED HER BEFORE, SO I NATURALLY THOUGHT SHE'D MAKE SLAVES OF YOU, AS SHE HAS ALL OF THE REST.
BUT TAKE CARE-- SHE'S WICKED AND FIERCE, AND MAY NOT ALLOW YOU TO DESTROY HER.
KEEP TO THE WEST, WHERE THE SUN SETS, AND YOU CANNOT FAIL TO FIND HER.
THE EMERALD CITY WAS SOON LEFT FAR BEHIND. IN THE AFTERNOON THE SUN SHONE HOT IN THEIR FACES.
BEFORE NIGHT DOROTHY AND TOTO AND THE LION WERE TIRED, AND LAY DOWN UPON THE GRASS AND FELL ASLEEP.
NOW, THE WICKED WITCH OF THE WEST HAD BUT ONE EYE.

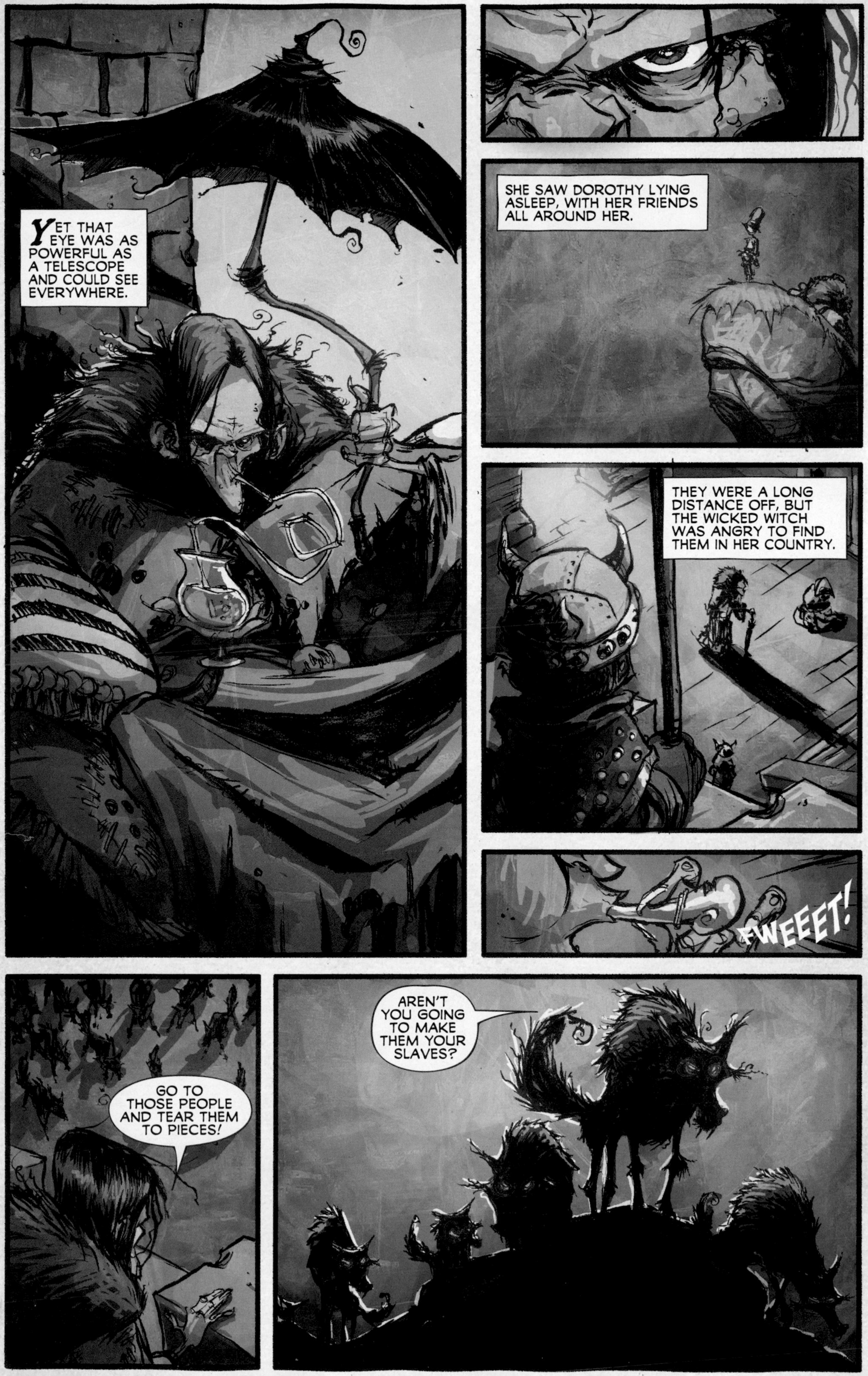
YET THAT EYE WAS AS POWERFUL AS A TELESCOPE AND COULD SEE EVERYWHERE.
SHE SAW DOROTHY LYING ASLEEP, WITH HER FRIENDS ALL AROUND HER.
THEY WERE A LONG DISTANCE OFF, BUT THE WICKED WITCH WAS ANGRY TO FIND THEM IN HER COUNTRY.
FWEEET!
GO TO THOSE PEOPLE AND TEAR THEM TO PIECES!
AREN'T YOU GOING TO MAKE THEM YOUR SLAVES?

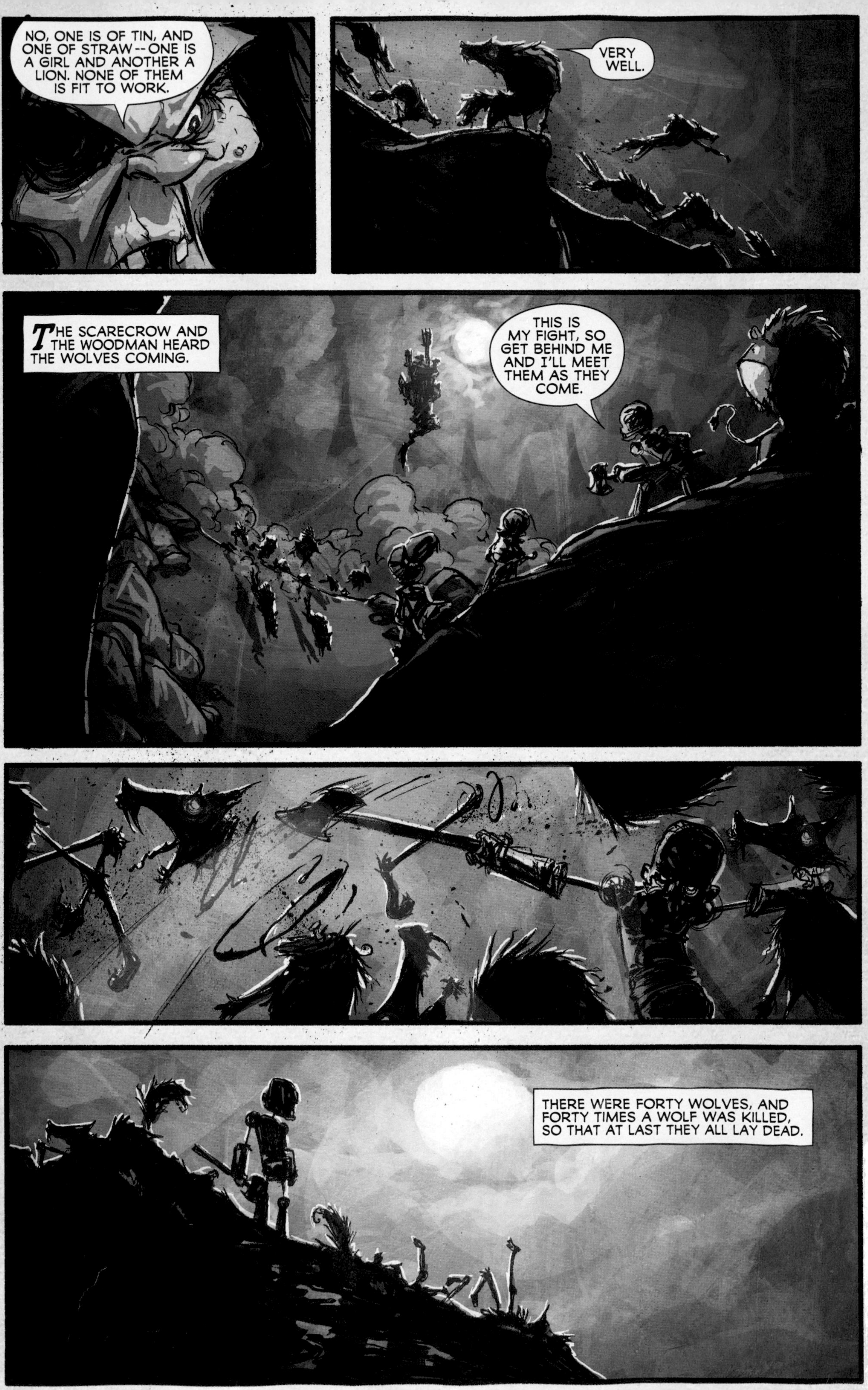
NO, ONE IS OF TIN, AND ONE OF STRAW--ONE IS A GIRL AND ANOTHER A LION. NONE OF THEM IS FIT TO WORK.
VERY WELL.
THE SCARECROW AND THE WOODMAN HEARD THE WOLVES COMING.
THIS IS MY FIGHT, SO GET BEHIND ME AND I'LL MEET THEM AS THEY COME.
THERE WERE FORTY WOLVES, AND FORTY TIMES A WOLF WAS KILLED, SO THAT AT LAST THEY ALL LAY DEAD.

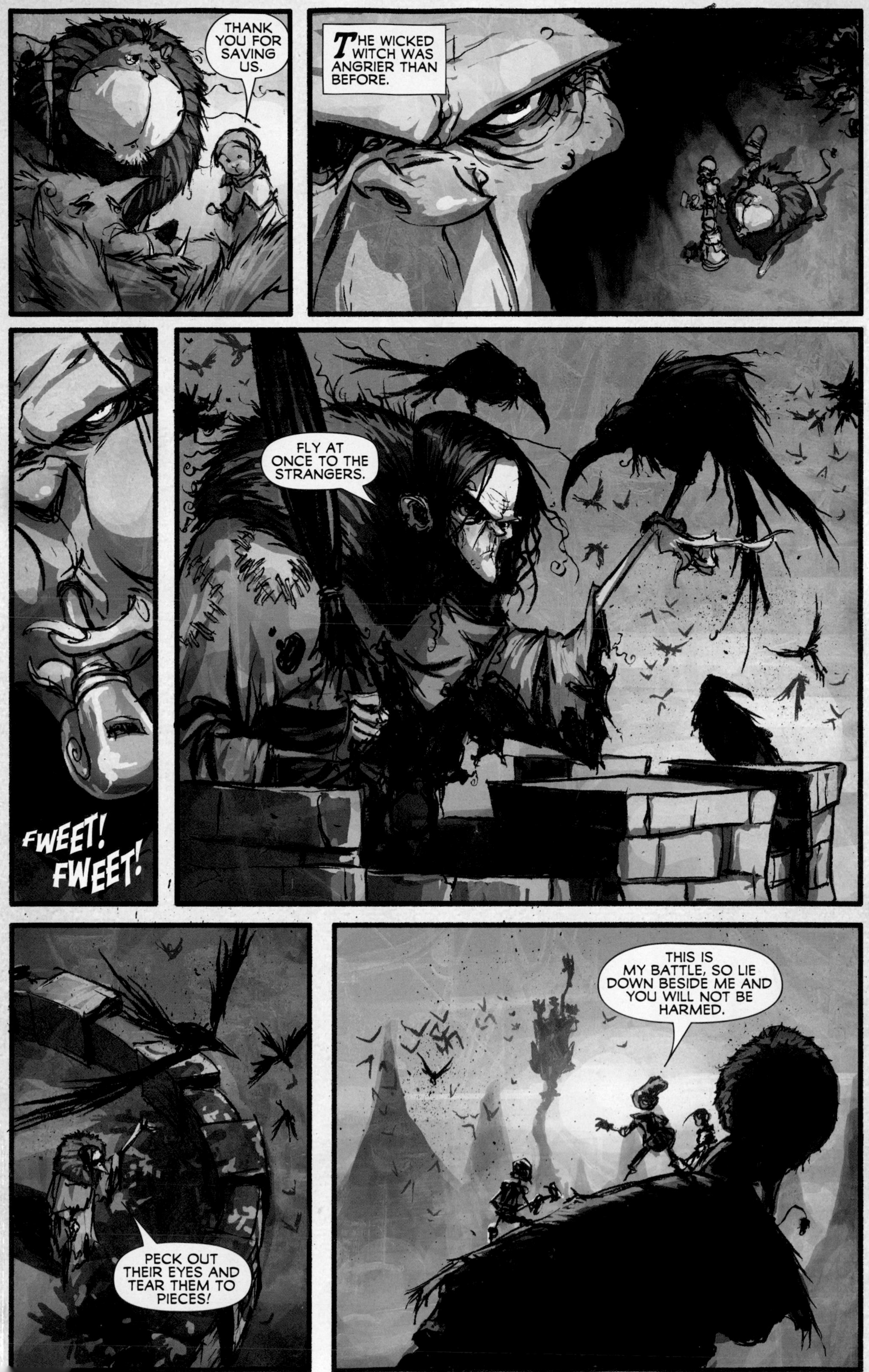

THANK YOU FOR SAVING US.
THE WICKED WITCH WAS ANGRIER THAN BEFORE.
FWEET! FWEET!
FLY AT ONCE TO THE STRANGERS.
PECK OUT THEIR EYES AND TEAR THEM TO PIECES!
THIS IS MY BATTLE, SO LIE DOWN BESIDE ME AND YOU WILL NOT BE HARMED.

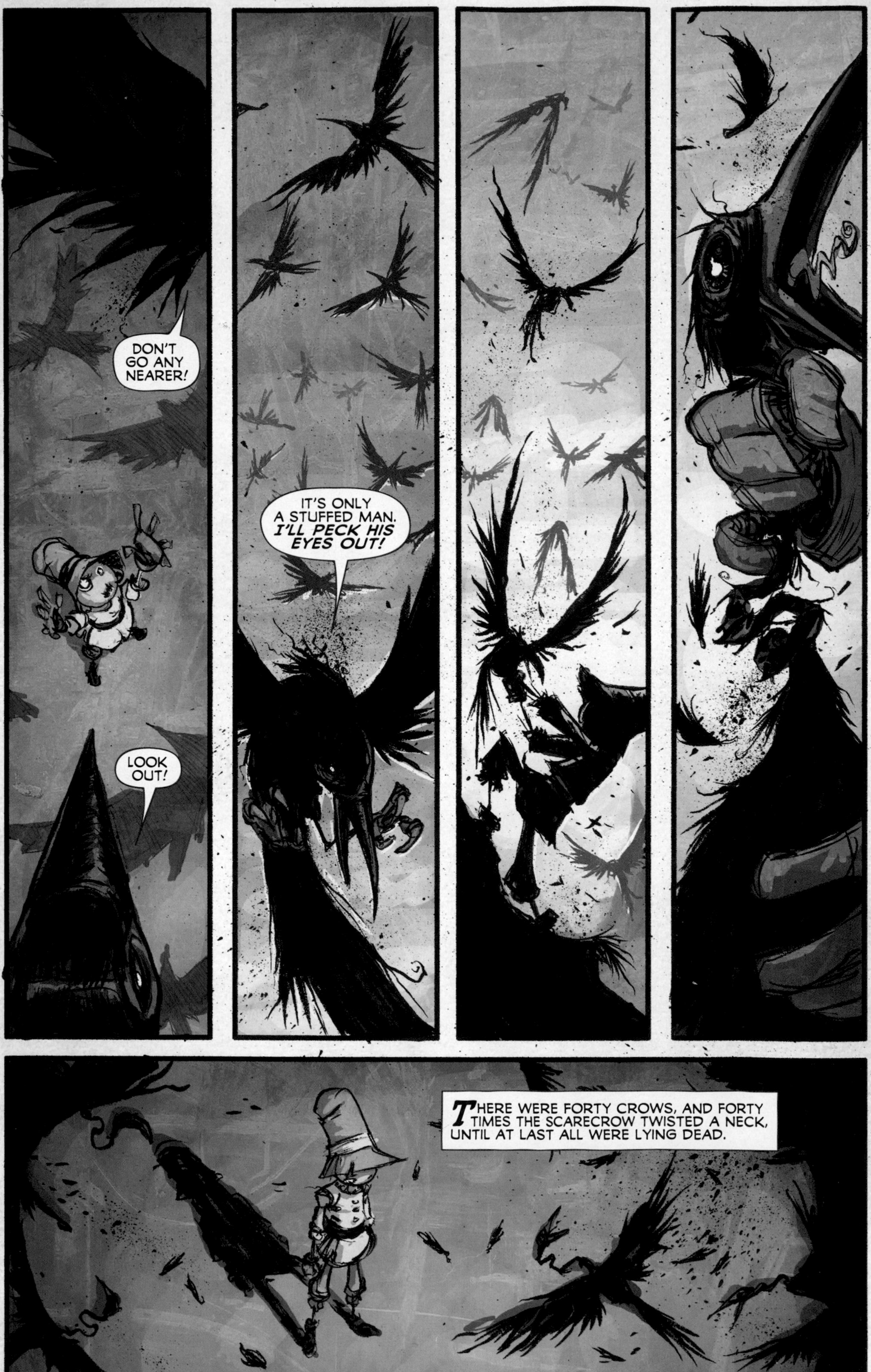
DON'T GO ANY NEARER!
LOOK OUT!
IT'S ONLY A STUFFED MAN. *I'LL PECK HIS EYES OUT!*
THERE WERE FORTY CROWS, AND FORTY TIMES THE SCARECROW TWISTED A NECK, UNTIL AT LAST ALL WERE LYING DEAD.

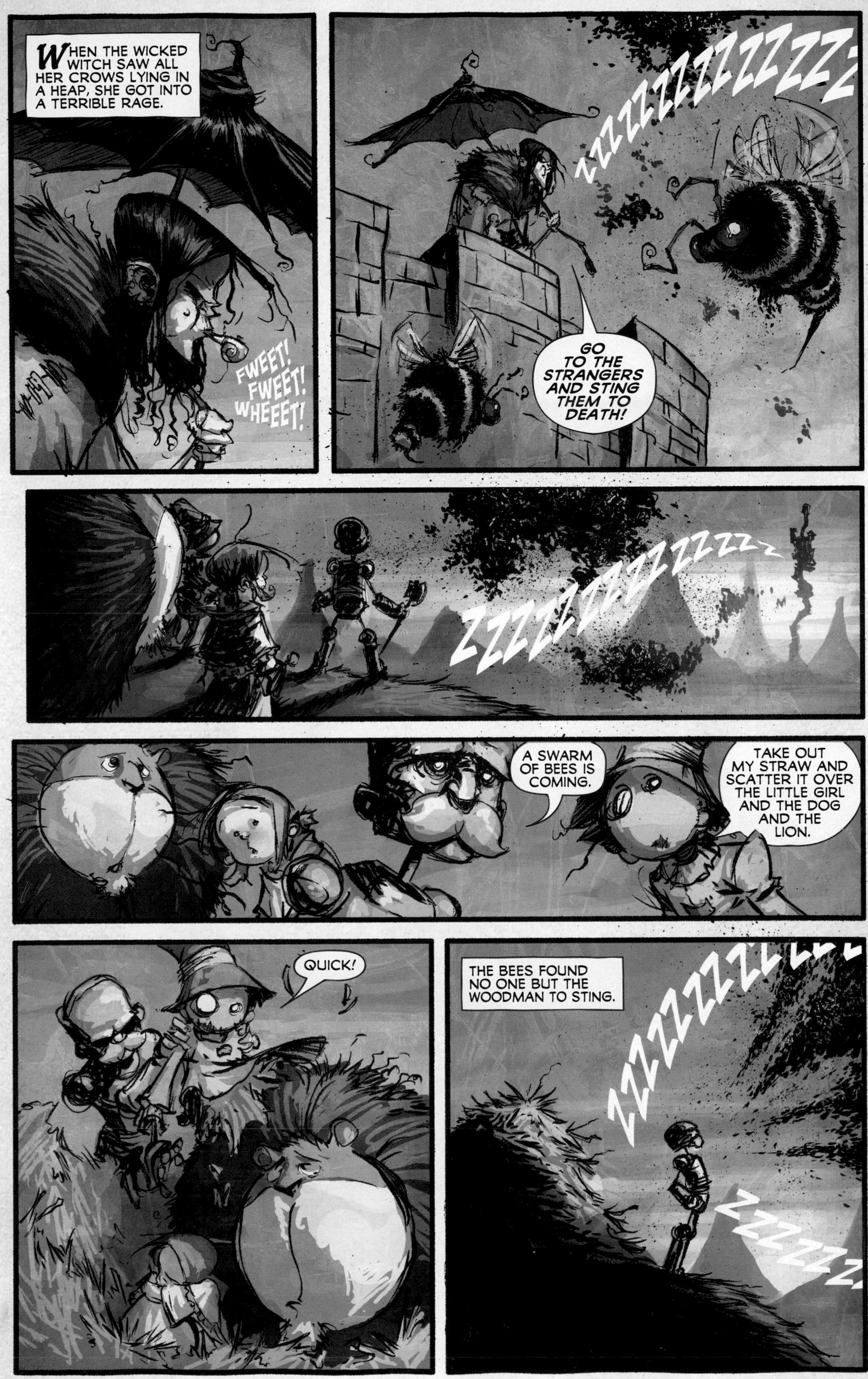
WHEN THE WICKED WITCH SAW ALL HER CROWS LYING IN A HEAP, SHE GOT INTO A TERRIBLE RAGE.
FWEET! FWEET! WHEEET!
ZZZZZZZZZZZZZZ
GO TO THE STRANGERS AND STING THEM TO DEATH!
ZZZZZZZZZZZZZZ
A SWARM OF BEES IS COMING.
TAKE OUT MY STRAW AND SCATTER IT OVER THE LITTLE GIRL AND THE DOG AND THE LION.
QUICK!
THE BEES FOUND NO ONE BUT THE WOODMAN TO STING.
ZZZZZZZZZZZZ
ZZZZZ

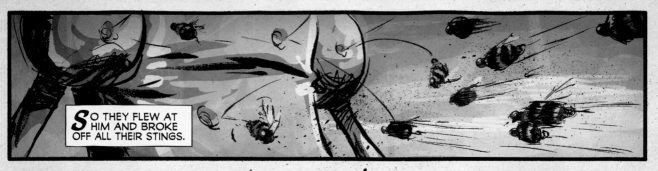

So they flew at him and broke off all their stings.

As bees cannot live when their stings are broken, that was the end of the black bees.

YAAH!

The wicked witch called a dozen of her slaves, who were the Winkies.

GO TO THE STRANGERS AND DESTROY THEM!

The Winkies were not a brave people.

RRROOOAAARR!

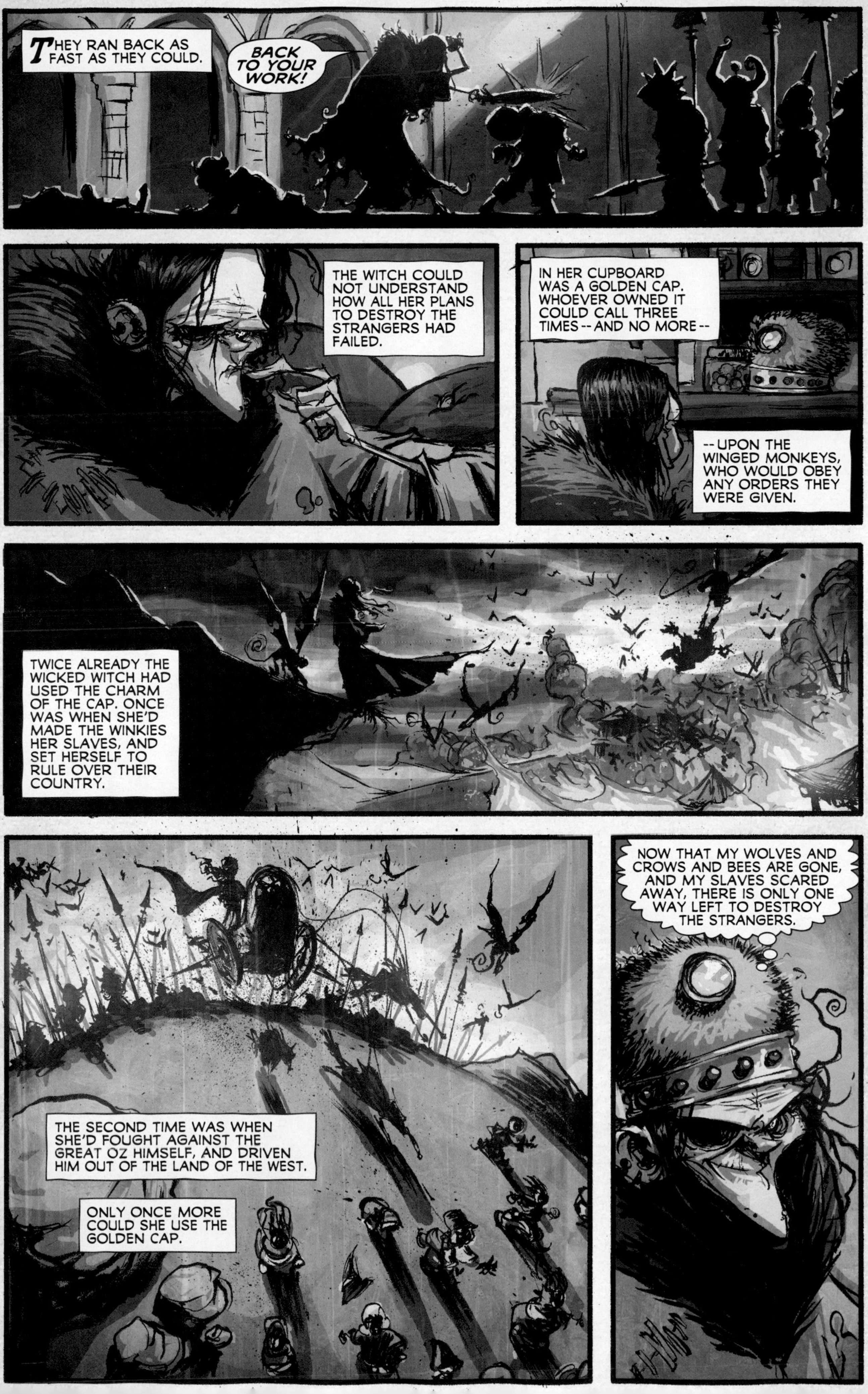
THEY RAN BACK AS FAST AS THEY COULD.
BACK TO YOUR WORK!
THE WITCH COULD NOT UNDERSTAND HOW ALL HER PLANS TO DESTROY THE STRANGERS HAD FAILED.
IN HER CUPBOARD WAS A GOLDEN CAP. WHOEVER OWNED IT COULD CALL THREE TIMES -- AND NO MORE --
-- UPON THE WINGED MONKEYS, WHO WOULD OBEY ANY ORDERS THEY WERE GIVEN.
TWICE ALREADY THE WICKED WITCH HAD USED THE CHARM OF THE CAP. ONCE WAS WHEN SHE'D MADE THE WINKIES HER SLAVES, AND SET HERSELF TO RULE OVER THEIR COUNTRY.
THE SECOND TIME WAS WHEN SHE'D FOUGHT AGAINST THE GREAT OZ HIMSELF, AND DRIVEN HIM OUT OF THE LAND OF THE WEST.
ONLY ONCE MORE COULD SHE USE THE GOLDEN CAP.
NOW THAT MY WOLVES AND CROWS AND BEES ARE GONE, AND MY SLAVES SCARED AWAY, THERE IS ONLY ONE WAY LEFT TO DESTROY THE STRANGERS.

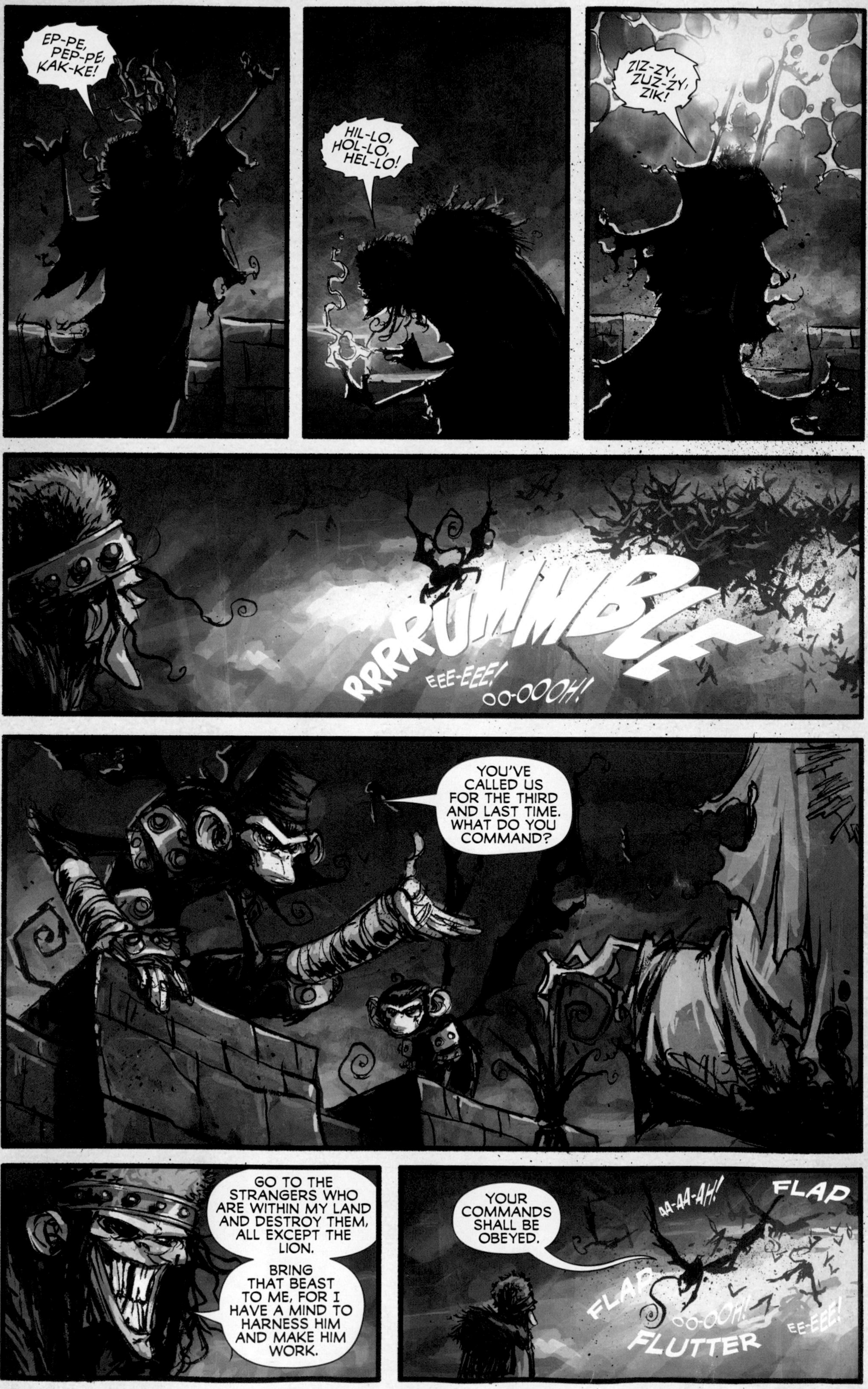
EP-PE, PEP-PE, KAK-KE!
HIL-LO, HOL-LO, HEL-LO!
ZIZ-ZY, ZUZ-ZY, ZIK!
RRRRUMMBLE
EEE-EEE!
OO-OOOH!
YOU'VE CALLED US FOR THE THIRD AND LAST TIME. WHAT DO YOU COMMAND?
GO TO THE STRANGERS WHO ARE WITHIN MY LAND AND DESTROY THEM, ALL EXCEPT THE LION.
BRING THAT BEAST TO ME, FOR I HAVE A MIND TO HARNESS HIM AND MAKE HIM WORK.
YOUR COMMANDS SHALL BE OBEYED.
AA-AA-AH!
FLAP
FLAP
OO-OOH!
EE-EEE!
FLUTTER

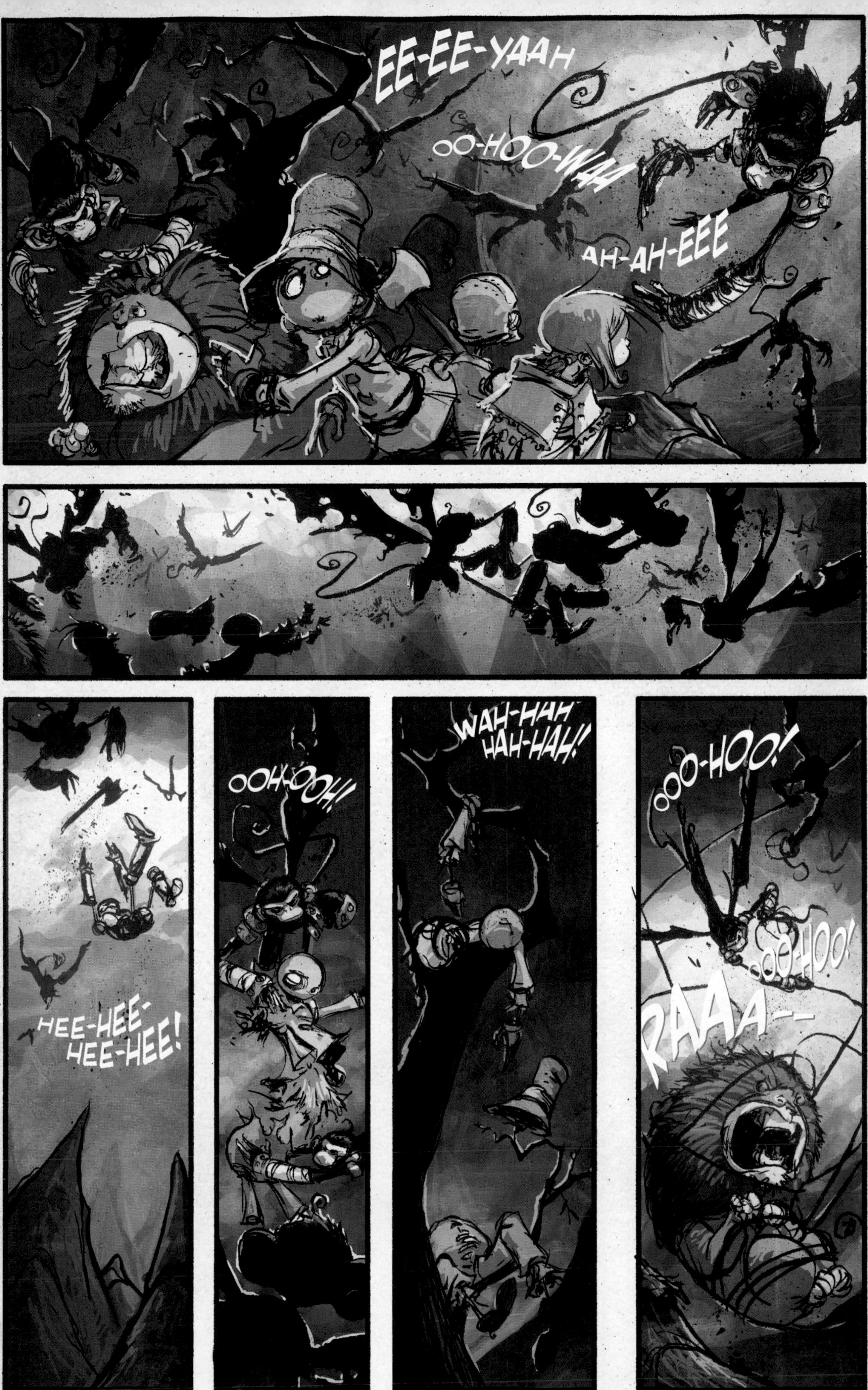
EE-EE-YAAH
OO-HOO-WAA
AH-AH-EEE
HEE-HEE-
HEE-HEE!
OOH-OOH!
WAH-HAH
HAH-HAH!
OOO-HOO!
OO-HOO!
RAAA--

EE-EE-
HAAH

OOH-
OOH

HEE-HEE-
EEE

HAAAA --

*T*HE LEADER OF THE WINGED MONKEYS SAW THE GOOD WITCH'S KISS UPON DOROTHY'S FOREHEAD.

OOH!

WE DARE NOT HARM THIS LITTLE GIRL.

ALL WE CAN DO IS CARRY HER TO THE CASTLE OF THE WICKED WITCH AND LEAVE HER THERE.

WE'VE OBEYED YOU AS FAR AS WE WERE ABLE. THE TIN WOODMAN AND THE SCARECROW ARE DESTROYED, AND THE LION IS TIED UP IN YOUR YARD.

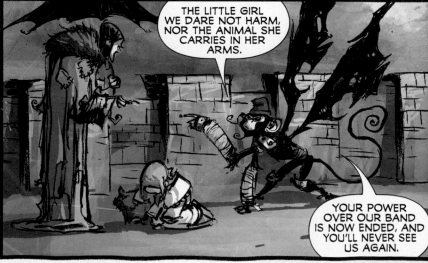

THE LITTLE GIRL WE DARE NOT HARM, NOR THE ANIMAL SHE CARRIES IN HER ARMS.

YOUR POWER OVER OUR BAND IS NOW ENDED, AND YOU'LL NEVER SEE US AGAIN.

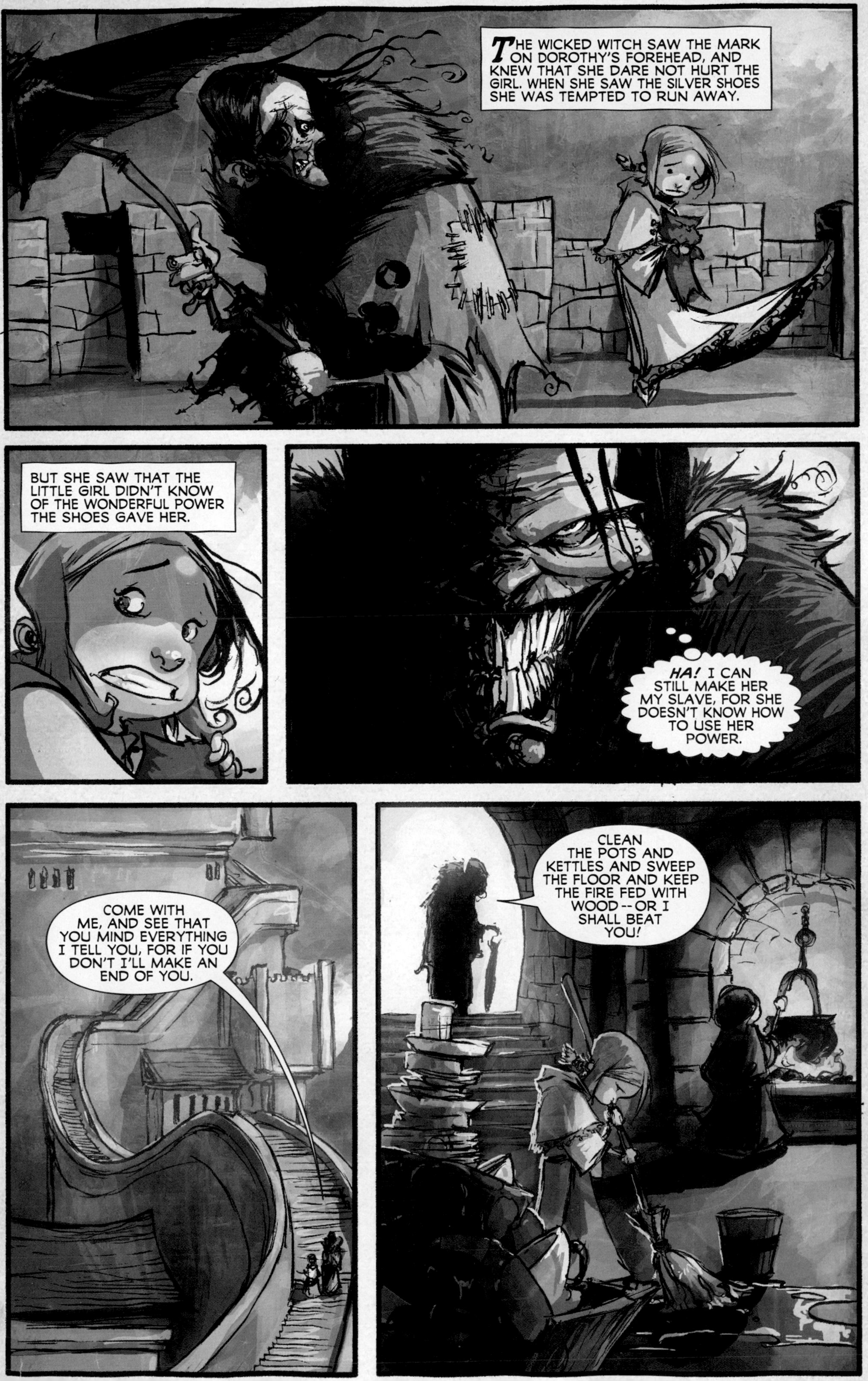
THE WICKED WITCH SAW THE MARK ON DOROTHY'S FOREHEAD, AND KNEW THAT SHE DARE NOT HURT THE GIRL. WHEN SHE SAW THE SILVER SHOES SHE WAS TEMPTED TO RUN AWAY.
BUT SHE SAW THAT THE LITTLE GIRL DIDN'T KNOW OF THE WONDERFUL POWER THE SHOES GAVE HER.
HA! I CAN STILL MAKE HER MY SLAVE, FOR SHE DOESN'T KNOW HOW TO USE HER POWER.
COME WITH ME, AND SEE THAT YOU MIND EVERYTHING I TELL YOU, FOR IF YOU DON'T I'LL MAKE AN END OF YOU.
CLEAN THE POTS AND KETTLES AND SWEEP THE FLOOR AND KEEP THE FIRE FED WITH WOOD -- OR I SHALL BEAT YOU!

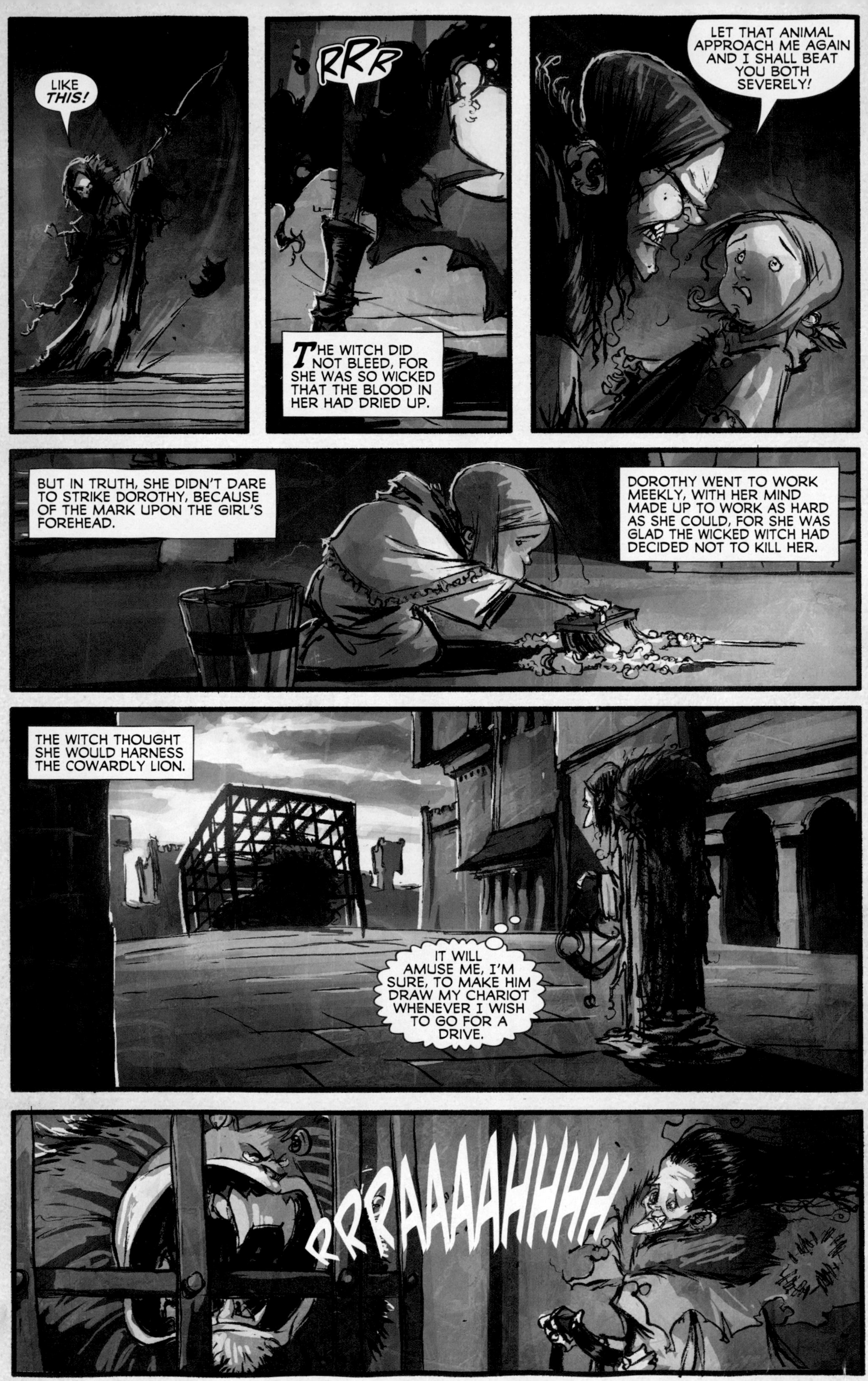
LIKE THIS!
RRR
THE WITCH DID NOT BLEED, FOR SHE WAS SO WICKED THAT THE BLOOD IN HER HAD DRIED UP.
LET THAT ANIMAL APPROACH ME AGAIN AND I SHALL BEAT YOU BOTH SEVERELY!
BUT IN TRUTH, SHE DIDN'T DARE TO STRIKE DOROTHY, BECAUSE OF THE MARK UPON THE GIRL'S FOREHEAD.
DOROTHY WENT TO WORK MEEKLY, WITH HER MIND MADE UP TO WORK AS HARD AS SHE COULD, FOR SHE WAS GLAD THE WICKED WITCH HAD DECIDED NOT TO KILL HER.
THE WITCH THOUGHT SHE WOULD HARNESS THE COWARDLY LION.
IT WILL AMUSE ME, I'M SURE, TO MAKE HIM DRAW MY CHARIOT WHENEVER I WISH TO GO FOR A DRIVE.
RRRAAAAHHHH

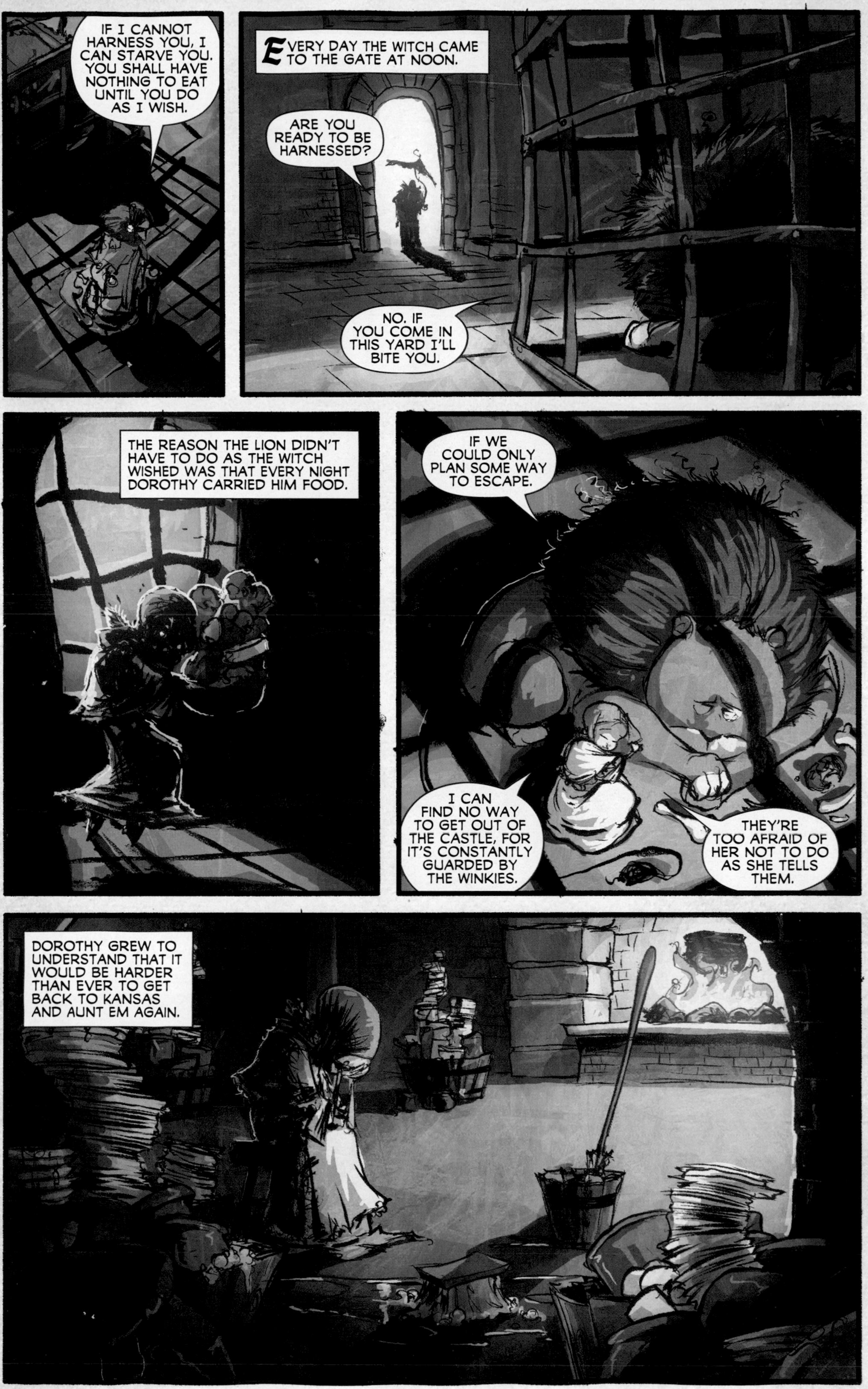
IF I CANNOT HARNESS YOU, I CAN STARVE YOU. YOU SHALL HAVE NOTHING TO EAT UNTIL YOU DO AS I WISH.
EVERY DAY THE WITCH CAME TO THE GATE AT NOON.
ARE YOU READY TO BE HARNESSED?
NO. IF YOU COME IN THIS YARD I'LL BITE YOU.
THE REASON THE LION DIDN'T HAVE TO DO AS THE WITCH WISHED WAS THAT EVERY NIGHT DOROTHY CARRIED HIM FOOD.
IF WE COULD ONLY PLAN SOME WAY TO ESCAPE.
I CAN FIND NO WAY TO GET OUT OF THE CASTLE, FOR IT'S CONSTANTLY GUARDED BY THE WINKIES.
THEY'RE TOO AFRAID OF HER NOT TO DO AS SHE TELLS THEM.
DOROTHY GREW TO UNDERSTAND THAT IT WOULD BE HARDER THAN EVER TO GET BACK TO KANSAS AND AUNT EM AGAIN.

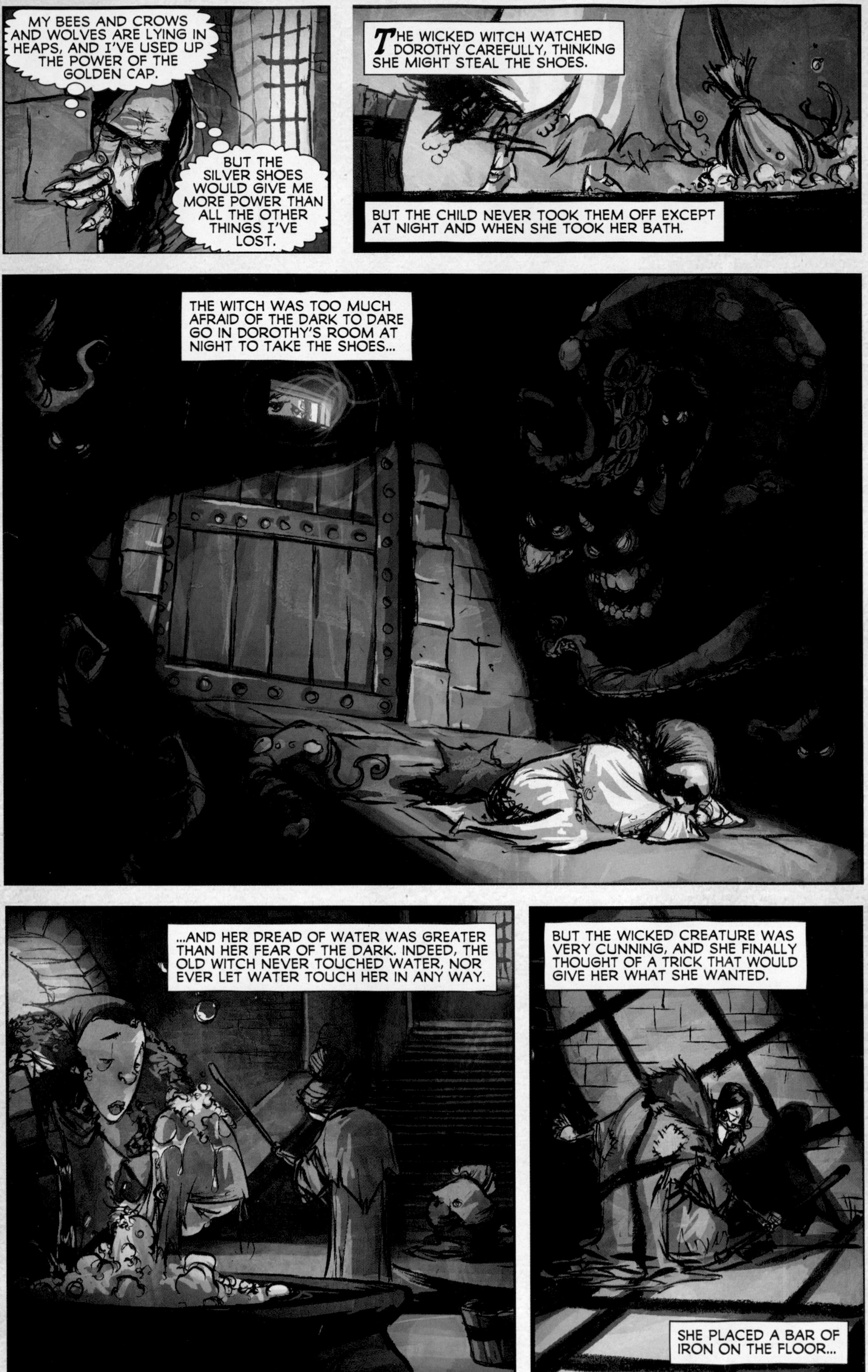

MY BEES AND CROWS AND WOLVES ARE LYING IN HEAPS, AND I'VE USED UP THE POWER OF THE GOLDEN CAP.
BUT THE SILVER SHOES WOULD GIVE ME MORE POWER THAN ALL THE OTHER THINGS I'VE LOST.
THE WICKED WITCH WATCHED DOROTHY CAREFULLY, THINKING SHE MIGHT STEAL THE SHOES.
BUT THE CHILD NEVER TOOK THEM OFF EXCEPT AT NIGHT AND WHEN SHE TOOK HER BATH.
THE WITCH WAS TOO MUCH AFRAID OF THE DARK TO DARE GO IN DOROTHY'S ROOM AT NIGHT TO TAKE THE SHOES...
...AND HER DREAD OF WATER WAS GREATER THAN HER FEAR OF THE DARK. INDEED, THE OLD WITCH NEVER TOUCHED WATER, NOR EVER LET WATER TOUCH HER IN ANY WAY.
BUT THE WICKED CREATURE WAS VERY CUNNING, AND SHE FINALLY THOUGHT OF A TRICK THAT WOULD GIVE HER WHAT SHE WANTED.
SHE PLACED A BAR OF IRON ON THE FLOOR...

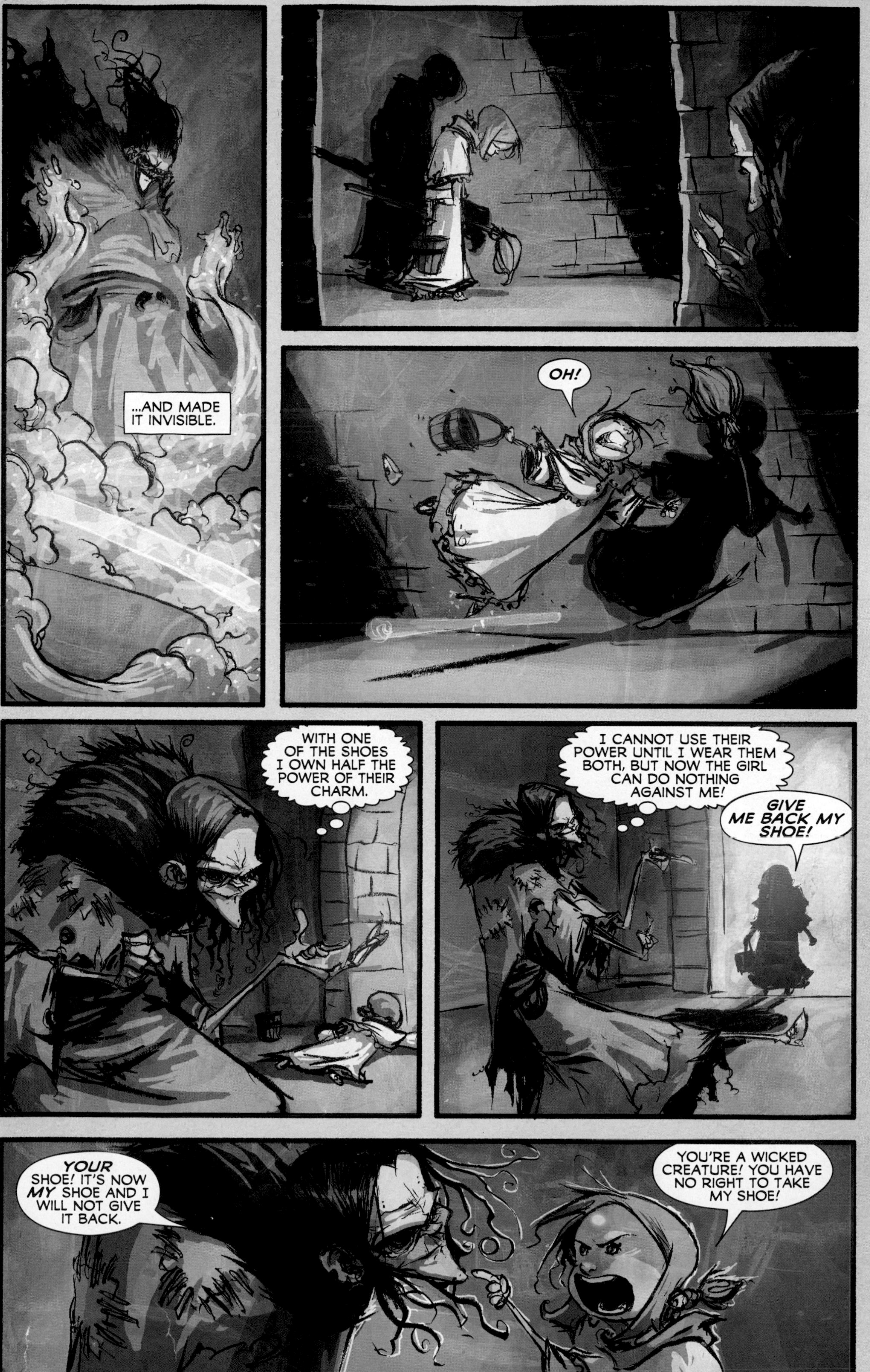
...AND MADE IT INVISIBLE.
OH!
WITH ONE OF THE SHOES I OWN HALF THE POWER OF THEIR CHARM.
I CANNOT USE THEIR POWER UNTIL I WEAR THEM BOTH, BUT NOW THE GIRL CAN DO NOTHING AGAINST ME!
GIVE ME BACK MY SHOE!
YOUR SHOE! IT'S NOW MY SHOE AND I WILL NOT GIVE IT BACK.
YOU'RE A WICKED CREATURE! YOU HAVE NO RIGHT TO TAKE MY SHOE!

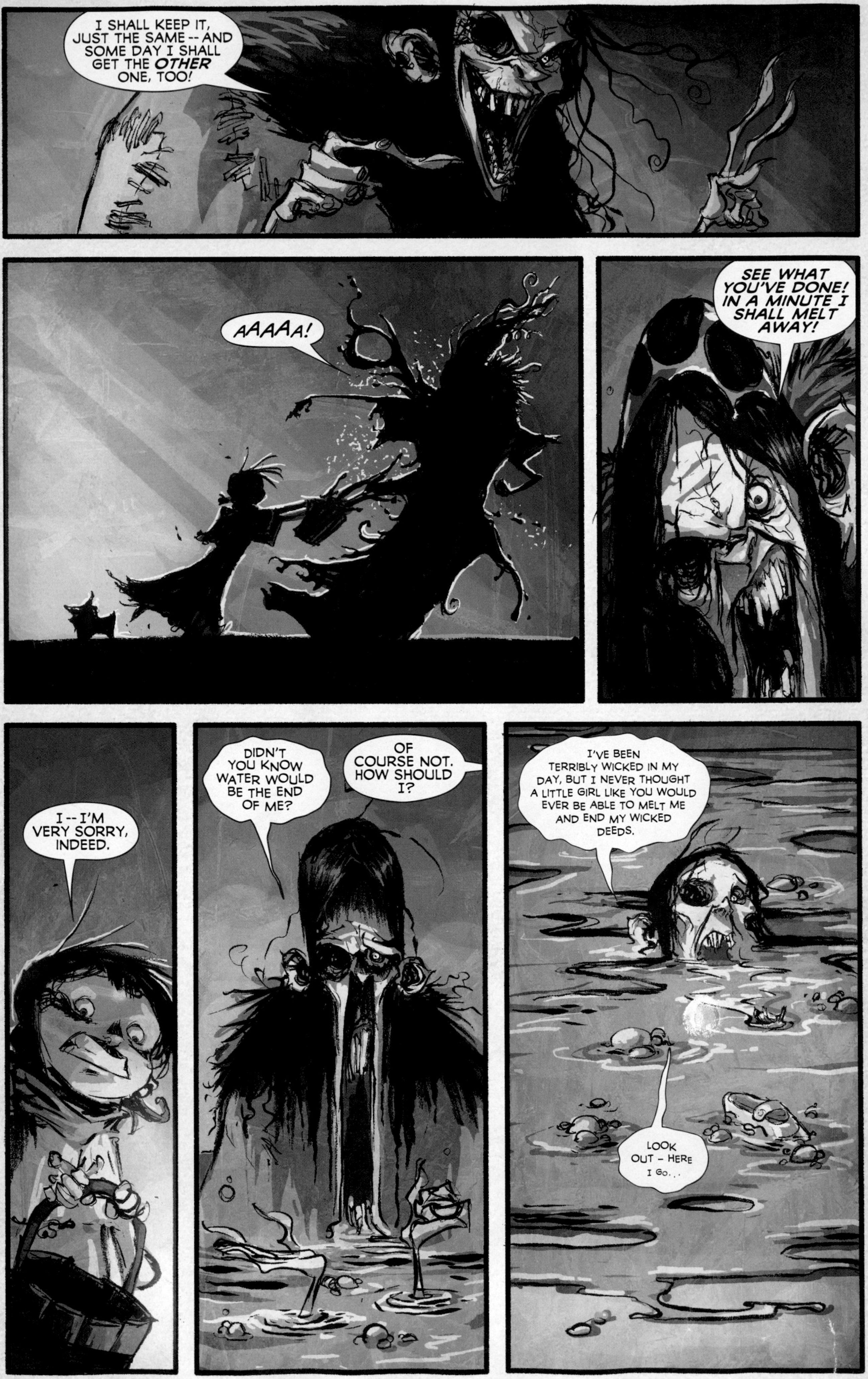
I SHALL KEEP IT, JUST THE SAME -- AND SOME DAY I SHALL GET THE *OTHER* ONE, TOO!
AAAAA!
SEE WHAT YOU'VE DONE! IN A MINUTE I SHALL MELT AWAY!
I -- I'M VERY SORRY, INDEED.
DIDN'T YOU KNOW WATER WOULD BE THE END OF ME?
OF COURSE NOT. HOW SHOULD I?
I'VE BEEN TERRIBLY WICKED IN MY DAY, BUT I NEVER THOUGHT A LITTLE GIRL LIKE YOU WOULD EVER BE ABLE TO MELT ME AND END MY WICKED DEEDS.
LOOK OUT - HERE I GO...

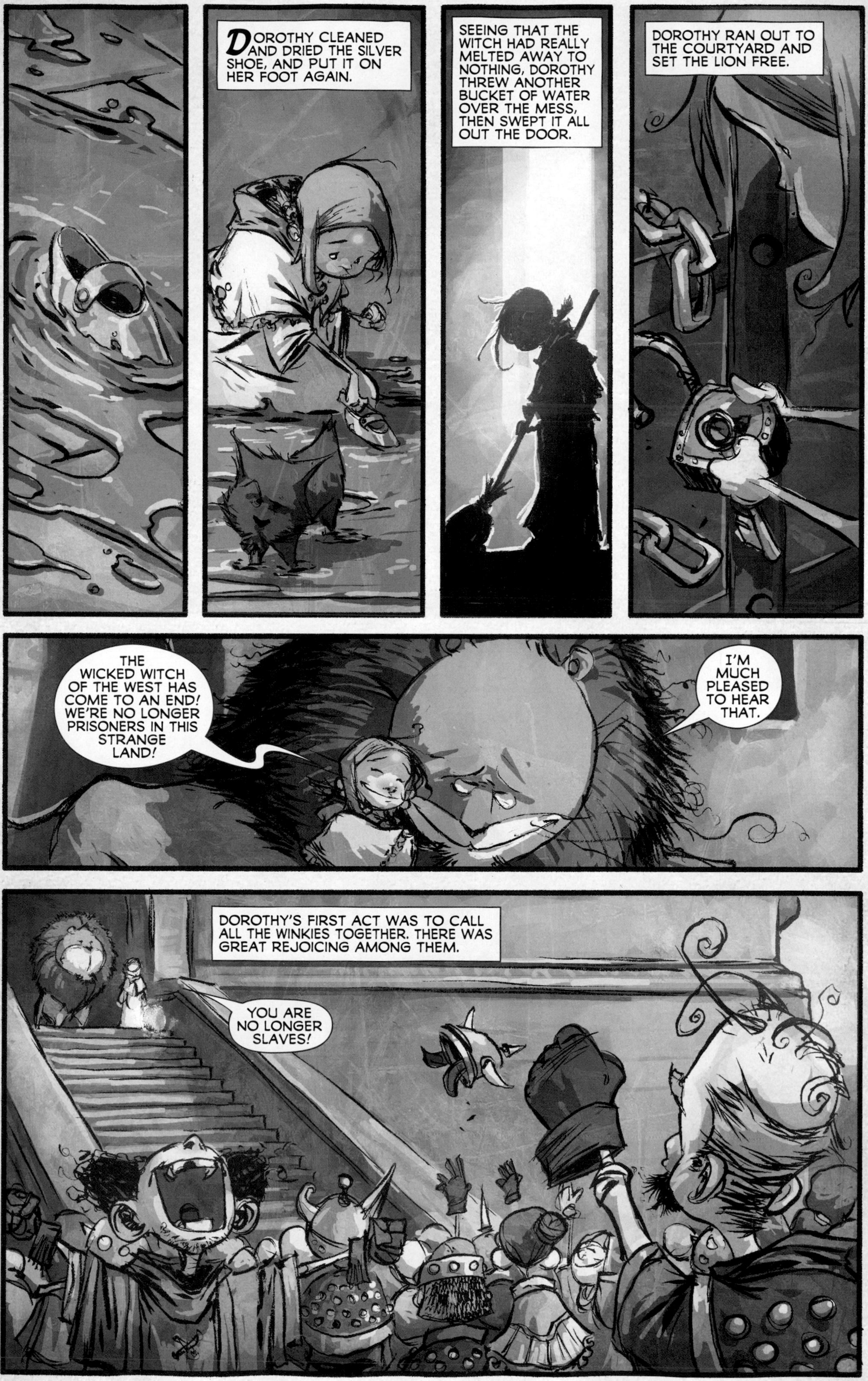
DOROTHY CLEANED AND DRIED THE SILVER SHOE, AND PUT IT ON HER FOOT AGAIN.
SEEING THAT THE WITCH HAD REALLY MELTED AWAY TO NOTHING, DOROTHY THREW ANOTHER BUCKET OF WATER OVER THE MESS, THEN SWEPT IT ALL OUT THE DOOR.
DOROTHY RAN OUT TO THE COURTYARD AND SET THE LION FREE.
THE WICKED WITCH OF THE WEST HAS COME TO AN END! WE'RE NO LONGER PRISONERS IN THIS STRANGE LAND!
I'M MUCH PLEASED TO HEAR THAT.
DOROTHY'S FIRST ACT WAS TO CALL ALL THE WINKIES TOGETHER. THERE WAS GREAT REJOICING AMONG THEM.
YOU ARE NO LONGER SLAVES!

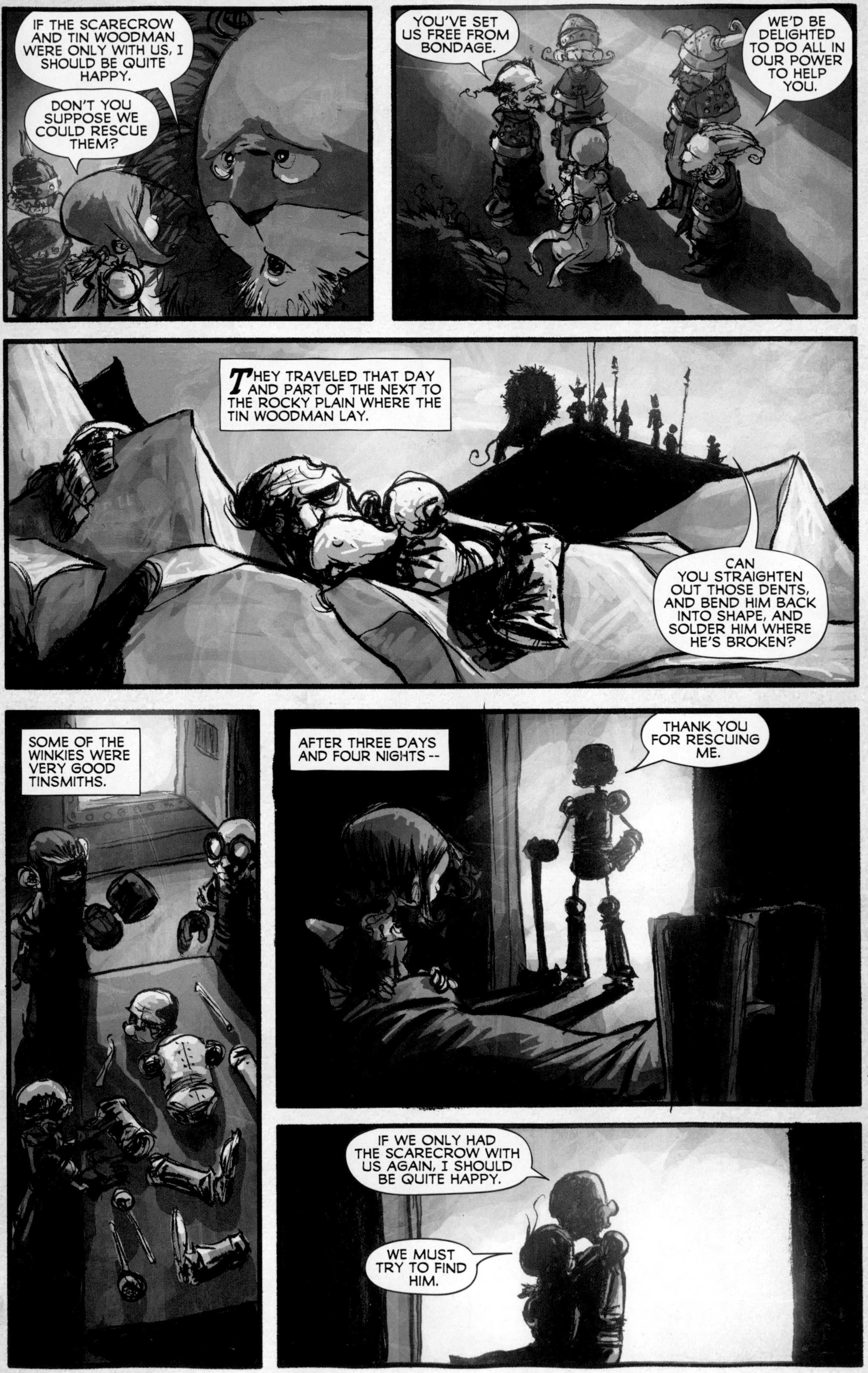
IF THE SCARECROW AND TIN WOODMAN WERE ONLY WITH US, I SHOULD BE QUITE HAPPY.
DON'T YOU SUPPOSE WE COULD RESCUE THEM?
YOU'VE SET US FREE FROM BONDAGE.
WE'D BE DELIGHTED TO DO ALL IN OUR POWER TO HELP YOU.
THEY TRAVELED THAT DAY AND PART OF THE NEXT TO THE ROCKY PLAIN WHERE THE TIN WOODMAN LAY.
CAN YOU STRAIGHTEN OUT THOSE DENTS, AND BEND HIM BACK INTO SHAPE, AND SOLDER HIM WHERE HE'S BROKEN?
SOME OF THE WINKIES WERE VERY GOOD TINSMITHS.
AFTER THREE DAYS AND FOUR NIGHTS --
THANK YOU FOR RESCUING ME.
IF WE ONLY HAD THE SCARECROW WITH US AGAIN, I SHOULD BE QUITE HAPPY.
WE MUST TRY TO FIND HIM.

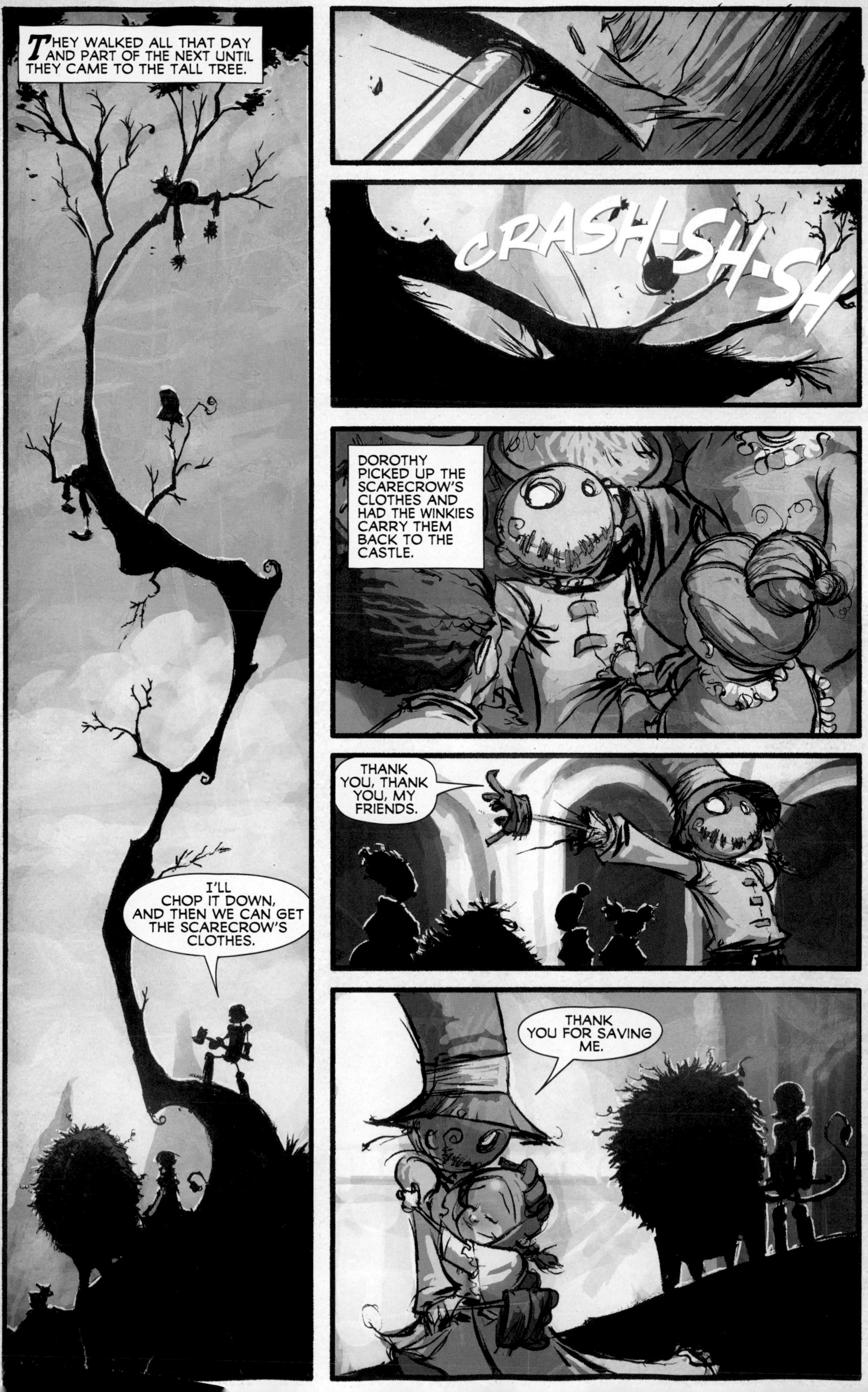
THEY WALKED ALL THAT DAY AND PART OF THE NEXT UNTIL THEY CAME TO THE TALL TREE.
I'LL CHOP IT DOWN, AND THEN WE CAN GET THE SCARECROW'S CLOTHES.
CRASH-SH-SH-SH
DOROTHY PICKED UP THE SCARECROW'S CLOTHES AND HAD THE WINKIES CARRY THEM BACK TO THE CASTLE.
THANK YOU, THANK YOU, MY FRIENDS.
THANK YOU FOR SAVING ME.

DOROTHY SPENT A FEW HAPPY DAYS AT THE YELLOW CASTLE. BUT ONE DAY SHE THOUGHT OF AUNT EM.

WE MUST GO BACK TO OZ AND CLAIM HIS PROMISE.

YES, AT LAST I SHALL GET MY BRAINS.

AND I SHALL GET MY COURAGE.

AND I SHALL GET MY HEART.

AND I SHALL GET BACK TO KANSAS!

LET'S START FOR THE EMERALD CITY TOMORROW!

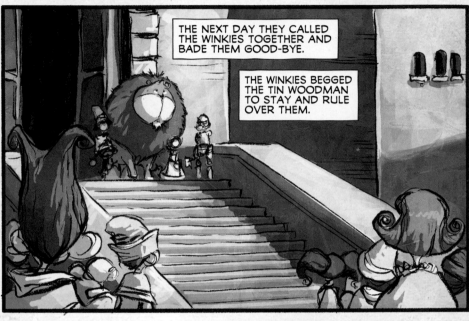

THE NEXT DAY THEY CALLED THE WINKIES TOGETHER AND BADE THEM GOOD-BYE.

THE WINKIES BEGGED THE TIN WOODMAN TO STAY AND RULE OVER THEM.

BUT FINDING THEY WERE DETERMINED TO GO, THE WINKIES PRESENTED A GIFT TO EACH --

-- AND ALL SHOOK HANDS UNTIL THEIR ARMS ACHED.

DOROTHY WENT TO FILL HER BASKET WITH FOOD AND FOUND THE GOLDEN CAP.

SHE DIDN'T KNOW ANYTHING ABOUT ITS CHARM, BUT SHE SAW THAT IT WAS PRETTY, SO SHE MADE UP HER MIND TO WEAR IT.

THEN THEY STARTED FOR THE EMERALD CITY. THE WINKIES GAVE THEM THREE CHEERS AND MANY GOOD WISHES TO CARRY WITH THEM.

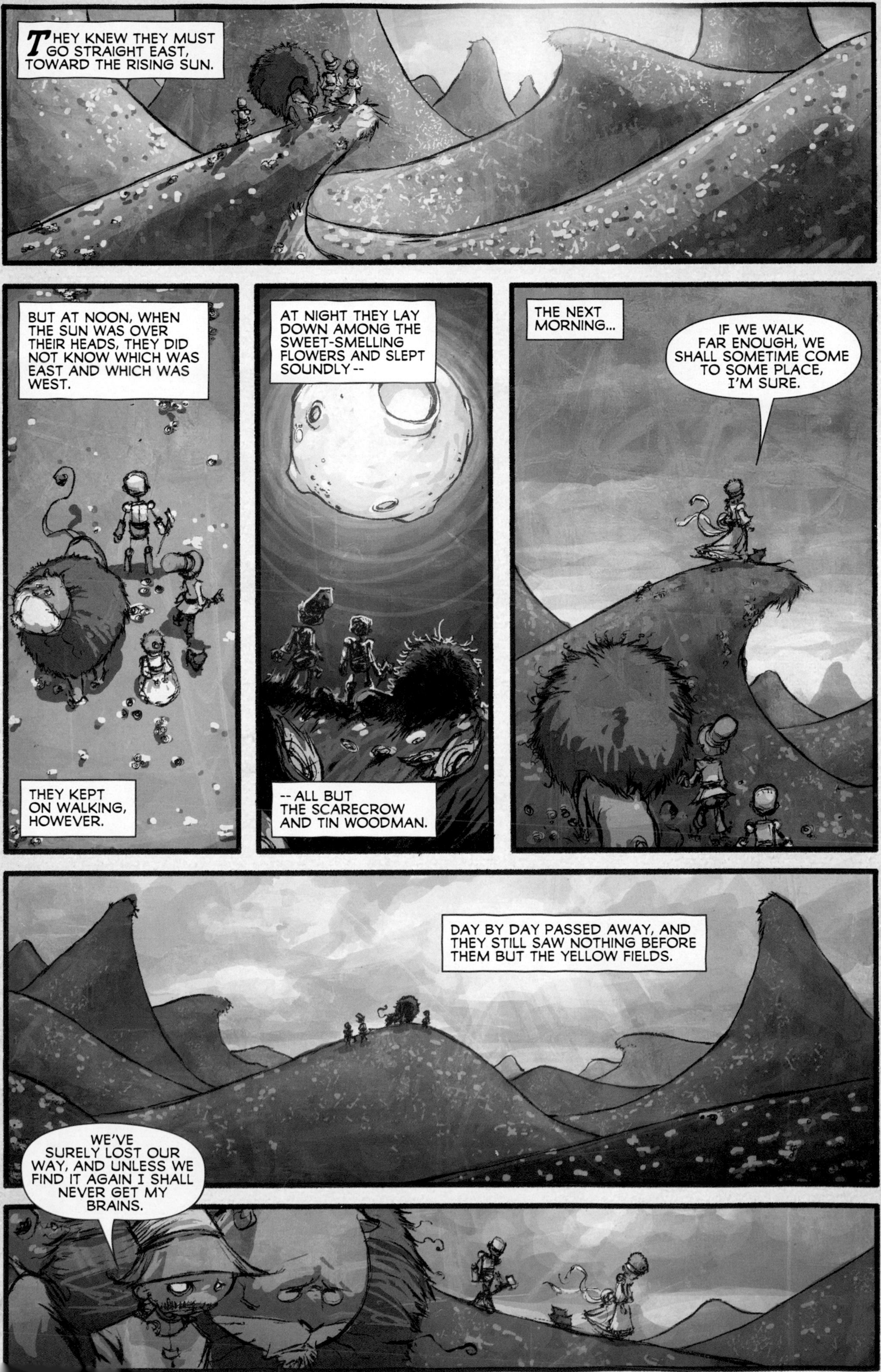
THEY KNEW THEY MUST GO STRAIGHT EAST, TOWARD THE RISING SUN.
BUT AT NOON, WHEN THE SUN WAS OVER THEIR HEADS, THEY DID NOT KNOW WHICH WAS EAST AND WHICH WAS WEST.
THEY KEPT ON WALKING, HOWEVER.
AT NIGHT THEY LAY DOWN AMONG THE SWEET-SMELLING FLOWERS AND SLEPT SOUNDLY --
-- ALL BUT THE SCARECROW AND TIN WOODMAN.
THE NEXT MORNING...
IF WE WALK FAR ENOUGH, WE SHALL SOMETIME COME TO SOME PLACE, I'M SURE.
DAY BY DAY PASSED AWAY, AND THEY STILL SAW NOTHING BEFORE THEM BUT THE YELLOW FIELDS.
WE'VE SURELY LOST OUR WAY, AND UNLESS WE FIND IT AGAIN I SHALL NEVER GET MY BRAINS.

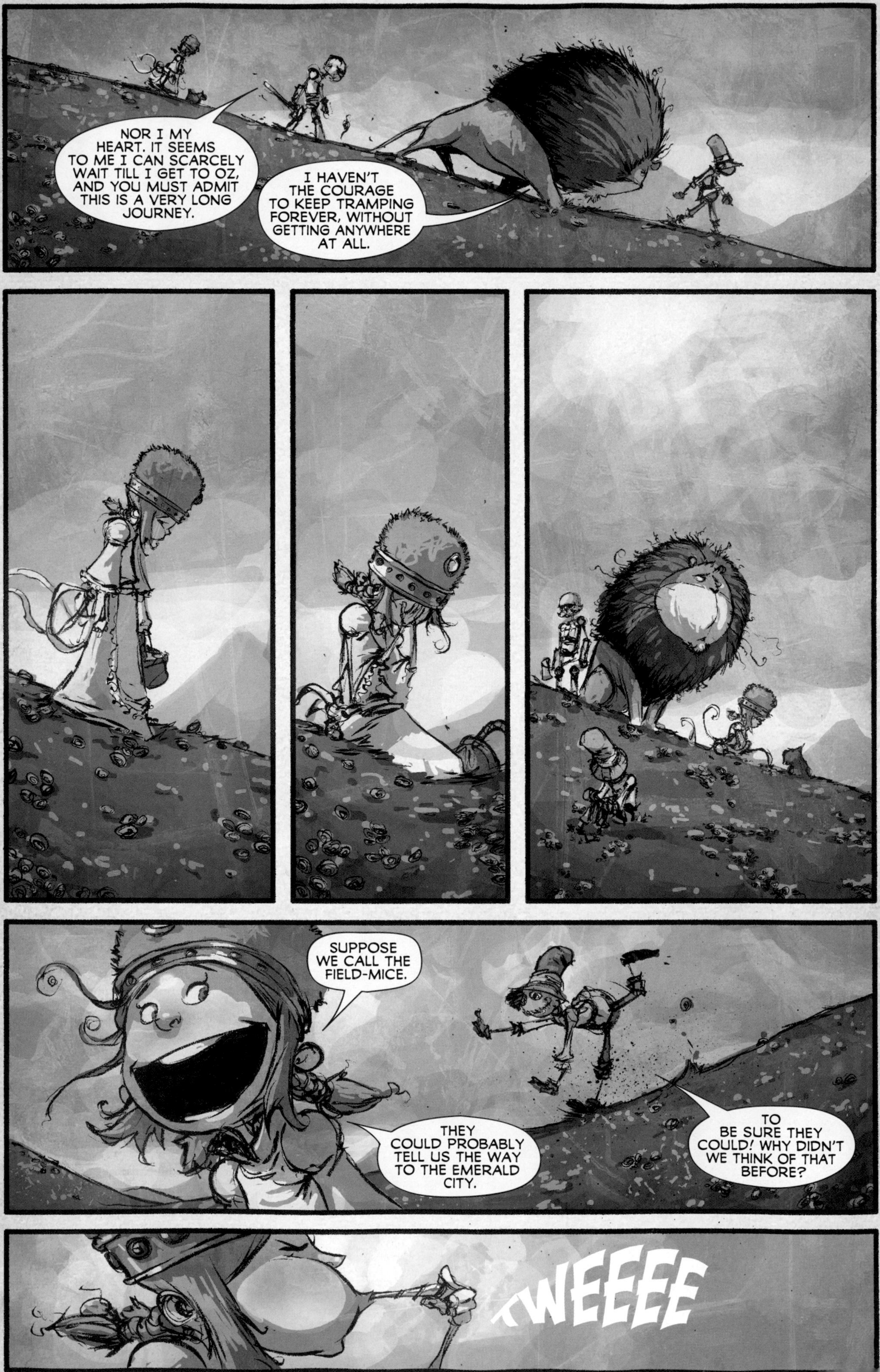
NOR I MY HEART. IT SEEMS TO ME I CAN SCARCELY WAIT TILL I GET TO OZ, AND YOU MUST ADMIT THIS IS A VERY LONG JOURNEY.
I HAVEN'T THE COURAGE TO KEEP TRAMPING FOREVER, WITHOUT GETTING ANYWHERE AT ALL.
SUPPOSE WE CALL THE FIELD-MICE.
THEY COULD PROBABLY TELL US THE WAY TO THE EMERALD CITY.
TO BE SURE THEY COULD! WHY DIDN'T WE THINK OF THAT BEFORE?
TWEEEE

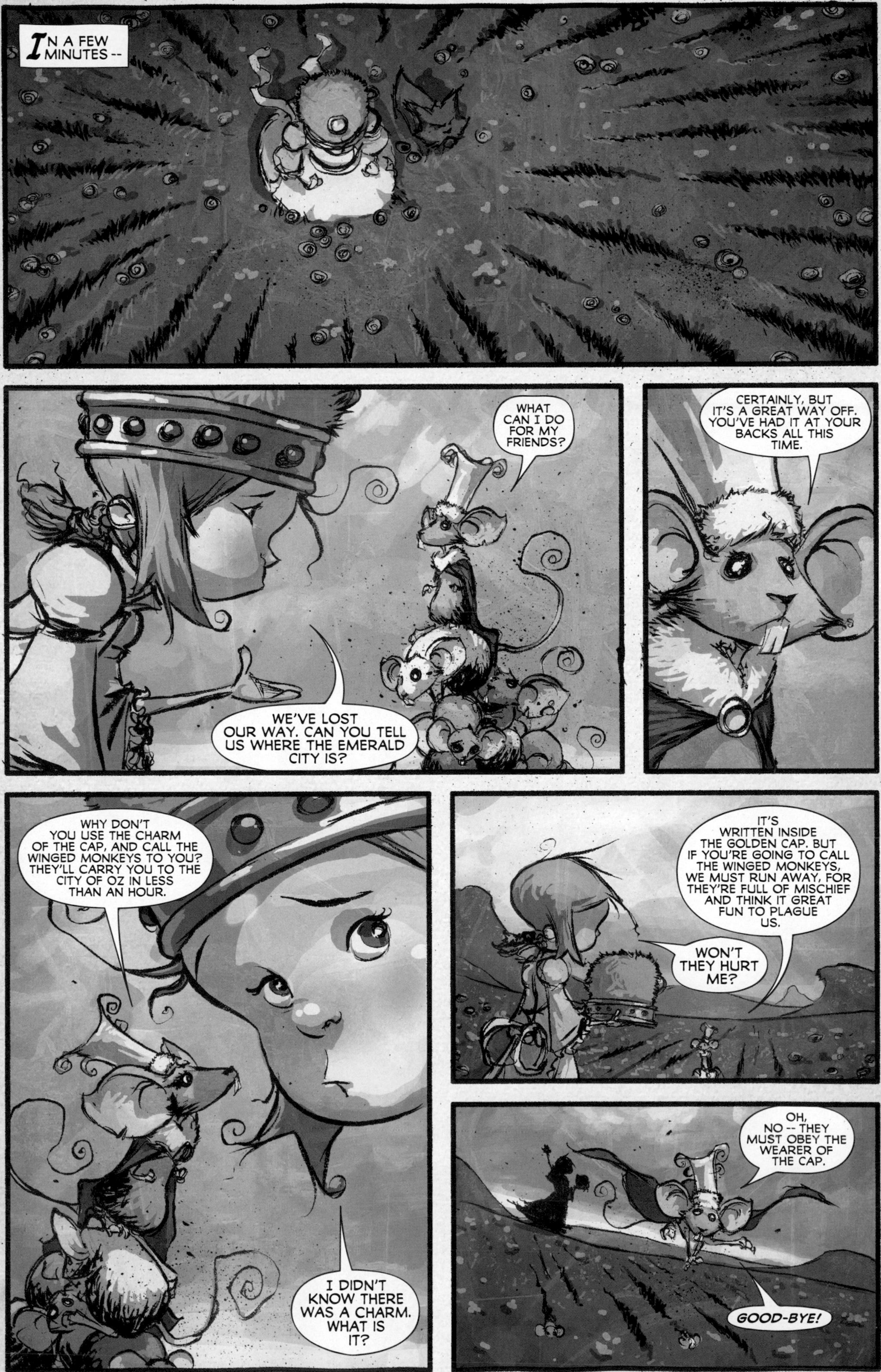
IN A FEW MINUTES --
WHAT CAN I DO FOR MY FRIENDS?
WE'VE LOST OUR WAY. CAN YOU TELL US WHERE THE EMERALD CITY IS?
CERTAINLY, BUT IT'S A GREAT WAY OFF. YOU'VE HAD IT AT YOUR BACKS ALL THIS TIME.
WHY DON'T YOU USE THE CHARM OF THE CAP, AND CALL THE WINGED MONKEYS TO YOU? THEY'LL CARRY YOU TO THE CITY OF OZ IN LESS THAN AN HOUR.
I DIDN'T KNOW THERE WAS A CHARM. WHAT IS IT?
IT'S WRITTEN INSIDE THE GOLDEN CAP. BUT IF YOU'RE GOING TO CALL THE WINGED MONKEYS, WE MUST RUN AWAY, FOR THEY'RE FULL OF MISCHIEF AND THINK IT GREAT FUN TO PLAGUE US.
WON'T THEY HURT ME?
OH, NO -- THEY MUST OBEY THE WEARER OF THE CAP.
GOOD-BYE!

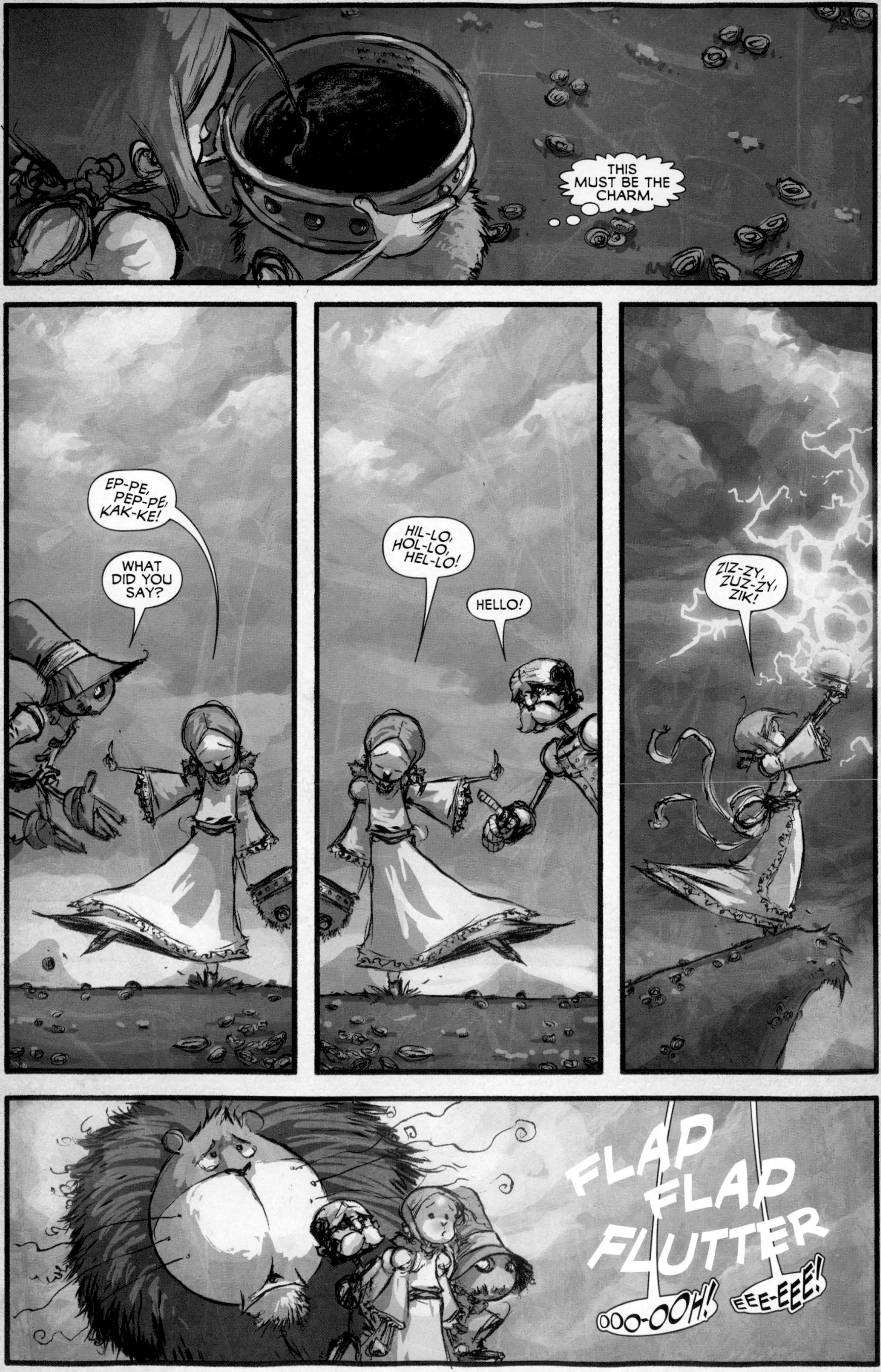
THIS MUST BE THE CHARM.
EP-PE, PEP-PE, KAK-KE!
WHAT DID YOU SAY?
HIL-LO, HOL-LO, HEL-LO!
HELLO!
ZIZ-ZY, ZUZ-ZY, ZIK!
FLAP FLAP FLUTTER
OOO-OOH!
EEE-EEE!

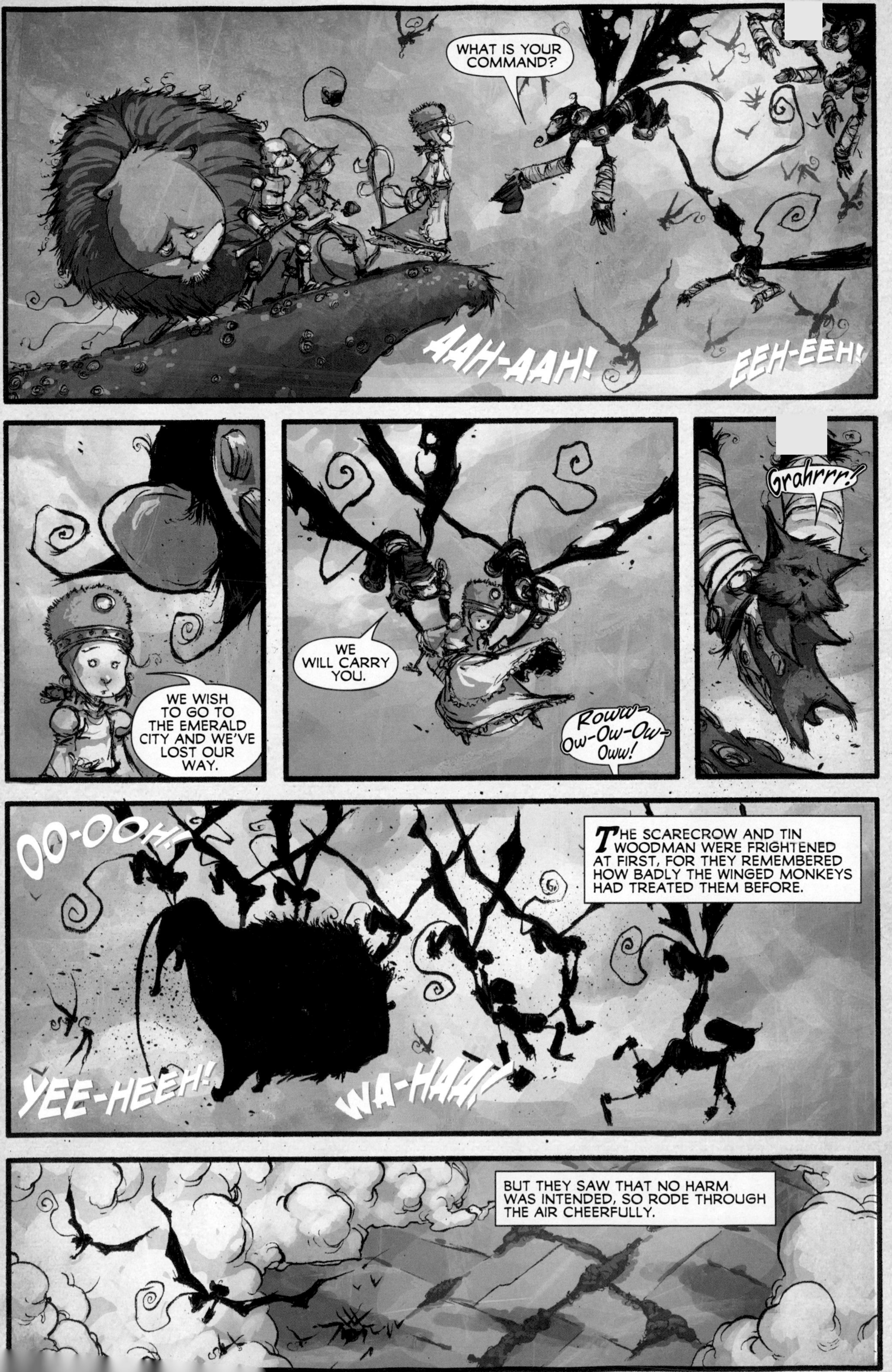
WHAT IS YOUR COMMAND?
AAH-AAH!
EEH-EEH!
WE WISH TO GO TO THE EMERALD CITY AND WE'VE LOST OUR WAY.
WE WILL CARRY YOU.
Roww-Ow-Ow-Ow-Oww!
Grahrrr!
THE SCARECROW AND TIN WOODMAN WERE FRIGHTENED AT FIRST, FOR THEY REMEMBERED HOW BADLY THE WINGED MONKEYS HAD TREATED THEM BEFORE.
OO-OOH!
YEE-HEEH!
WA-HAA!
BUT THEY SAW THAT NO HARM WAS INTENDED, SO RODE THROUGH THE AIR CHEERFULLY.

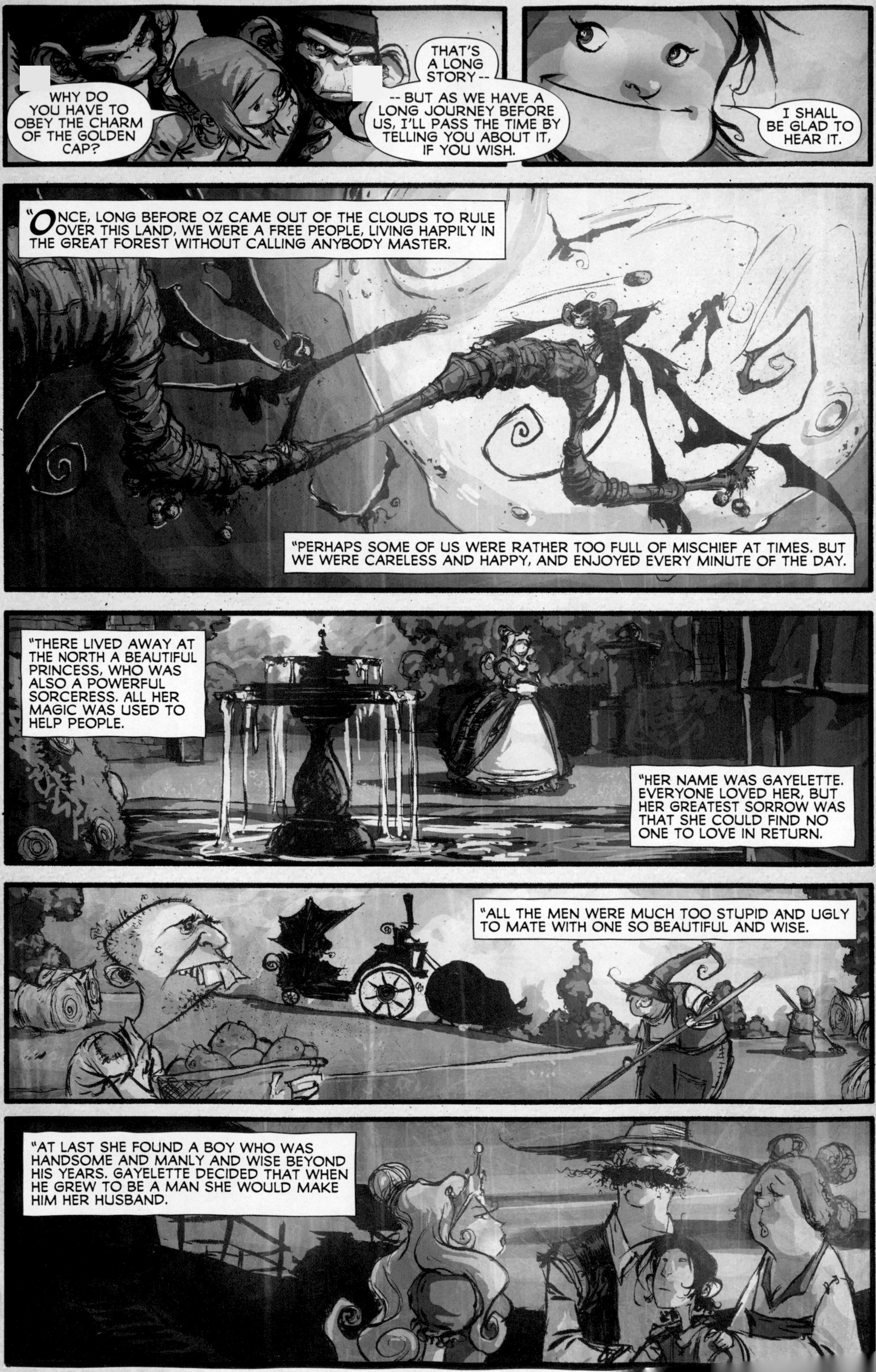
WHY DO YOU HAVE TO OBEY THE CHARM OF THE GOLDEN CAP?
THAT'S A LONG STORY --
-- BUT AS WE HAVE A LONG JOURNEY BEFORE US, I'LL PASS THE TIME BY TELLING YOU ABOUT IT, IF YOU WISH.
I SHALL BE GLAD TO HEAR IT.
"ONCE, LONG BEFORE OZ CAME OUT OF THE CLOUDS TO RULE OVER THIS LAND, WE WERE A FREE PEOPLE, LIVING HAPPILY IN THE GREAT FOREST WITHOUT CALLING ANYBODY MASTER.
"PERHAPS SOME OF US WERE RATHER TOO FULL OF MISCHIEF AT TIMES. BUT WE WERE CARELESS AND HAPPY, AND ENJOYED EVERY MINUTE OF THE DAY.
"THERE LIVED AWAY AT THE NORTH A BEAUTIFUL PRINCESS, WHO WAS ALSO A POWERFUL SORCERESS. ALL HER MAGIC WAS USED TO HELP PEOPLE.
"HER NAME WAS GAYELETTE. EVERYONE LOVED HER, BUT HER GREATEST SORROW WAS THAT SHE COULD FIND NO ONE TO LOVE IN RETURN.
"ALL THE MEN WERE MUCH TOO STUPID AND UGLY TO MATE WITH ONE SO BEAUTIFUL AND WISE.
"AT LAST SHE FOUND A BOY WHO WAS HANDSOME AND MANLY AND WISE BEYOND HIS YEARS. GAYELETTE DECIDED THAT WHEN HE GREW TO BE A MAN SHE WOULD MAKE HIM HER HUSBAND.

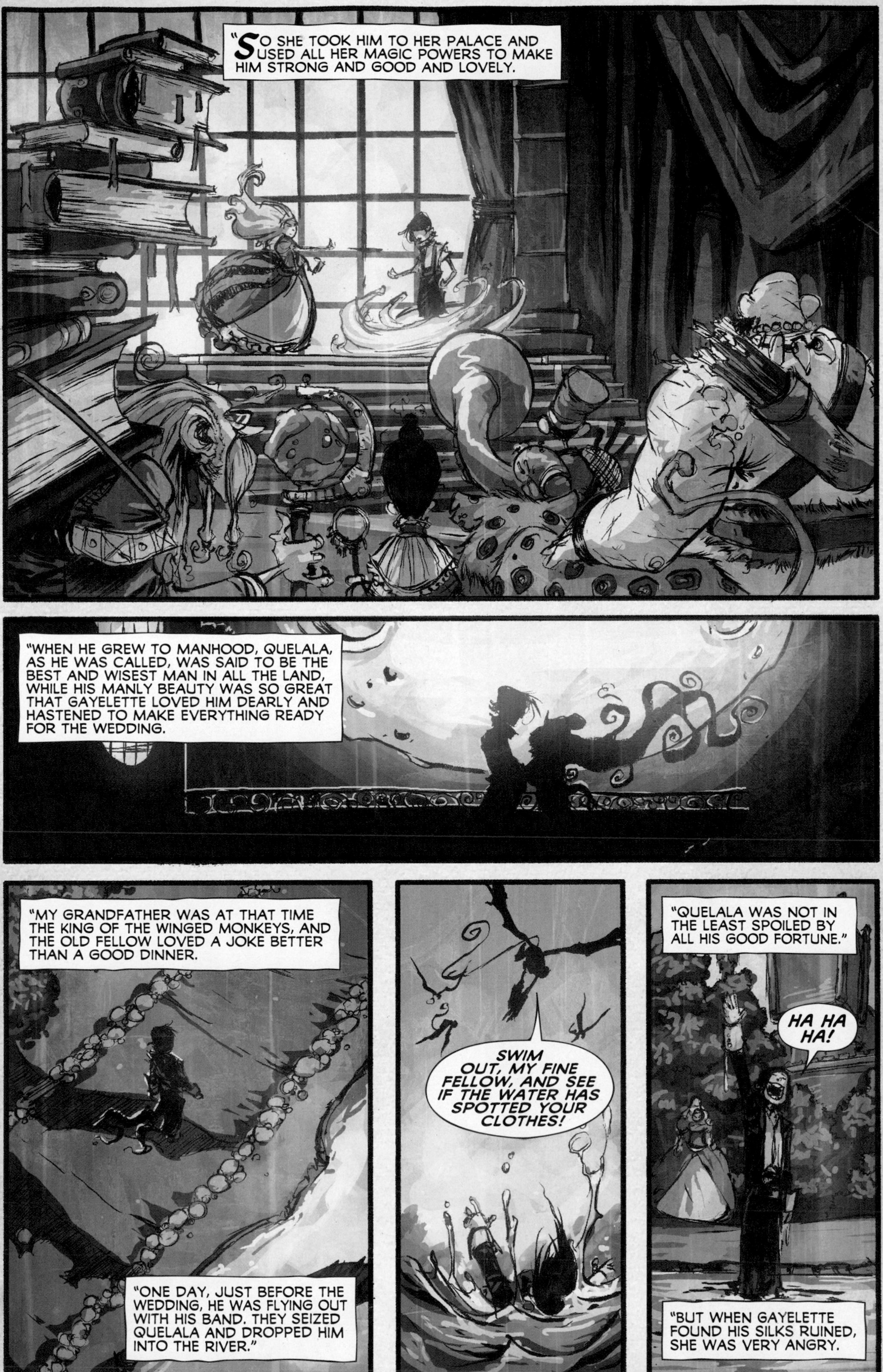
"SO SHE TOOK HIM TO HER PALACE AND USED ALL HER MAGIC POWERS TO MAKE HIM STRONG AND GOOD AND LOVELY.
"WHEN HE GREW TO MANHOOD, QUELALA, AS HE WAS CALLED, WAS SAID TO BE THE BEST AND WISEST MAN IN ALL THE LAND, WHILE HIS MANLY BEAUTY WAS SO GREAT THAT GAYELETTE LOVED HIM DEARLY AND HASTENED TO MAKE EVERYTHING READY FOR THE WEDDING.
"MY GRANDFATHER WAS AT THAT TIME THE KING OF THE WINGED MONKEYS, AND THE OLD FELLOW LOVED A JOKE BETTER THAN A GOOD DINNER.
"ONE DAY, JUST BEFORE THE WEDDING, HE WAS FLYING OUT WITH HIS BAND. THEY SEIZED QUELALA AND DROPPED HIM INTO THE RIVER."
SWIM OUT, MY FINE FELLOW, AND SEE IF THE WATER HAS SPOTTED YOUR CLOTHES!
"QUELALA WAS NOT IN THE LEAST SPOILED BY ALL HIS GOOD FORTUNE."
HA HA HA!
"BUT WHEN GAYELETTE FOUND HIS SILKS RUINED, SHE WAS VERY ANGRY.

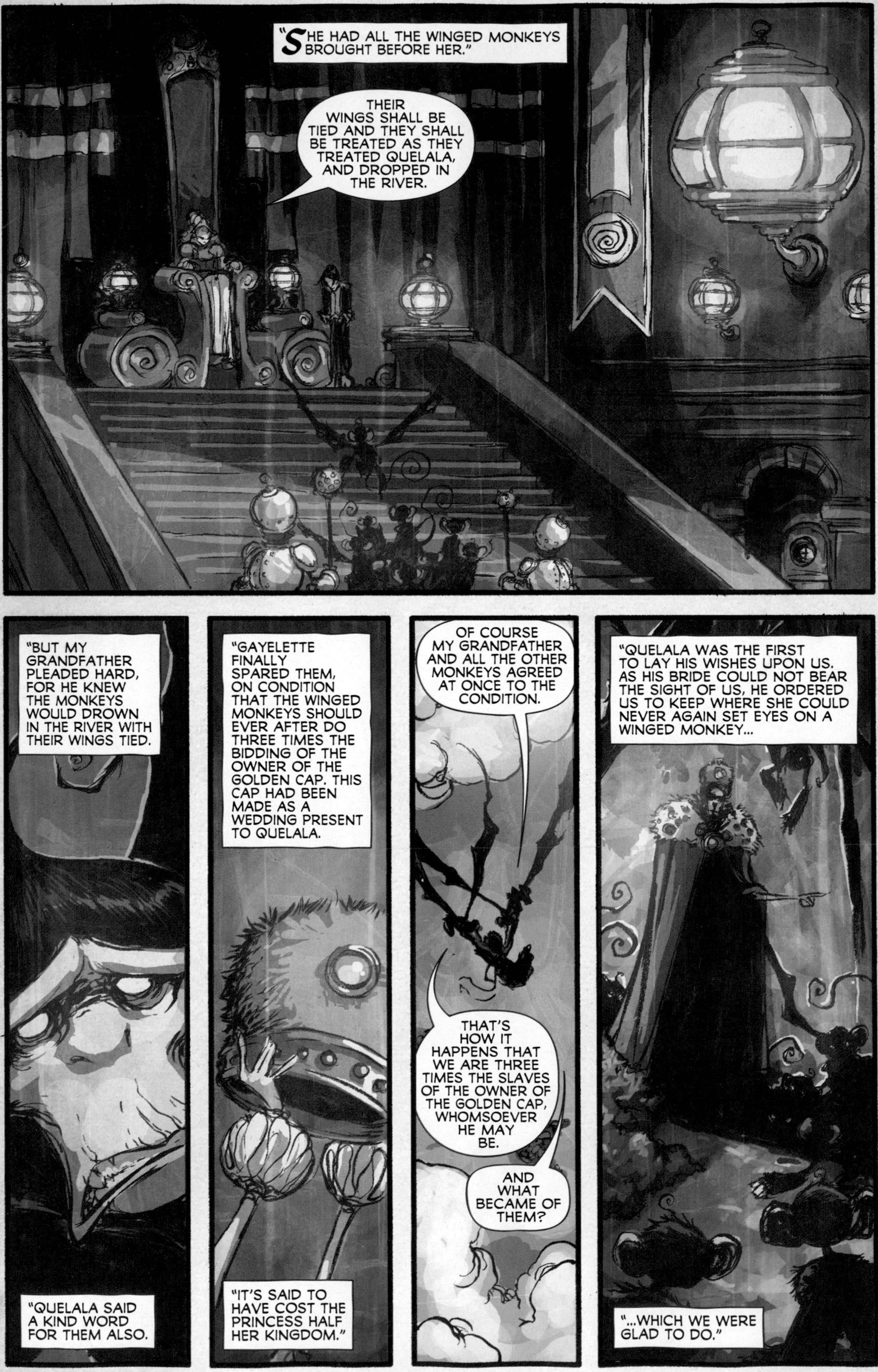
"SHE HAD ALL THE WINGED MONKEYS BROUGHT BEFORE HER."
THEIR WINGS SHALL BE TIED AND THEY SHALL BE TREATED AS THEY TREATED QUELALA, AND DROPPED IN THE RIVER.
"BUT MY GRANDFATHER PLEADED HARD, FOR HE KNEW THE MONKEYS WOULD DROWN IN THE RIVER WITH THEIR WINGS TIED.
"QUELALA SAID A KIND WORD FOR THEM ALSO.
"GAYELETTE FINALLY SPARED THEM, ON CONDITION THAT THE WINGED MONKEYS SHOULD EVER AFTER DO THREE TIMES THE BIDDING OF THE OWNER OF THE GOLDEN CAP. THIS CAP HAD BEEN MADE AS A WEDDING PRESENT TO QUELALA.
"IT'S SAID TO HAVE COST THE PRINCESS HALF HER KINGDOM."
OF COURSE MY GRANDFATHER AND ALL THE OTHER MONKEYS AGREED AT ONCE TO THE CONDITION.
THAT'S HOW IT HAPPENS THAT WE ARE THREE TIMES THE SLAVES OF THE OWNER OF THE GOLDEN CAP, WHOMSOEVER HE MAY BE.
AND WHAT BECAME OF THEM?
"QUELALA WAS THE FIRST TO LAY HIS WISHES UPON US. AS HIS BRIDE COULD NOT BEAR THE SIGHT OF US, HE ORDERED US TO KEEP WHERE SHE COULD NEVER AGAIN SET EYES ON A WINGED MONKEY...
"...WHICH WE WERE GLAD TO DO."

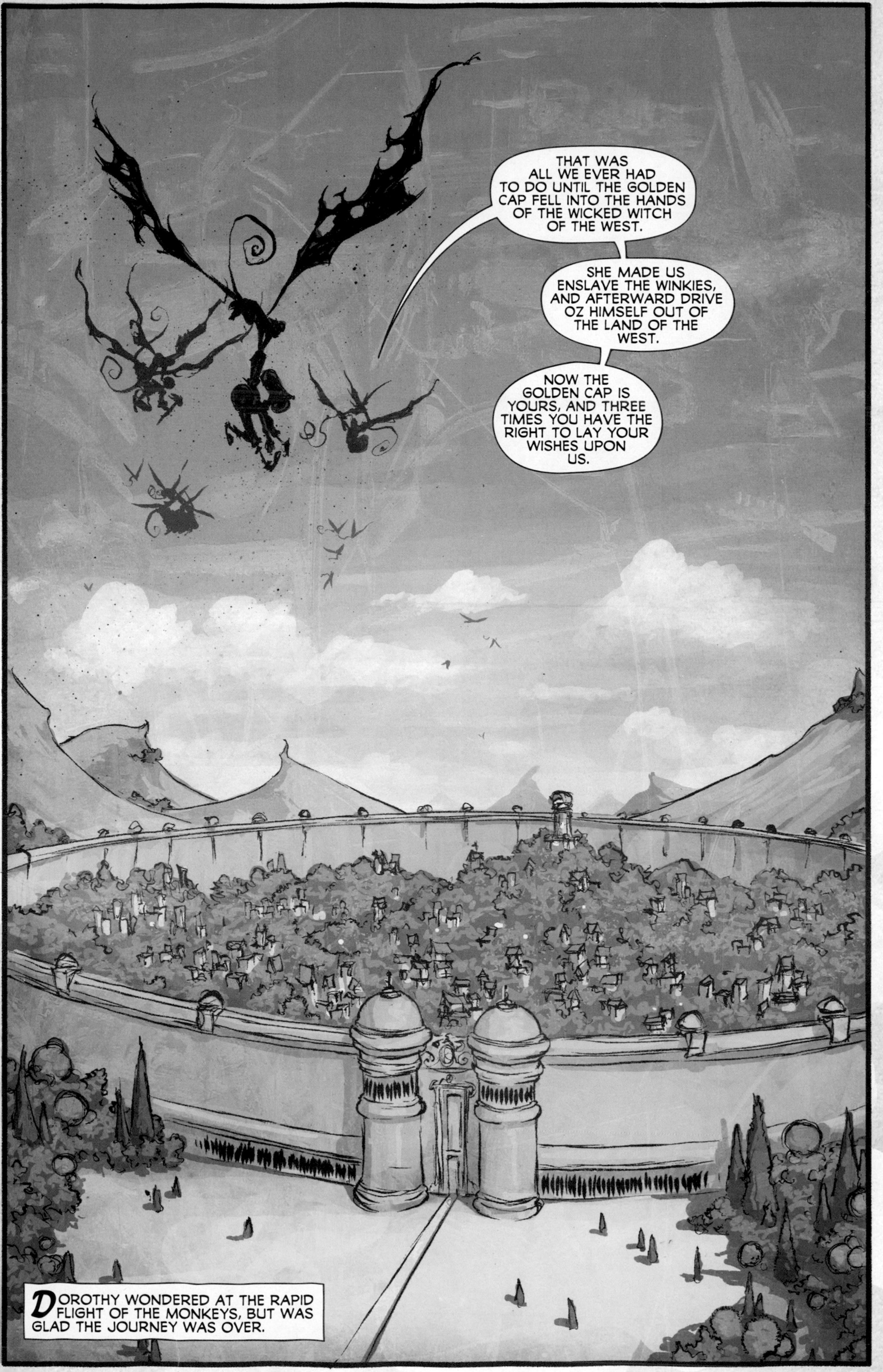
THAT WAS ALL WE EVER HAD TO DO UNTIL THE GOLDEN CAP FELL INTO THE HANDS OF THE WICKED WITCH OF THE WEST.
SHE MADE US ENSLAVE THE WINKIES, AND AFTERWARD DRIVE OZ HIMSELF OUT OF THE LAND OF THE WEST.
NOW THE GOLDEN CAP IS YOURS, AND THREE TIMES YOU HAVE THE RIGHT TO LAY YOUR WISHES UPON US.
DOROTHY WONDERED AT THE RAPID FLIGHT OF THE MONKEYS, BUT WAS GLAD THE JOURNEY WAS OVER.

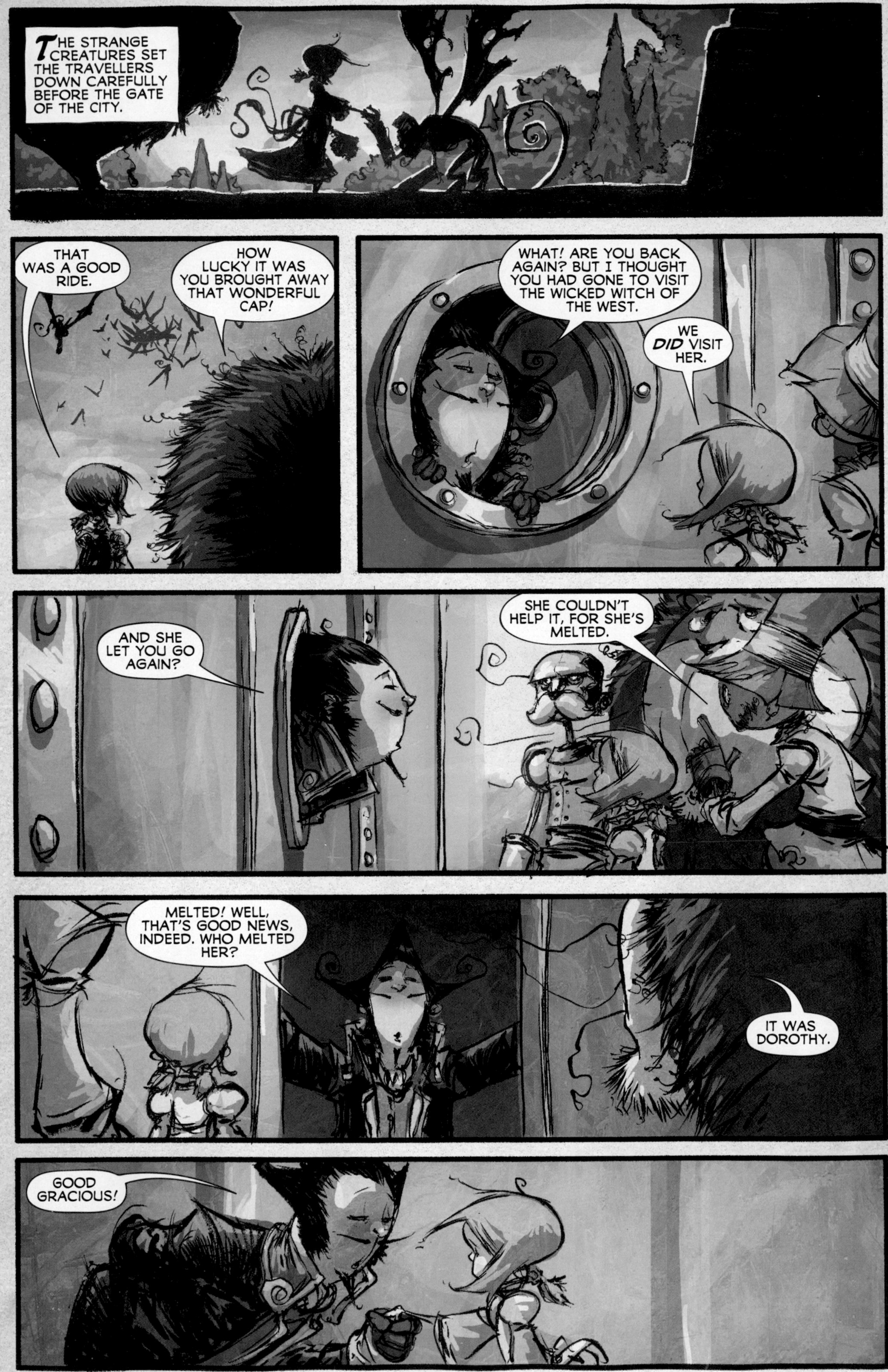
THE STRANGE CREATURES SET THE TRAVELLERS DOWN CAREFULLY BEFORE THE GATE OF THE CITY.
THAT WAS A GOOD RIDE.
HOW LUCKY IT WAS YOU BROUGHT AWAY THAT WONDERFUL CAP!
WHAT! ARE YOU BACK AGAIN? BUT I THOUGHT YOU HAD GONE TO VISIT THE WICKED WITCH OF THE WEST.
WE *DID* VISIT HER.
AND SHE LET YOU GO AGAIN?
SHE COULDN'T HELP IT, FOR SHE'S MELTED.
MELTED! WELL, THAT'S GOOD NEWS, INDEED. WHO MELTED HER?
IT WAS DOROTHY.
GOOD GRACIOUS!

When the people heard from the Guardian of the Gates that Dorothy had melted the Wicked Witch of the West, they all gathered around and followed in a great crowd to the palace of Oz.

The Soldier with the Green Whiskers let the travellers in at once.

They were met by the beautiful green girl who showed each of them to their old rooms.

The Soldier had the news carried straight to Oz that the travellers had come back again after destroying the Wicked Witch.

But Oz made no reply.

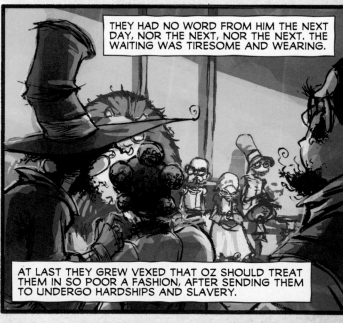

They had no word from him the next day, nor the next, nor the next. The waiting was tiresome and wearing.

At last they grew vexed that Oz should treat them in so poor a fashion, after sending them to undergo hardships and slavery.

So the Scarecrow asked the green girl to take another message to Oz.

IF HE DOESN'T LET US SEE HIM AT ONCE, WE'LL CALL THE WINGED MONKEYS AND FIND OUT WHETHER HE KEEPS HIS PROMISES OR NOT.

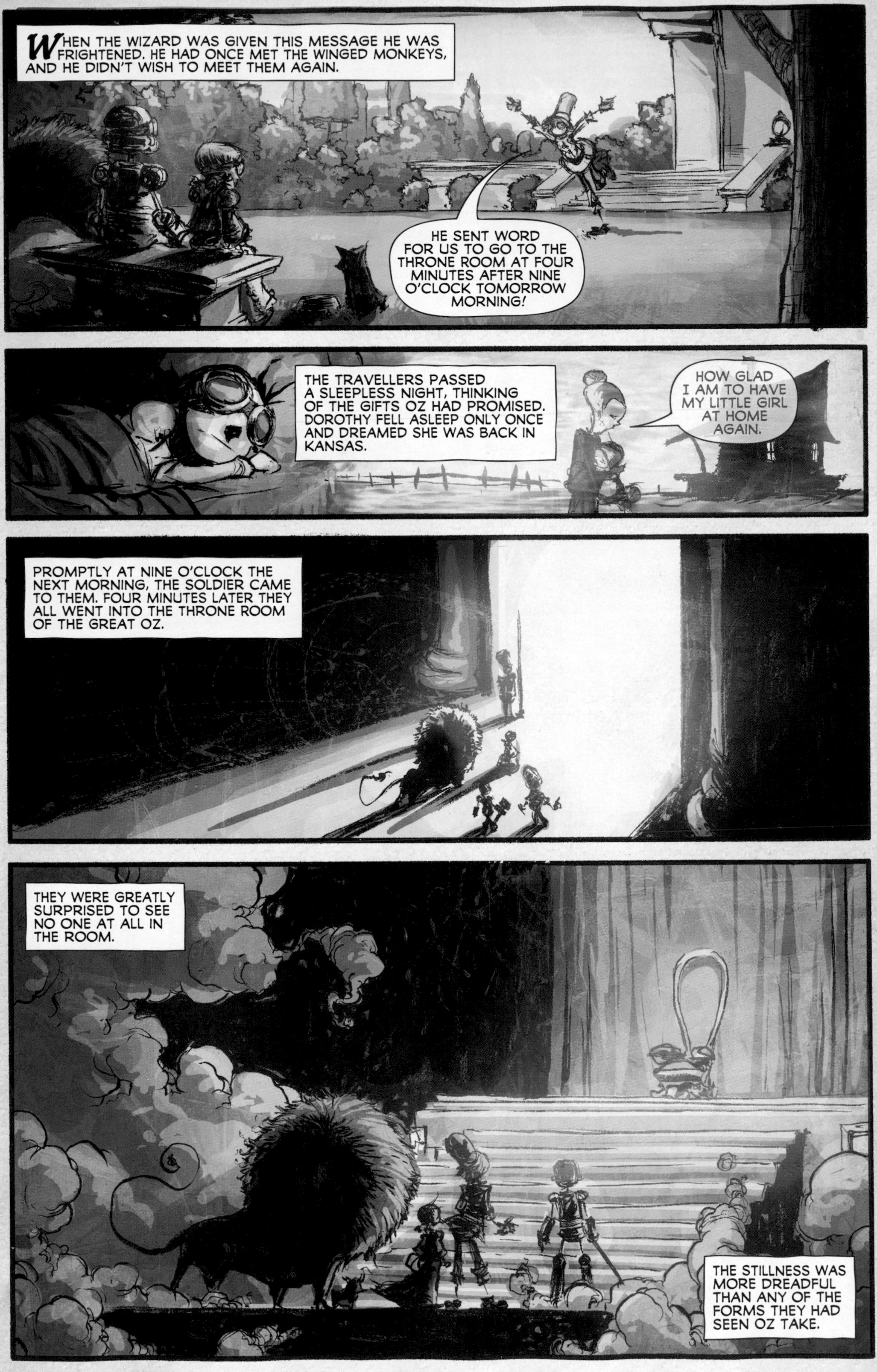
WHEN THE WIZARD WAS GIVEN THIS MESSAGE HE WAS FRIGHTENED. HE HAD ONCE MET THE WINGED MONKEYS, AND HE DIDN'T WISH TO MEET THEM AGAIN.
HE SENT WORD FOR US TO GO TO THE THRONE ROOM AT FOUR MINUTES AFTER NINE O'CLOCK TOMORROW MORNING!
THE TRAVELLERS PASSED A SLEEPLESS NIGHT, THINKING OF THE GIFTS OZ HAD PROMISED. DOROTHY FELL ASLEEP ONLY ONCE AND DREAMED SHE WAS BACK IN KANSAS.
HOW GLAD I AM TO HAVE MY LITTLE GIRL AT HOME AGAIN.
PROMPTLY AT NINE O'CLOCK THE NEXT MORNING, THE SOLDIER CAME TO THEM. FOUR MINUTES LATER THEY ALL WENT INTO THE THRONE ROOM OF THE GREAT OZ.
THEY WERE GREATLY SURPRISED TO SEE NO ONE AT ALL IN THE ROOM.
THE STILLNESS WAS MORE DREADFUL THAN ANY OF THE FORMS THEY HAD SEEN OZ TAKE.

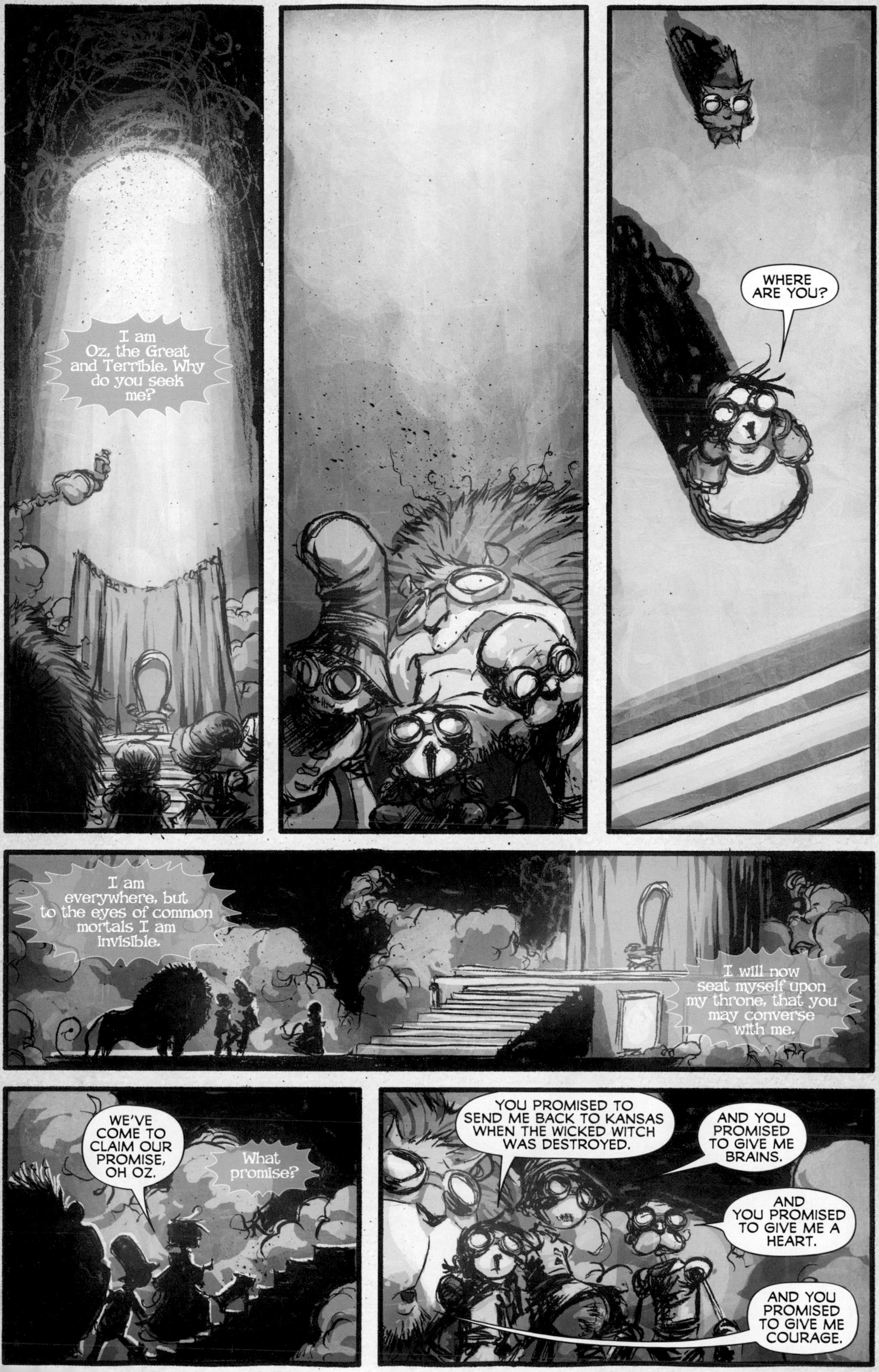
I am Oz, the Great and Terrible. Why do you seek me?
WHERE ARE YOU?
I am everywhere, but to the eyes of common mortals I am invisible.
I will now seat myself upon my throne, that you may converse with me.
WE'VE COME TO CLAIM OUR PROMISE, OH OZ.
What promise?
YOU PROMISED TO SEND ME BACK TO KANSAS WHEN THE WICKED WITCH WAS DESTROYED.
AND YOU PROMISED TO GIVE ME BRAINS.
AND YOU PROMISED TO GIVE ME A HEART.
AND YOU PROMISED TO GIVE ME COURAGE.

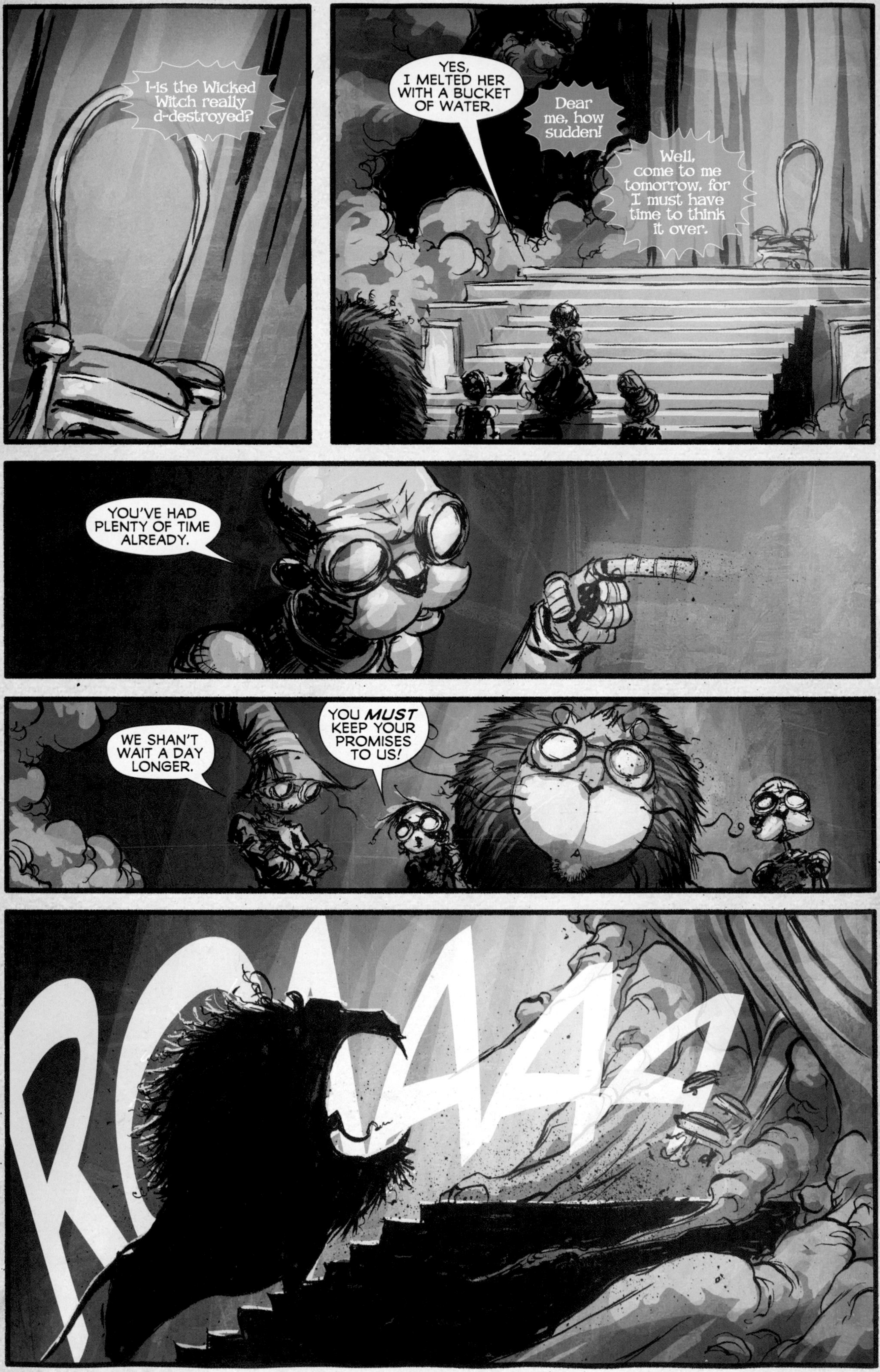
I-is the Wicked Witch really d-destroyed?
YES, I MELTED HER WITH A BUCKET OF WATER.
Dear me, how sudden!
Well, come to me tomorrow, for I must have time to think it over.
YOU'VE HAD PLENTY OF TIME ALREADY.
WE SHAN'T WAIT A DAY LONGER.
YOU MUST KEEP YOUR PROMISES TO US!
ROAAA

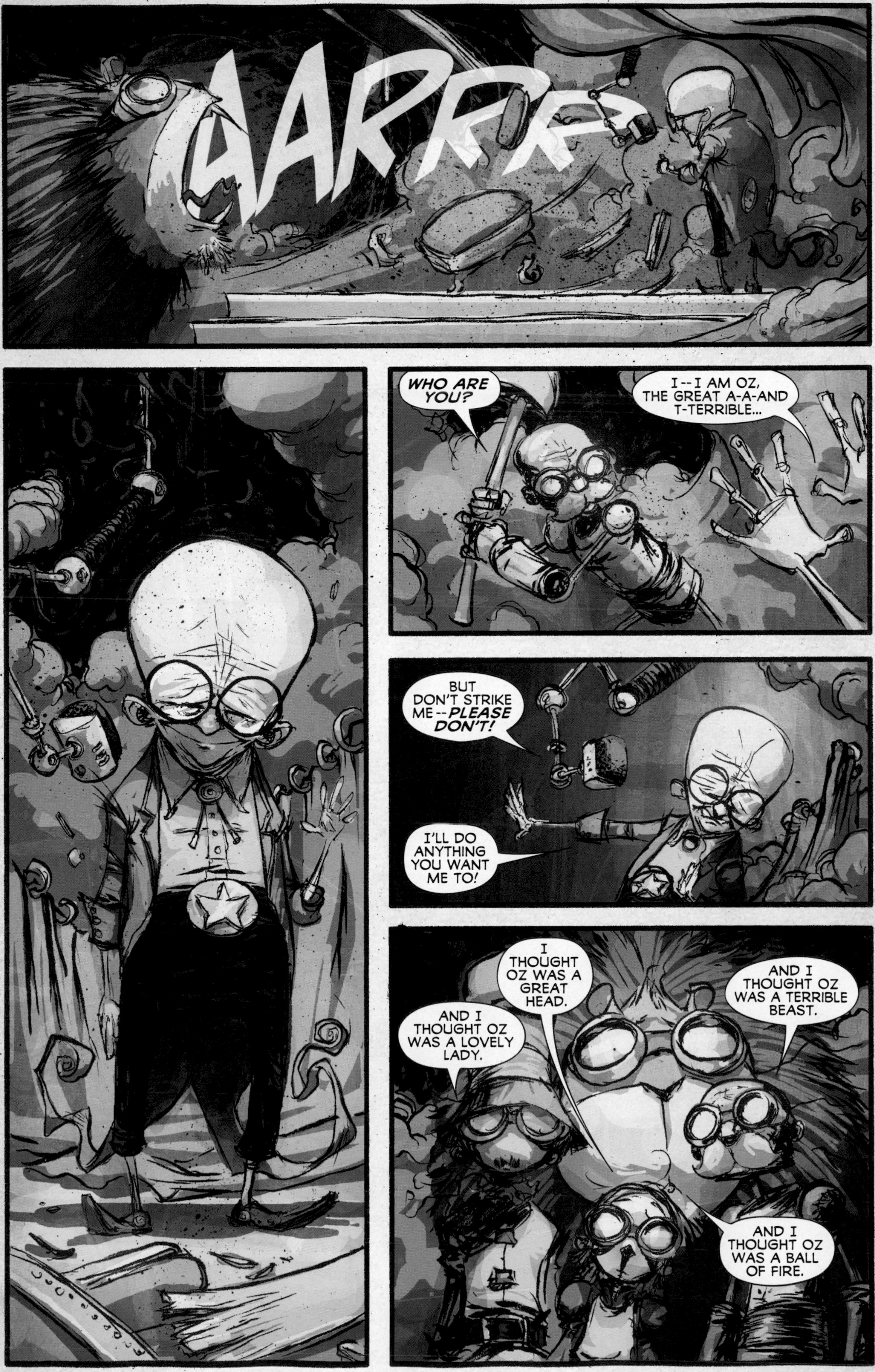

AARRRR
WHO ARE YOU?
I--I AM OZ, THE GREAT A-A-AND T-TERRIBLE...
BUT DON'T STRIKE ME--*PLEASE DON'T!*
I'LL DO ANYTHING YOU WANT ME TO!
I THOUGHT OZ WAS A GREAT HEAD.
AND I THOUGHT OZ WAS A LOVELY LADY.
AND I THOUGHT OZ WAS A TERRIBLE BEAST.
AND I THOUGHT OZ WAS A BALL OF FIRE.

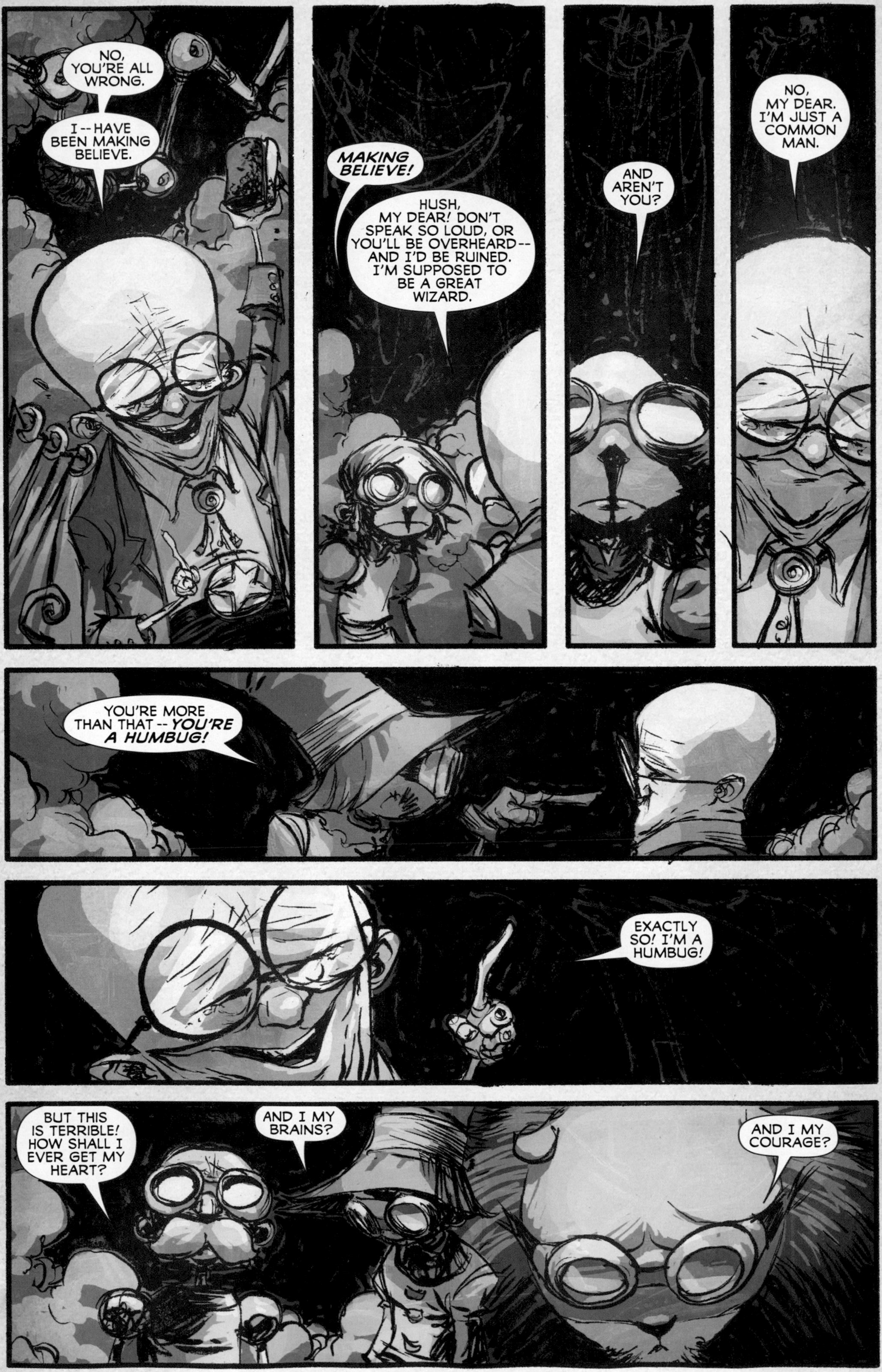
NO, YOU'RE ALL WRONG.
I -- HAVE BEEN MAKING BELIEVE.
MAKING BELIEVE!
HUSH, MY DEAR! DON'T SPEAK SO LOUD, OR YOU'LL BE OVERHEARD -- AND I'D BE RUINED. I'M SUPPOSED TO BE A GREAT WIZARD.
AND AREN'T YOU?
NO, MY DEAR. I'M JUST A COMMON MAN.
YOU'RE MORE THAN THAT -- YOU'RE A HUMBUG!
EXACTLY SO! I'M A HUMBUG!
BUT THIS IS TERRIBLE! HOW SHALL I EVER GET MY HEART?
AND I MY BRAINS?
AND I MY COURAGE?

MY DEAR FRIENDS, I PRAY YOU NOT TO SPEAK OF THESE LITTLE THINGS.

THINK OF ME, AND THE TERRIBLE TROUBLE I'M IN AT BEING FOUND OUT.

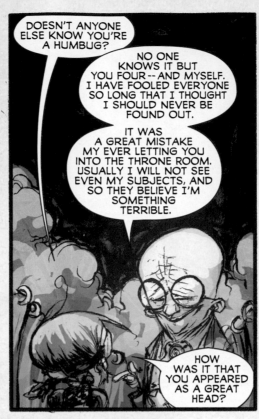

DOESN'T ANYONE ELSE KNOW YOU'RE A HUMBUG?

NO ONE KNOWS IT BUT YOU FOUR -- AND MYSELF. I HAVE FOOLED EVERYONE SO LONG THAT I THOUGHT I SHOULD NEVER BE FOUND OUT.

IT WAS A GREAT MISTAKE MY EVER LETTING YOU INTO THE THRONE ROOM. USUALLY I WILL NOT SEE EVEN MY SUBJECTS, AND SO THEY BELIEVE I'M SOMETHING TERRIBLE.

HOW WAS IT THAT YOU APPEARED AS A GREAT HEAD?

THAT WAS ONE OF MY TRICKS. STEP THIS WAY, PLEASE.

THIS I HUNG FROM THE CEILING BY A WIRE. I STOOD BEHIND THE SCREEN AND PULLED A THREAD, TO MAKE THE EYES MOVE AND THE MOUTH OPEN.

BUT HOW ABOUT THE VOICE?

OH, I'M A VENTRILOQUIST, AND I CAN THROW THE SOUND OF MY VOICE WHEREVER I WISH, SO THAT YOU THOUGHT IT WAS COMING OUT OF THE HEAD.

HERE ARE THE OTHER THINGS I USED TO DECEIVE YOU.

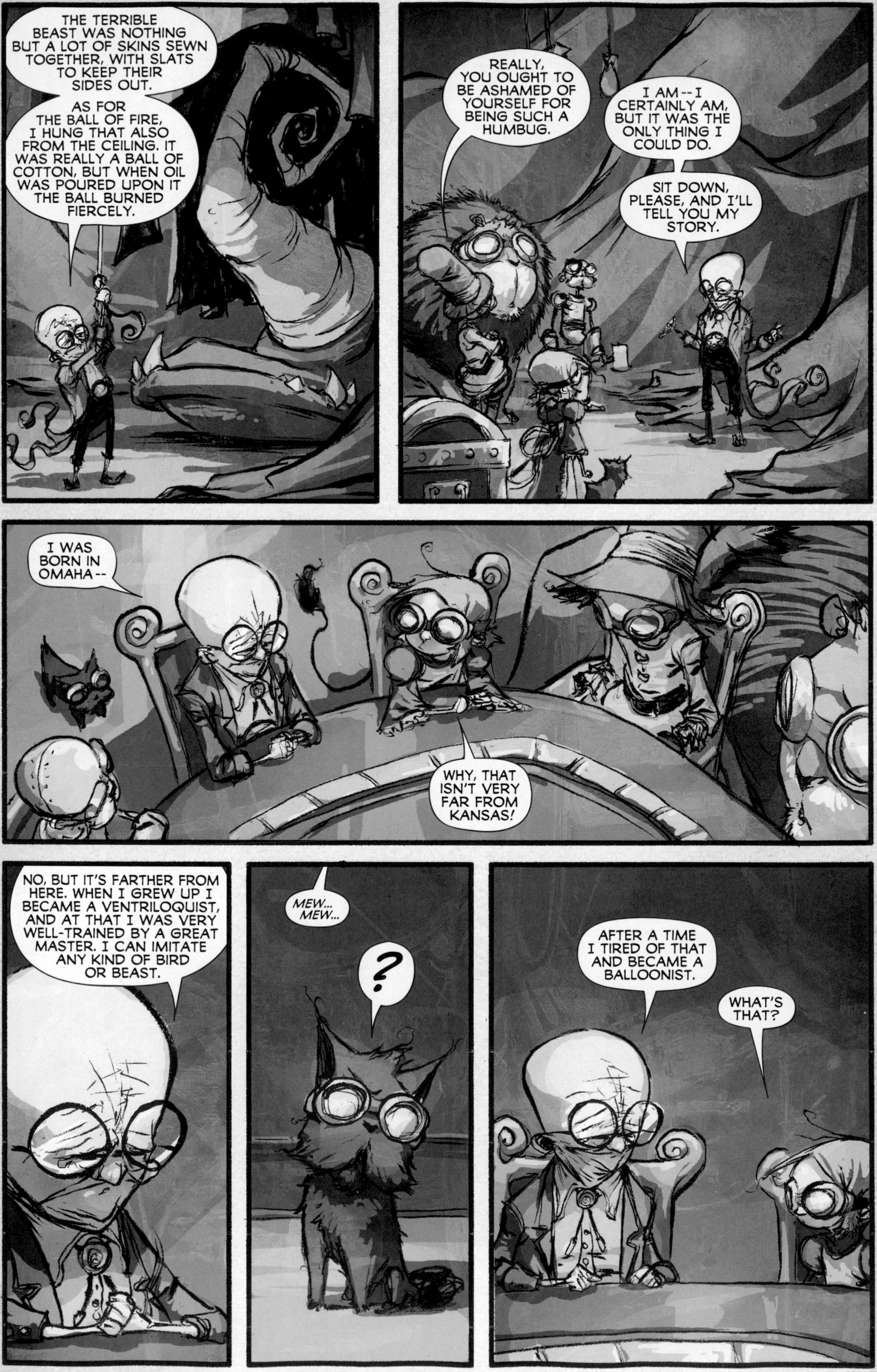
THE TERRIBLE BEAST WAS NOTHING BUT A LOT OF SKINS SEWN TOGETHER, WITH SLATS TO KEEP THEIR SIDES OUT.
AS FOR THE BALL OF FIRE, I HUNG THAT ALSO FROM THE CEILING. IT WAS REALLY A BALL OF COTTON, BUT WHEN OIL WAS POURED UPON IT THE BALL BURNED FIERCELY.
REALLY, YOU OUGHT TO BE ASHAMED OF YOURSELF FOR BEING SUCH A HUMBUG.
I AM -- I CERTAINLY AM, BUT IT WAS THE ONLY THING I COULD DO.
SIT DOWN, PLEASE, AND I'LL TELL YOU MY STORY.
I WAS BORN IN OMAHA --
WHY, THAT ISN'T VERY FAR FROM KANSAS!
NO, BUT IT'S FARTHER FROM HERE. WHEN I GREW UP I BECAME A VENTRILOQUIST, AND AT THAT I WAS VERY WELL-TRAINED BY A GREAT MASTER. I CAN IMITATE ANY KIND OF BIRD OR BEAST.
MEW... MEW...
?
AFTER A TIME I TIRED OF THAT AND BECAME A BALLOONIST.
WHAT'S THAT?

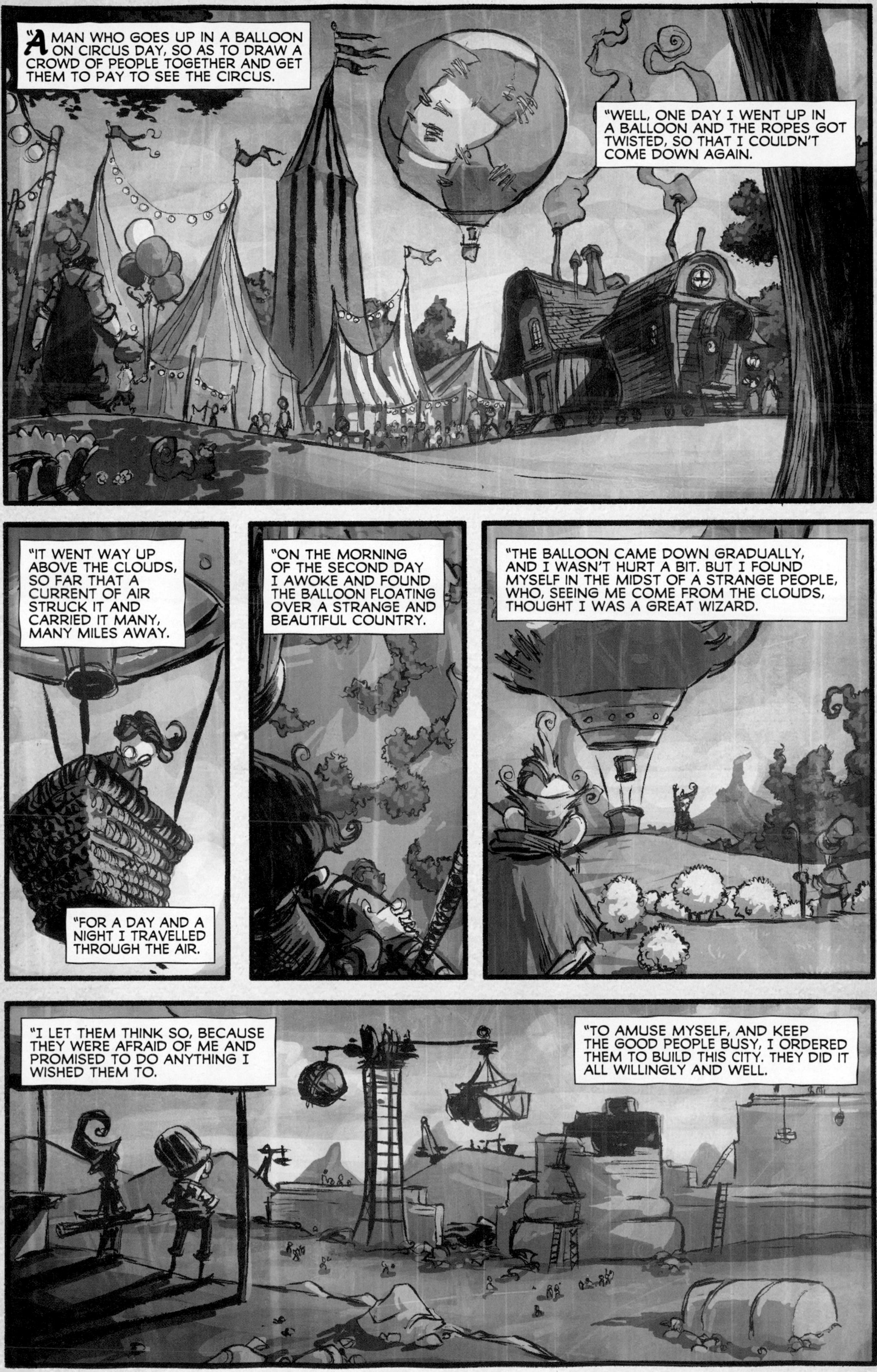
"A MAN WHO GOES UP IN A BALLOON ON CIRCUS DAY, SO AS TO DRAW A CROWD OF PEOPLE TOGETHER AND GET THEM TO PAY TO SEE THE CIRCUS.
"WELL, ONE DAY I WENT UP IN A BALLOON AND THE ROPES GOT TWISTED, SO THAT I COULDN'T COME DOWN AGAIN.
"IT WENT WAY UP ABOVE THE CLOUDS, SO FAR THAT A CURRENT OF AIR STRUCK IT AND CARRIED IT MANY, MANY MILES AWAY.
"FOR A DAY AND A NIGHT I TRAVELLED THROUGH THE AIR.
"ON THE MORNING OF THE SECOND DAY I AWOKE AND FOUND THE BALLOON FLOATING OVER A STRANGE AND BEAUTIFUL COUNTRY.
"THE BALLOON CAME DOWN GRADUALLY, AND I WASN'T HURT A BIT. BUT I FOUND MYSELF IN THE MIDST OF A STRANGE PEOPLE, WHO, SEEING ME COME FROM THE CLOUDS, THOUGHT I WAS A GREAT WIZARD.
"I LET THEM THINK SO, BECAUSE THEY WERE AFRAID OF ME AND PROMISED TO DO ANYTHING I WISHED THEM TO.
"TO AMUSE MYSELF, AND KEEP THE GOOD PEOPLE BUSY, I ORDERED THEM TO BUILD THIS CITY. THEY DID IT ALL WILLINGLY AND WELL.

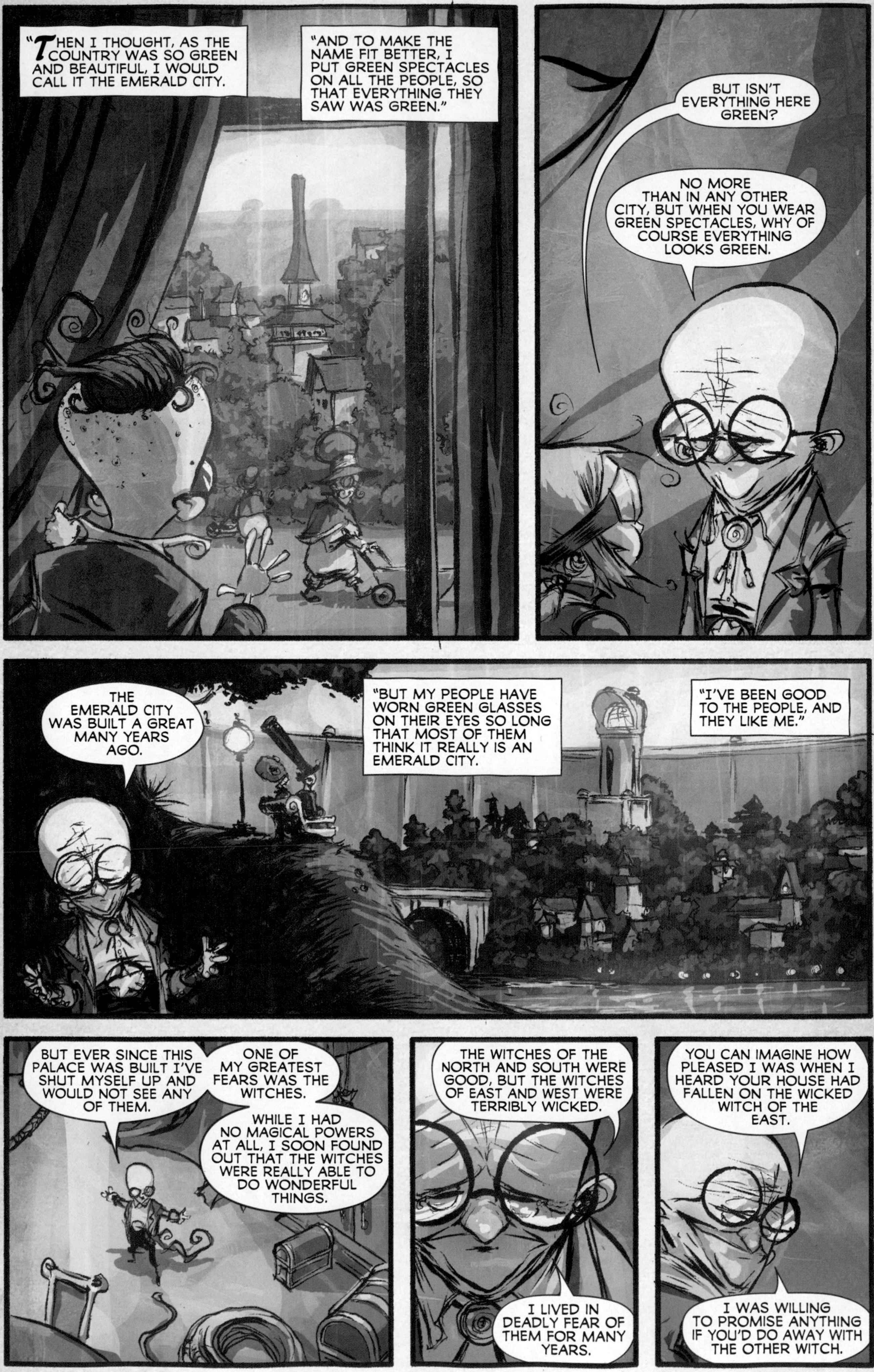
"THEN I THOUGHT, AS THE COUNTRY WAS SO GREEN AND BEAUTIFUL, I WOULD CALL IT THE EMERALD CITY.
"AND TO MAKE THE NAME FIT BETTER, I PUT GREEN SPECTACLES ON ALL THE PEOPLE, SO THAT EVERYTHING THEY SAW WAS GREEN."
BUT ISN'T EVERYTHING HERE GREEN?
NO MORE THAN IN ANY OTHER CITY, BUT WHEN YOU WEAR GREEN SPECTACLES, WHY OF COURSE EVERYTHING LOOKS GREEN.
THE EMERALD CITY WAS BUILT A GREAT MANY YEARS AGO.
"BUT MY PEOPLE HAVE WORN GREEN GLASSES ON THEIR EYES SO LONG THAT MOST OF THEM THINK IT REALLY IS AN EMERALD CITY.
"I'VE BEEN GOOD TO THE PEOPLE, AND THEY LIKE ME."
BUT EVER SINCE THIS PALACE WAS BUILT I'VE SHUT MYSELF UP AND WOULD NOT SEE ANY OF THEM.
ONE OF MY GREATEST FEARS WAS THE WITCHES.
WHILE I HAD NO MAGICAL POWERS AT ALL, I SOON FOUND OUT THAT THE WITCHES WERE REALLY ABLE TO DO WONDERFUL THINGS.
THE WITCHES OF THE NORTH AND SOUTH WERE GOOD, BUT THE WITCHES OF EAST AND WEST WERE TERRIBLY WICKED.
I LIVED IN DEADLY FEAR OF THEM FOR MANY YEARS.
YOU CAN IMAGINE HOW PLEASED I WAS WHEN I HEARD YOUR HOUSE HAD FALLEN ON THE WICKED WITCH OF THE EAST.
I WAS WILLING TO PROMISE ANYTHING IF YOU'D DO AWAY WITH THE OTHER WITCH.

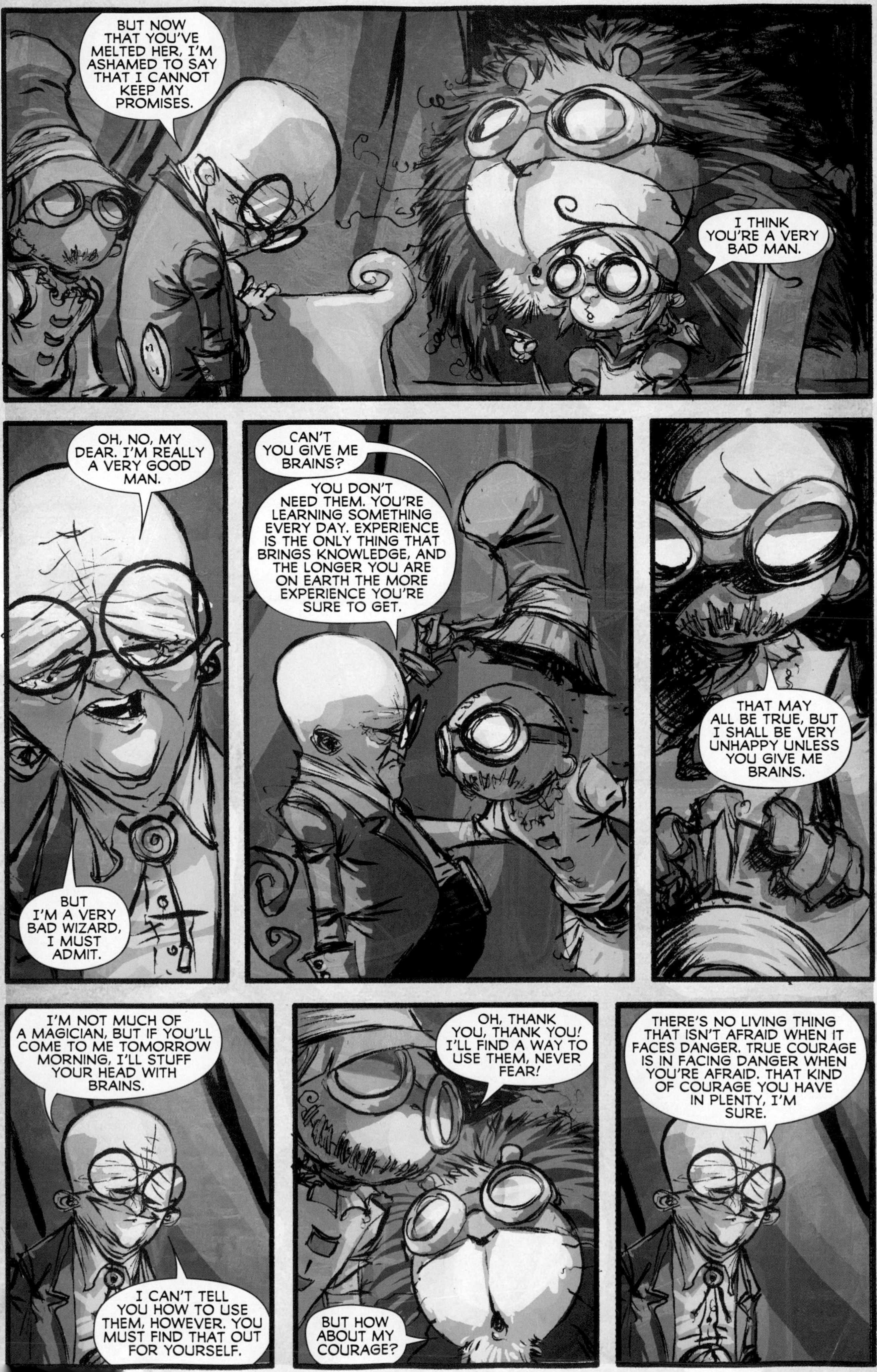
BUT NOW THAT YOU'VE MELTED HER, I'M ASHAMED TO SAY THAT I CANNOT KEEP MY PROMISES.
I THINK YOU'RE A VERY BAD MAN.
OH, NO, MY DEAR. I'M REALLY A VERY GOOD MAN.
BUT I'M A VERY BAD WIZARD, I MUST ADMIT.
CAN'T YOU GIVE ME BRAINS?
YOU DON'T NEED THEM. YOU'RE LEARNING SOMETHING EVERY DAY. EXPERIENCE IS THE ONLY THING THAT BRINGS KNOWLEDGE, AND THE LONGER YOU ARE ON EARTH THE MORE EXPERIENCE YOU'RE SURE TO GET.
THAT MAY ALL BE TRUE, BUT I SHALL BE VERY UNHAPPY UNLESS YOU GIVE ME BRAINS.
I'M NOT MUCH OF A MAGICIAN, BUT IF YOU'LL COME TO ME TOMORROW MORNING, I'LL STUFF YOUR HEAD WITH BRAINS.
I CAN'T TELL YOU HOW TO USE THEM, HOWEVER. YOU MUST FIND THAT OUT FOR YOURSELF.
OH, THANK YOU, THANK YOU! I'LL FIND A WAY TO USE THEM, NEVER FEAR!
BUT HOW ABOUT MY COURAGE?
THERE'S NO LIVING THING THAT ISN'T AFRAID WHEN IT FACES DANGER. TRUE COURAGE IS IN FACING DANGER WHEN YOU'RE AFRAID. THAT KIND OF COURAGE YOU HAVE IN PLENTY, I'M SURE.

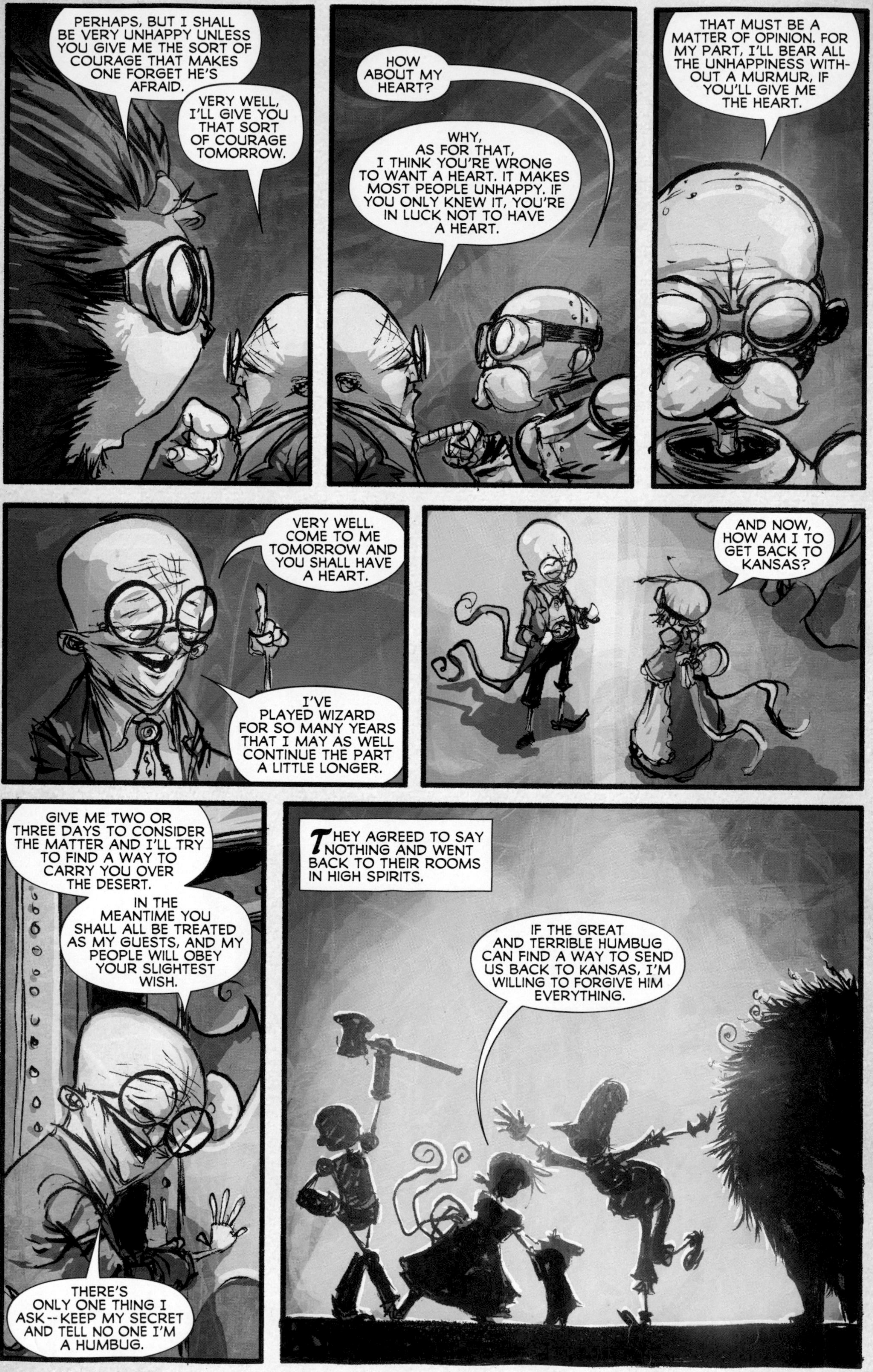
PERHAPS, BUT I SHALL BE VERY UNHAPPY UNLESS YOU GIVE ME THE SORT OF COURAGE THAT MAKES ONE FORGET HE'S AFRAID.
VERY WELL, I'LL GIVE YOU THAT SORT OF COURAGE TOMORROW.
HOW ABOUT MY HEART?
WHY, AS FOR THAT, I THINK YOU'RE WRONG TO WANT A HEART. IT MAKES MOST PEOPLE UNHAPPY. IF YOU ONLY KNEW IT, YOU'RE IN LUCK NOT TO HAVE A HEART.
THAT MUST BE A MATTER OF OPINION. FOR MY PART, I'LL BEAR ALL THE UNHAPPINESS WITHOUT A MURMUR, IF YOU'LL GIVE ME THE HEART.
VERY WELL. COME TO ME TOMORROW AND YOU SHALL HAVE A HEART.
I'VE PLAYED WIZARD FOR SO MANY YEARS THAT I MAY AS WELL CONTINUE THE PART A LITTLE LONGER.
AND NOW, HOW AM I TO GET BACK TO KANSAS?
GIVE ME TWO OR THREE DAYS TO CONSIDER THE MATTER AND I'LL TRY TO FIND A WAY TO CARRY YOU OVER THE DESERT.
IN THE MEANTIME YOU SHALL ALL BE TREATED AS MY GUESTS, AND MY PEOPLE WILL OBEY YOUR SLIGHTEST WISH.
THERE'S ONLY ONE THING I ASK--KEEP MY SECRET AND TELL NO ONE I'M A HUMBUG.
THEY AGREED TO SAY NOTHING AND WENT BACK TO THEIR ROOMS IN HIGH SPIRITS.
IF THE GREAT AND TERRIBLE HUMBUG CAN FIND A WAY TO SEND US BACK TO KANSAS, I'M WILLING TO FORGIVE HIM EVERYTHING.

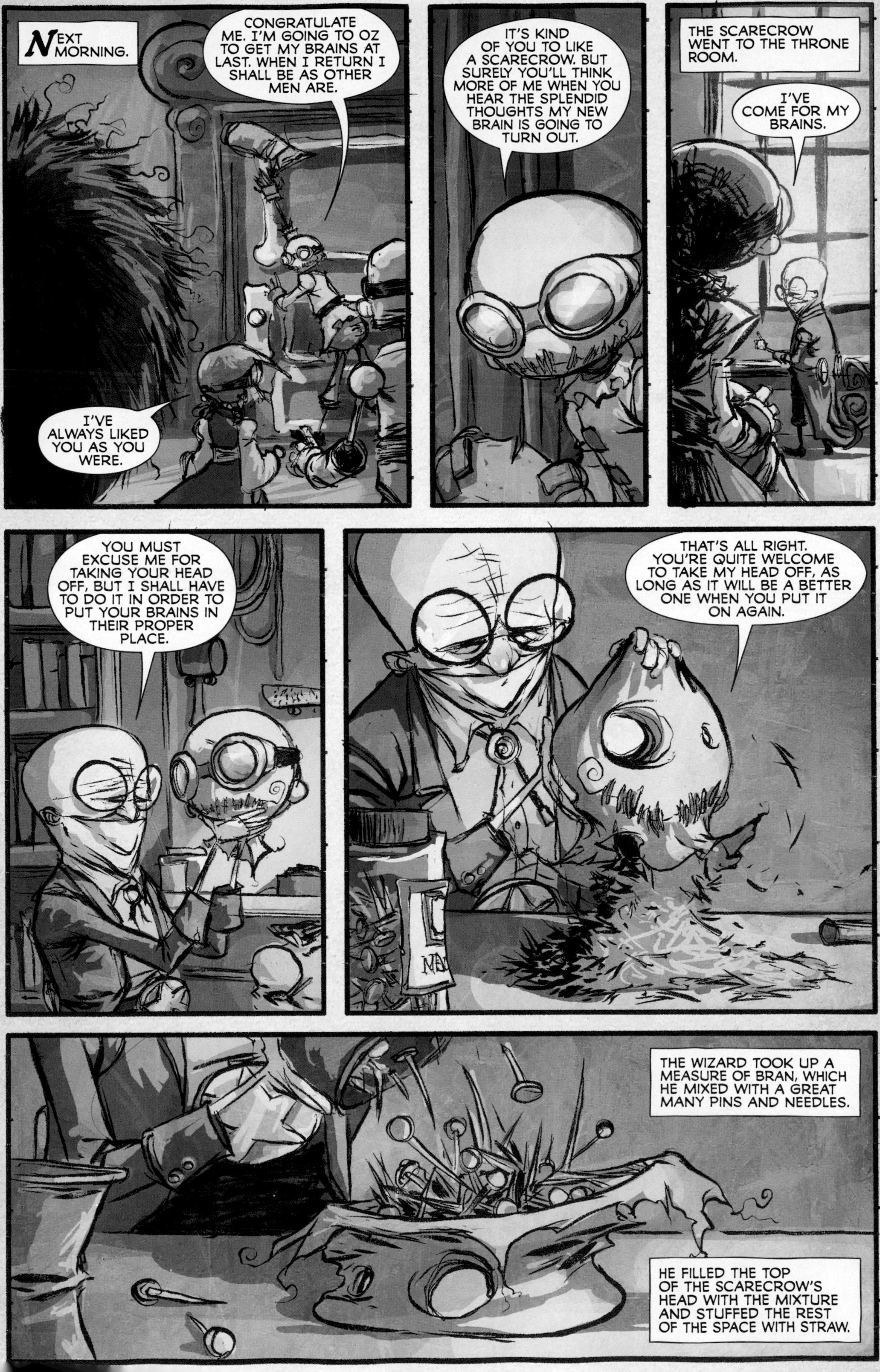
NEXT MORNING.
CONGRATULATE ME. I'M GOING TO OZ TO GET MY BRAINS AT LAST. WHEN I RETURN I SHALL BE AS OTHER MEN ARE.
I'VE ALWAYS LIKED YOU AS YOU WERE.
IT'S KIND OF YOU TO LIKE A SCARECROW. BUT SURELY YOU'LL THINK MORE OF ME WHEN YOU HEAR THE SPLENDID THOUGHTS MY NEW BRAIN IS GOING TO TURN OUT.
THE SCARECROW WENT TO THE THRONE ROOM.
I'VE COME FOR MY BRAINS.
YOU MUST EXCUSE ME FOR TAKING YOUR HEAD OFF, BUT I SHALL HAVE TO DO IT IN ORDER TO PUT YOUR BRAINS IN THEIR PROPER PLACE.
THAT'S ALL RIGHT. YOU'RE QUITE WELCOME TO TAKE MY HEAD OFF, AS LONG AS IT WILL BE A BETTER ONE WHEN YOU PUT IT ON AGAIN.
THE WIZARD TOOK UP A MEASURE OF BRAN, WHICH HE MIXED WITH A GREAT MANY PINS AND NEEDLES.
HE FILLED THE TOP OF THE SCARECROW'S HEAD WITH THE MIXTURE AND STUFFED THE REST OF THE SPACE WITH STRAW.

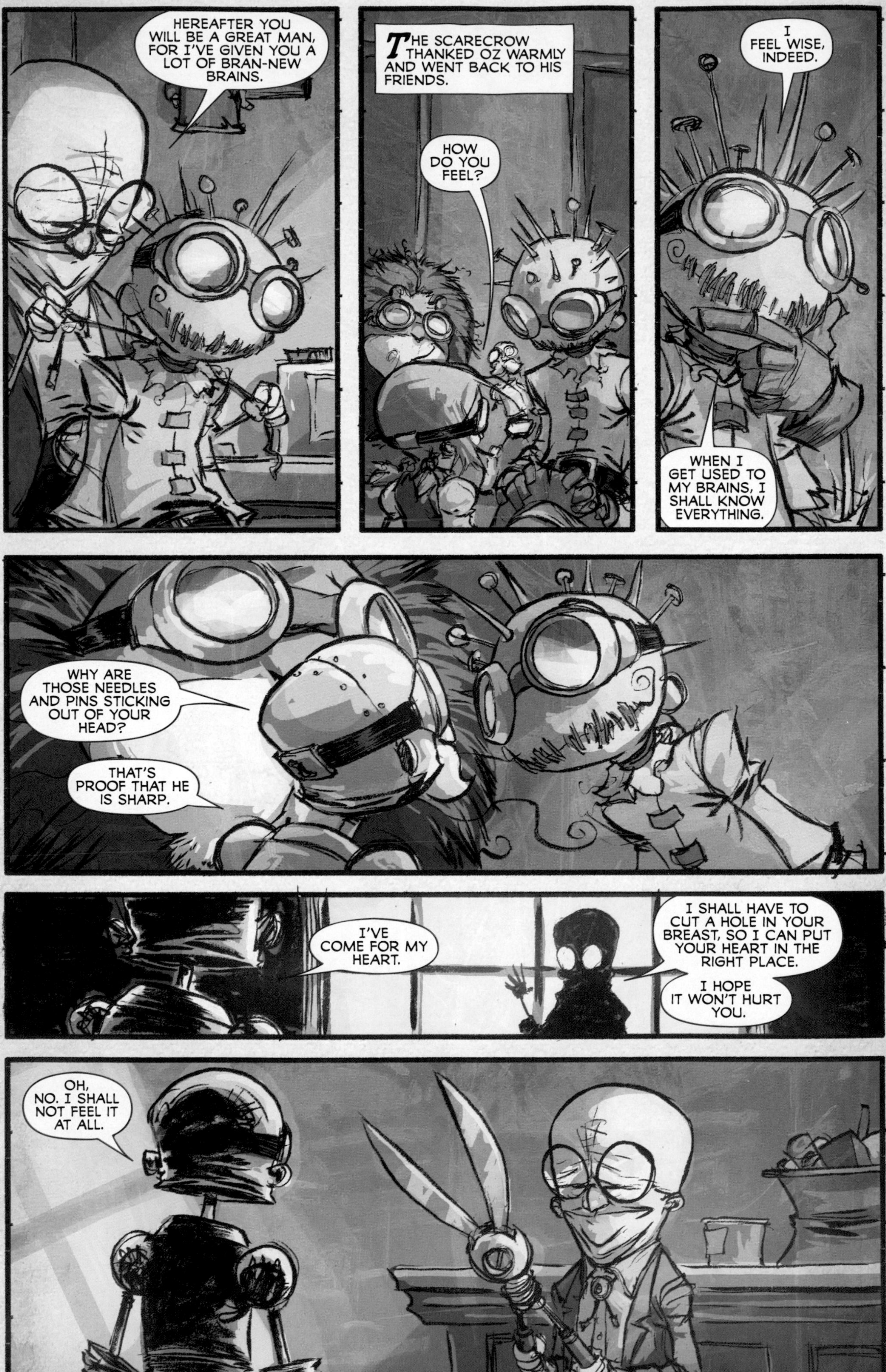
HEREAFTER YOU WILL BE A GREAT MAN, FOR I'VE GIVEN YOU A LOT OF BRAN-NEW BRAINS.
THE SCARECROW THANKED OZ WARMLY AND WENT BACK TO HIS FRIENDS.
HOW DO YOU FEEL?
I FEEL WISE, INDEED.
WHEN I GET USED TO MY BRAINS, I SHALL KNOW EVERYTHING.
WHY ARE THOSE NEEDLES AND PINS STICKING OUT OF YOUR HEAD?
THAT'S PROOF THAT HE IS SHARP.
I'VE COME FOR MY HEART.
I SHALL HAVE TO CUT A HOLE IN YOUR BREAST, SO I CAN PUT YOUR HEART IN THE RIGHT PLACE.
I HOPE IT WON'T HURT YOU.
OH, NO. I SHALL NOT FEEL IT AT ALL.

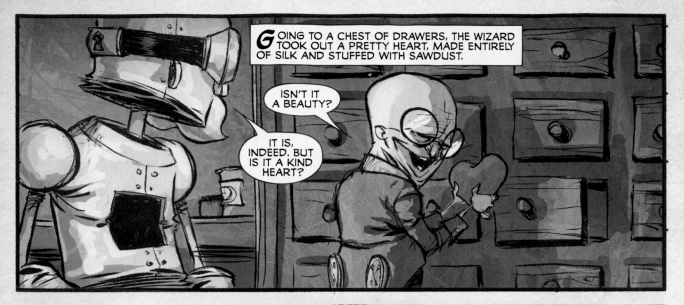

GOING TO A CHEST OF DRAWERS, THE WIZARD TOOK OUT A PRETTY HEART, MADE ENTIRELY OF SILK AND STUFFED WITH SAWDUST.

ISN'T IT A BEAUTY?

IT IS, INDEED. BUT IS IT A KIND HEART?

OH, VERY!

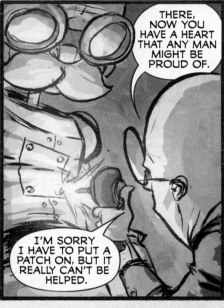

THERE, NOW YOU HAVE A HEART THAT ANY MAN MIGHT BE PROUD OF.

I'M SORRY I HAVE TO PUT A PATCH ON, BUT IT REALLY CAN'T BE HELPED.

NEVER MIND THE PATCH. I'M GRATEFUL TO YOU, AND SHALL NEVER FORGET YOUR KINDNESS.

DON'T SPEAK OF IT.

THE TIN WOODMAN WENT BACK TO HIS FRIENDS.

WE WISH YOU EVERY JOY ON ACCOUNT OF YOUR GOOD FORTUNE!

COME IN.

I'VE COME FOR MY COURAGE.

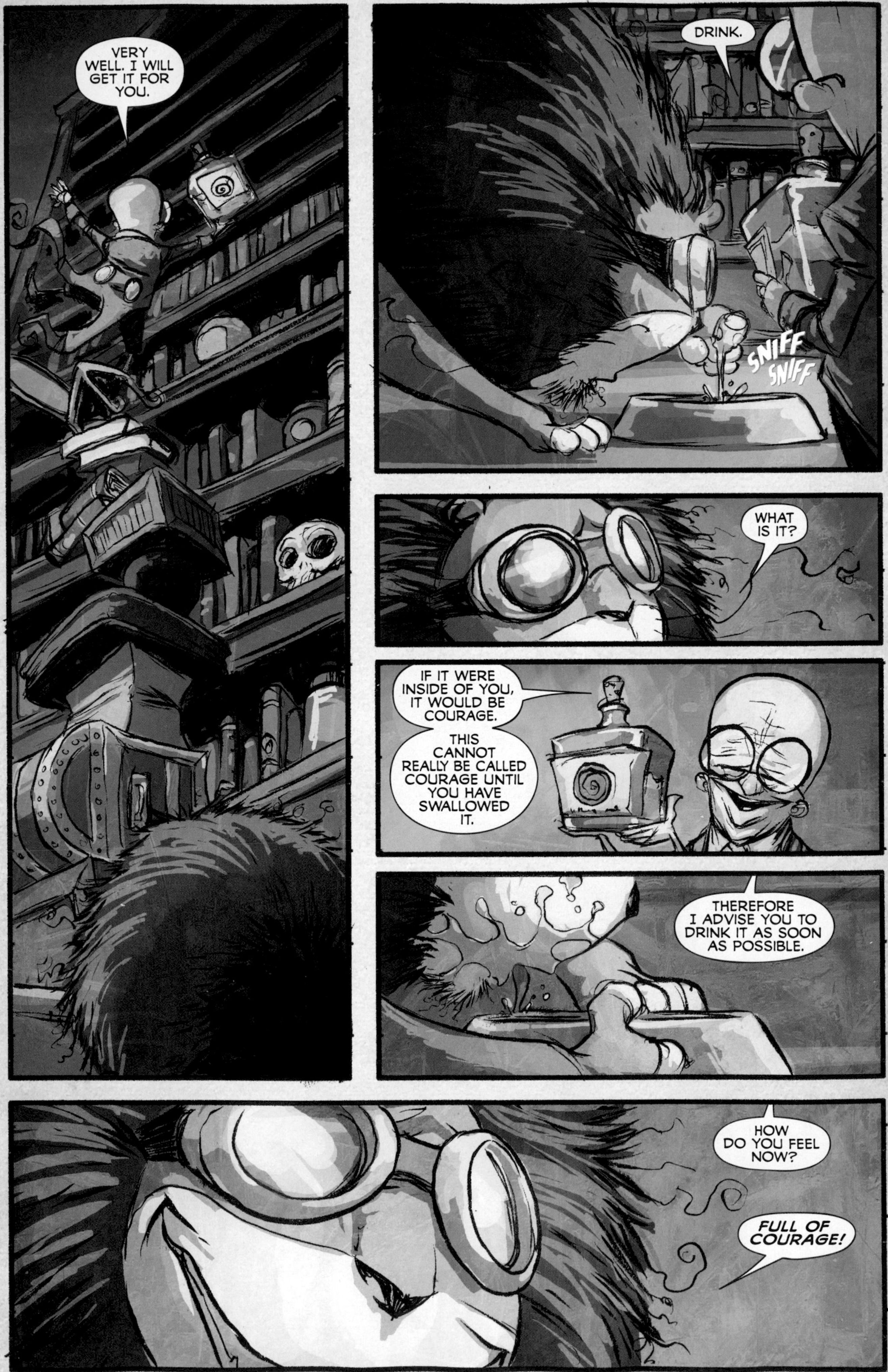
VERY WELL. I WILL GET IT FOR YOU.
DRINK.
SNIFF SNIFF
WHAT IS IT?
IF IT WERE INSIDE OF YOU, IT WOULD BE COURAGE.
THIS CANNOT REALLY BE CALLED COURAGE UNTIL YOU HAVE SWALLOWED IT.
THEREFORE I ADVISE YOU TO DRINK IT AS SOON AS POSSIBLE.
HOW DO YOU FEEL NOW?
FULL OF COURAGE!

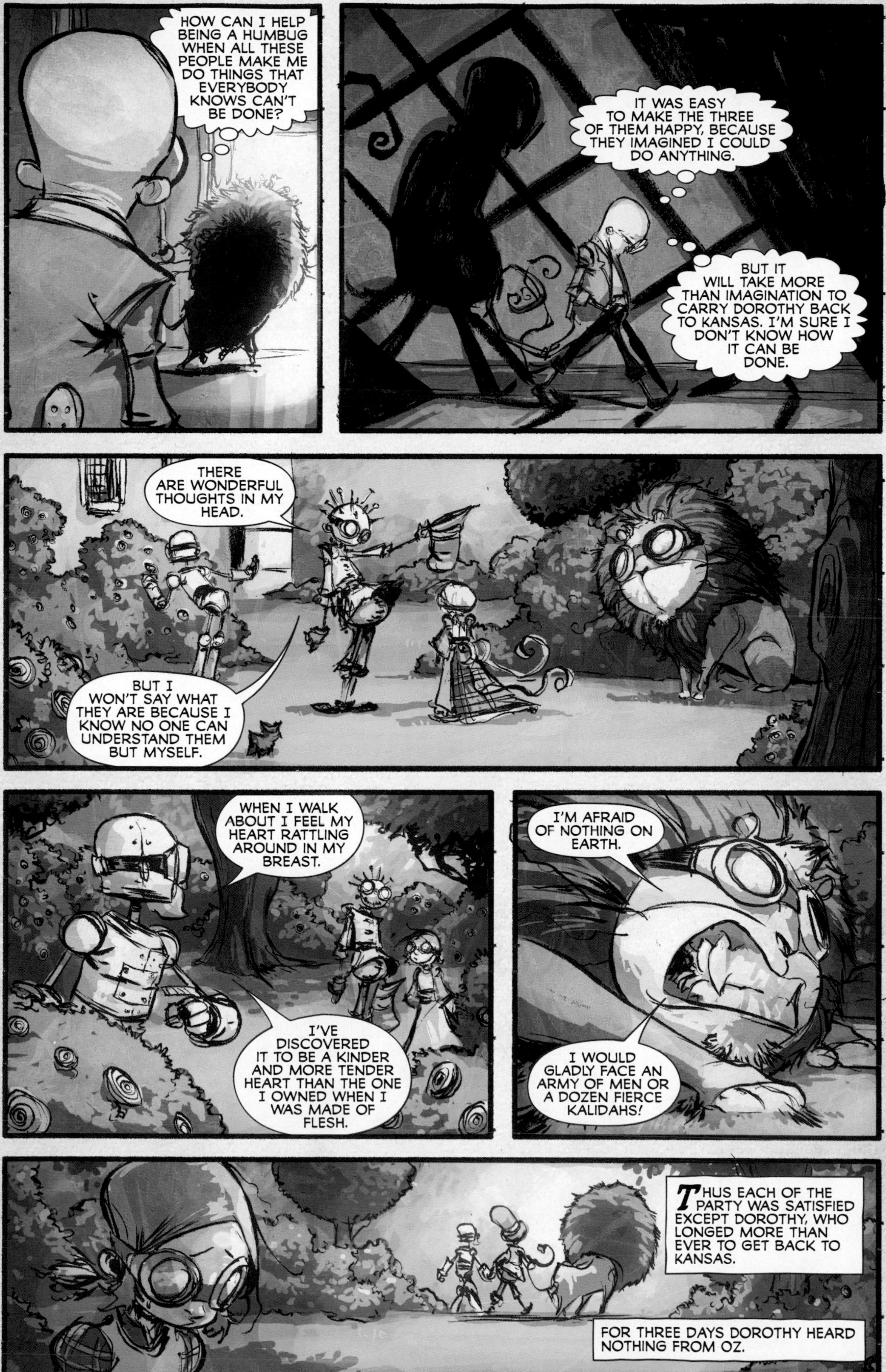
HOW CAN I HELP BEING A HUMBUG WHEN ALL THESE PEOPLE MAKE ME DO THINGS THAT EVERYBODY KNOWS CAN'T BE DONE?
IT WAS EASY TO MAKE THE THREE OF THEM HAPPY, BECAUSE THEY IMAGINED I COULD DO ANYTHING.
BUT IT WILL TAKE MORE THAN IMAGINATION TO CARRY DOROTHY BACK TO KANSAS. I'M SURE I DON'T KNOW HOW IT CAN BE DONE.
THERE ARE WONDERFUL THOUGHTS IN MY HEAD.
BUT I WON'T SAY WHAT THEY ARE BECAUSE I KNOW NO ONE CAN UNDERSTAND THEM BUT MYSELF.
WHEN I WALK ABOUT I FEEL MY HEART RATTLING AROUND IN MY BREAST.
I'VE DISCOVERED IT TO BE A KINDER AND MORE TENDER HEART THAN THE ONE I OWNED WHEN I WAS MADE OF FLESH.
I'M AFRAID OF NOTHING ON EARTH.
I WOULD GLADLY FACE AN ARMY OF MEN OR A DOZEN FIERCE KALIDAHS!
THUS EACH OF THE PARTY WAS SATISFIED EXCEPT DOROTHY, WHO LONGED MORE THAN EVER TO GET BACK TO KANSAS.
FOR THREE DAYS DOROTHY HEARD NOTHING FROM OZ.

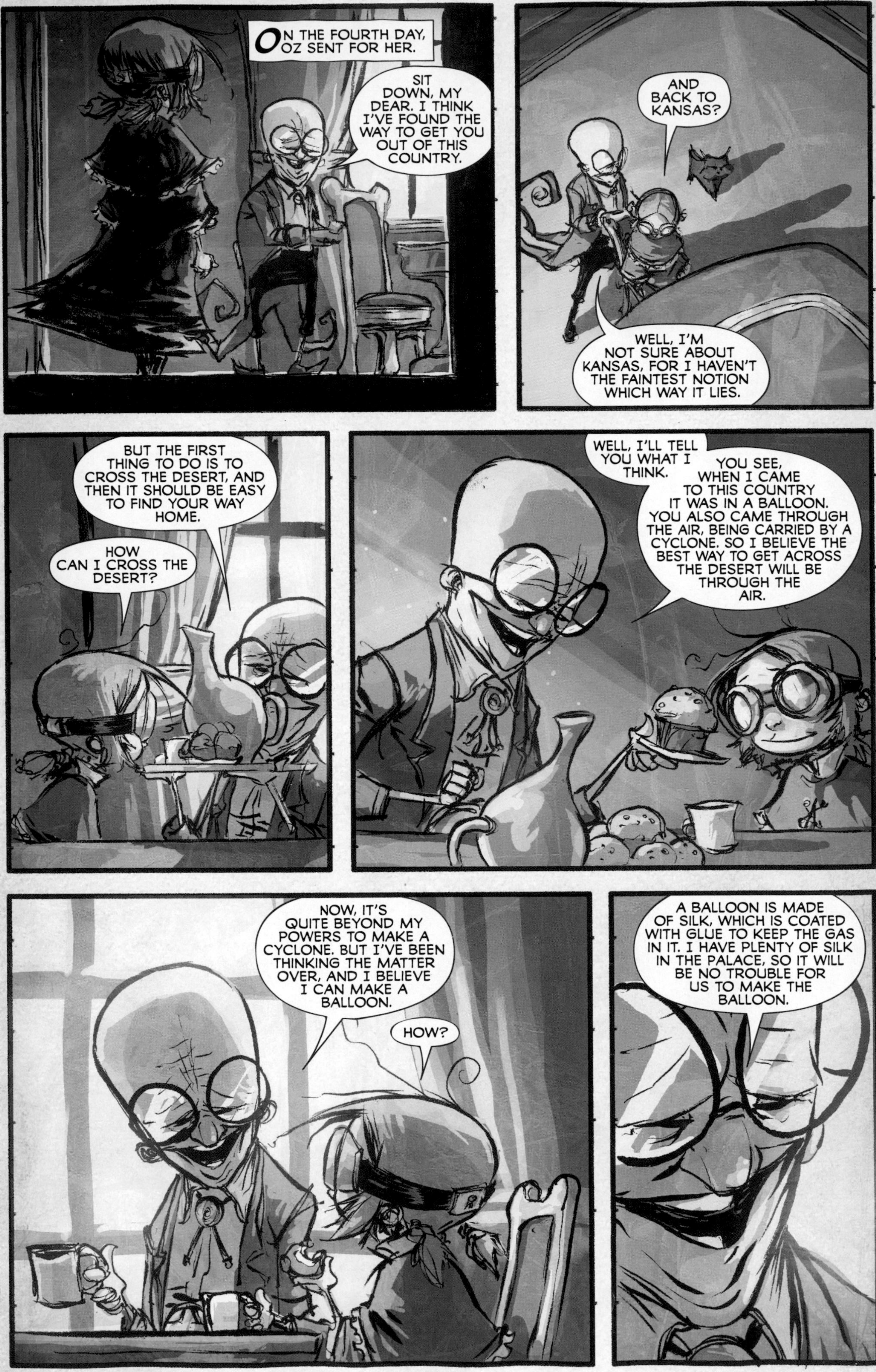
ON THE FOURTH DAY, OZ SENT FOR HER.
SIT DOWN, MY DEAR. I THINK I'VE FOUND THE WAY TO GET YOU OUT OF THIS COUNTRY.
AND BACK TO KANSAS?
WELL, I'M NOT SURE ABOUT KANSAS, FOR I HAVEN'T THE FAINTEST NOTION WHICH WAY IT LIES.
BUT THE FIRST THING TO DO IS TO CROSS THE DESERT, AND THEN IT SHOULD BE EASY TO FIND YOUR WAY HOME.
HOW CAN I CROSS THE DESERT?
WELL, I'LL TELL YOU WHAT I THINK.
YOU SEE, WHEN I CAME TO THIS COUNTRY IT WAS IN A BALLOON. YOU ALSO CAME THROUGH THE AIR, BEING CARRIED BY A CYCLONE. SO I BELIEVE THE BEST WAY TO GET ACROSS THE DESERT WILL BE THROUGH THE AIR.
NOW, IT'S QUITE BEYOND MY POWERS TO MAKE A CYCLONE. BUT I'VE BEEN THINKING THE MATTER OVER, AND I BELIEVE I CAN MAKE A BALLOON.
HOW?
A BALLOON IS MADE OF SILK, WHICH IS COATED WITH GLUE TO KEEP THE GAS IN IT. I HAVE PLENTY OF SILK IN THE PALACE, SO IT WILL BE NO TROUBLE FOR US TO MAKE THE BALLOON.

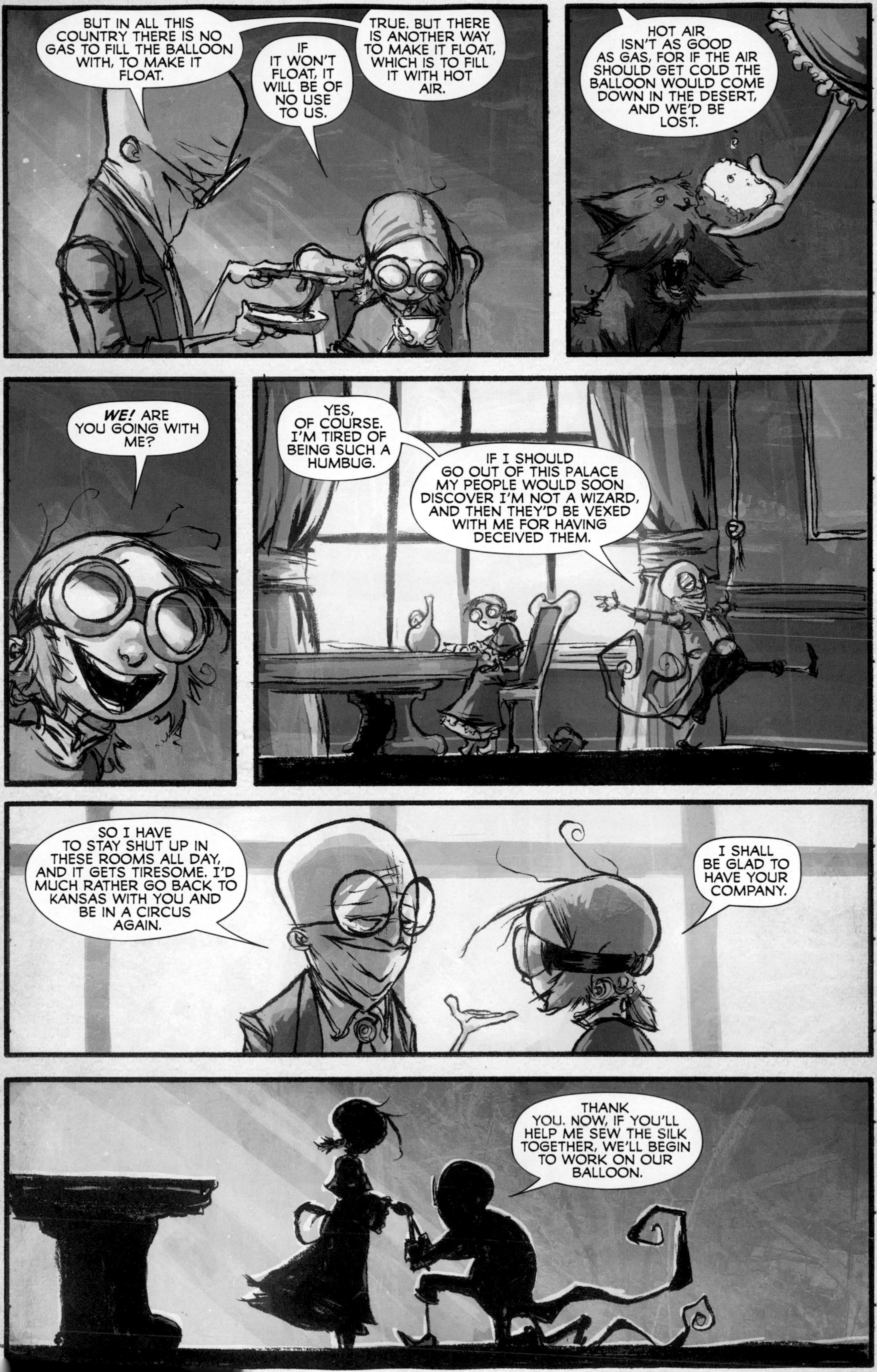
BUT IN ALL THIS COUNTRY THERE IS NO GAS TO FILL THE BALLOON WITH, TO MAKE IT FLOAT.
IF IT WON'T FLOAT, IT WILL BE OF NO USE TO US.
TRUE. BUT THERE IS ANOTHER WAY TO MAKE IT FLOAT, WHICH IS TO FILL IT WITH HOT AIR.
HOT AIR ISN'T AS GOOD AS GAS, FOR IF THE AIR SHOULD GET COLD THE BALLOON WOULD COME DOWN IN THE DESERT, AND WE'D BE LOST.
WE! ARE YOU GOING WITH ME?
YES, OF COURSE. I'M TIRED OF BEING SUCH A HUMBUG.
IF I SHOULD GO OUT OF THIS PALACE MY PEOPLE WOULD SOON DISCOVER I'M NOT A WIZARD, AND THEN THEY'D BE VEXED WITH ME FOR HAVING DECEIVED THEM.
SO I HAVE TO STAY SHUT UP IN THESE ROOMS ALL DAY, AND IT GETS TIRESOME. I'D MUCH RATHER GO BACK TO KANSAS WITH YOU AND BE IN A CIRCUS AGAIN.
I SHALL BE GLAD TO HAVE YOUR COMPANY.
THANK YOU. NOW, IF YOU'LL HELP ME SEW THE SILK TOGETHER, WE'LL BEGIN TO WORK ON OUR BALLOON.

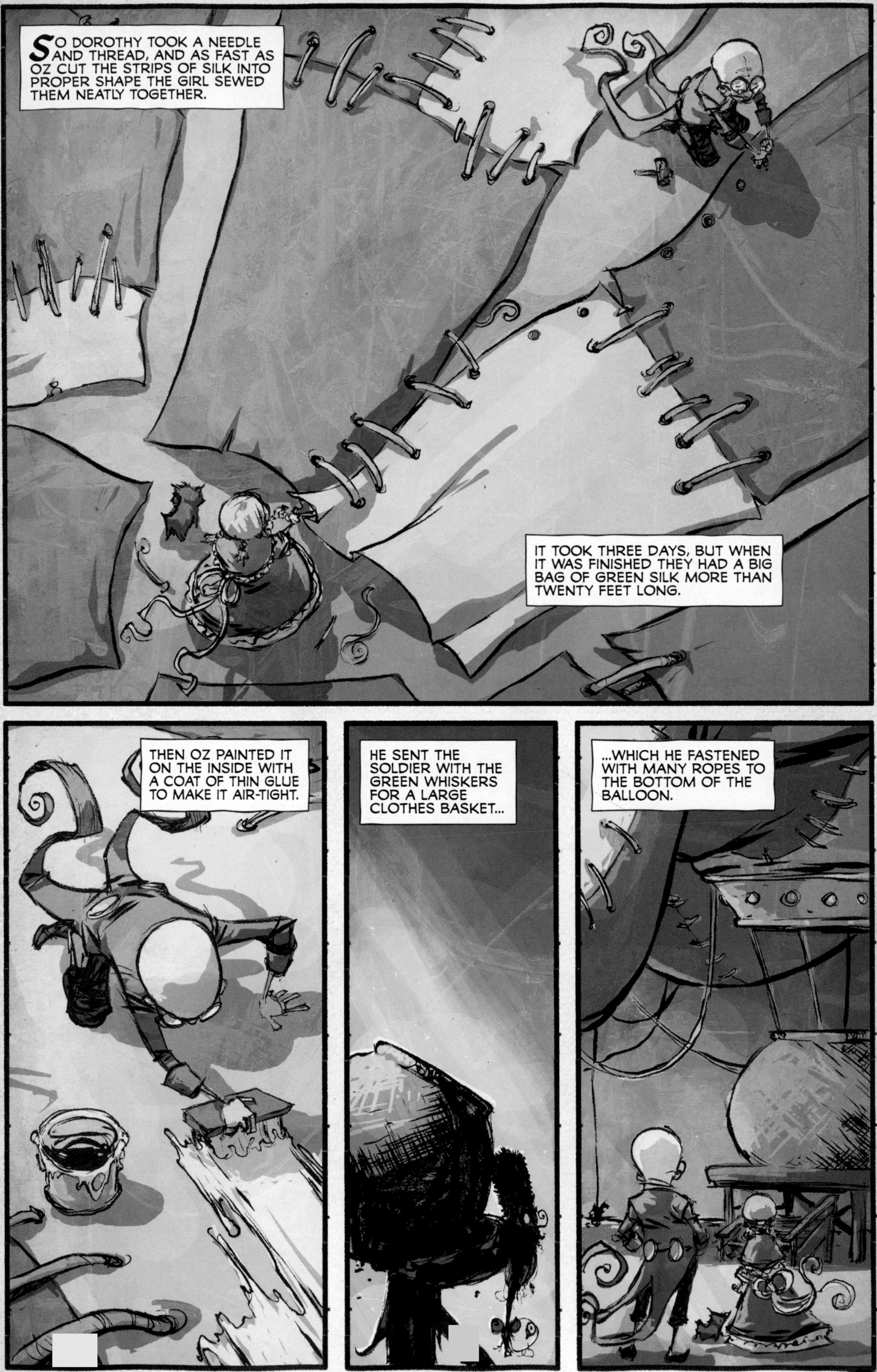
SO DOROTHY TOOK A NEEDLE AND THREAD, AND AS FAST AS OZ CUT THE STRIPS OF SILK INTO PROPER SHAPE THE GIRL SEWED THEM NEATLY TOGETHER.
IT TOOK THREE DAYS, BUT WHEN IT WAS FINISHED THEY HAD A BIG BAG OF GREEN SILK MORE THAN TWENTY FEET LONG.
THEN OZ PAINTED IT ON THE INSIDE WITH A COAT OF THIN GLUE TO MAKE IT AIR-TIGHT.
HE SENT THE SOLDIER WITH THE GREEN WHISKERS FOR A LARGE CLOTHES BASKET...
...WHICH HE FASTENED WITH MANY ROPES TO THE BOTTOM OF THE BALLOON.

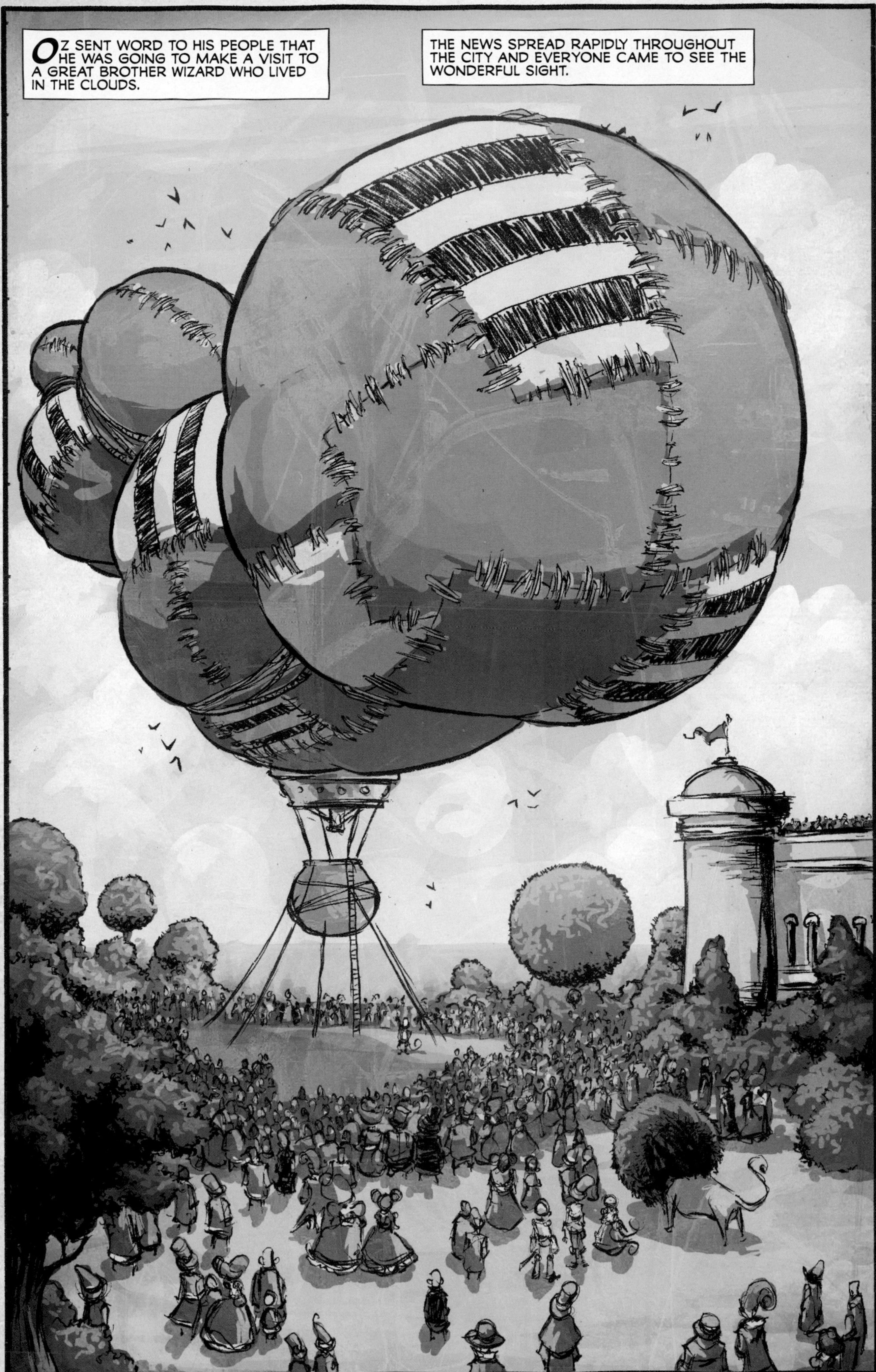
OZ SENT WORD TO HIS PEOPLE THAT HE WAS GOING TO MAKE A VISIT TO A GREAT BROTHER WIZARD WHO LIVED IN THE CLOUDS.
THE NEWS SPREAD RAPIDLY THROUGHOUT THE CITY AND EVERYONE CAME TO SEE THE WONDERFUL SIGHT.

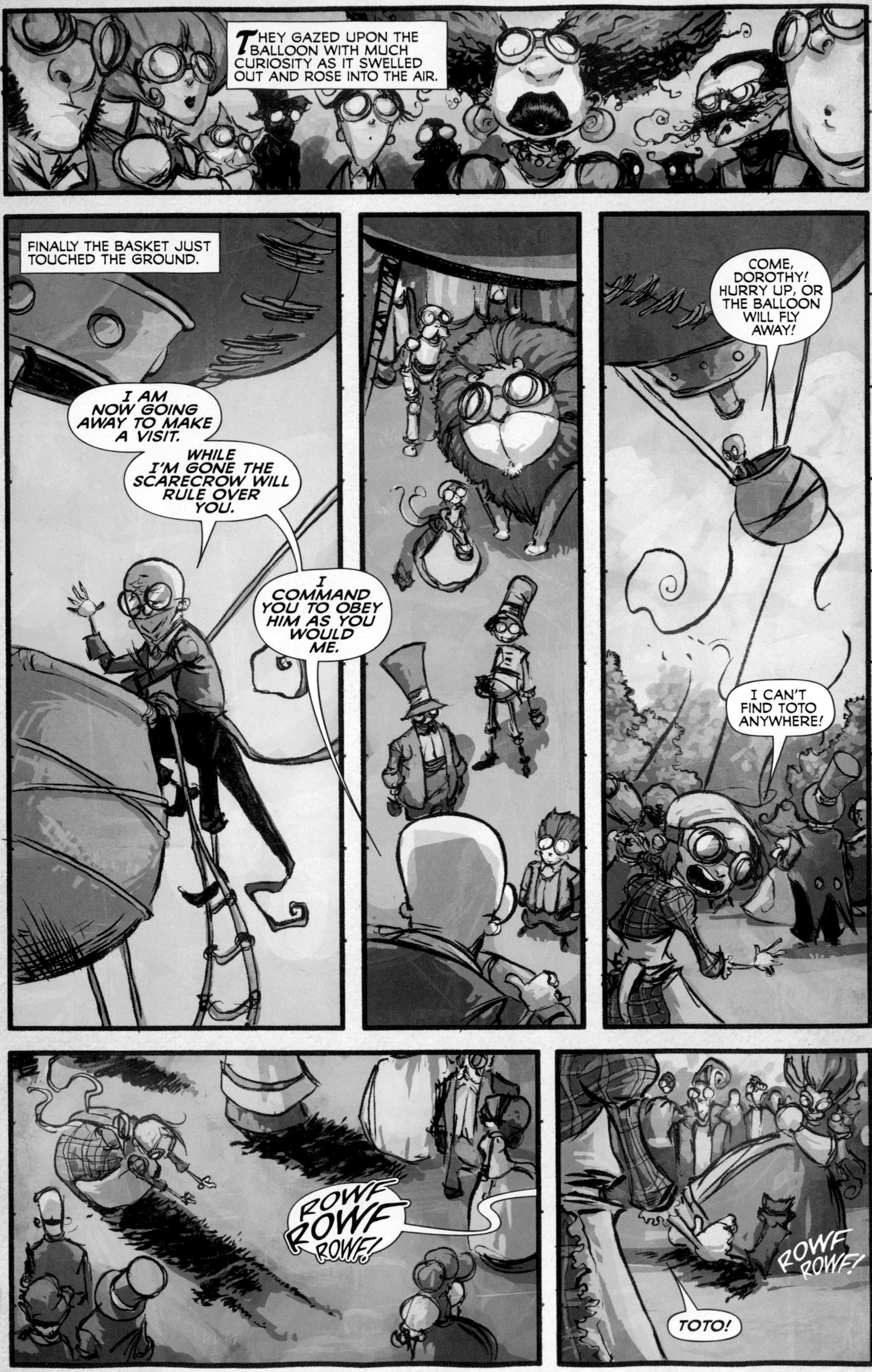
THEY GAZED UPON THE BALLOON WITH MUCH CURIOSITY AS IT SWELLED OUT AND ROSE INTO THE AIR.
FINALLY THE BASKET JUST TOUCHED THE GROUND.
I AM NOW GOING AWAY TO MAKE A VISIT.
WHILE I'M GONE THE SCARECROW WILL RULE OVER YOU.
I COMMAND YOU TO OBEY HIM AS YOU WOULD ME.
COME, DOROTHY! HURRY UP, OR THE BALLOON WILL FLY AWAY!
I CAN'T FIND TOTO ANYWHERE!
ROWF ROWF ROWF!
ROWF ROWF!
TOTO!

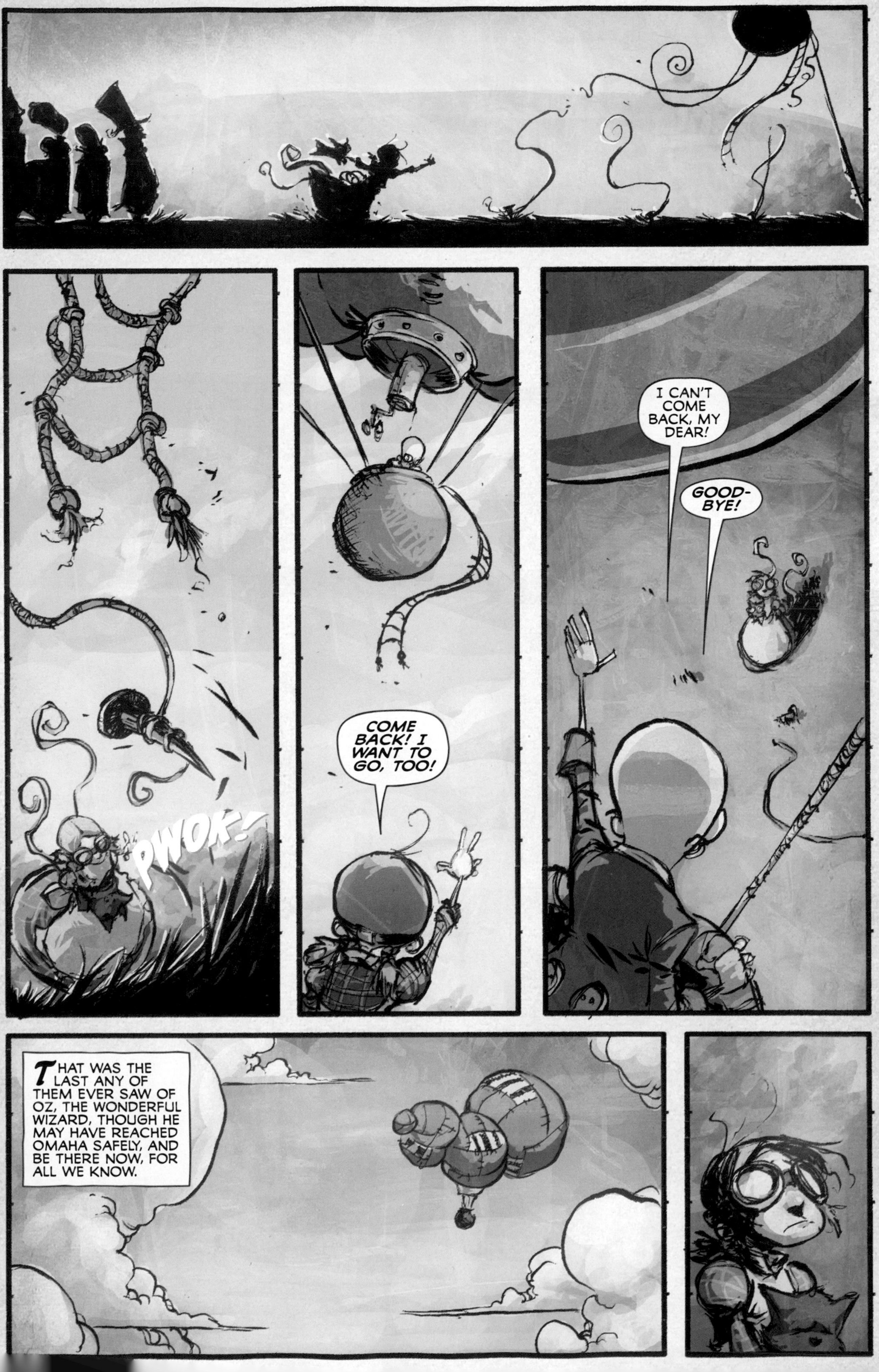

PWOK!
COME BACK! I WANT TO GO, TOO!
I CAN'T COME BACK, MY DEAR!
GOOD-BYE!
THAT WAS THE LAST ANY OF THEM EVER SAW OF OZ, THE WONDERFUL WIZARD, THOUGH HE MAY HAVE REACHED OMAHA SAFELY, AND BE THERE NOW, FOR ALL WE KNOW.

BUT THE PEOPLE REMEMBERED HIM LOVINGLY.

AND HE'S LEFT THE WISE SCARECROW TO RULE OVER US.

OZ WAS ALWAYS OUR FRIEND.

HE BUILT THIS BEAUTIFUL EMERALD CITY.

THERE ISN'T ANOTHER CITY IN ALL THE WORLD THAT'S RULED BY A STUFFED MAN.

AND, SO FAR AS THEY KNEW, THEY WERE QUITE RIGHT.

DOROTHY WEPT BITTERLY AT THE PASSING OF HER HOPE TO GET HOME TO KANSAS AGAIN. BUT WHEN SHE THOUGHT IT ALL OVER, SHE WAS GLAD SHE HAD NOT GONE UP IN A BALLOON.

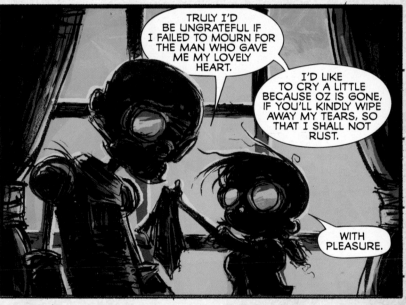

TRULY I'D BE UNGRATEFUL IF I FAILED TO MOURN FOR THE MAN WHO GAVE ME MY LOVELY HEART.

I'D LIKE TO CRY A LITTLE BECAUSE OZ IS GONE, IF YOU'LL KINDLY WIPE AWAY MY TEARS, SO THAT I SHALL NOT RUST.

WITH PLEASURE.

THE MORNING AFTER.

WE'RE NOT SO UNLUCKY, FOR THIS PALACE AND THE EMERALD CITY BELONG TO US, AND WE CAN DO JUST AS WE PLEASE.

WHEN I REMEMBER THAT A SHORT TIME AGO I WAS UP ON A POLE IN A FARMER'S CORNFIELD, AND THAT NOW I'M THE RULER OF THIS BEAUTIFUL CITY, I'M QUITE SATISFIED WITH MY LOT.

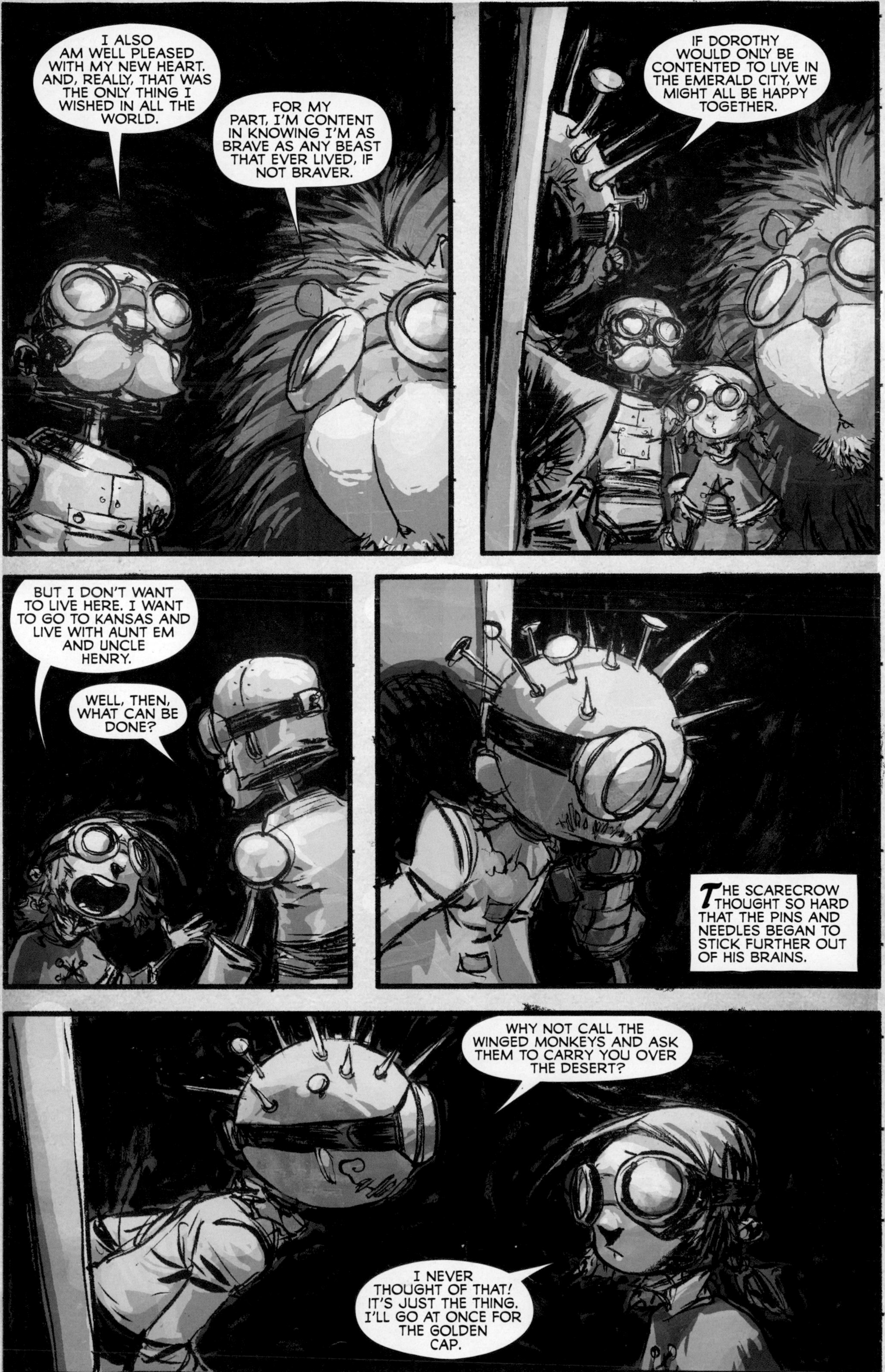
I ALSO AM WELL PLEASED WITH MY NEW HEART. AND, REALLY, THAT WAS THE ONLY THING I WISHED IN ALL THE WORLD.
FOR MY PART, I'M CONTENT IN KNOWING I'M AS BRAVE AS ANY BEAST THAT EVER LIVED, IF NOT BRAVER.
IF DOROTHY WOULD ONLY BE CONTENTED TO LIVE IN THE EMERALD CITY, WE MIGHT ALL BE HAPPY TOGETHER.
BUT I DON'T WANT TO LIVE HERE. I WANT TO GO TO KANSAS AND LIVE WITH AUNT EM AND UNCLE HENRY.
WELL, THEN, WHAT CAN BE DONE?
THE SCARECROW THOUGHT SO HARD THAT THE PINS AND NEEDLES BEGAN TO STICK FURTHER OUT OF HIS BRAINS.
WHY NOT CALL THE WINGED MONKEYS AND ASK THEM TO CARRY YOU OVER THE DESERT?
I NEVER THOUGHT OF THAT! IT'S JUST THE THING. I'LL GO AT ONCE FOR THE GOLDEN CAP.

THAT CANNOT BE DONE.

WE BELONG TO THIS COUNTRY ALONE, AND CANNOT LEAVE IT. THERE HAS NEVER BEEN A WINGED MONKEY IN KANSAS YET.

DOROTHY BROUGHT IT INTO THE THRONE ROOM AND SPOKE THE MAGIC WORDS.

THIS IS THE SECOND TIME YOU HAVE CALLED US. WHAT DO YOU WISH?

I WANT YOU TO FLY WITH ME TO KANSAS.

WE SHALL BE GLAD TO SERVE YOU IN ANY WAY IN OUR POWER, BUT WE CANNOT CROSS THE DESERT. GOOD-BYE.

I'VE WASTED THE CHARM OF THE GOLDEN CAP TO NO PURPOSE!

IT'S CERTAINLY TOO BAD!

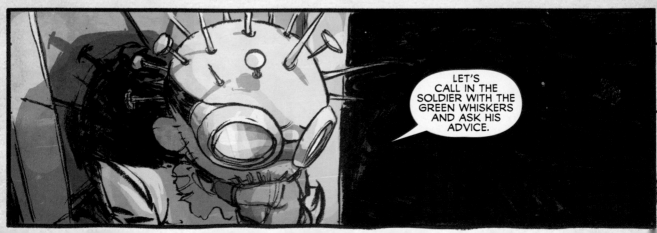

LET'S CALL IN THE SOLDIER WITH THE GREEN WHISKERS AND ASK HIS ADVICE.

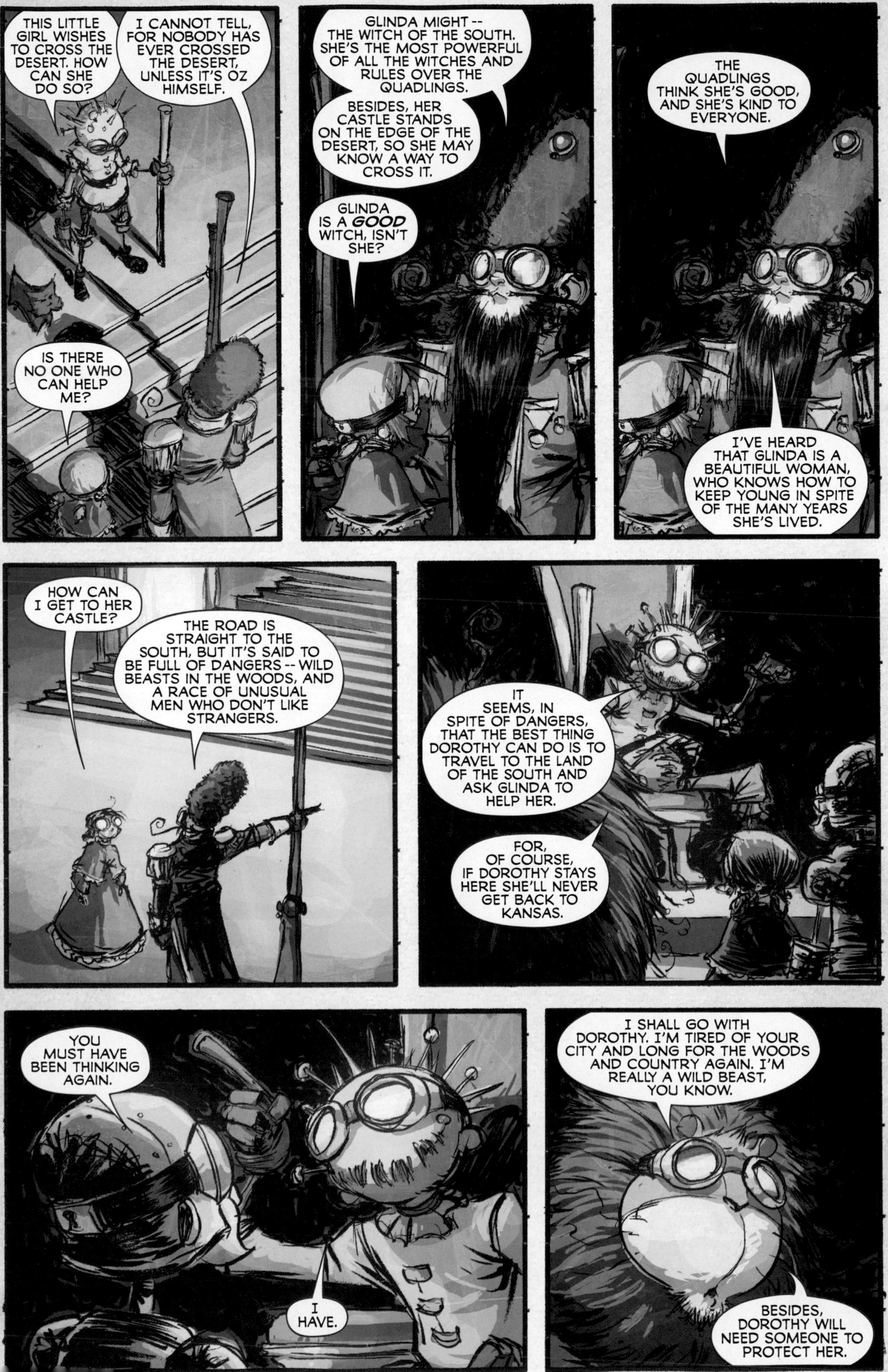
THIS LITTLE GIRL WISHES TO CROSS THE DESERT. HOW CAN SHE DO SO?
I CANNOT TELL, FOR NOBODY HAS EVER CROSSED THE DESERT, UNLESS IT'S OZ HIMSELF.
IS THERE NO ONE WHO CAN HELP ME?
GLINDA MIGHT -- THE WITCH OF THE SOUTH. SHE'S THE MOST POWERFUL OF ALL THE WITCHES AND RULES OVER THE QUADLINGS.
BESIDES, HER CASTLE STANDS ON THE EDGE OF THE DESERT, SO SHE MAY KNOW A WAY TO CROSS IT.
GLINDA IS A *GOOD* WITCH, ISN'T SHE?
THE QUADLINGS THINK SHE'S GOOD, AND SHE'S KIND TO EVERYONE.
I'VE HEARD THAT GLINDA IS A BEAUTIFUL WOMAN, WHO KNOWS HOW TO KEEP YOUNG IN SPITE OF THE MANY YEARS SHE'S LIVED.
HOW CAN I GET TO HER CASTLE?
THE ROAD IS STRAIGHT TO THE SOUTH, BUT IT'S SAID TO BE FULL OF DANGERS -- WILD BEASTS IN THE WOODS, AND A RACE OF UNUSUAL MEN WHO DON'T LIKE STRANGERS.
IT SEEMS, IN SPITE OF DANGERS, THAT THE BEST THING DOROTHY CAN DO IS TO TRAVEL TO THE LAND OF THE SOUTH AND ASK GLINDA TO HELP HER.
FOR, OF COURSE, IF DOROTHY STAYS HERE SHE'LL NEVER GET BACK TO KANSAS.
YOU MUST HAVE BEEN THINKING AGAIN.
I HAVE.
I SHALL GO WITH DOROTHY. I'M TIRED OF YOUR CITY AND LONG FOR THE WOODS AND COUNTRY AGAIN. I'M REALLY A WILD BEAST, YOU KNOW.
BESIDES, DOROTHY WILL NEED SOMEONE TO PROTECT HER.

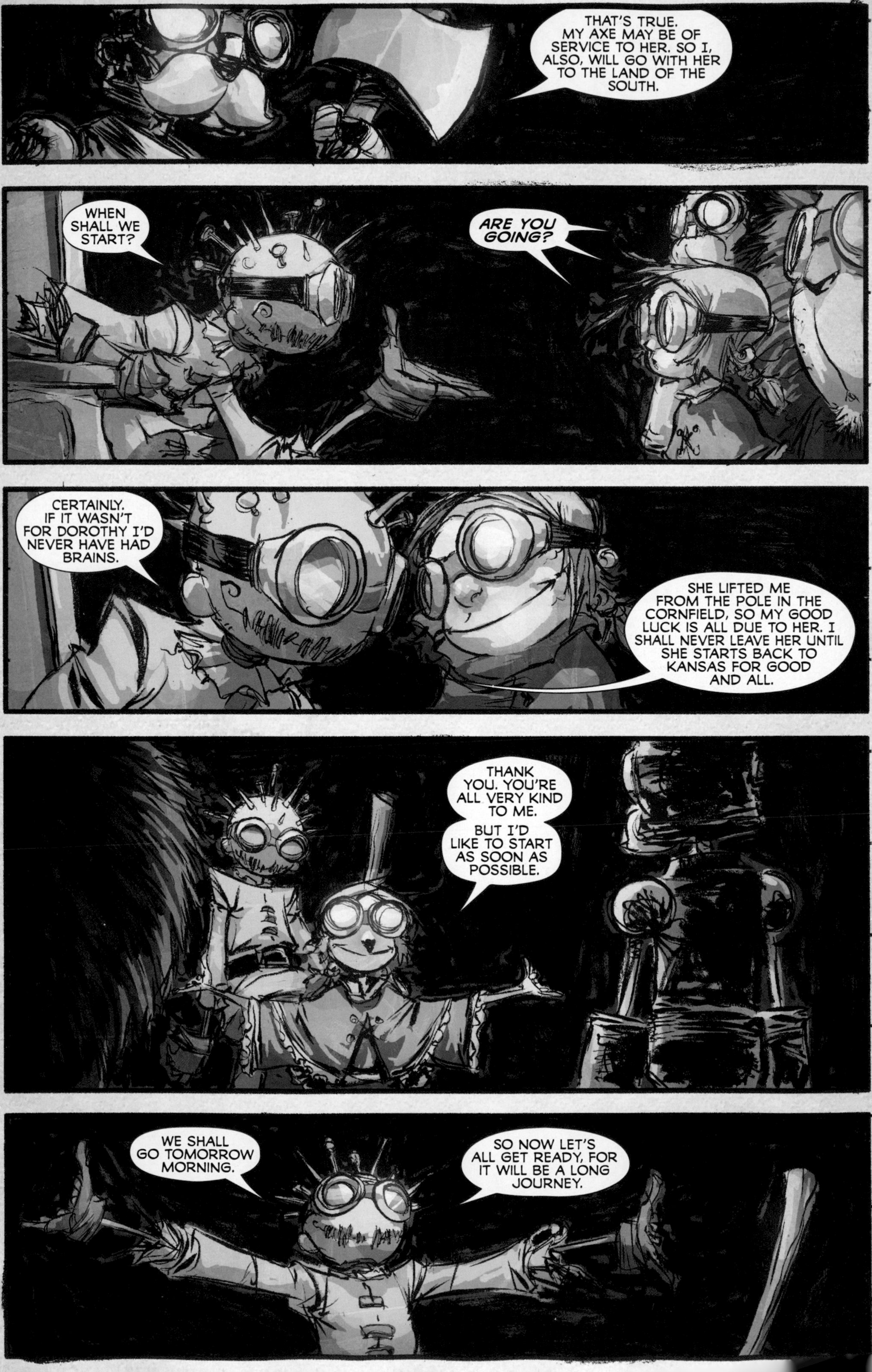
THAT'S TRUE. MY AXE MAY BE OF SERVICE TO HER. SO I, ALSO, WILL GO WITH HER TO THE LAND OF THE SOUTH.
WHEN SHALL WE START?
ARE YOU GOING?
CERTAINLY. IF IT WASN'T FOR DOROTHY I'D NEVER HAVE HAD BRAINS.
SHE LIFTED ME FROM THE POLE IN THE CORNFIELD, SO MY GOOD LUCK IS ALL DUE TO HER. I SHALL NEVER LEAVE HER UNTIL SHE STARTS BACK TO KANSAS FOR GOOD AND ALL.
THANK YOU. YOU'RE ALL VERY KIND TO ME.
BUT I'D LIKE TO START AS SOON AS POSSIBLE.
WE SHALL GO TOMORROW MORNING.
SO NOW LET'S ALL GET READY, FOR IT WILL BE A LONG JOURNEY.

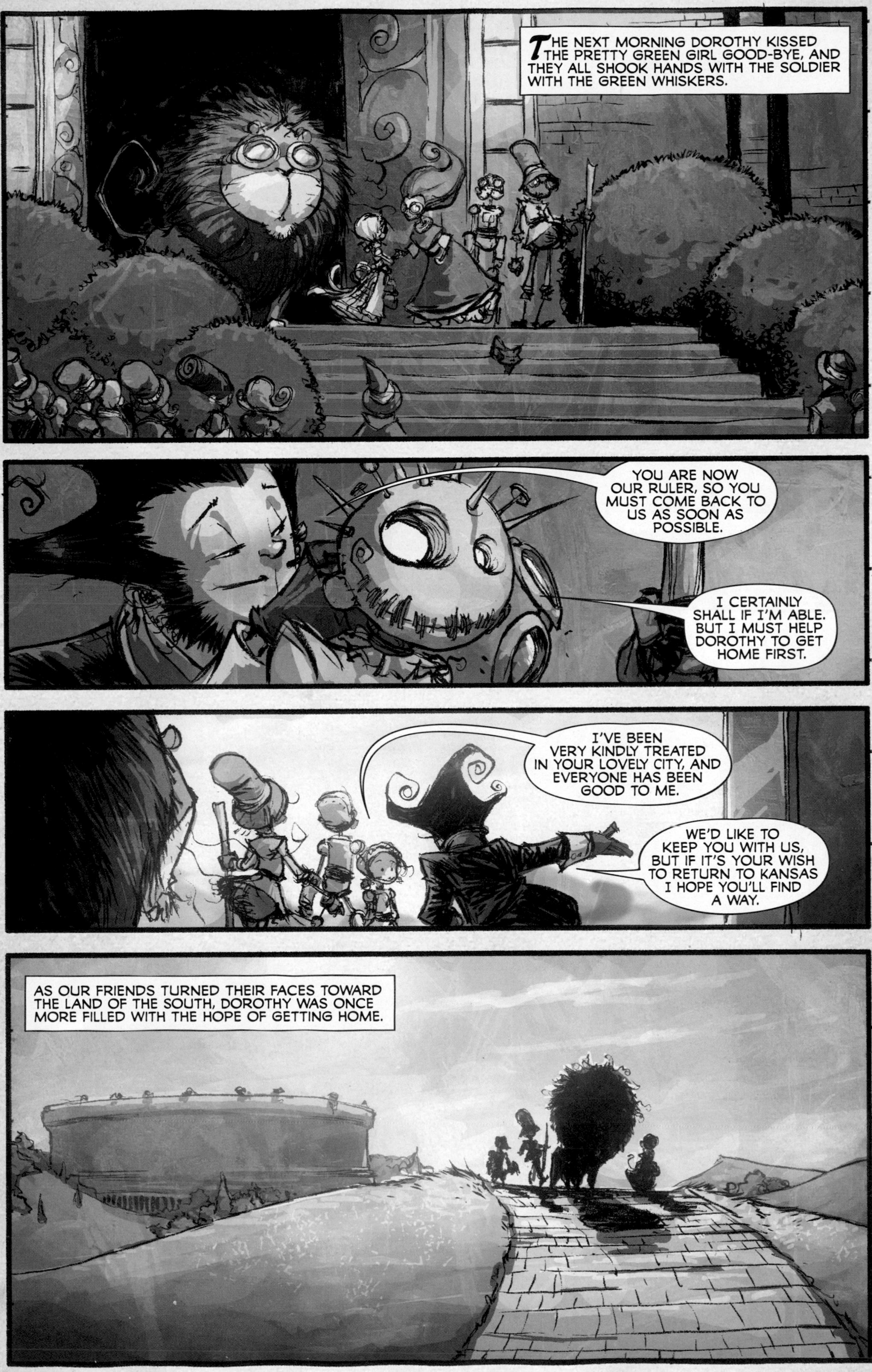
THE NEXT MORNING DOROTHY KISSED THE PRETTY GREEN GIRL GOOD-BYE, AND THEY ALL SHOOK HANDS WITH THE SOLDIER WITH THE GREEN WHISKERS.
YOU ARE NOW OUR RULER, SO YOU MUST COME BACK TO US AS SOON AS POSSIBLE.
I CERTAINLY SHALL IF I'M ABLE. BUT I MUST HELP DOROTHY TO GET HOME FIRST.
I'VE BEEN VERY KINDLY TREATED IN YOUR LOVELY CITY, AND EVERYONE HAS BEEN GOOD TO ME.
WE'D LIKE TO KEEP YOU WITH US, BUT IF IT'S YOUR WISH TO RETURN TO KANSAS I HOPE YOU'LL FIND A WAY.
AS OUR FRIENDS TURNED THEIR FACES TOWARD THE LAND OF THE SOUTH, DOROTHY WAS ONCE MORE FILLED WITH THE HOPE OF GETTING HOME.

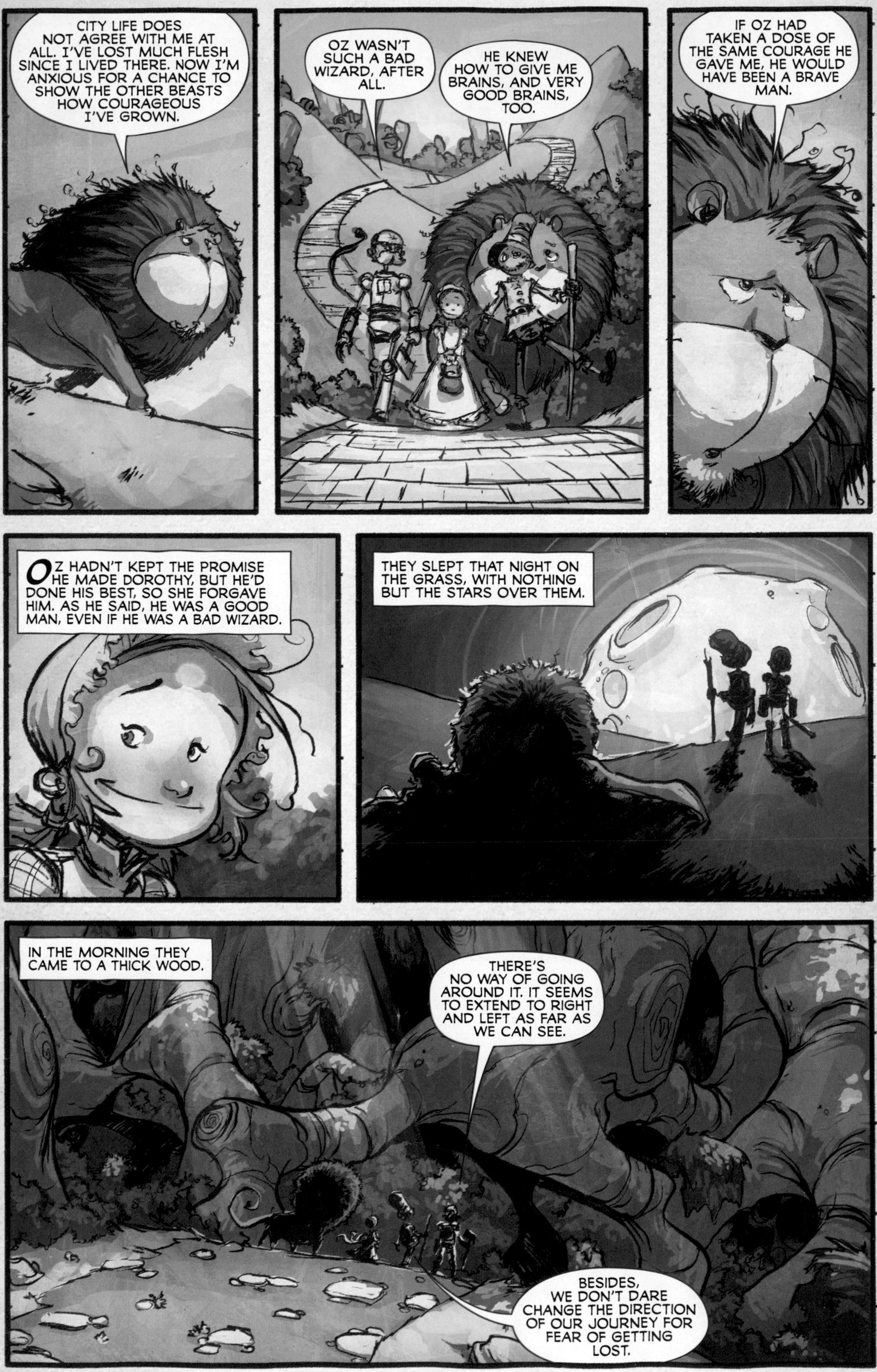
CITY LIFE DOES NOT AGREE WITH ME AT ALL. I'VE LOST MUCH FLESH SINCE I LIVED THERE. NOW I'M ANXIOUS FOR A CHANCE TO SHOW THE OTHER BEASTS HOW COURAGEOUS I'VE GROWN.
OZ WASN'T SUCH A BAD WIZARD, AFTER ALL.
HE KNEW HOW TO GIVE ME BRAINS, AND VERY GOOD BRAINS, TOO.
IF OZ HAD TAKEN A DOSE OF THE SAME COURAGE HE GAVE ME, HE WOULD HAVE BEEN A BRAVE MAN.
OZ HADN'T KEPT THE PROMISE HE MADE DOROTHY, BUT HE'D DONE HIS BEST, SO SHE FORGAVE HIM. AS HE SAID, HE WAS A GOOD MAN, EVEN IF HE WAS A BAD WIZARD.
THEY SLEPT THAT NIGHT ON THE GRASS, WITH NOTHING BUT THE STARS OVER THEM.
IN THE MORNING THEY CAME TO A THICK WOOD.
THERE'S NO WAY OF GOING AROUND IT. IT SEEMS TO EXTEND TO RIGHT AND LEFT AS FAR AS WE CAN SEE.
BESIDES, WE DON'T DARE CHANGE THE DIRECTION OF OUR JOURNEY FOR FEAR OF GETTING LOST.

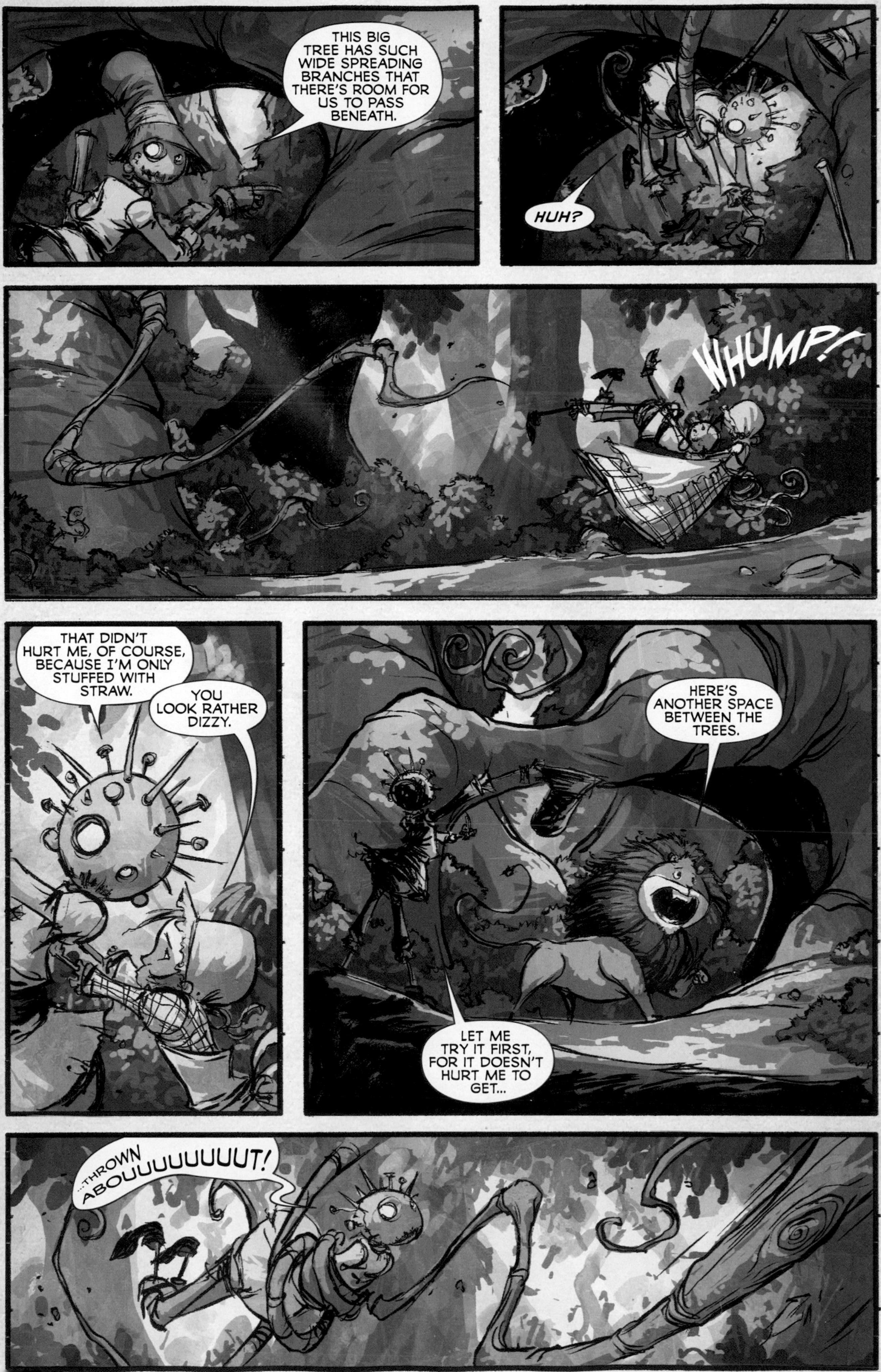
THIS BIG TREE HAS SUCH WIDE SPREADING BRANCHES THAT THERE'S ROOM FOR US TO PASS BENEATH.
HUH?
WHUMP!
THAT DIDN'T HURT ME, OF COURSE, BECAUSE I'M ONLY STUFFED WITH STRAW.
YOU LOOK RATHER DIZZY.
HERE'S ANOTHER SPACE BETWEEN THE TREES.
LET ME TRY IT FIRST, FOR IT DOESN'T HURT ME TO GET...
...THROWN ABOUUUUUUUUT!

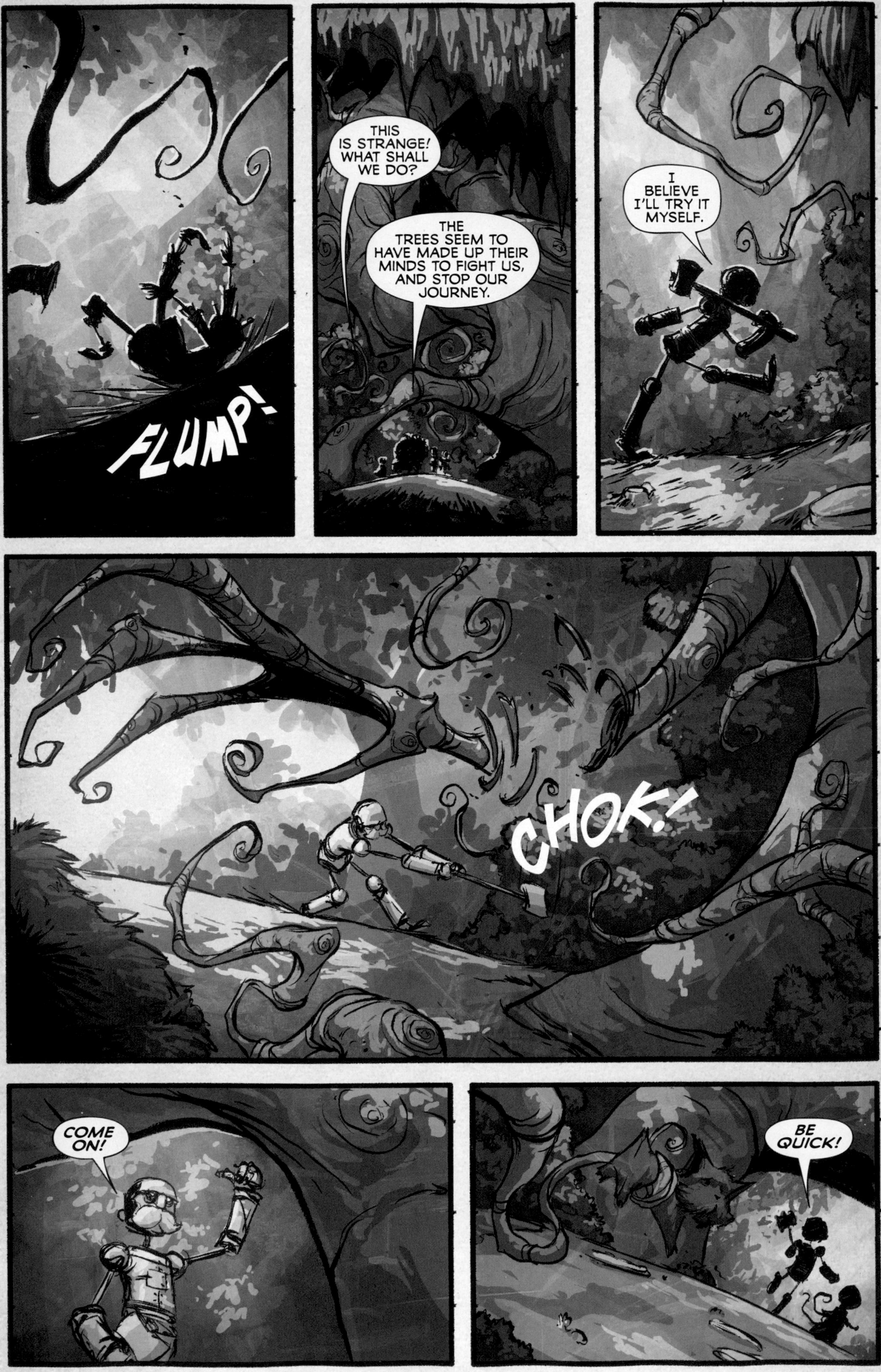
FLUMP!
THIS IS STRANGE! WHAT SHALL WE DO?
THE TREES SEEM TO HAVE MADE UP THEIR MINDS TO FIGHT US, AND STOP OUR JOURNEY.
I BELIEVE I'LL TRY IT MYSELF.
CHOK!
COME ON!
BE QUICK!

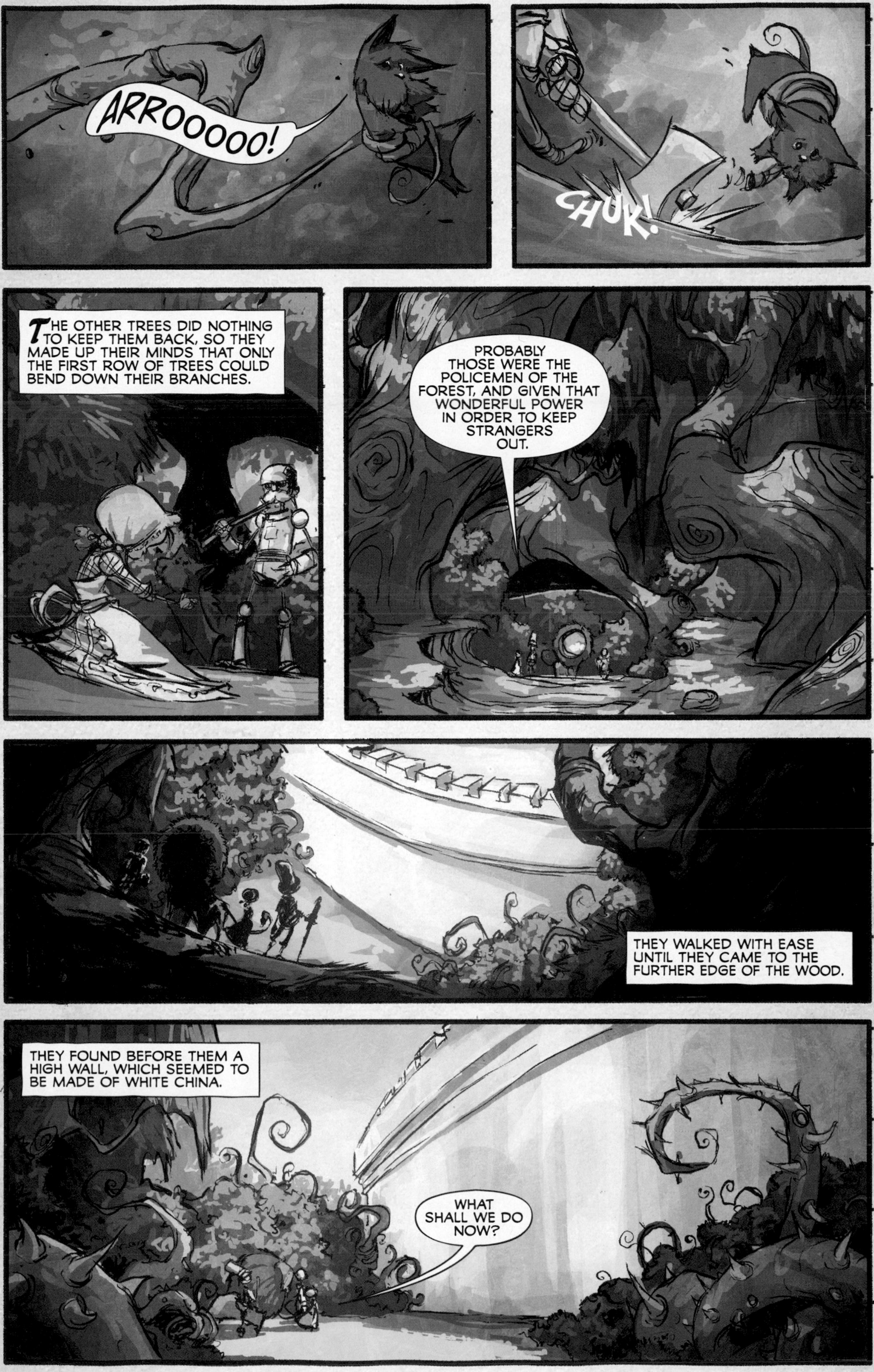
ARROOOOO!
CHUK!
THE OTHER TREES DID NOTHING TO KEEP THEM BACK, SO THEY MADE UP THEIR MINDS THAT ONLY THE FIRST ROW OF TREES COULD BEND DOWN THEIR BRANCHES.
PROBABLY THOSE WERE THE POLICEMEN OF THE FOREST, AND GIVEN THAT WONDERFUL POWER IN ORDER TO KEEP STRANGERS OUT.
THEY WALKED WITH EASE UNTIL THEY CAME TO THE FURTHER EDGE OF THE WOOD.
THEY FOUND BEFORE THEM A HIGH WALL, WHICH SEEMED TO BE MADE OF WHITE CHINA.
WHAT SHALL WE DO NOW?

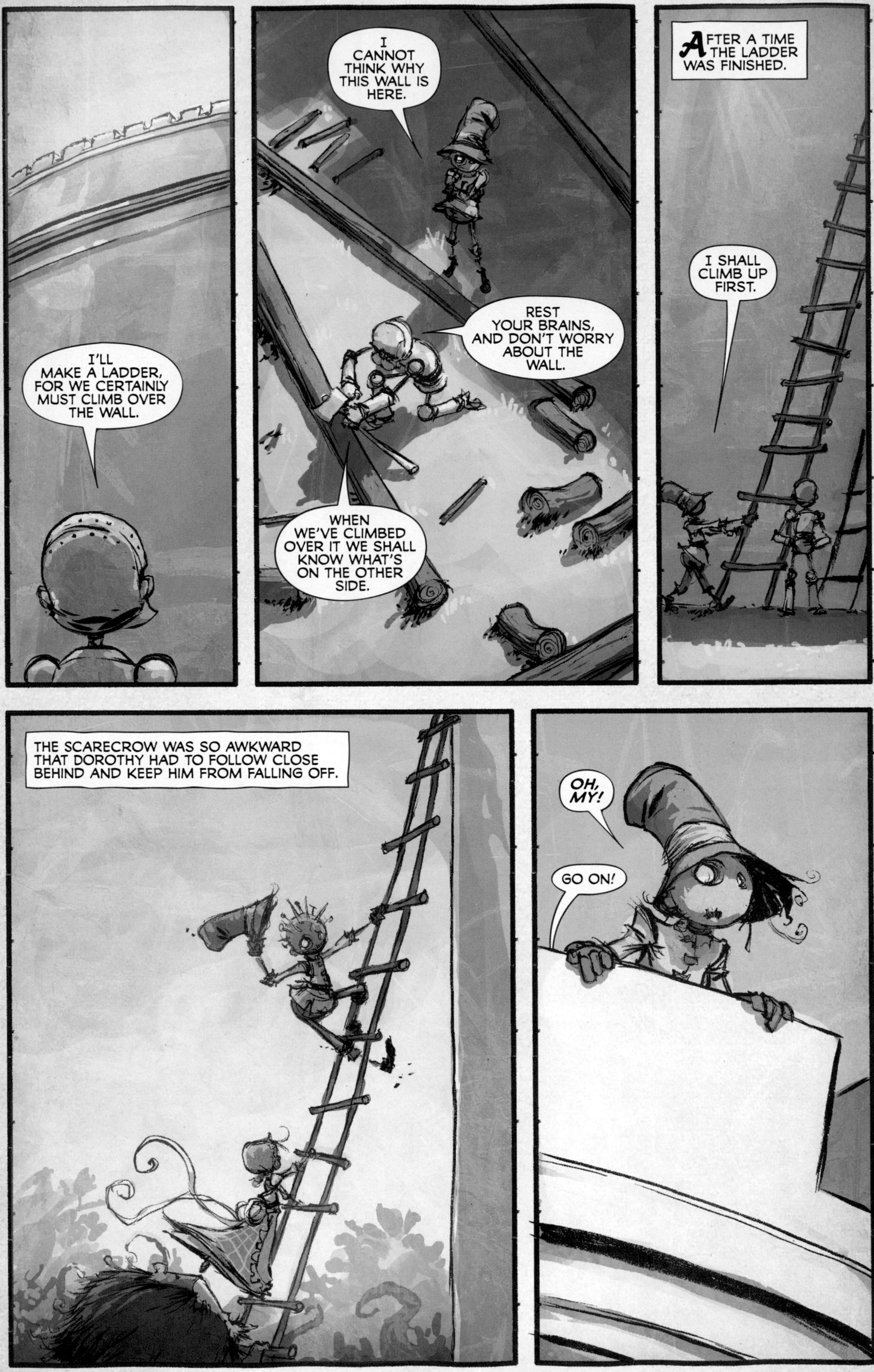
I'LL MAKE A LADDER, FOR WE CERTAINLY MUST CLIMB OVER THE WALL.
I CANNOT THINK WHY THIS WALL IS HERE.
REST YOUR BRAINS, AND DON'T WORRY ABOUT THE WALL.
WHEN WE'VE CLIMBED OVER IT WE SHALL KNOW WHAT'S ON THE OTHER SIDE.
AFTER A TIME THE LADDER WAS FINISHED.
I SHALL CLIMB UP FIRST.
THE SCARECROW WAS SO AWKWARD THAT DOROTHY HAD TO FOLLOW CLOSE BEHIND AND KEEP HIM FROM FALLING OFF.
OH, MY!
GO ON!

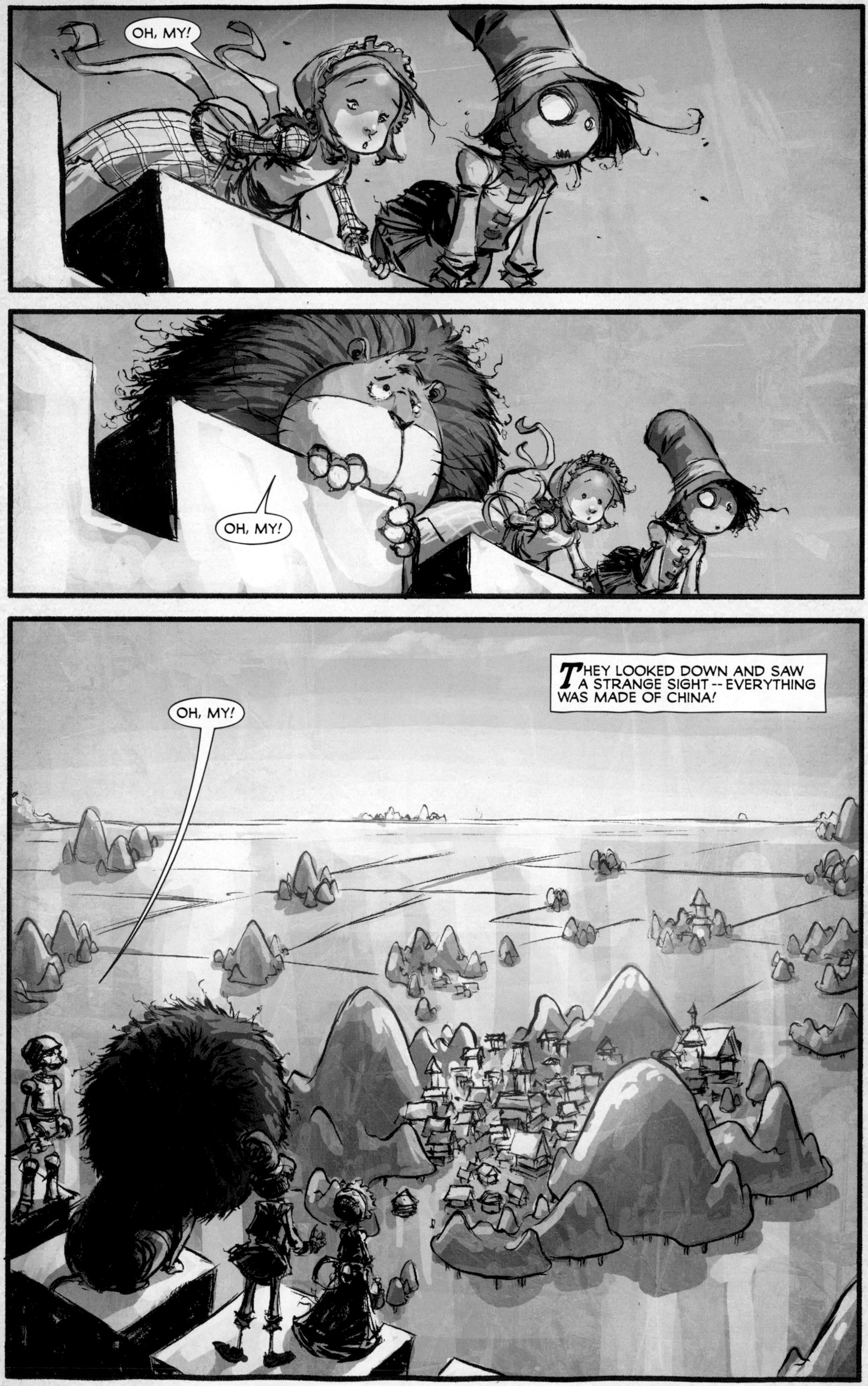
OH, MY!
OH, MY!
THEY LOOKED DOWN AND SAW A STRANGE SIGHT -- EVERYTHING WAS MADE OF CHINA!
OH, MY!

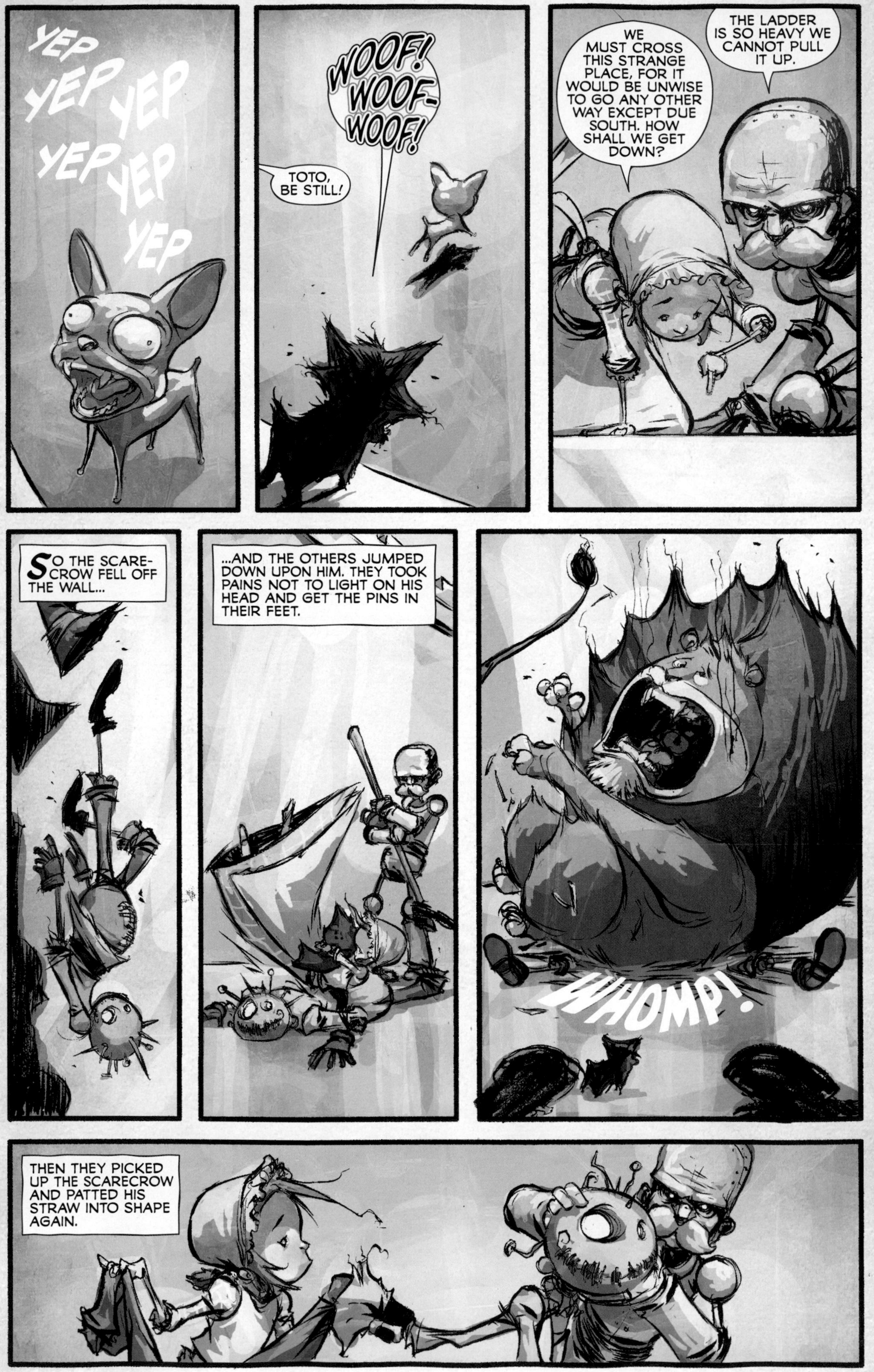
YEP YEP YEP YEP YEP YEP
WOOF! WOOF-WOOF!
TOTO, BE STILL!
WE MUST CROSS THIS STRANGE PLACE, FOR IT WOULD BE UNWISE TO GO ANY OTHER WAY EXCEPT DUE SOUTH. HOW SHALL WE GET DOWN?
THE LADDER IS SO HEAVY WE CANNOT PULL IT UP.
SO THE SCARECROW FELL OFF THE WALL...
...AND THE OTHERS JUMPED DOWN UPON HIM. THEY TOOK PAINS NOT TO LIGHT ON HIS HEAD AND GET THE PINS IN THEIR FEET.
WHOMP!
THEN THEY PICKED UP THE SCARECROW AND PATTED HIS STRAW INTO SHAPE AGAIN.

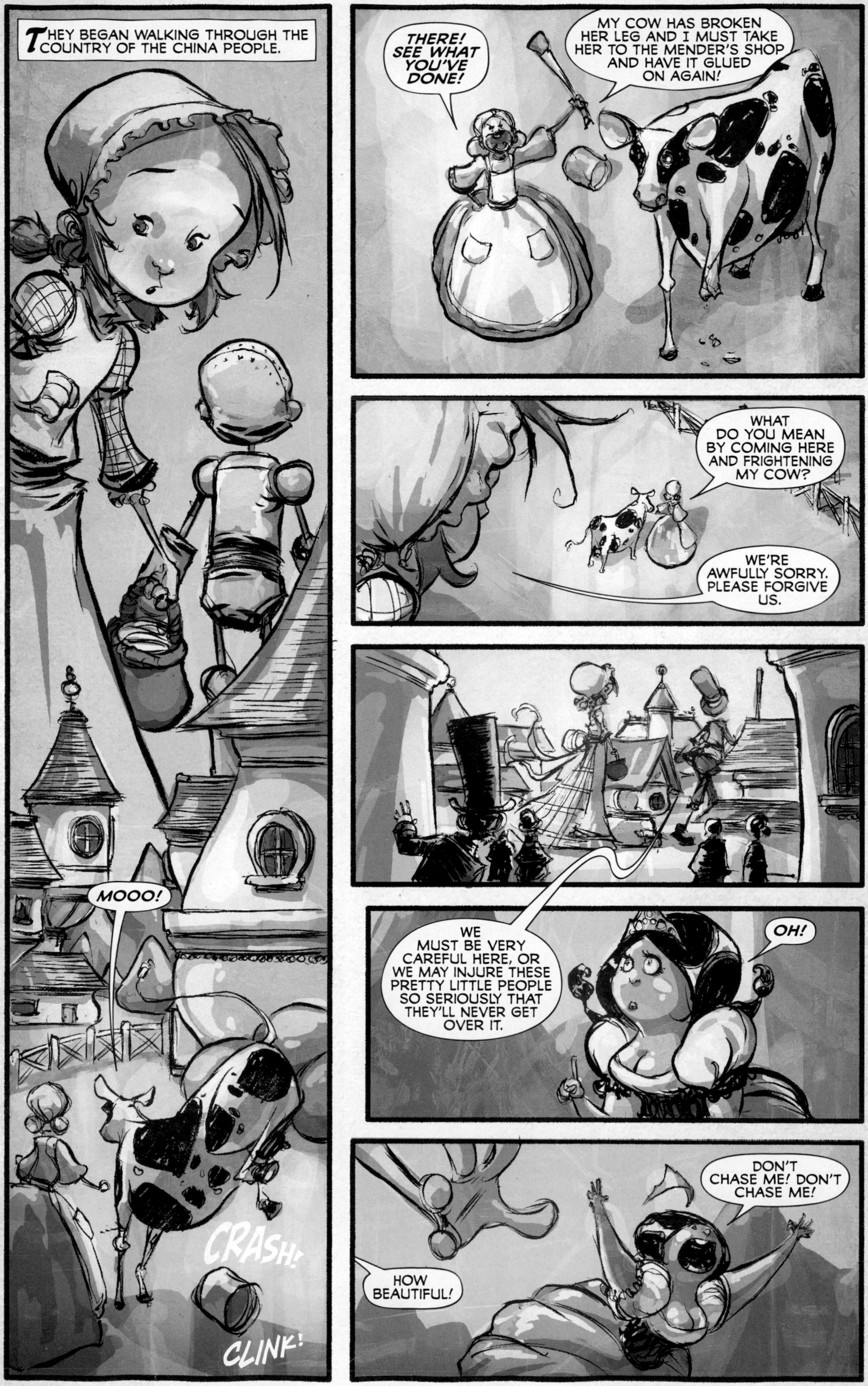
THEY BEGAN WALKING THROUGH THE COUNTRY OF THE CHINA PEOPLE.
MOOO!
CRASH!
CLINK!
THERE! SEE WHAT YOU'VE DONE!
MY COW HAS BROKEN HER LEG AND I MUST TAKE HER TO THE MENDER'S SHOP AND HAVE IT GLUED ON AGAIN!
WHAT DO YOU MEAN BY COMING HERE AND FRIGHTENING MY COW?
WE'RE AWFULLY SORRY. PLEASE FORGIVE US.
WE MUST BE VERY CAREFUL HERE, OR WE MAY INJURE THESE PRETTY LITTLE PEOPLE SO SERIOUSLY THAT THEY'LL NEVER GET OVER IT.
OH!
DON'T CHASE ME! DON'T CHASE ME!
HOW BEAUTIFUL!

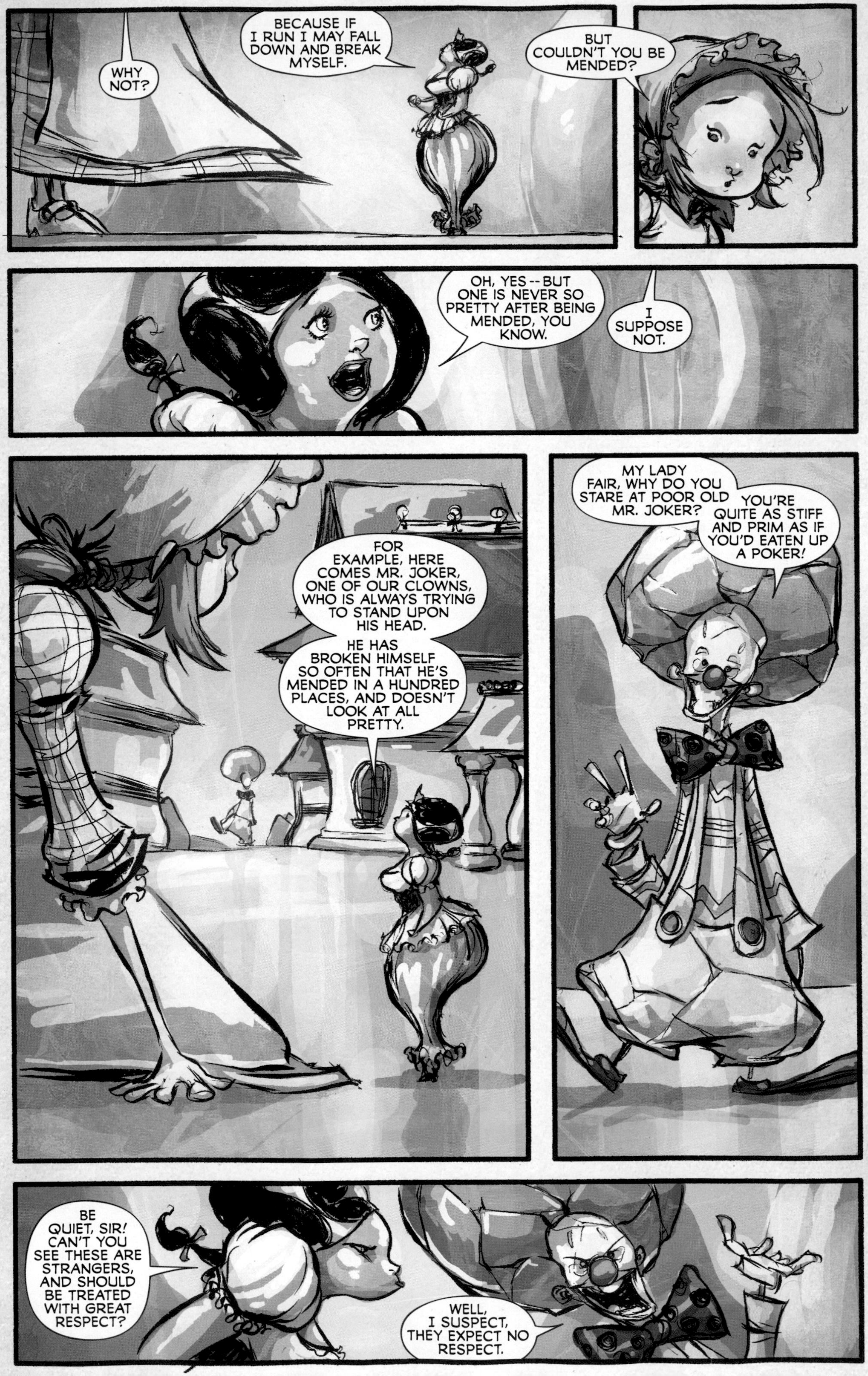
WHY NOT?
BECAUSE IF I RUN I MAY FALL DOWN AND BREAK MYSELF.
BUT COULDN'T YOU BE MENDED?
OH, YES -- BUT ONE IS NEVER SO PRETTY AFTER BEING MENDED, YOU KNOW.
I SUPPOSE NOT.
FOR EXAMPLE, HERE COMES MR. JOKER, ONE OF OUR CLOWNS, WHO IS ALWAYS TRYING TO STAND UPON HIS HEAD.
HE HAS BROKEN HIMSELF SO OFTEN THAT HE'S MENDED IN A HUNDRED PLACES, AND DOESN'T LOOK AT ALL PRETTY.
MY LADY FAIR, WHY DO YOU STARE AT POOR OLD MR. JOKER?
YOU'RE QUITE AS STIFF AND PRIM AS IF YOU'D EATEN UP A POKER!
BE QUIET, SIR! CAN'T YOU SEE THESE ARE STRANGERS, AND SHOULD BE TREATED WITH GREAT RESPECT?
WELL, I SUSPECT, THEY EXPECT NO RESPECT.

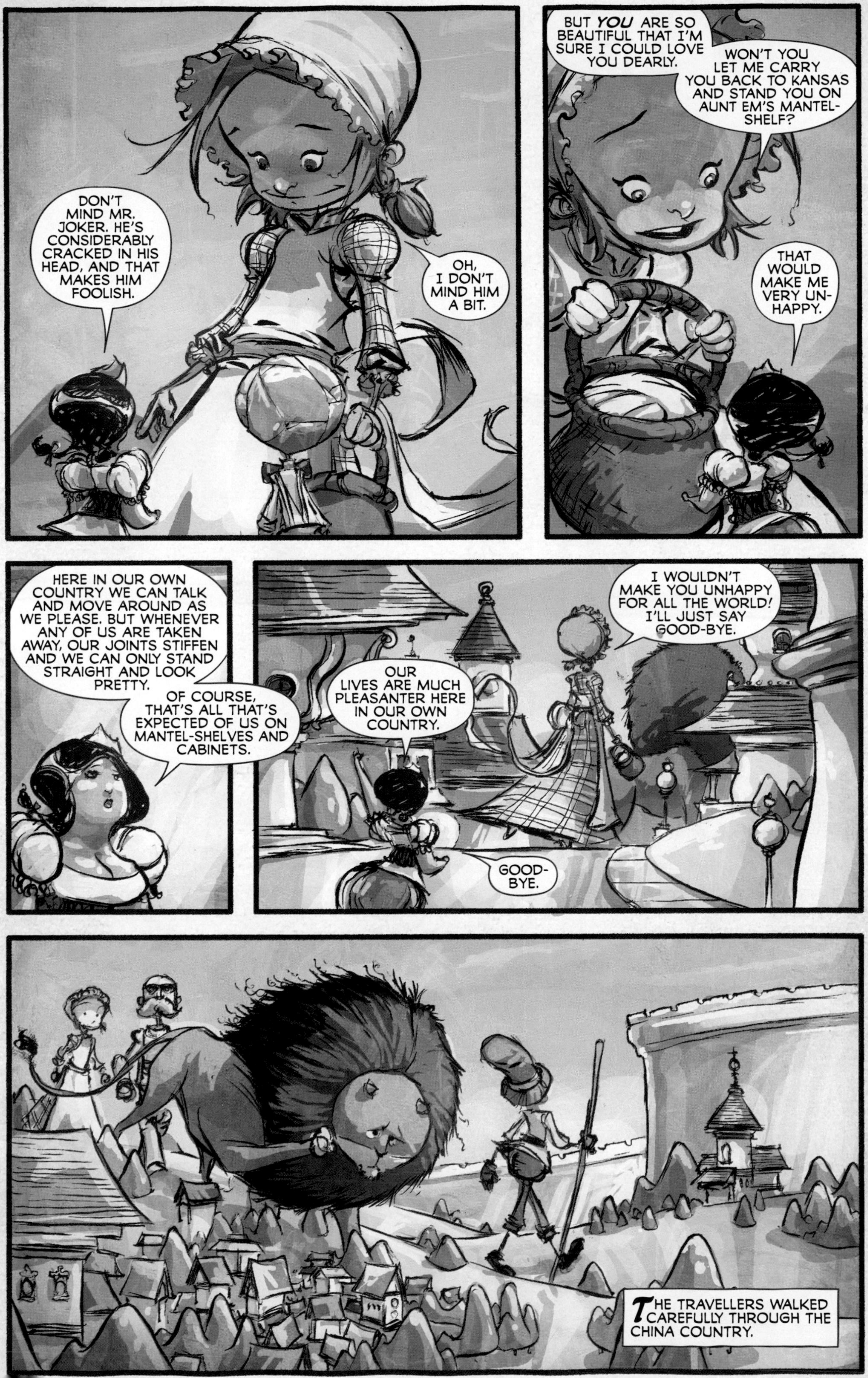
DON'T MIND MR. JOKER. HE'S CONSIDERABLY CRACKED IN HIS HEAD, AND THAT MAKES HIM FOOLISH.
OH, I DON'T MIND HIM A BIT.
BUT YOU ARE SO BEAUTIFUL THAT I'M SURE I COULD LOVE YOU DEARLY.
WON'T YOU LET ME CARRY YOU BACK TO KANSAS AND STAND YOU ON AUNT EM'S MANTEL-SHELF?
THAT WOULD MAKE ME VERY UN-HAPPY.
HERE IN OUR OWN COUNTRY WE CAN TALK AND MOVE AROUND AS WE PLEASE. BUT WHENEVER ANY OF US ARE TAKEN AWAY, OUR JOINTS STIFFEN AND WE CAN ONLY STAND STRAIGHT AND LOOK PRETTY.
OF COURSE, THAT'S ALL THAT'S EXPECTED OF US ON MANTEL-SHELVES AND CABINETS.
OUR LIVES ARE MUCH PLEASANTER HERE IN OUR OWN COUNTRY.
I WOULDN'T MAKE YOU UNHAPPY FOR ALL THE WORLD! I'LL JUST SAY GOOD-BYE.
GOOD-BYE.
THE TRAVELLERS WALKED CAREFULLY THROUGH THE CHINA COUNTRY.

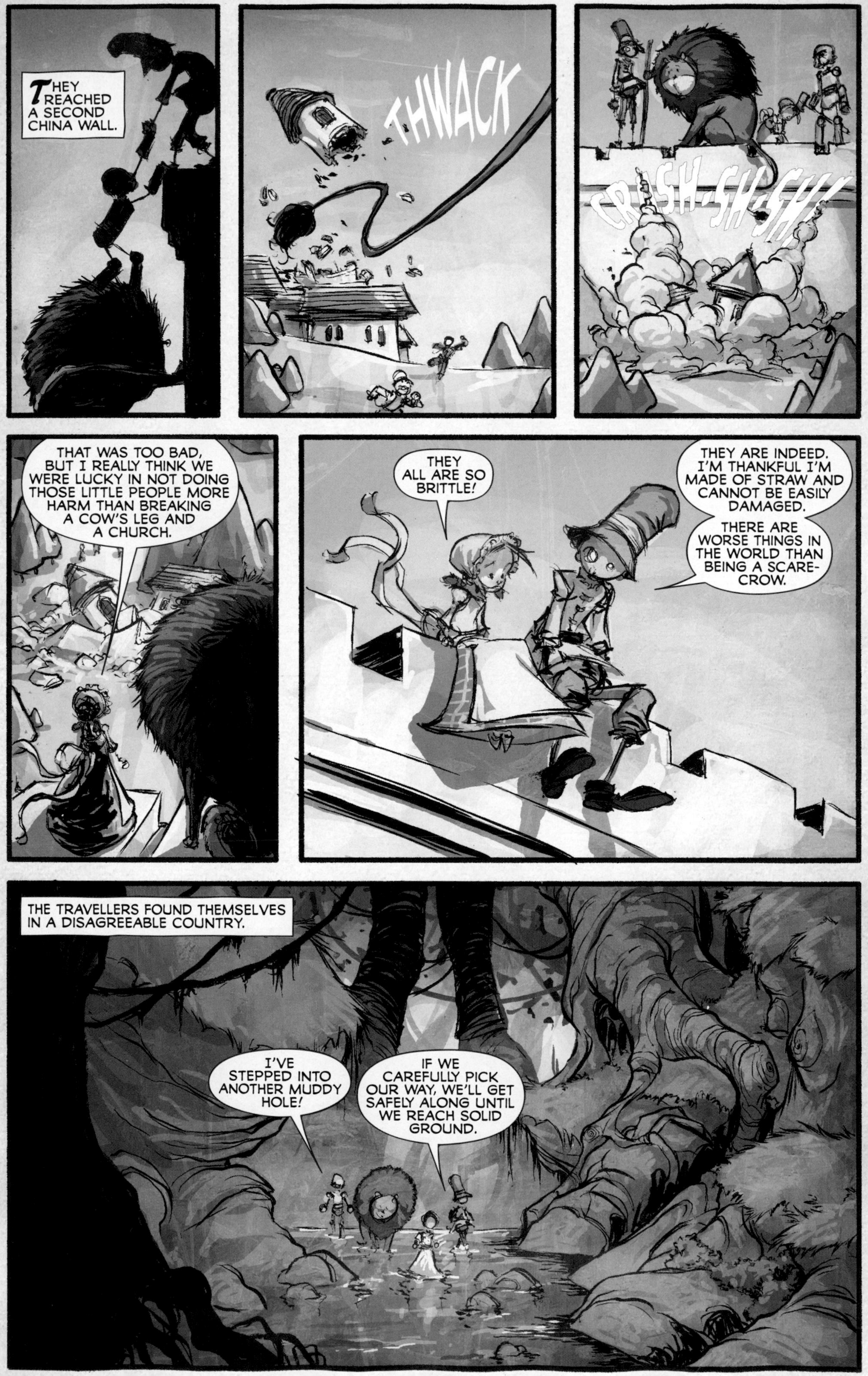
THEY REACHED A SECOND CHINA WALL.
THWACK
CRASH-SH-SH-SH!
THAT WAS TOO BAD, BUT I REALLY THINK WE WERE LUCKY IN NOT DOING THOSE LITTLE PEOPLE MORE HARM THAN BREAKING A COW'S LEG AND A CHURCH.
THEY ALL ARE SO BRITTLE!
THEY ARE INDEED. I'M THANKFUL I'M MADE OF STRAW AND CANNOT BE EASILY DAMAGED.
THERE ARE WORSE THINGS IN THE WORLD THAN BEING A SCARE-CROW.
THE TRAVELLERS FOUND THEMSELVES IN A DISAGREEABLE COUNTRY.
I'VE STEPPED INTO ANOTHER MUDDY HOLE!
IF WE CAREFULLY PICK OUR WAY, WE'LL GET SAFELY ALONG UNTIL WE REACH SOLID GROUND.

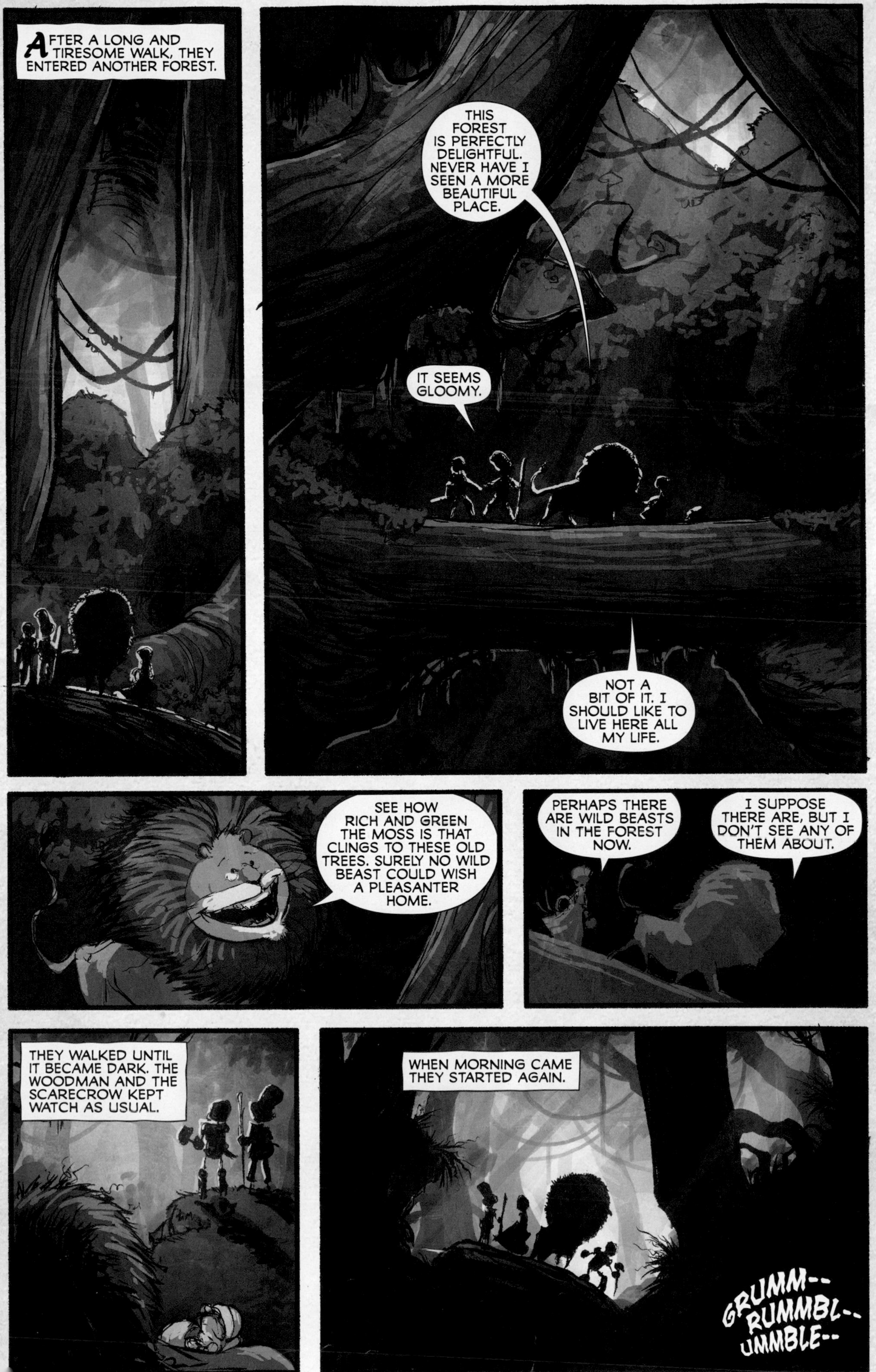
AFTER A LONG AND TIRESOME WALK, THEY ENTERED ANOTHER FOREST.
THIS FOREST IS PERFECTLY DELIGHTFUL. NEVER HAVE I SEEN A MORE BEAUTIFUL PLACE.
IT SEEMS GLOOMY.
NOT A BIT OF IT. I SHOULD LIKE TO LIVE HERE ALL MY LIFE.
SEE HOW RICH AND GREEN THE MOSS IS THAT CLINGS TO THESE OLD TREES. SURELY NO WILD BEAST COULD WISH A PLEASANTER HOME.
PERHAPS THERE ARE WILD BEASTS IN THE FOREST NOW.
I SUPPOSE THERE ARE, BUT I DON'T SEE ANY OF THEM ABOUT.
THEY WALKED UNTIL IT BECAME DARK. THE WOODMAN AND THE SCARECROW KEPT WATCH AS USUAL.
WHEN MORNING CAME THEY STARTED AGAIN.
GRUMM-- RUMMBL-- UMMBLE--

RRAAARRP--ROWWWL--ARROWR--KAAARR

THE ANIMALS ARE HOLDING A MEETING. I JUDGE BY THEIR SNARLING AND GROWLING THAT THEY'RE IN GREAT TROUBLE.

GRROWW-- RRAAAAHH--

WELCOME, O KING OF BEASTS! YOU'VE COME IN GOOD TIME TO FIGHT OUR ENEMY AND BRING PEACE TO ALL THE ANIMALS OF THE FOREST ONCE MORE.

WHAT IS YOUR TROUBLE?

WE'RE ALL THREATENED BY A FIERCE ENEMY WHICH HAS LATELY COME INTO THIS FOREST.

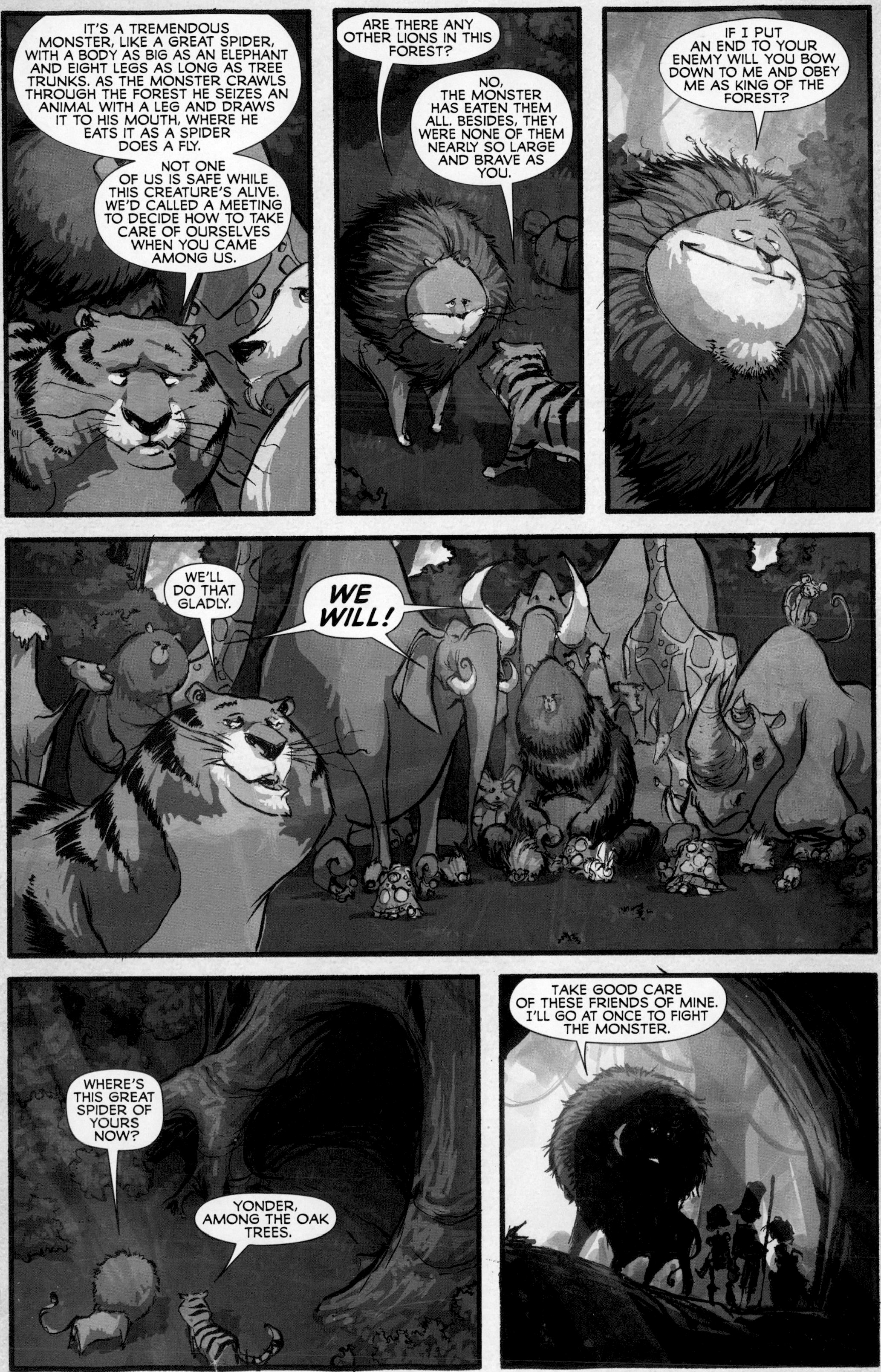
IT'S A TREMENDOUS MONSTER, LIKE A GREAT SPIDER, WITH A BODY AS BIG AS AN ELEPHANT AND EIGHT LEGS AS LONG AS TREE TRUNKS. AS THE MONSTER CRAWLS THROUGH THE FOREST HE SEIZES AN ANIMAL WITH A LEG AND DRAWS IT TO HIS MOUTH, WHERE HE EATS IT AS A SPIDER DOES A FLY.
NOT ONE OF US IS SAFE WHILE THIS CREATURE'S ALIVE. WE'D CALLED A MEETING TO DECIDE HOW TO TAKE CARE OF OURSELVES WHEN YOU CAME AMONG US.
ARE THERE ANY OTHER LIONS IN THIS FOREST?
NO, THE MONSTER HAS EATEN THEM ALL. BESIDES, THEY WERE NONE OF THEM NEARLY SO LARGE AND BRAVE AS YOU.
IF I PUT AN END TO YOUR ENEMY WILL YOU BOW DOWN TO ME AND OBEY ME AS KING OF THE FOREST?
WE'LL DO THAT GLADLY.
WE WILL!
WHERE'S THIS GREAT SPIDER OF YOURS NOW?
YONDER, AMONG THE OAK TREES.
TAKE GOOD CARE OF THESE FRIENDS OF MINE. I'LL GO AT ONCE TO FIGHT THE MONSTER.

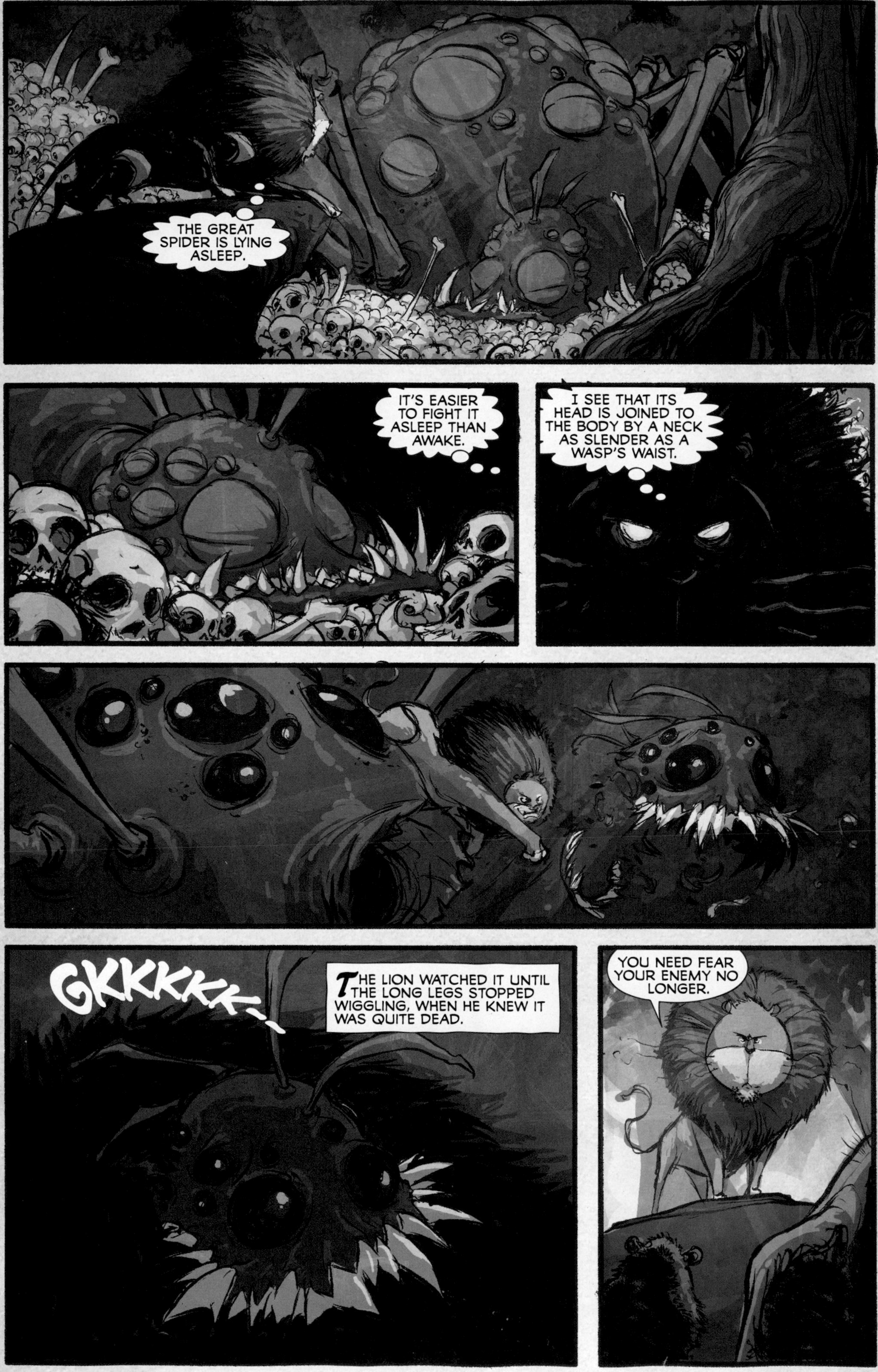
THE GREAT SPIDER IS LYING ASLEEP.
IT'S EASIER TO FIGHT IT ASLEEP THAN AWAKE.
I SEE THAT ITS HEAD IS JOINED TO THE BODY BY A NECK AS SLENDER AS A WASP'S WAIST.
GKKKKK--
THE LION WATCHED IT UNTIL THE LONG LEGS STOPPED WIGGLING, WHEN HE KNEW IT WAS QUITE DEAD.
YOU NEED FEAR YOUR ENEMY NO LONGER.

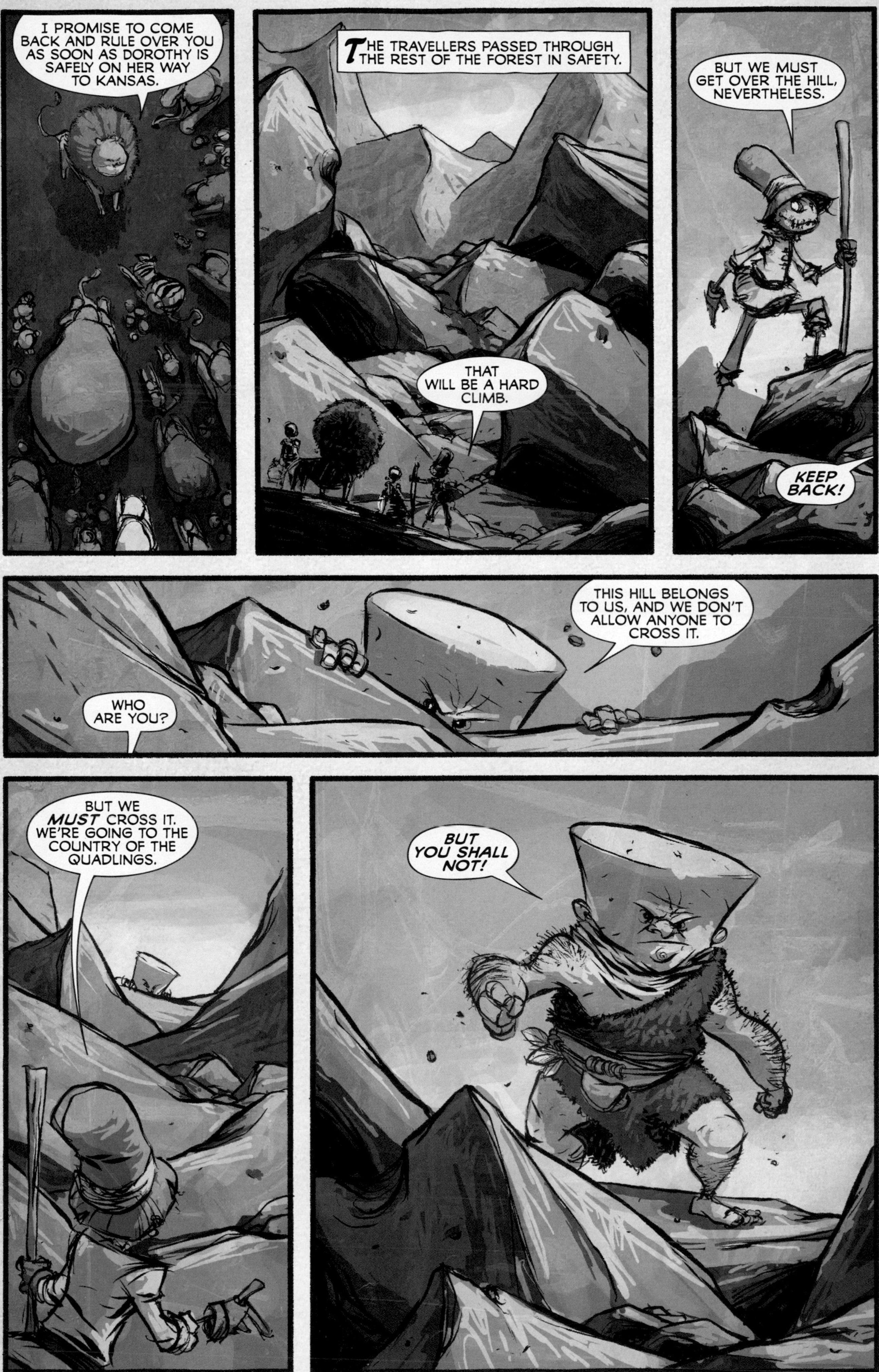
I PROMISE TO COME BACK AND RULE OVER YOU AS SOON AS DOROTHY IS SAFELY ON HER WAY TO KANSAS.
THE TRAVELLERS PASSED THROUGH THE REST OF THE FOREST IN SAFETY.
THAT WILL BE A HARD CLIMB.
BUT WE MUST GET OVER THE HILL, NEVERTHELESS.
KEEP BACK!
WHO ARE YOU?
THIS HILL BELONGS TO US, AND WE DON'T ALLOW ANYONE TO CROSS IT.
BUT WE *MUST* CROSS IT. WE'RE GOING TO THE COUNTRY OF THE QUADLINGS.
BUT YOU SHALL NOT!

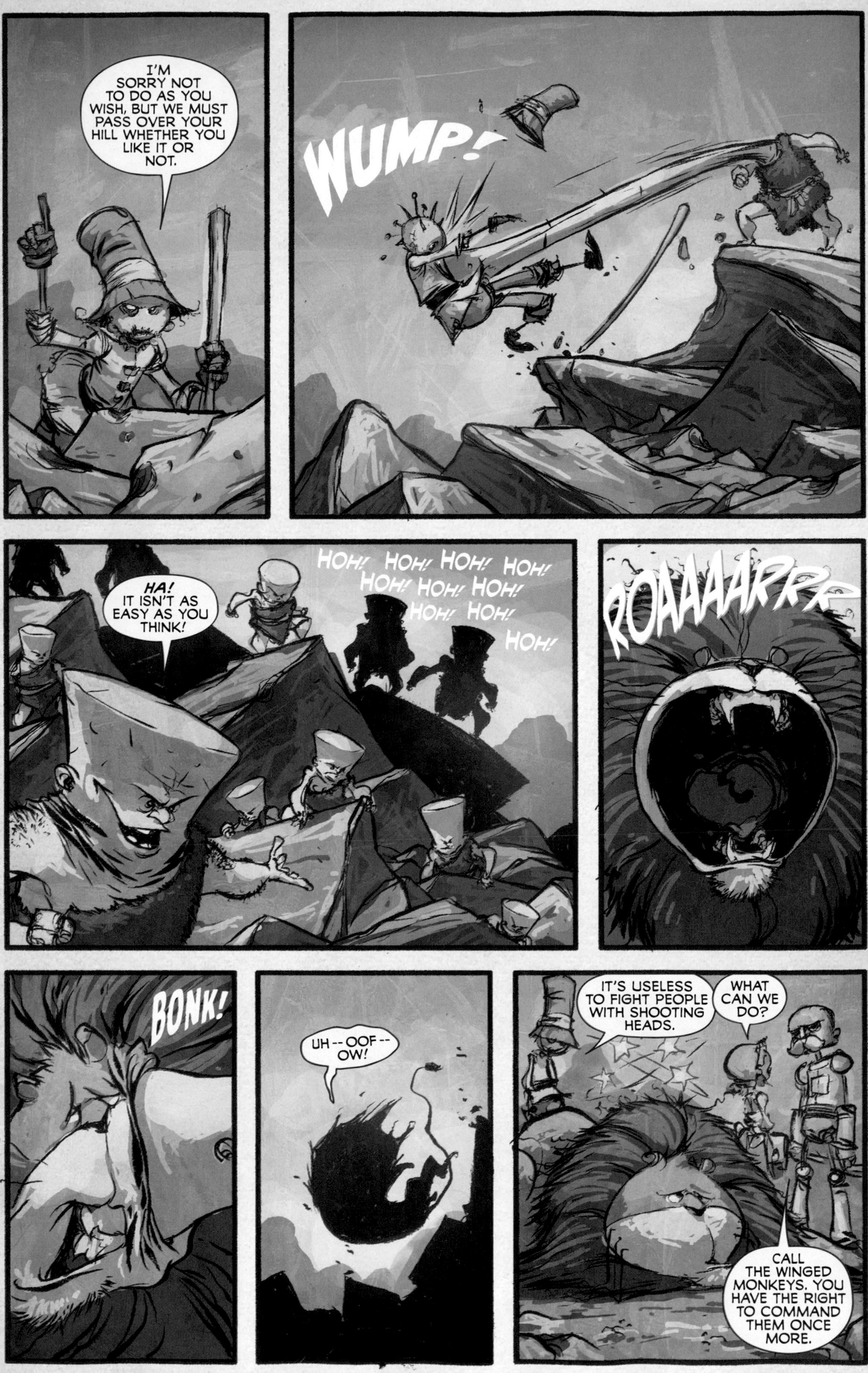

I'M SORRY NOT TO DO AS YOU WISH, BUT WE MUST PASS OVER YOUR HILL WHETHER YOU LIKE IT OR NOT.
WUMP!
HA! IT ISN'T AS EASY AS YOU THINK!
HOH! HOH! HOH! HOH! HOH! HOH! HOH! HOH! HOH! HOH!
ROAAAAARRR
BONK!
UH -- OOF -- OW!
IT'S USELESS TO FIGHT PEOPLE WITH SHOOTING HEADS.
WHAT CAN WE DO?
CALL THE WINGED MONKEYS. YOU HAVE THE RIGHT TO COMMAND THEM ONCE MORE.

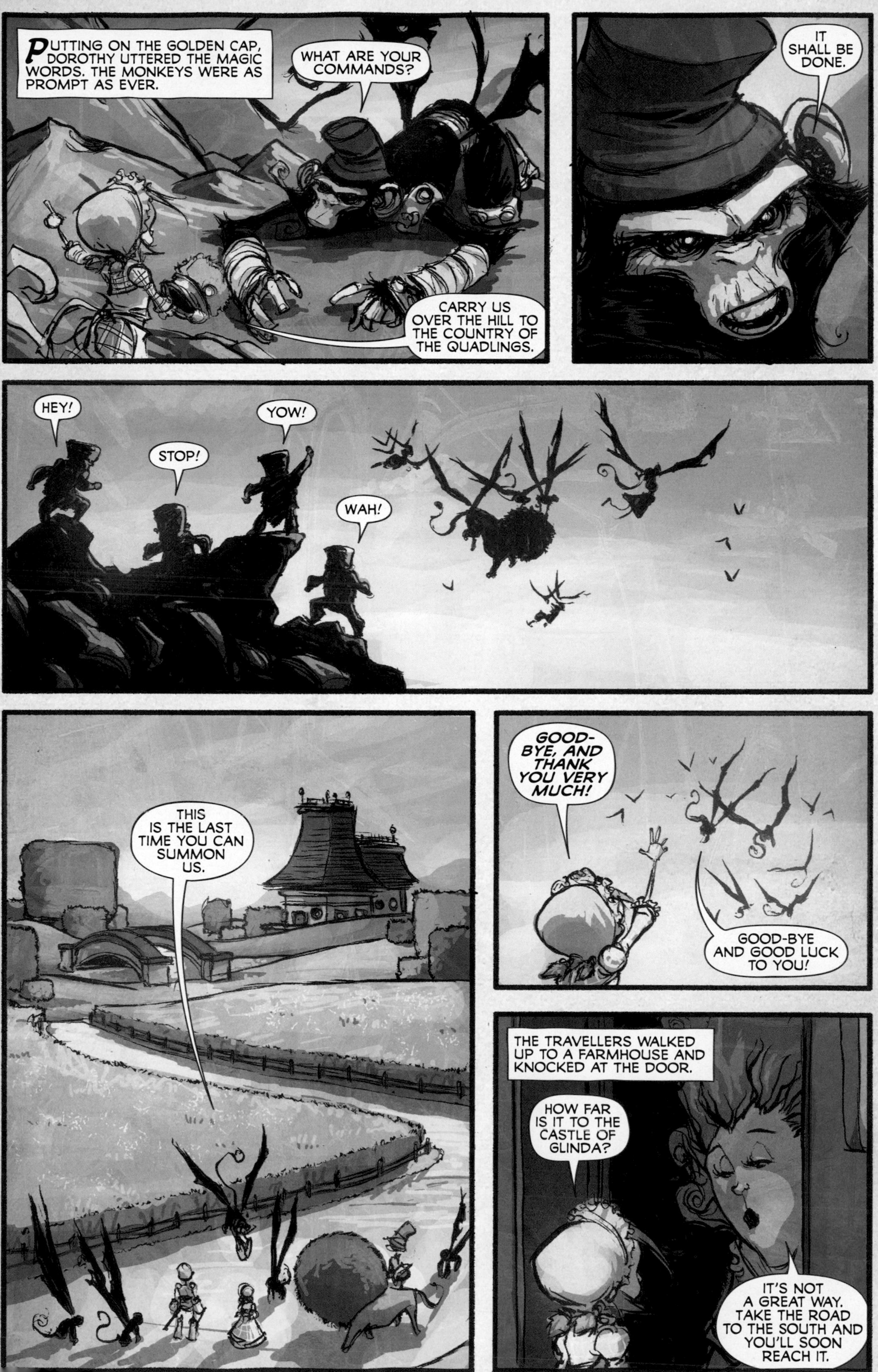
PUTTING ON THE GOLDEN CAP, DOROTHY UTTERED THE MAGIC WORDS. THE MONKEYS WERE AS PROMPT AS EVER.
WHAT ARE YOUR COMMANDS?
CARRY US OVER THE HILL TO THE COUNTRY OF THE QUADLINGS.
IT SHALL BE DONE.
HEY!
STOP!
YOW!
WAH!
THIS IS THE LAST TIME YOU CAN SUMMON US.
GOOD-BYE, AND THANK YOU VERY MUCH!
GOOD-BYE AND GOOD LUCK TO YOU!
THE TRAVELLERS WALKED UP TO A FARMHOUSE AND KNOCKED AT THE DOOR.
HOW FAR IS IT TO THE CASTLE OF GLINDA?
IT'S NOT A GREAT WAY. TAKE THE ROAD TO THE SOUTH AND YOU'LL SOON REACH IT.

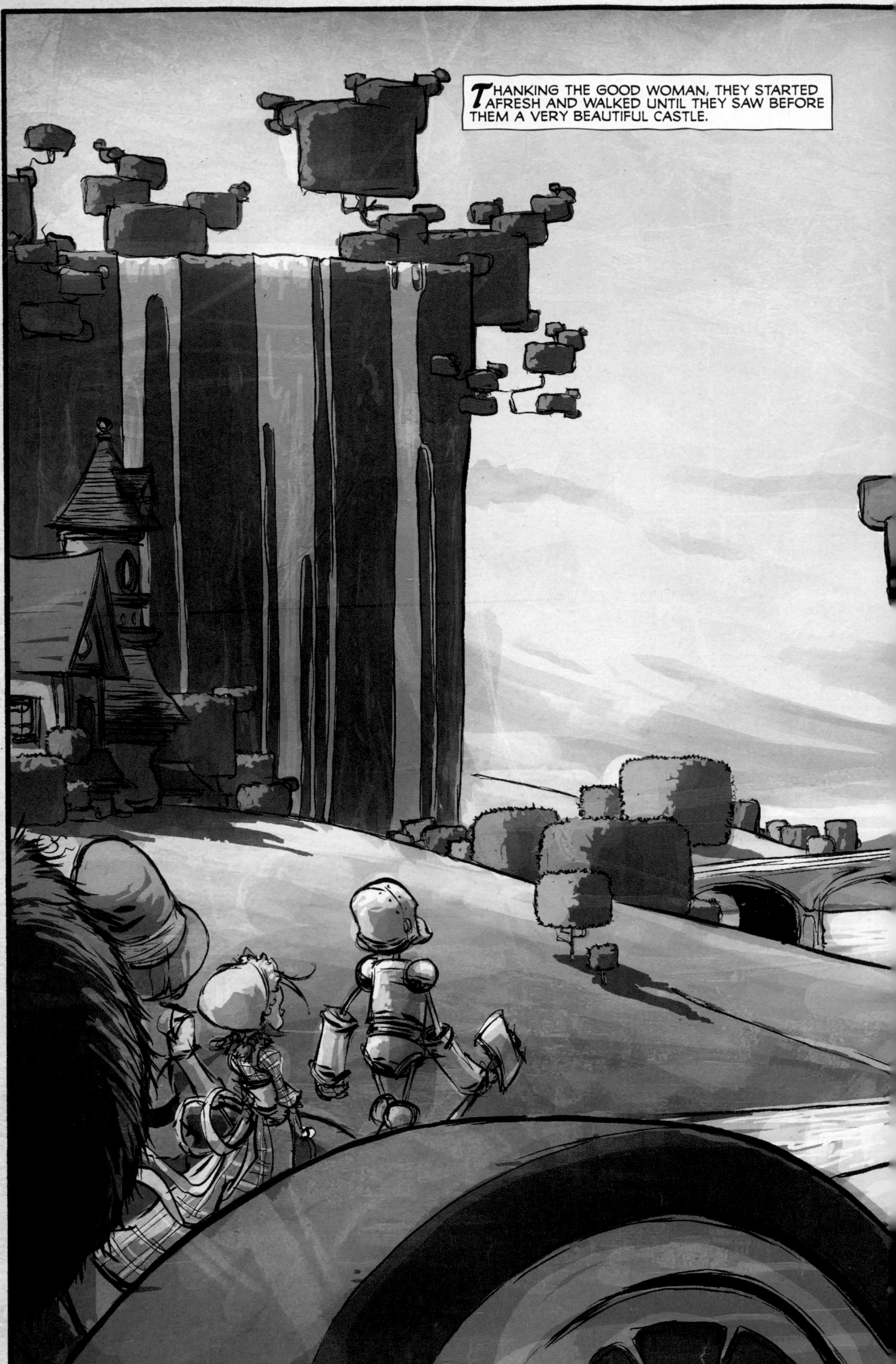
THANKING THE GOOD WOMAN, THEY STARTED AFRESH AND WALKED UNTIL THEY SAW BEFORE THEM A VERY BEAUTIFUL CASTLE.

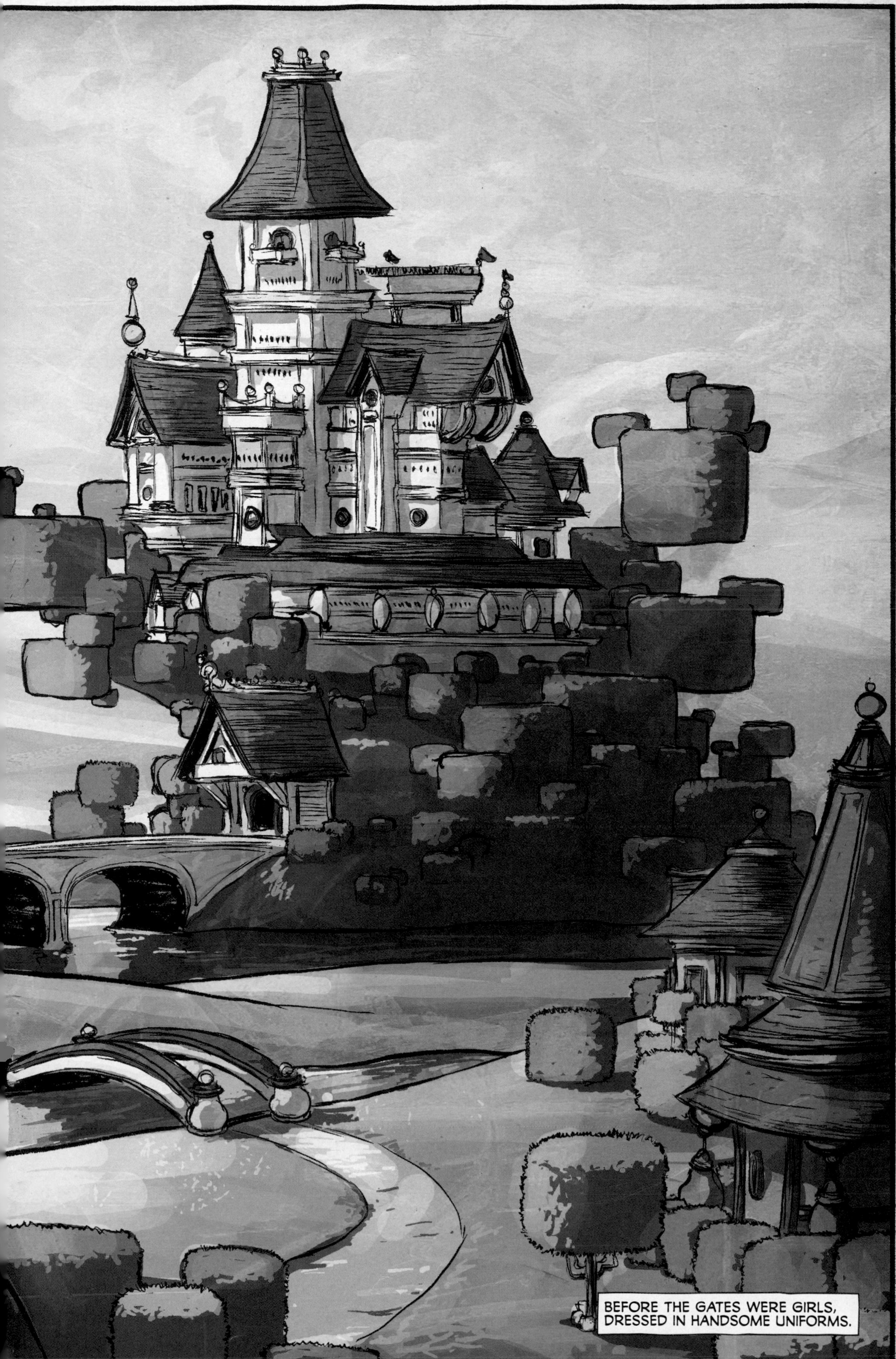
BEFORE THE GATES WERE GIRLS, DRESSED IN HANDSOME UNIFORMS.

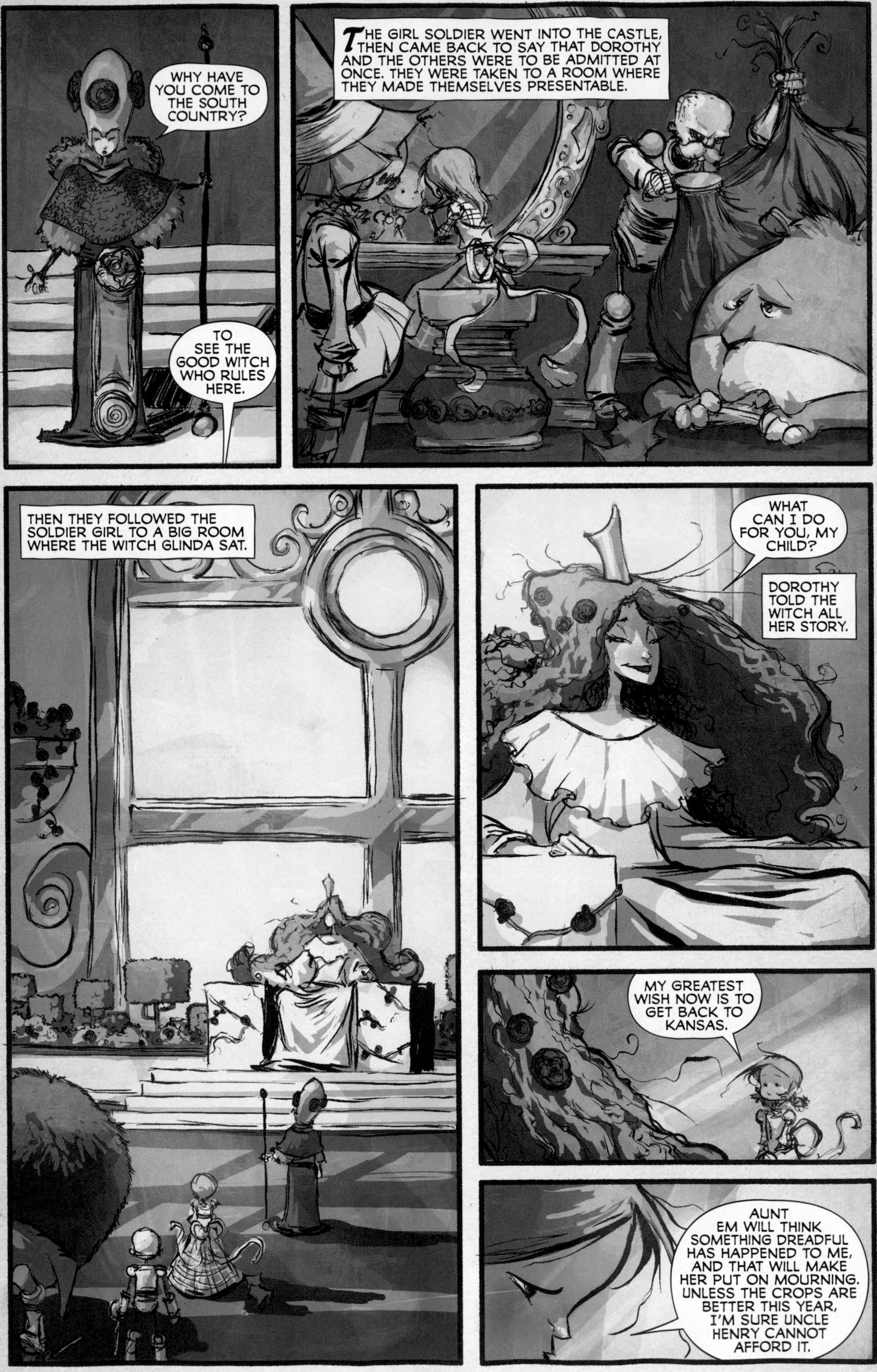
WHY HAVE YOU COME TO THE SOUTH COUNTRY?
TO SEE THE GOOD WITCH WHO RULES HERE.
THE GIRL SOLDIER WENT INTO THE CASTLE, THEN CAME BACK TO SAY THAT DOROTHY AND THE OTHERS WERE TO BE ADMITTED AT ONCE. THEY WERE TAKEN TO A ROOM WHERE THEY MADE THEMSELVES PRESENTABLE.
THEN THEY FOLLOWED THE SOLDIER GIRL TO A BIG ROOM WHERE THE WITCH GLINDA SAT.
WHAT CAN I DO FOR YOU, MY CHILD?
DOROTHY TOLD THE WITCH ALL HER STORY.
MY GREATEST WISH NOW IS TO GET BACK TO KANSAS.
AUNT EM WILL THINK SOMETHING DREADFUL HAS HAPPENED TO ME, AND THAT WILL MAKE HER PUT ON MOURNING. UNLESS THE CROPS ARE BETTER THIS YEAR, I'M SURE UNCLE HENRY CANNOT AFFORD IT.

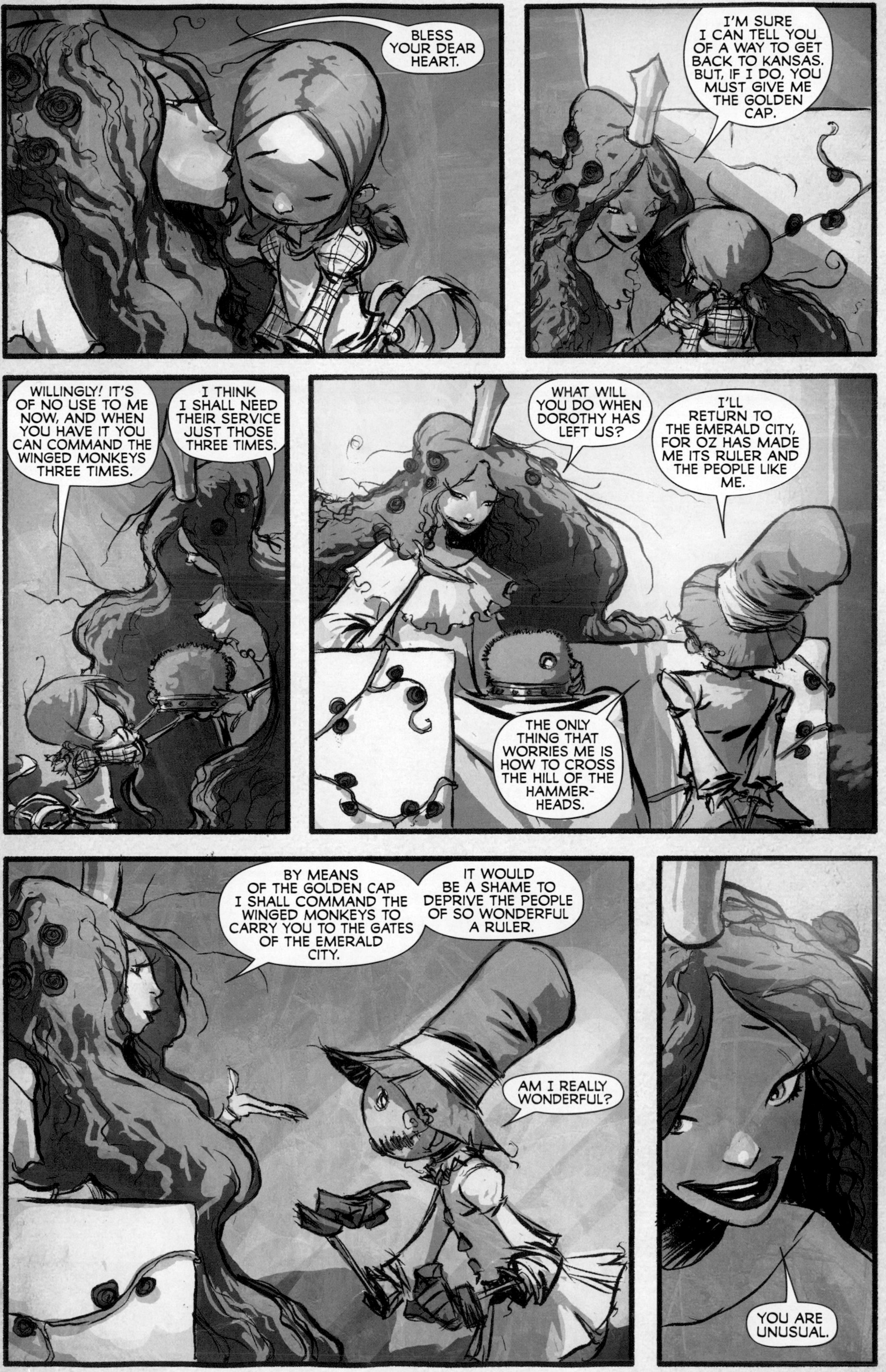
BLESS YOUR DEAR HEART.
I'M SURE I CAN TELL YOU OF A WAY TO GET BACK TO KANSAS. BUT, IF I DO, YOU MUST GIVE ME THE GOLDEN CAP.
WILLINGLY! IT'S OF NO USE TO ME NOW, AND WHEN YOU HAVE IT YOU CAN COMMAND THE WINGED MONKEYS THREE TIMES.
I THINK I SHALL NEED THEIR SERVICE JUST THOSE THREE TIMES.
WHAT WILL YOU DO WHEN DOROTHY HAS LEFT US?
I'LL RETURN TO THE EMERALD CITY, FOR OZ HAS MADE ME ITS RULER AND THE PEOPLE LIKE ME.
THE ONLY THING THAT WORRIES ME IS HOW TO CROSS THE HILL OF THE HAMMER-HEADS.
BY MEANS OF THE GOLDEN CAP I SHALL COMMAND THE WINGED MONKEYS TO CARRY YOU TO THE GATES OF THE EMERALD CITY.
IT WOULD BE A SHAME TO DEPRIVE THE PEOPLE OF SO WONDERFUL A RULER.
AM I REALLY WONDERFUL?
YOU ARE UNUSUAL.

WHAT WILL BECOME OF YOU WHEN DOROTHY LEAVES THIS COUNTRY?

THE WINKIES WERE VERY KIND TO ME AND WANTED ME TO RULE OVER THEM AFTER THE WICKED WITCH DIED.

IF I COULD GET BACK TO THE COUNTRY OF THE WEST I SHOULD LIKE NOTHING BETTER THAN TO RULE OVER THEM FOREVER.

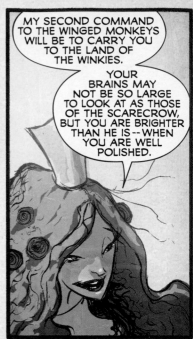

MY SECOND COMMAND TO THE WINGED MONKEYS WILL BE TO CARRY YOU TO THE LAND OF THE WINKIES.

YOUR BRAINS MAY NOT BE SO LARGE TO LOOK AT AS THOSE OF THE SCARECROW, BUT YOU ARE BRIGHTER THAN HE IS -- WHEN YOU ARE WELL POLISHED.

WHEN DOROTHY HAS RETURNED TO HER OWN HOME, WHAT WILL BECOME OF YOU?

OVER THE HILL OF THE HAMMER-HEADS LIES A GRAND OLD FOREST, AND ALL THE BEASTS THAT LIVE THERE HAVE MADE ME THEIR KING.

IF I COULD ONLY GET BACK TO THIS FOREST I'D PASS MY LIFE VERY HAPPILY THERE.

MY THIRD COMMAND TO THE WINGED MONKEYS SHALL BE TO CARRY YOU TO YOUR FOREST.

THEN, HAVING USED UP THE POWERS OF THE GOLDEN CAP, I SHALL GIVE IT TO THE KING OF THE MONKEYS, THAT HE AND HIS BAND MAY THEREAFTER BE FREE FOREVERMORE.

YOU'RE CERTAINLY AS GOOD AS YOU ARE BEAUTIFUL! BUT YOU HAVEN'T YET TOLD ME HOW TO GET BACK TO KANSAS.

YOUR SILVER SHOES WILL CARRY YOU OVER THE DESERT.

IF YOU HAD KNOWN THEIR POWER YOU COULD HAVE GONE BACK TO YOUR AUNT EM THE VERY FIRST DAY YOU CAME TO THIS COUNTRY.

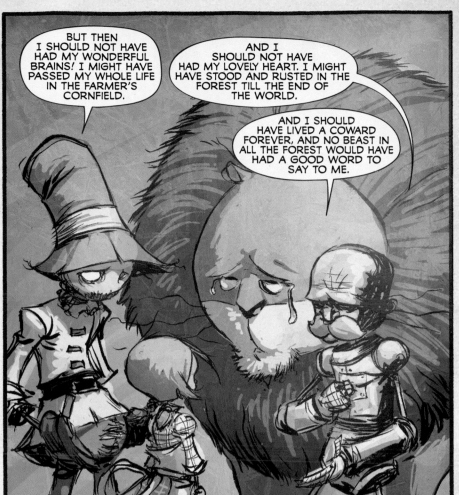

BUT THEN I SHOULD NOT HAVE HAD MY WONDERFUL BRAINS! I MIGHT HAVE PASSED MY WHOLE LIFE IN THE FARMER'S CORNFIELD.

AND I SHOULD NOT HAVE HAD MY LOVELY HEART. I MIGHT HAVE STOOD AND RUSTED IN THE FOREST TILL THE END OF THE WORLD.

AND I SHOULD HAVE LIVED A COWARD FOREVER, AND NO BEAST IN ALL THE FOREST WOULD HAVE HAD A GOOD WORD TO SAY TO ME.

THIS IS ALL TRUE, AND I'M GLAD I WAS OF USE TO THESE GOOD FRIENDS.

BUT NOW THAT EACH OF THEM HAS WHAT HE MOST DESIRED, AND EACH IS HAPPY TO HAVE A KINGDOM TO RULE, I SHOULD LIKE TO GO BACK TO KANSAS.

THE SILVER SHOES CAN CARRY YOU TO ANY PLACE IN THE WORLD IN THREE STEPS, AND EACH STEP WILL BE MADE IN THE WINK OF AN EYE.

ALL YOU HAVE TO DO IS KNOCK THE HEELS TOGETHER THREE TIMES AND COMMAND THE SHOES TO CARRY YOU WHEREVER YOU WISH TO GO.

IF THAT'S SO, I'LL ASK THEM TO CARRY ME BACK TO KANSAS AT ONCE.

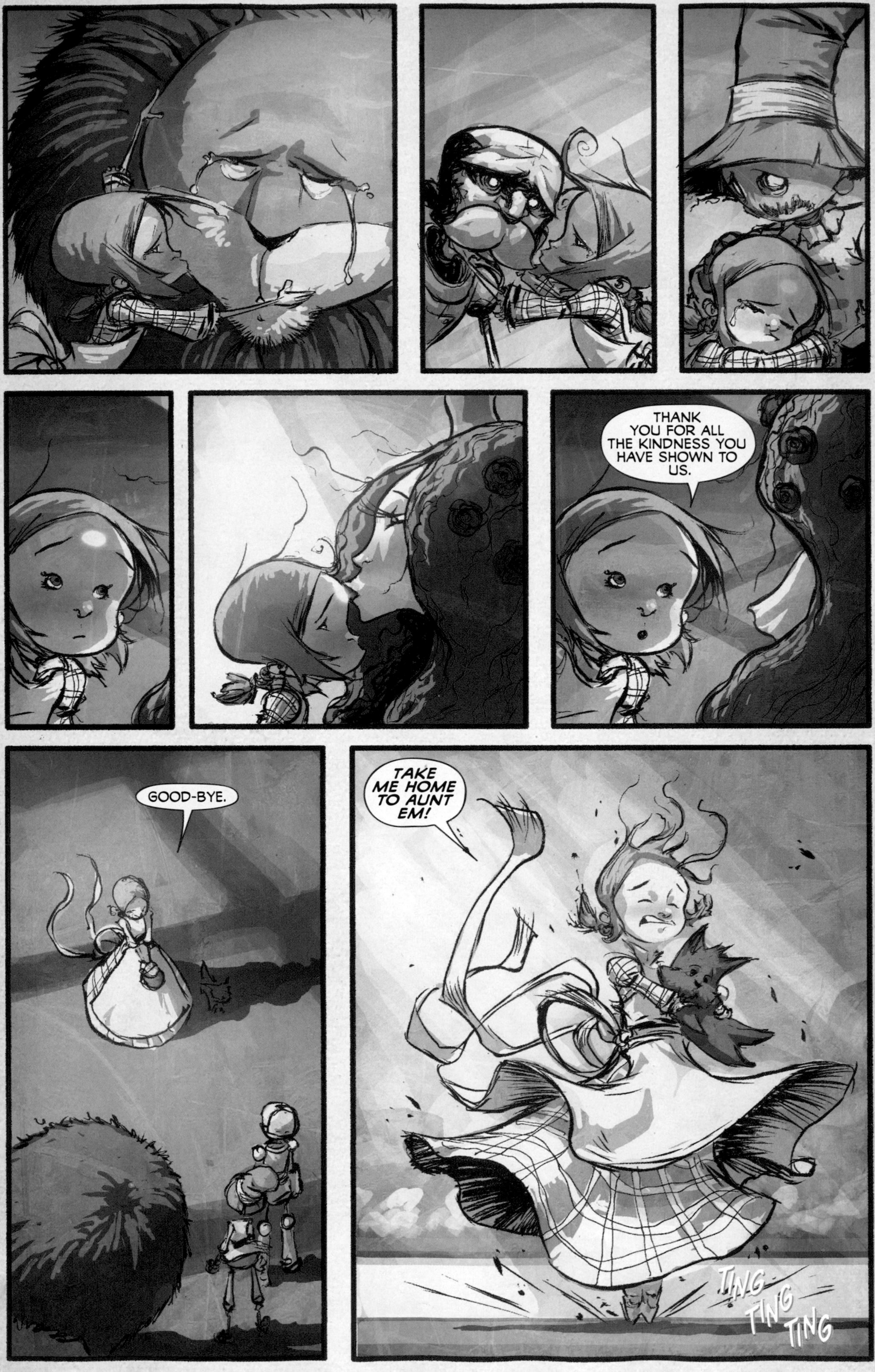
THANK YOU FOR ALL THE KINDNESS YOU HAVE SHOWN TO US.
GOOD-BYE.
TAKE ME HOME TO AUNT EM!
TING TING TING

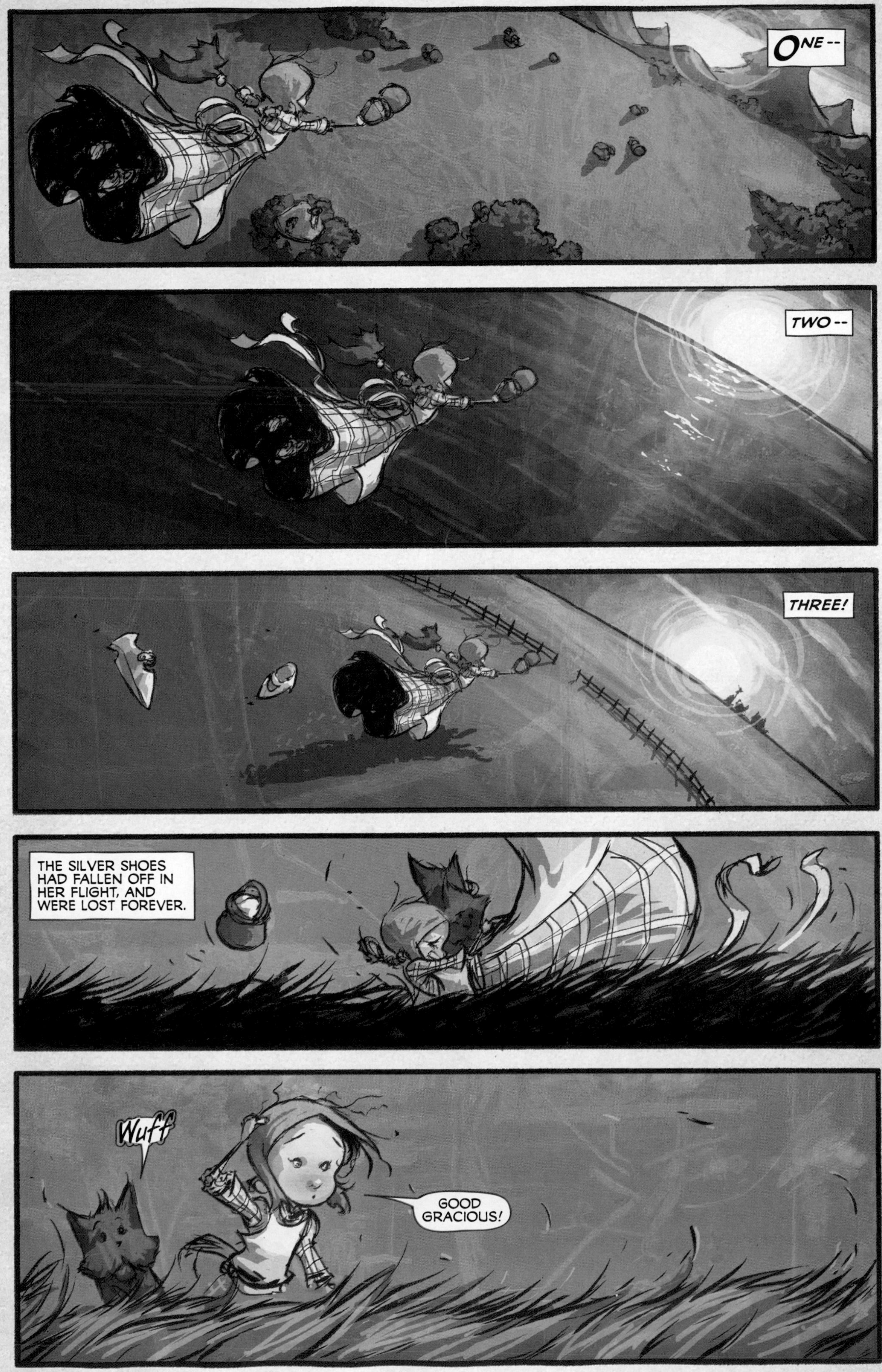
ONE--
TWO--
THREE!
THE SILVER SHOES HAD FALLEN OFF IN HER FLIGHT, AND WERE LOST FOREVER.
Wuff
GOOD GRACIOUS!

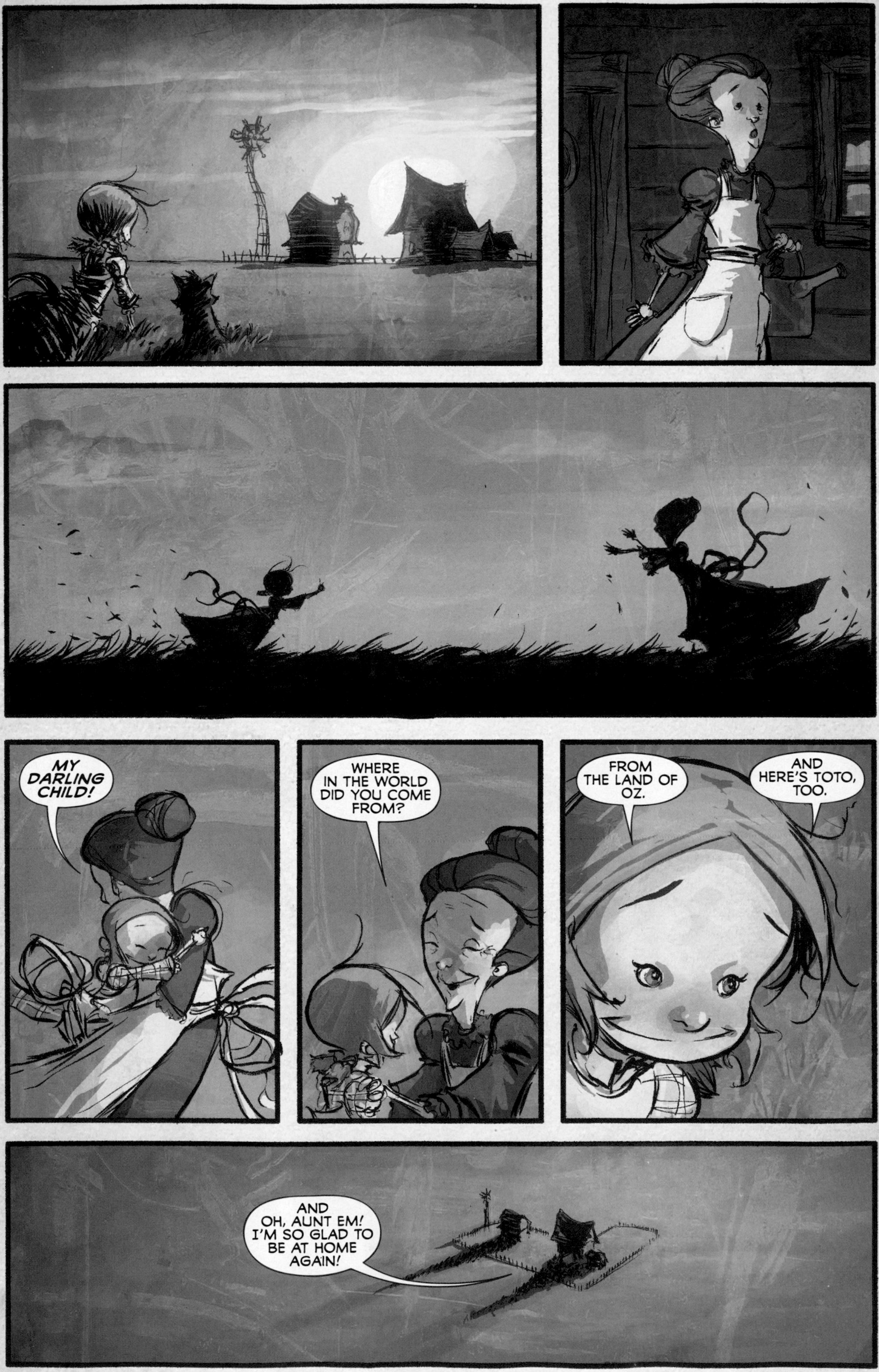
MY DARLING CHILD!
WHERE IN THE WORLD DID YOU COME FROM?
FROM THE LAND OF OZ.
AND HERE'S TOTO, TOO.
AND OH, AUNT EM! I'M SO GLAD TO BE AT HOME AGAIN!

The story continues in...

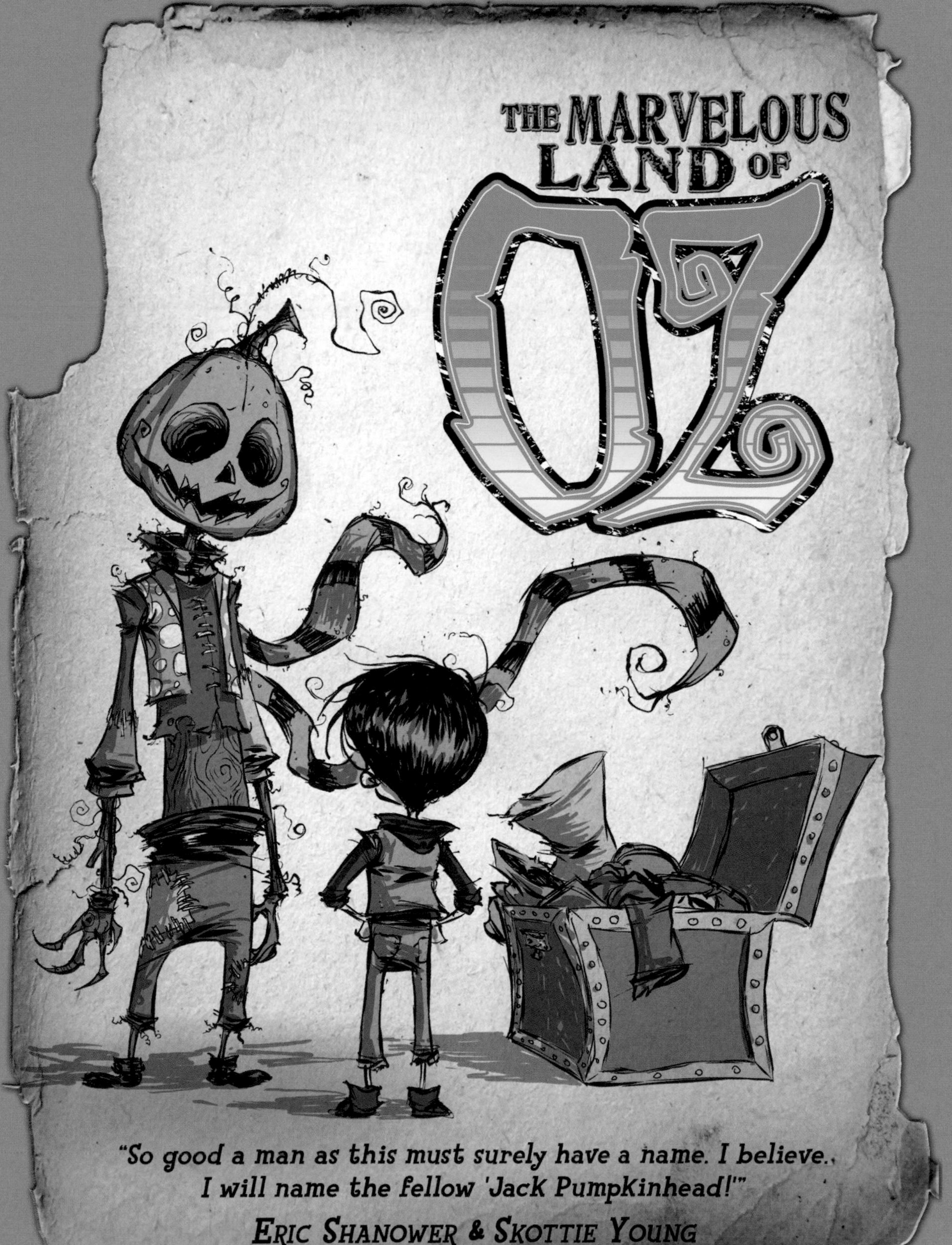
THE MARVELOUS LAND OF OZ
"So good a man as this must surely have a name. I believe. I will name the fellow 'Jack Pumpkinhead!'"
ERIC SHANOWER & SKOTTIE YOUNG

ONE

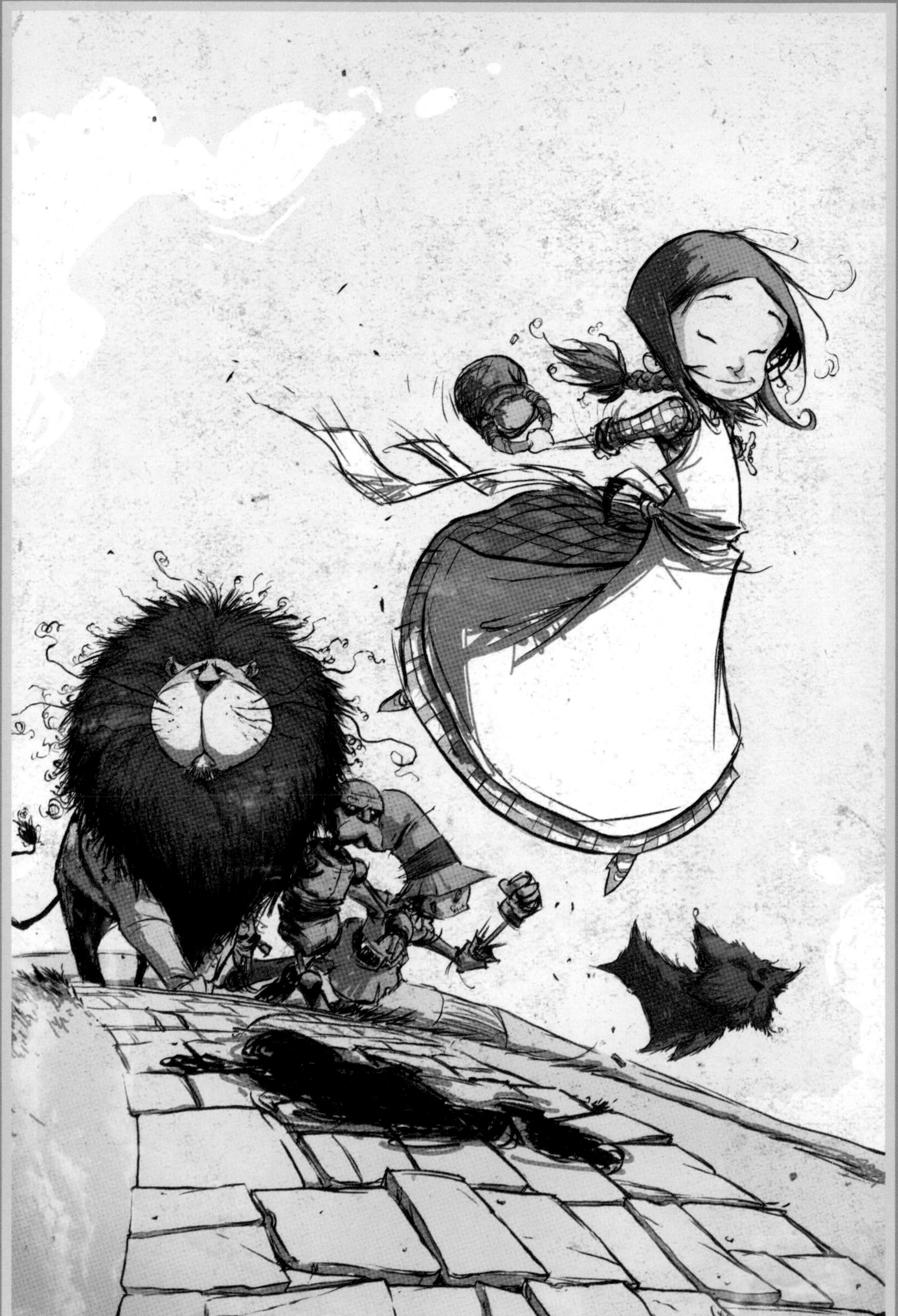

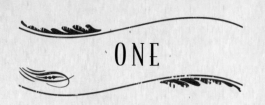

ONE

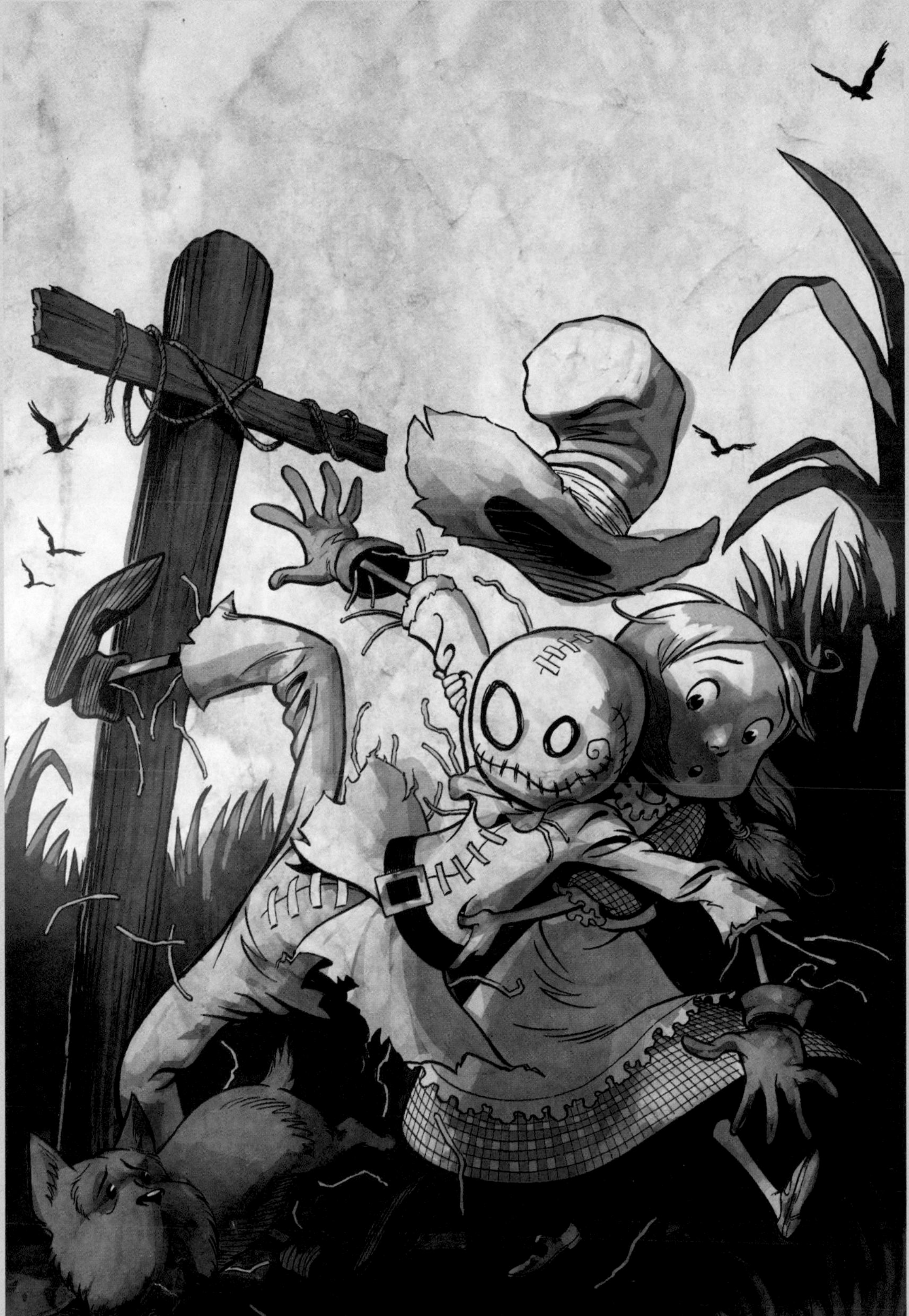

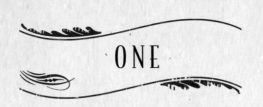

Variant Cover by Eric Shanower

ONE

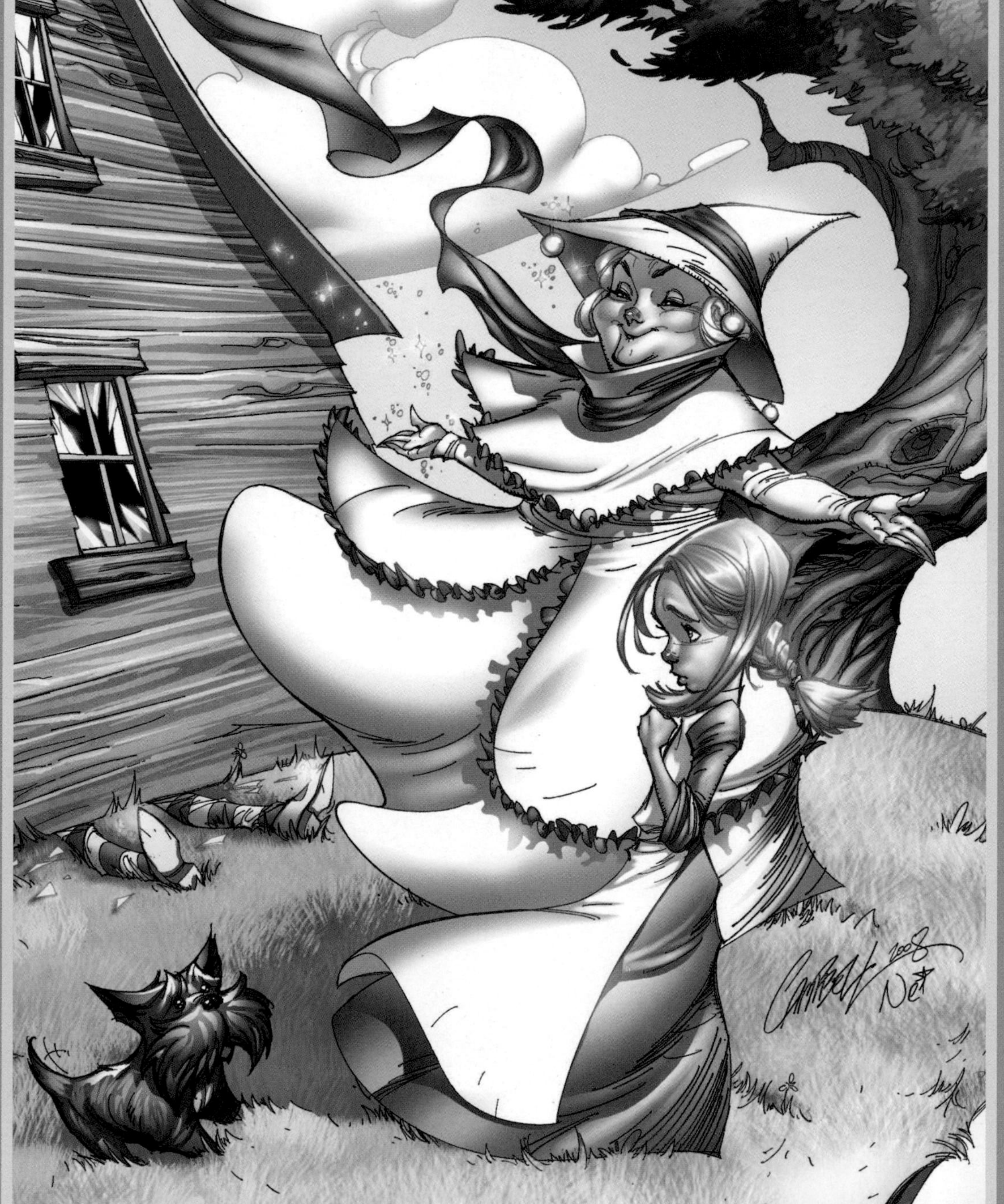
Campbell 2008
Net

Variant Cover by J. Scott Campbell

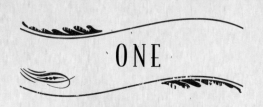

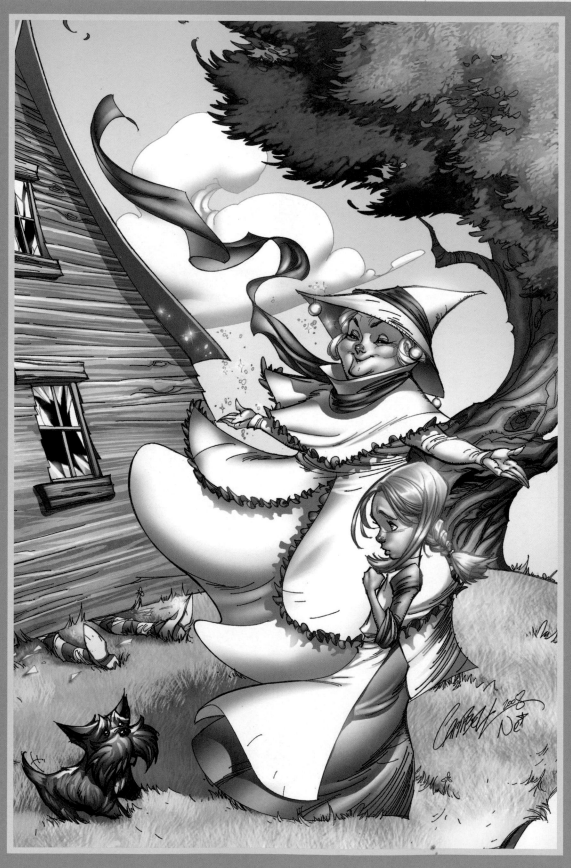

TWO

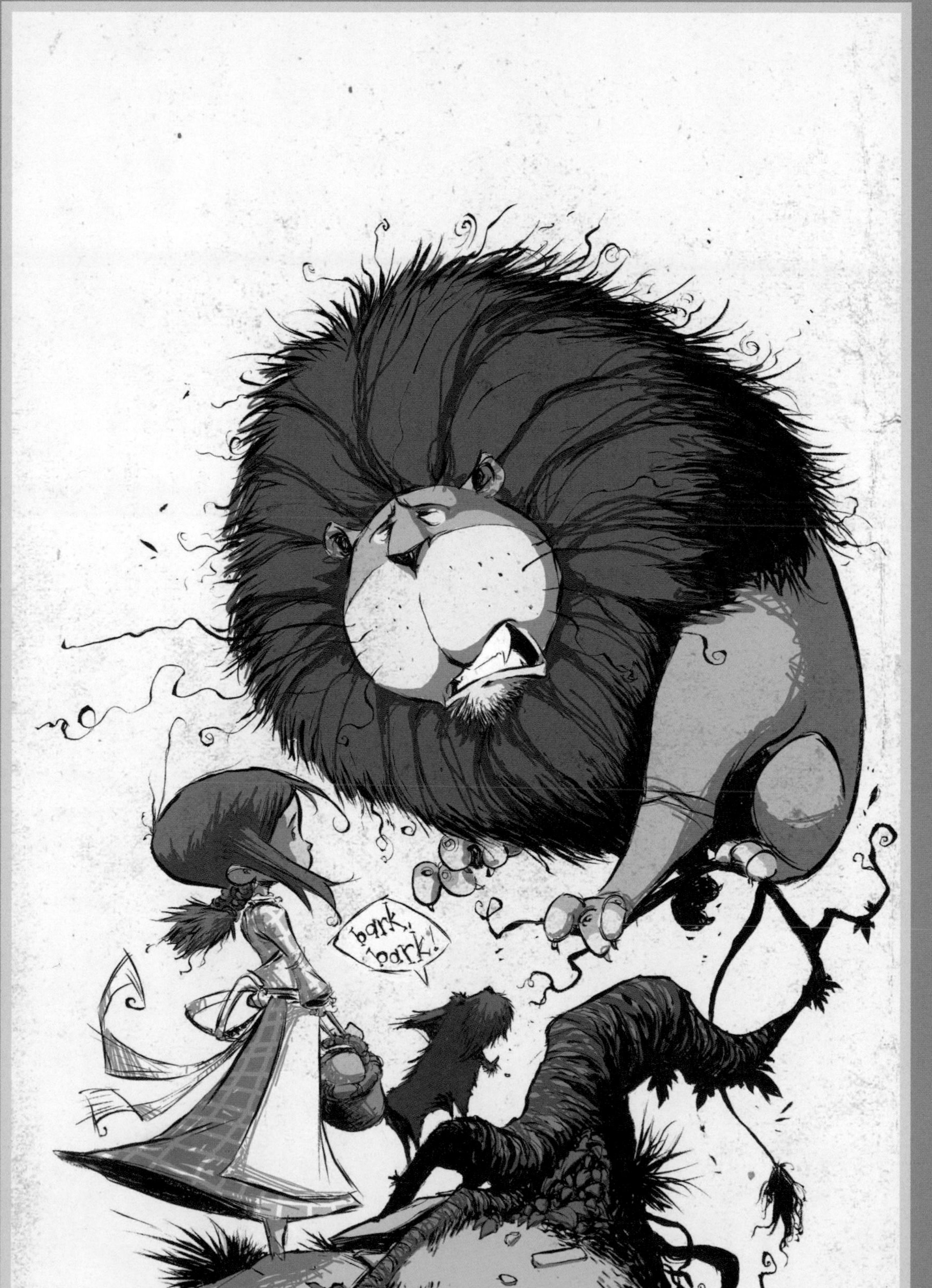
bark, bark!

THREE

zzZ

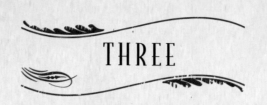

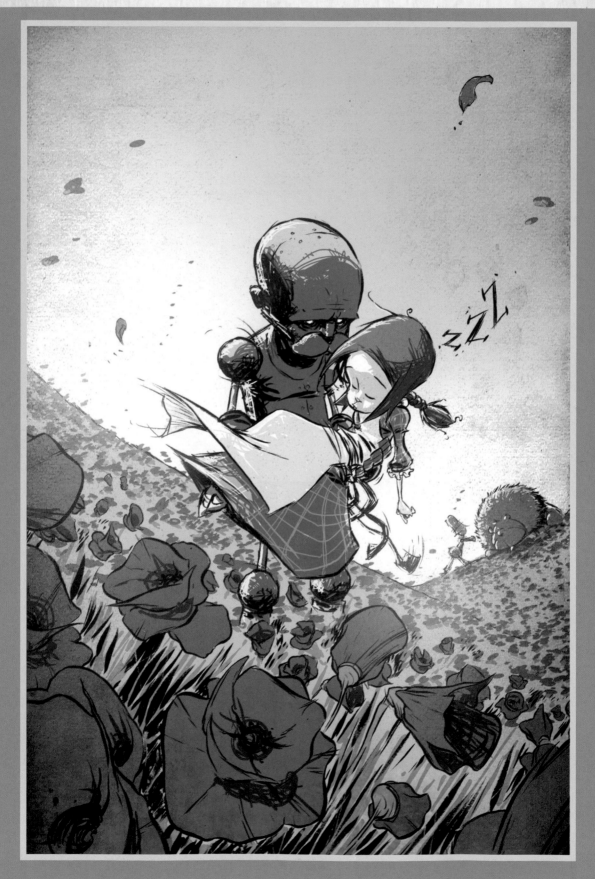

FOUR

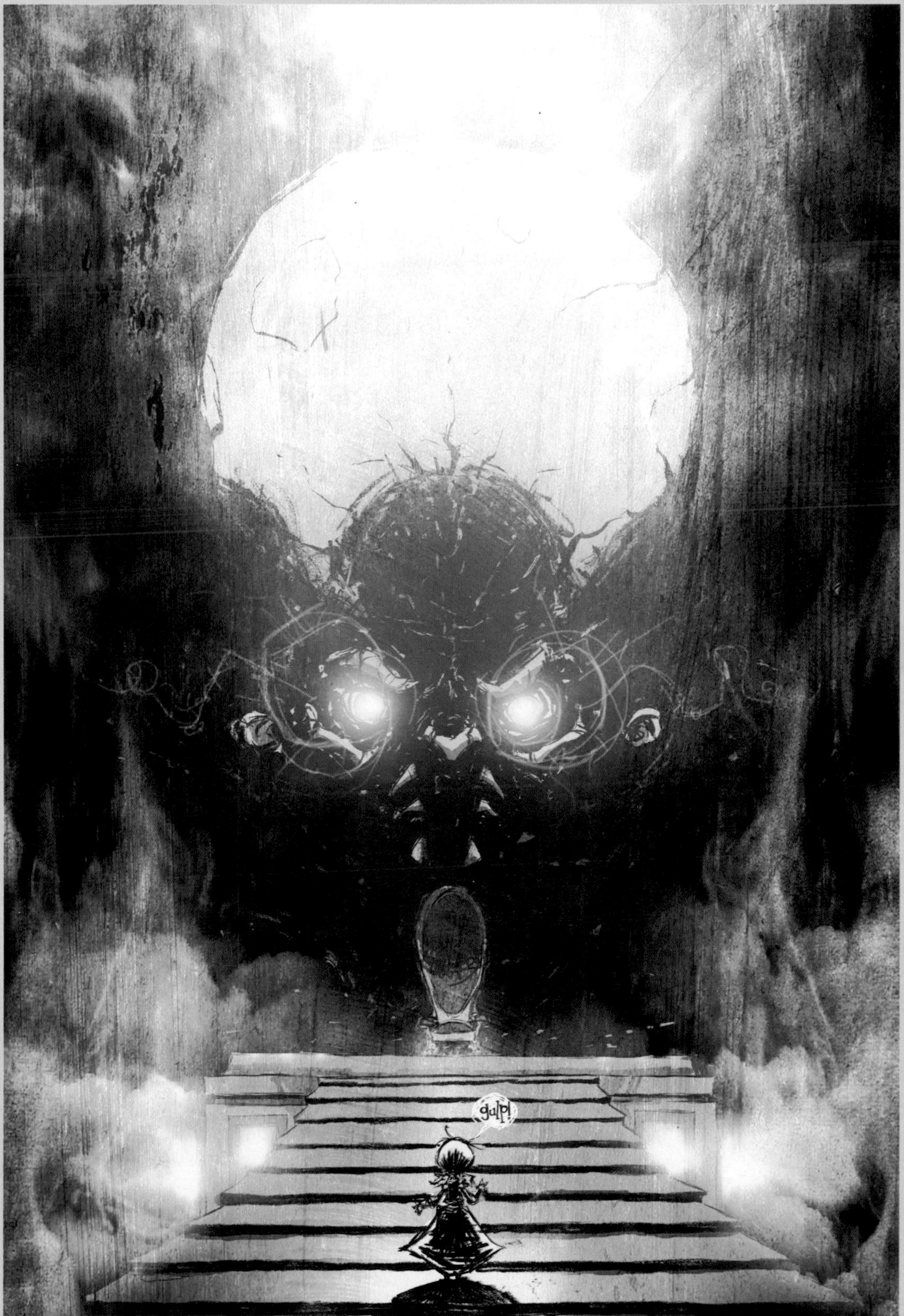
gulp!

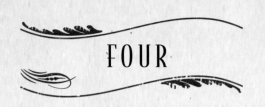

FIVE

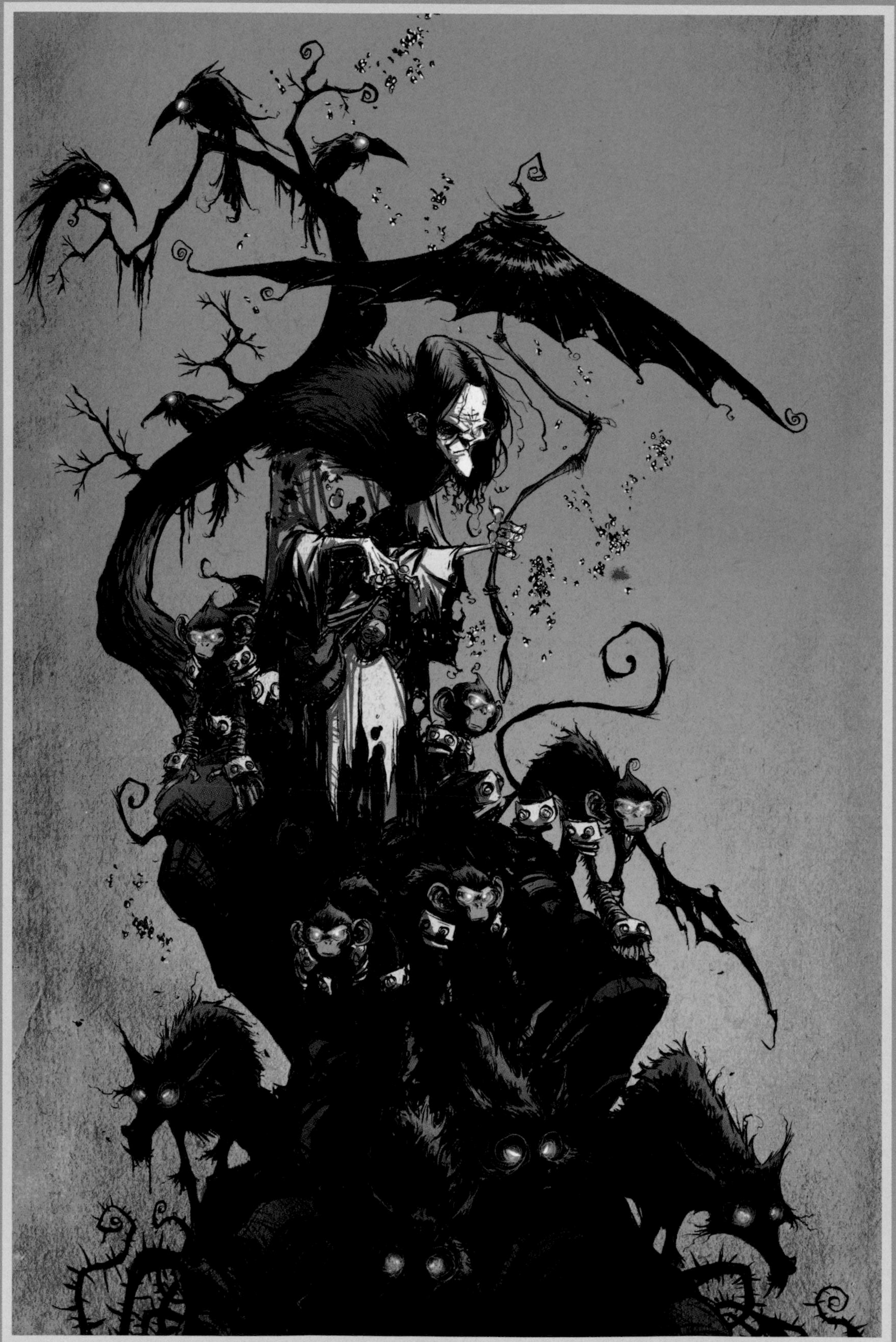

SIX

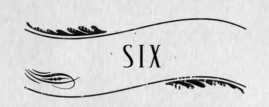

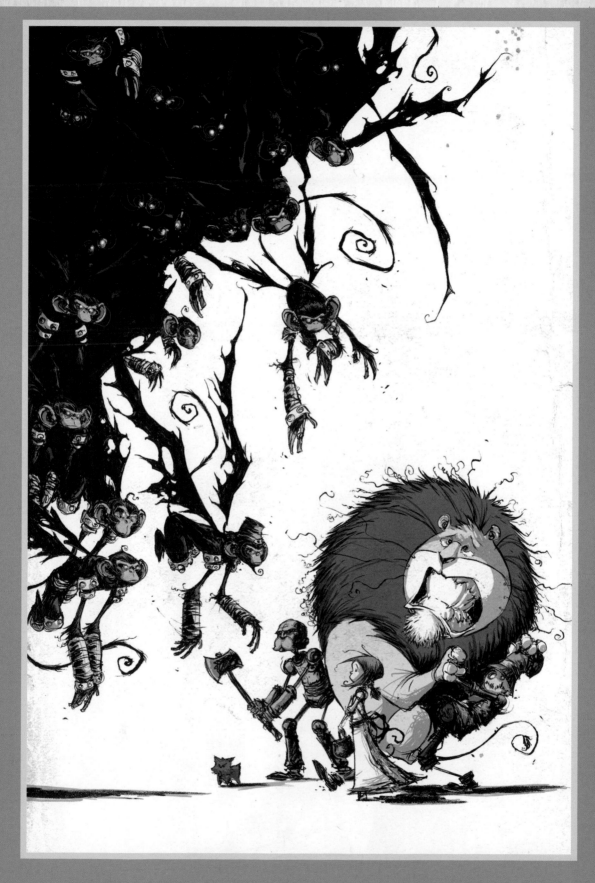

SEVEN

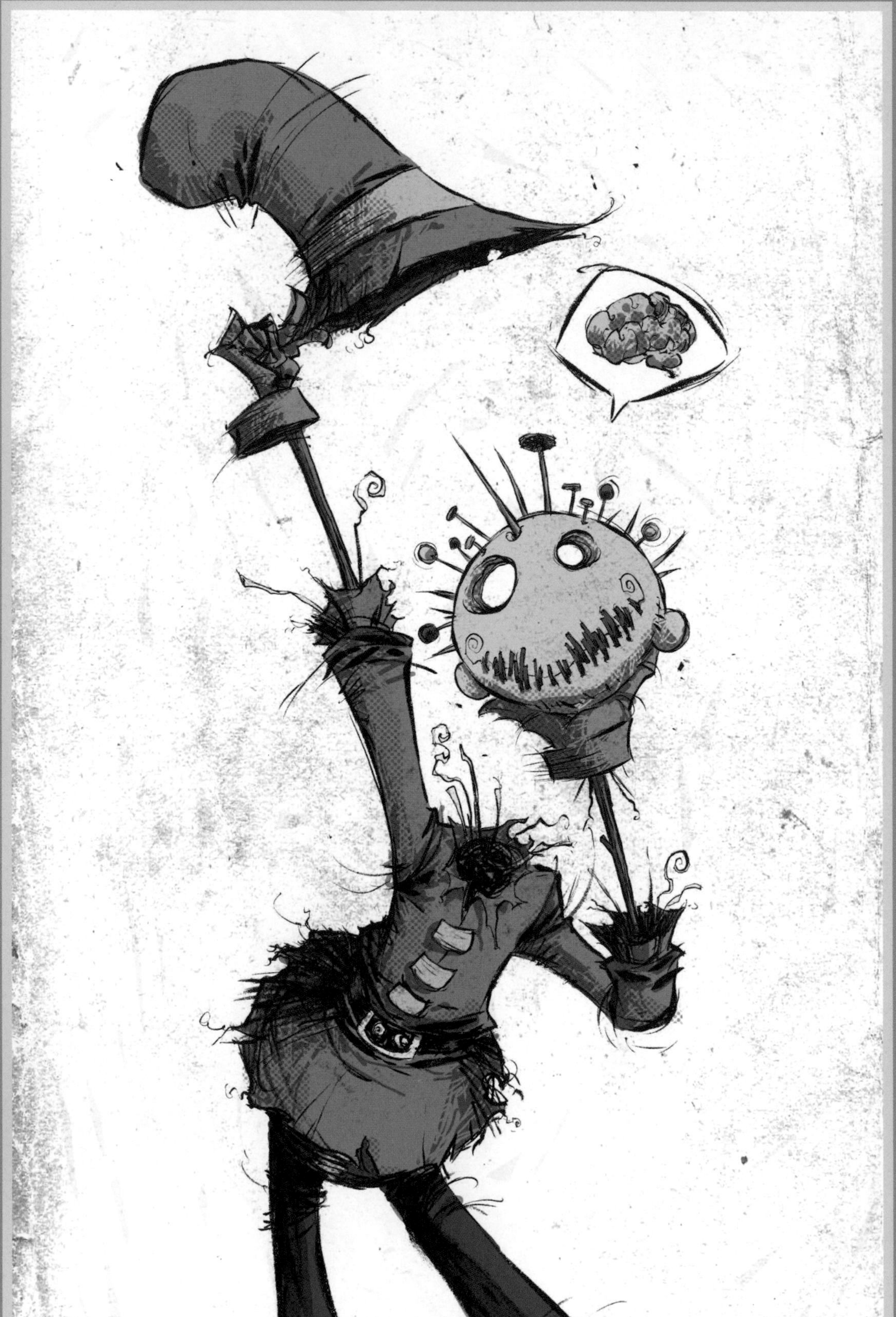

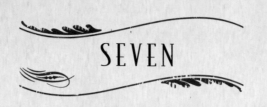

EIGHT

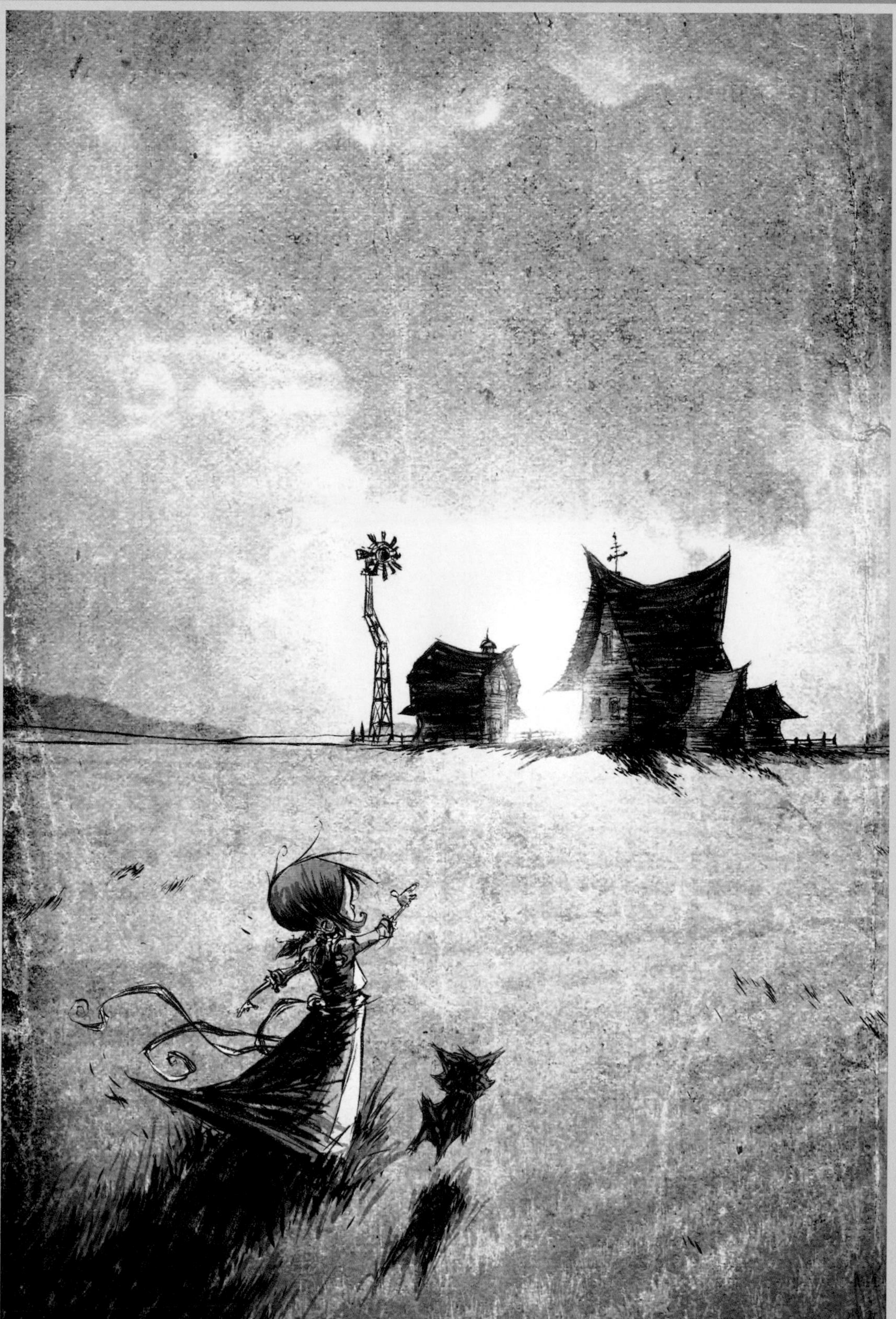

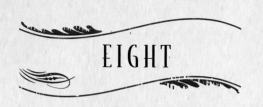

SKETCHBOOK

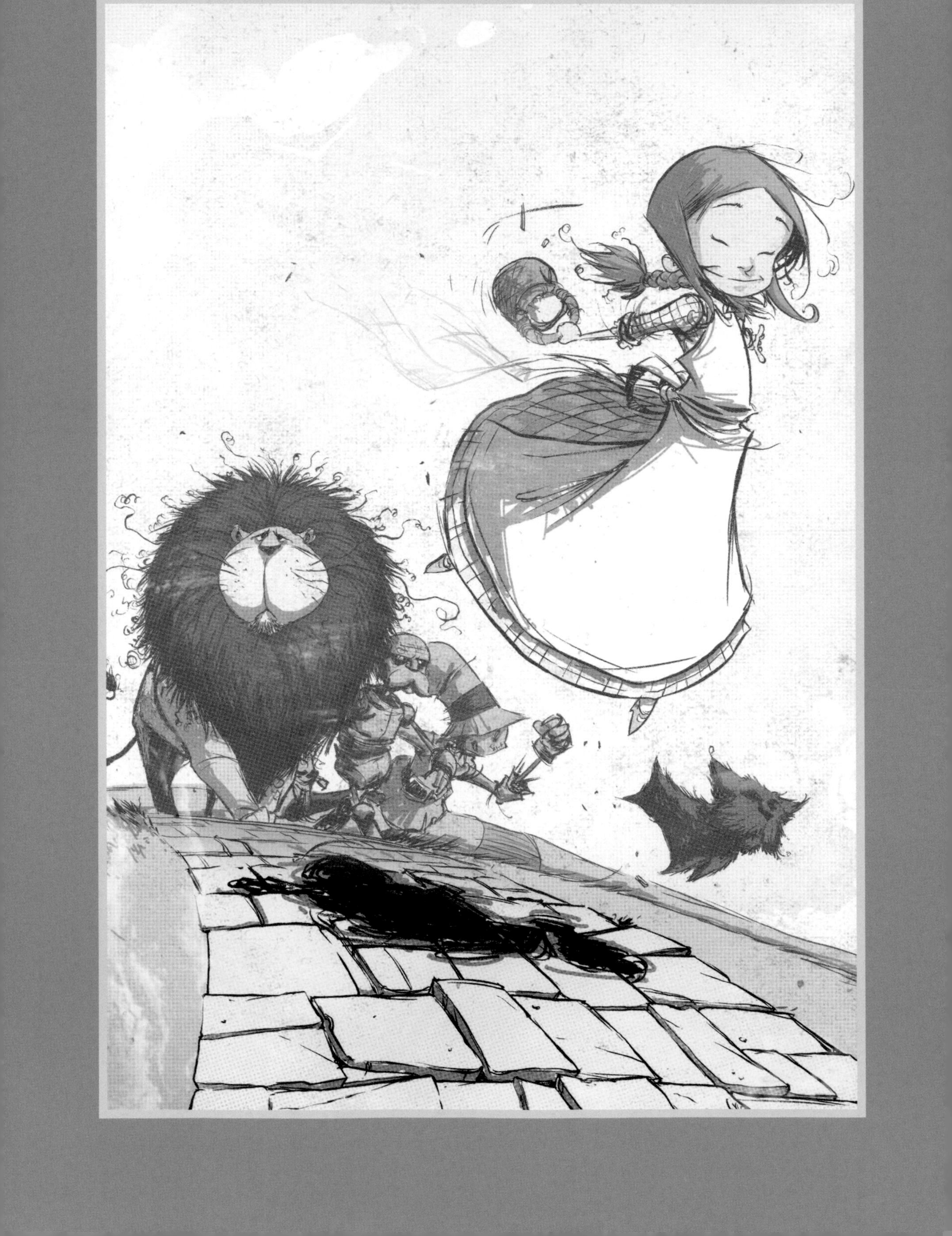

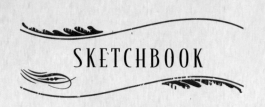

The Wonderful Wizard of Oz

by L. Frank Baum earned the status of bestseller almost immediately upon publication in 1900. Its lavish illustrations by W. W. Denslow raised the bar for excellence in book design. Baum's story, too, set a new standard. This wasn't the first time an American author had created a fantasy using American themes, setting aside elves, fairies, and the trappings of medieval Europe. But it was the first time an American fairy tale struck a lasting chord with readers and took its place on the shelves of great American literature.

Shortly after the book's publication, adaptations began. Baum took his story to Broadway, where *The Wizard of Oz* became the most popular show of 1903. This success prompted first a sequel to the book, then a whole series of Oz books, while more stage shows and films quickly followed. The book series proved so popular that it outlived Baum, officially continued by six writers through 1963 and unofficially continued by dozens of writers since.

The motion picture adaptation of *The Wizard of Oz* starring Judy Garland opened in 1939 and is now considered one of the most popular movies of all time. Since 1956, when the book entered the public domain, newly illustrated editions have proliferated worldwide. Russian children enjoy *The Wizard of the Emerald City*, the 1939 translation by Alexander Volkov, who spun off his own series of books, continued by others after Volkov's death.

Comic adaptations of Oz flourished alongside the other adaptations. Newspapers in 1904-05 carried two separate Oz series—one by author Baum, another by illustrator Denslow—featuring adventures of Oz characters in the USA. A daily newspaper comic strip by Walt Spouse adapted Baum's Oz books in the 1930s. In 1956 the first stand-alone comic book adaptation of *The Wizard of Oz* appeared, *Dell Junior Treasury* #5.

Since then Oz comics have flourished. Twenty-first century Oz comics are surprisingly varied. Dark overtones, steampunk backgrounds, team-ups with other children's book characters, Japanese manga, Korean manwha, French bande dessinée, web comics—it's all there. Now, Marvel is taking Oz back to its roots with a faithful comics adaptation of the book that began it all, *The Wonderful Wizard of Oz*, with a script by yours truly and glorious art by Skottie Young.

Young has set aside previous versions of Oz and reached inside himself for his own response to Baum's story. He's brought forth a brand new vision of Oz, firmly rooted in the original, yet with life bursting out all around. Young's Dorothy is unmistakably a Kansas farm girl, whisked away to a magical land. It's a journey we're glad to take with her because she is so obviously sensible, human, and down-to-earth. Young's solid designs of Dorothy's companions, the Scarecrow and the Tin Woodman, make these preposterous creatures easy to believe in. And Young's Cowardly Lion . . . well, Young's big, bashful fur ball is my favorite.

Just turn the page, take a look, and see if you don't agree.

—ERIC SHANOWER

Dorothy

Skottie was obviously trying several different looks for Dorothy Gale here. The character can't be too specific since she's a sort of Everywoman. Skottie's final design for Dorothy is perfect. It's just what the story calls for.
—Eric

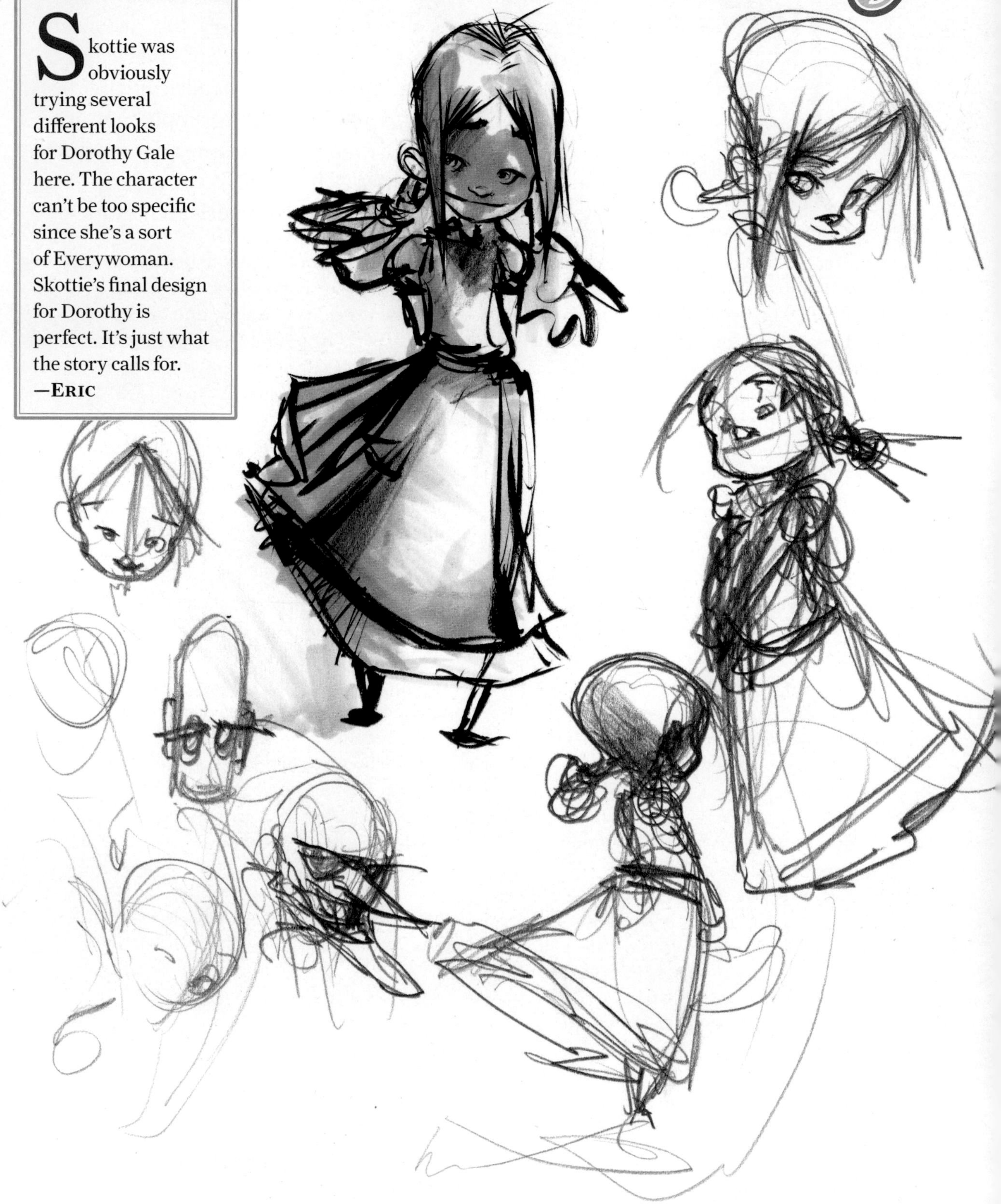

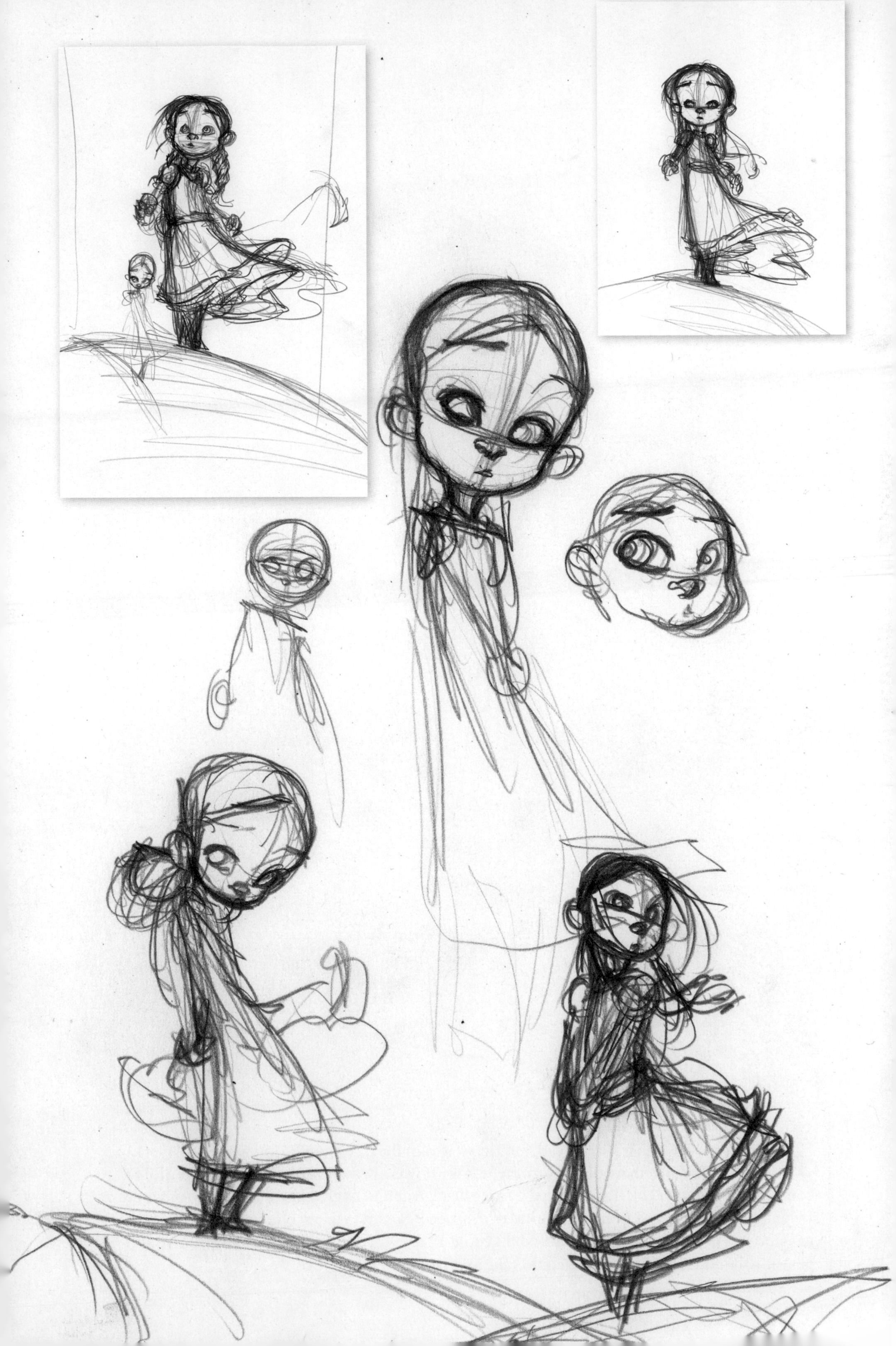

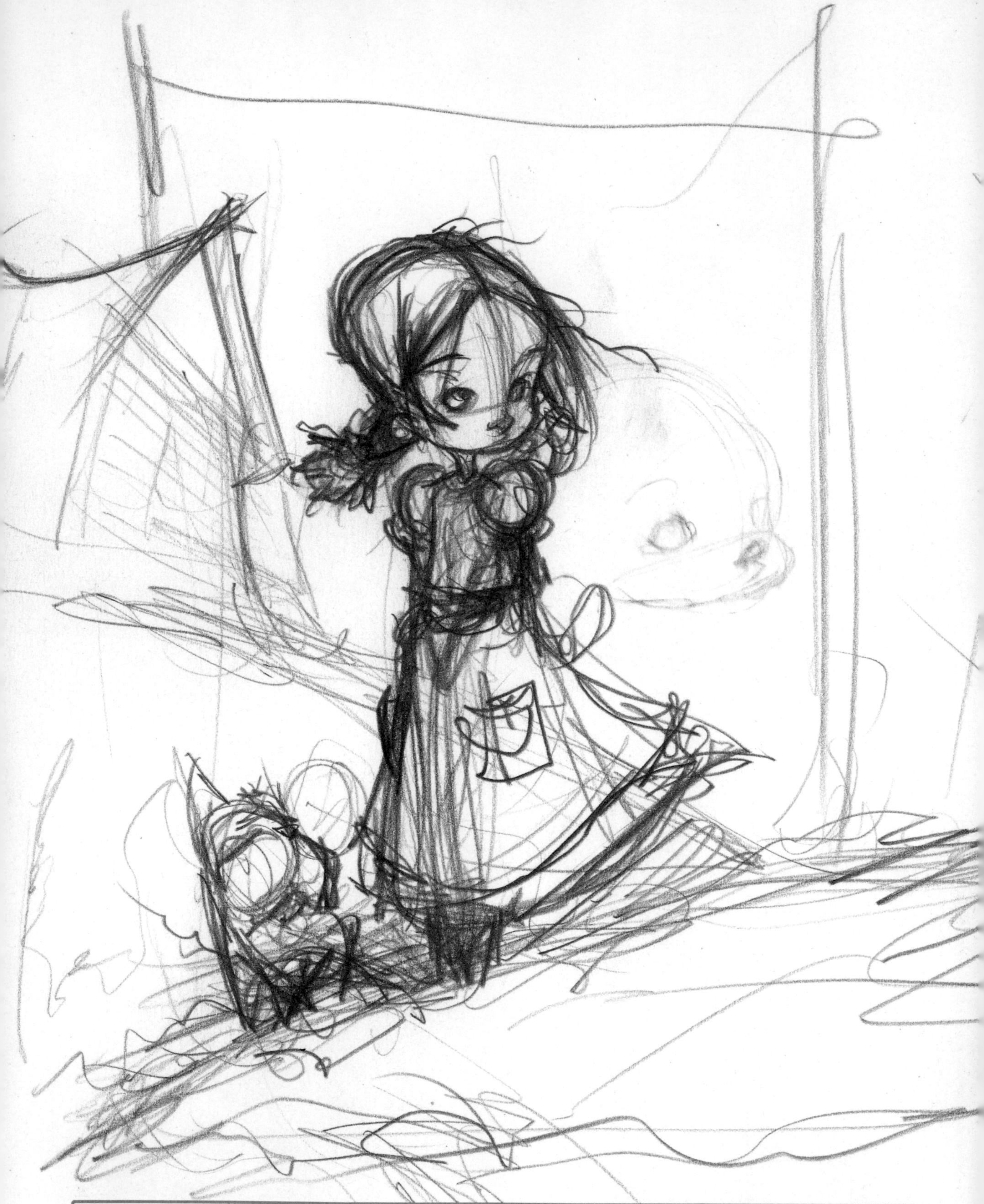

I may have drawn Dorothy's head 300 times. From the day I got the job while still working on X-Men, I started doodling Dorothy heads. It was always a very subtle change and to someone else it may look like I drew the same head over and over. I had a good idea of where I wanted her to go, but I tried every kind of eye, nose, ear, and strand of hair you could think of. Dorothy is the soul of this story and if I couldn't convince you to love her within two seconds of seeing her on the page, then I should take another job. —**SKOTTIE**

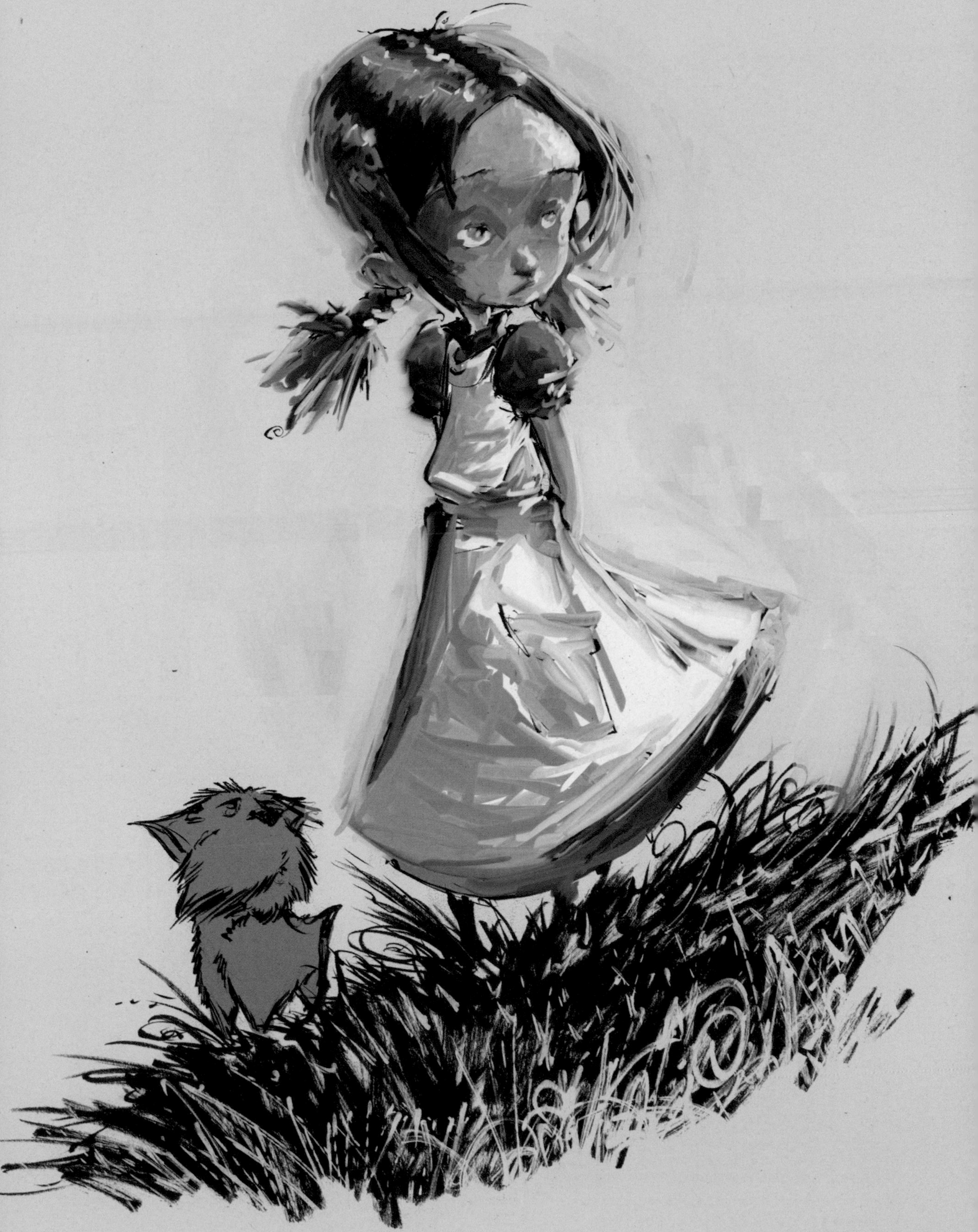

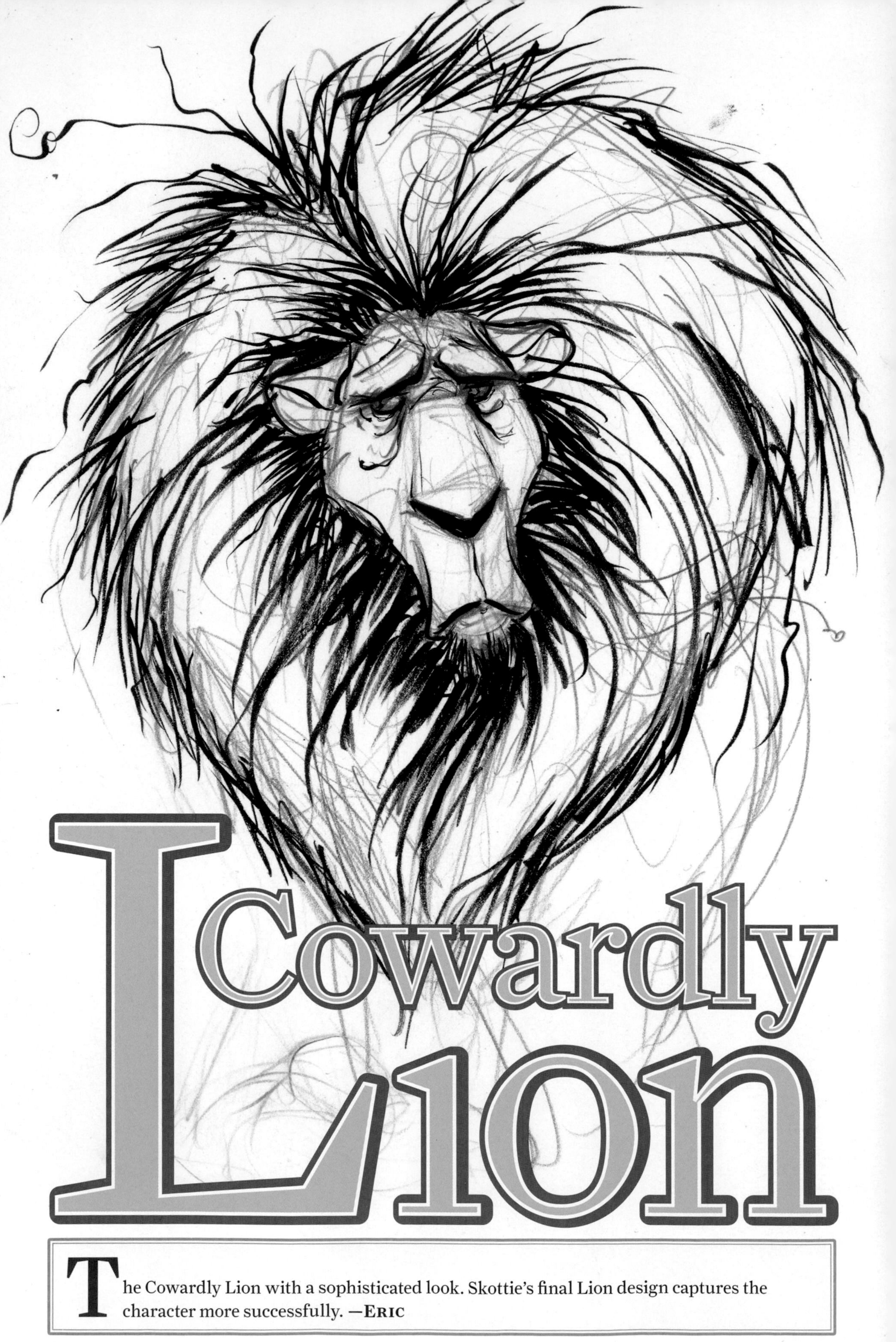

Cowardly Lion

The Cowardly Lion with a sophisticated look. Skottie's final Lion design captures the character more successfully. —Eric

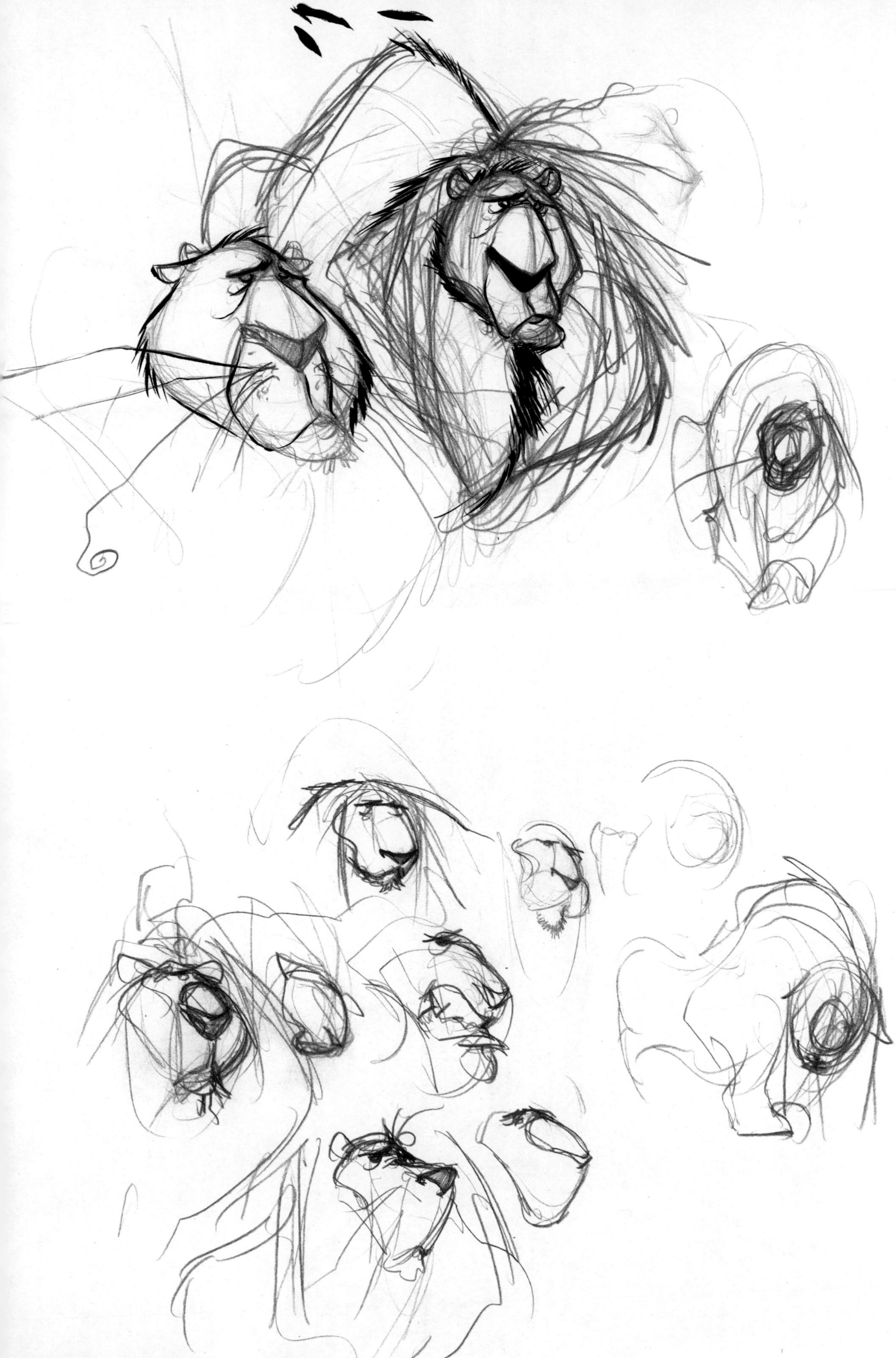

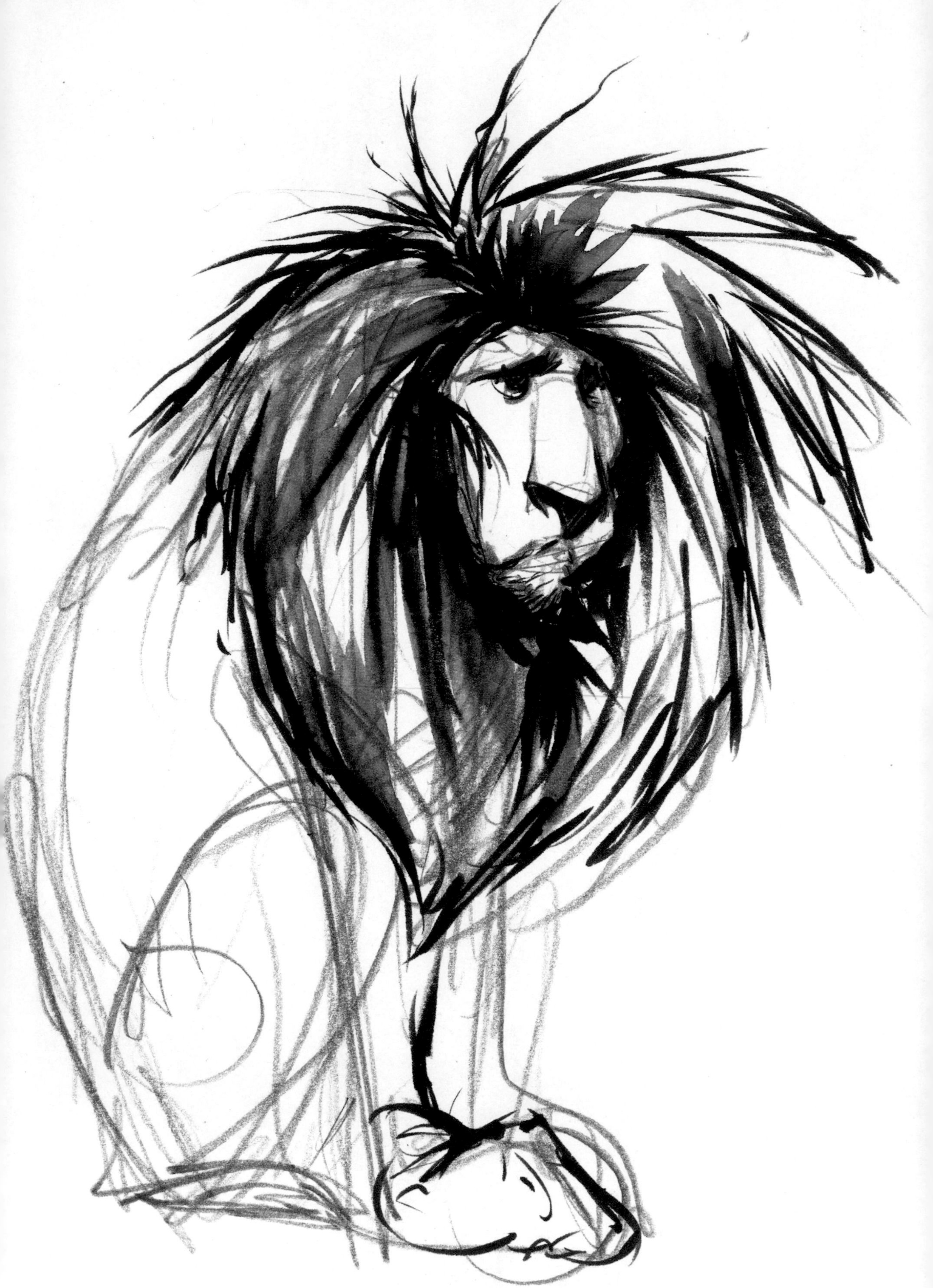

The lion was tough because when you think of lions you think of beautiful, majestic beasts. But we need you to think, "What a pussy cat." You can see that I first played with more traditional lion shapes but ended up somewhere very different. I needed to be soft and nothing says soft like big, round, puffy circles. I went with that for the face. Just a big circle with all the trappings of a lions face inside of it. Add a big frizzed-out mane of hair and we've got a lion out of a shape that you might not think screams lion. —SKOTTIE

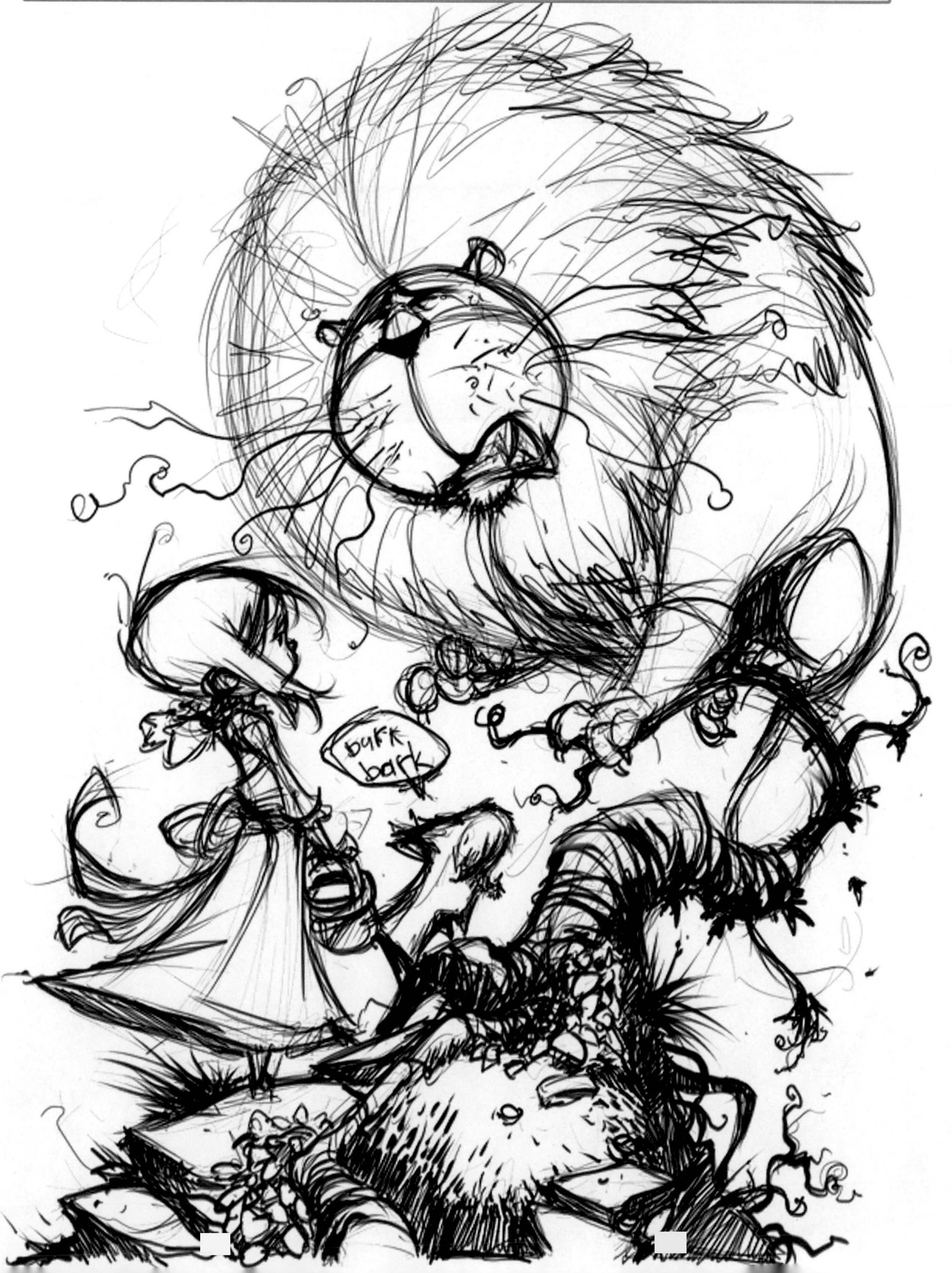
bark
bark

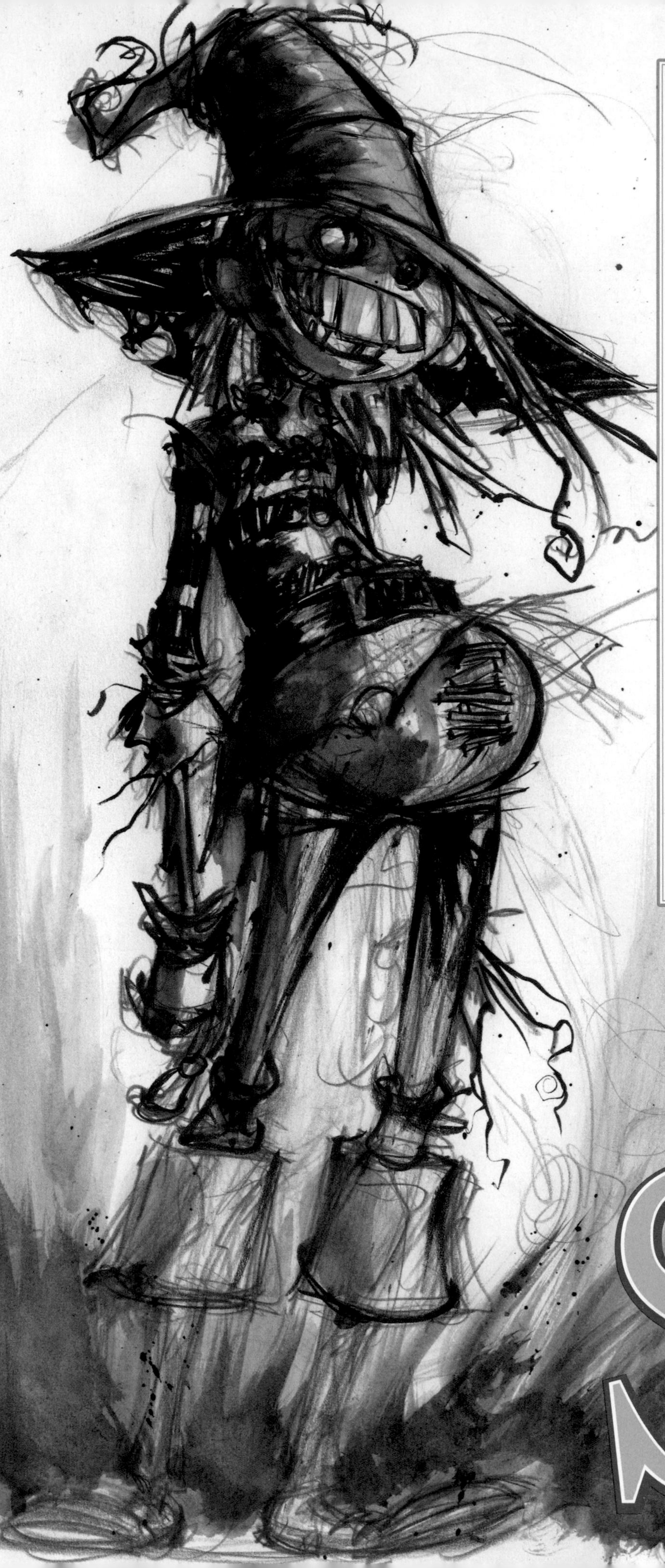

Get the Scarecrow to a dentist—quick!—**Eric**

As you'll notice, my first version of the Scarecrow was a tad over the top. I loved this version, but elements didn't illustrate Baum's vision very well. I gave him a fully functioning mouth, but he should really be more Scarecrow than person. Once I took him back to being more of a stuffed man, I tried to focus on the hat. After going through many versions of the traditional pointy hat, I landed on a bit more of a rounded one. I felt it gave him a great shape and matched the round theme I had going through his body.
—**Skottie**

Sc

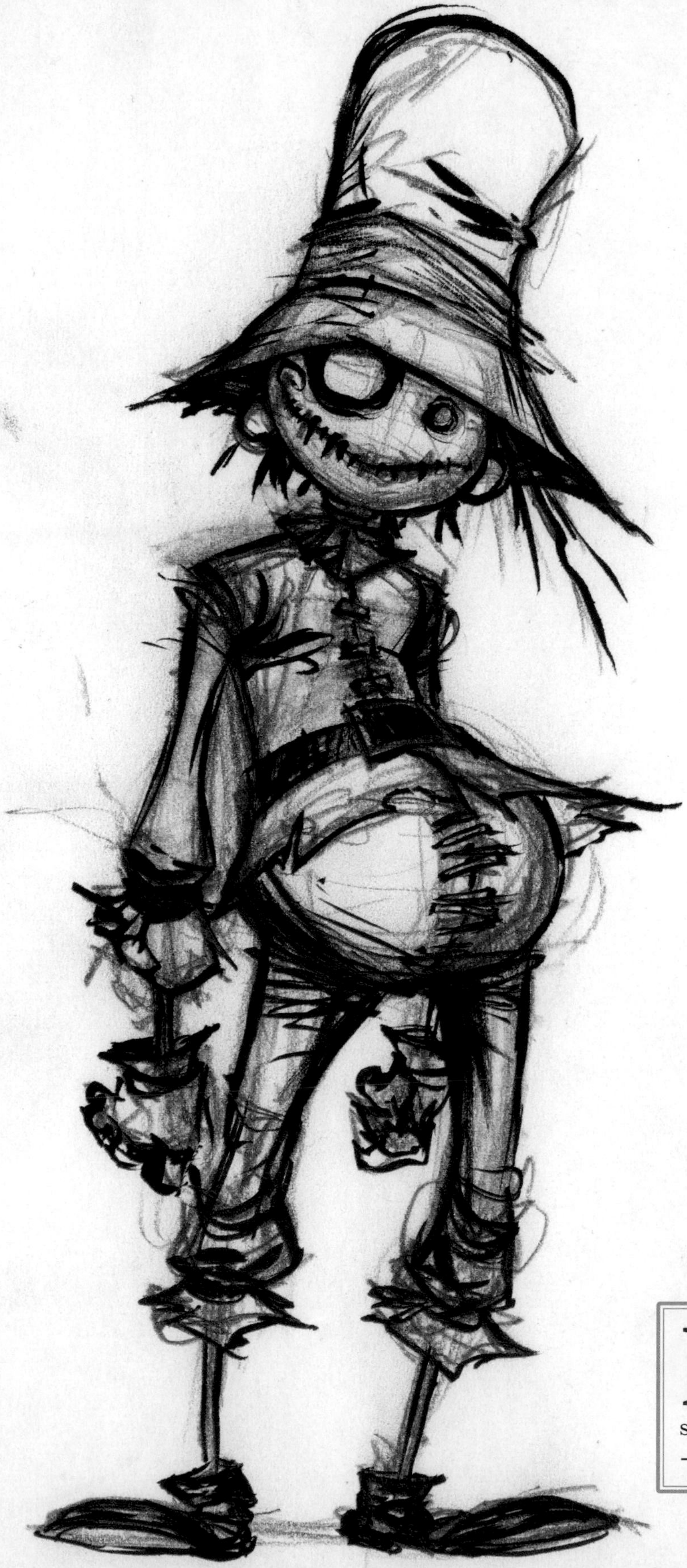

Everyone's favorite straw man.
—Eric

arecrow

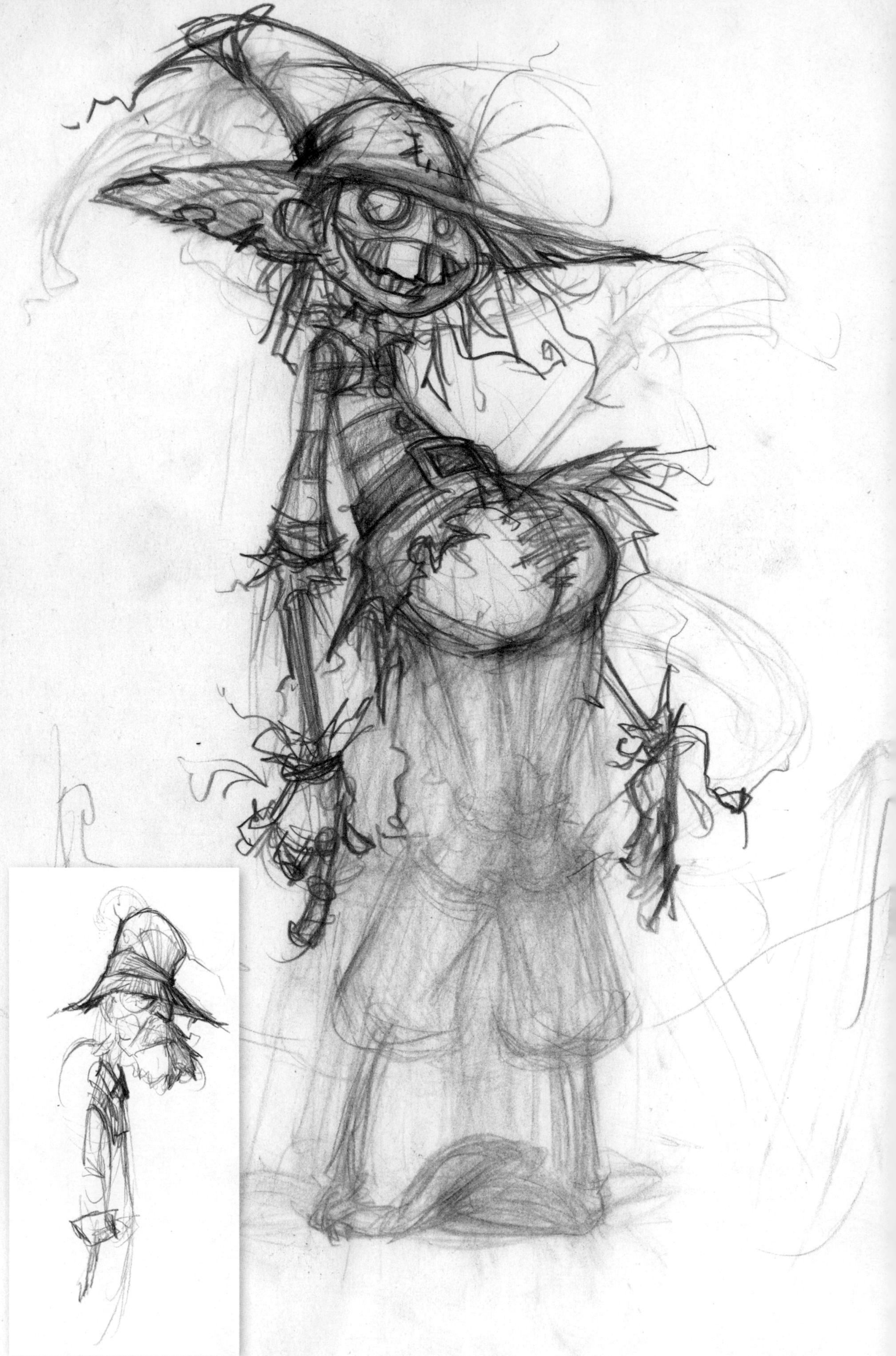

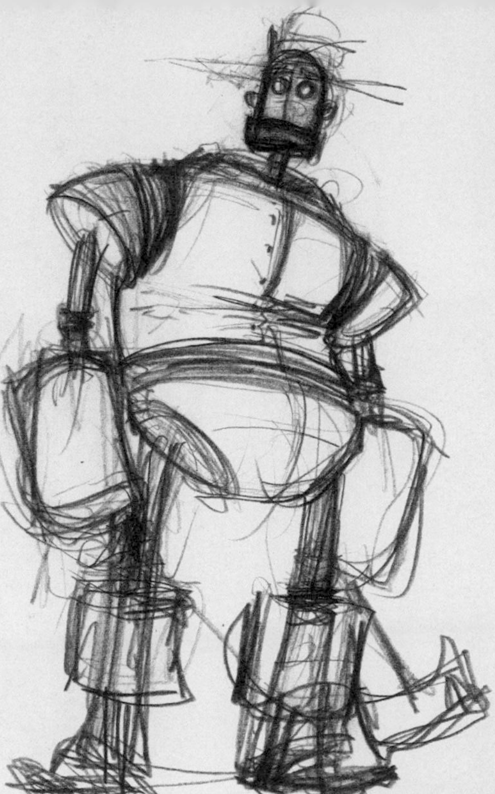

Tin Woodman

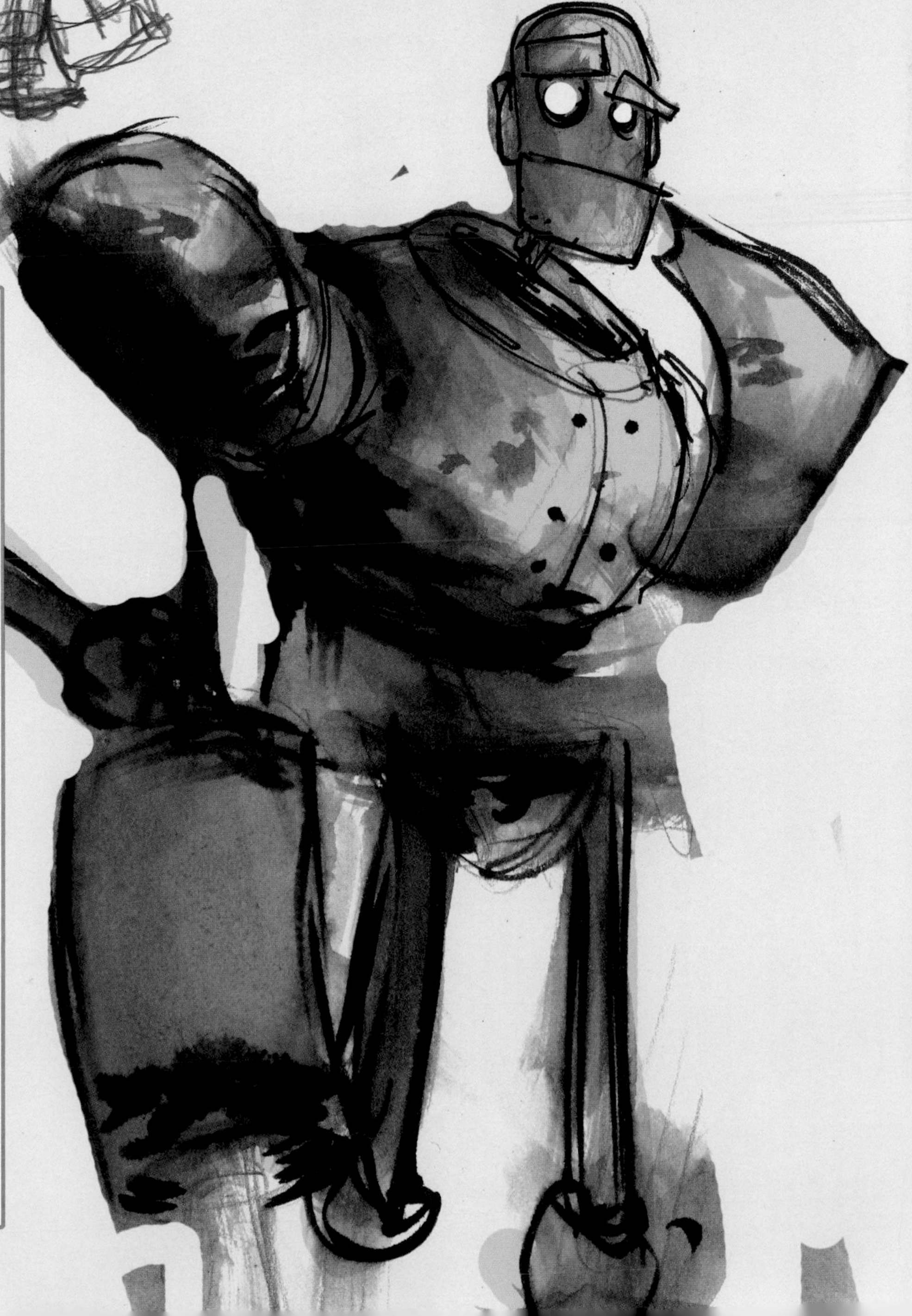

This Tin Woodman doesn't look like he'd need an axe to chop down trees.
—Eric

At first you can see that I was wanting to go super-big and more robotic. I wanted to show off how crazy I could make shapes. In the end I brought it back to the spirit of the character and who he is. I needed him to have a few features that could be pushed and pulled to lend some emotion that the "big cool robot" style just didn't give.
—Skottie

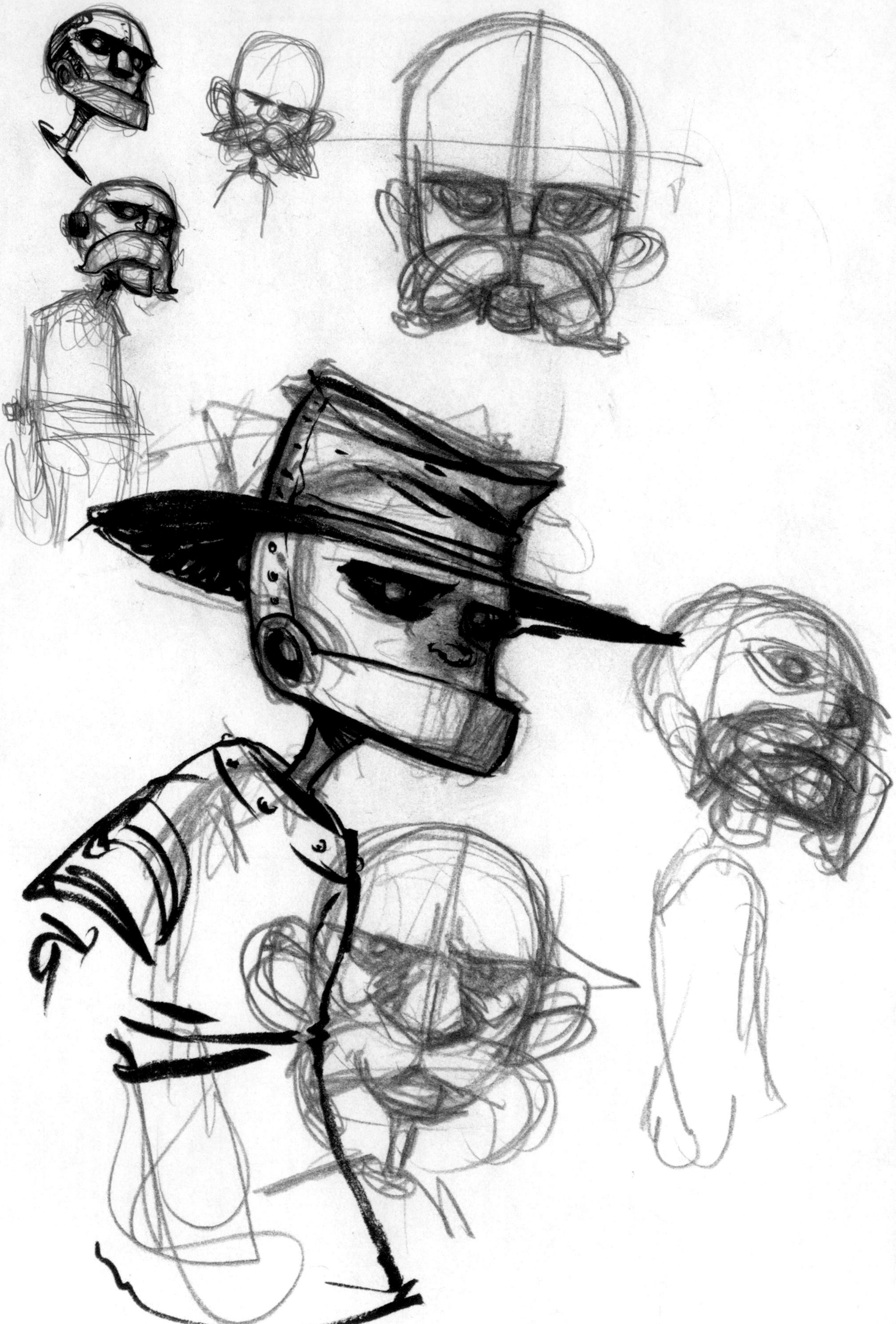

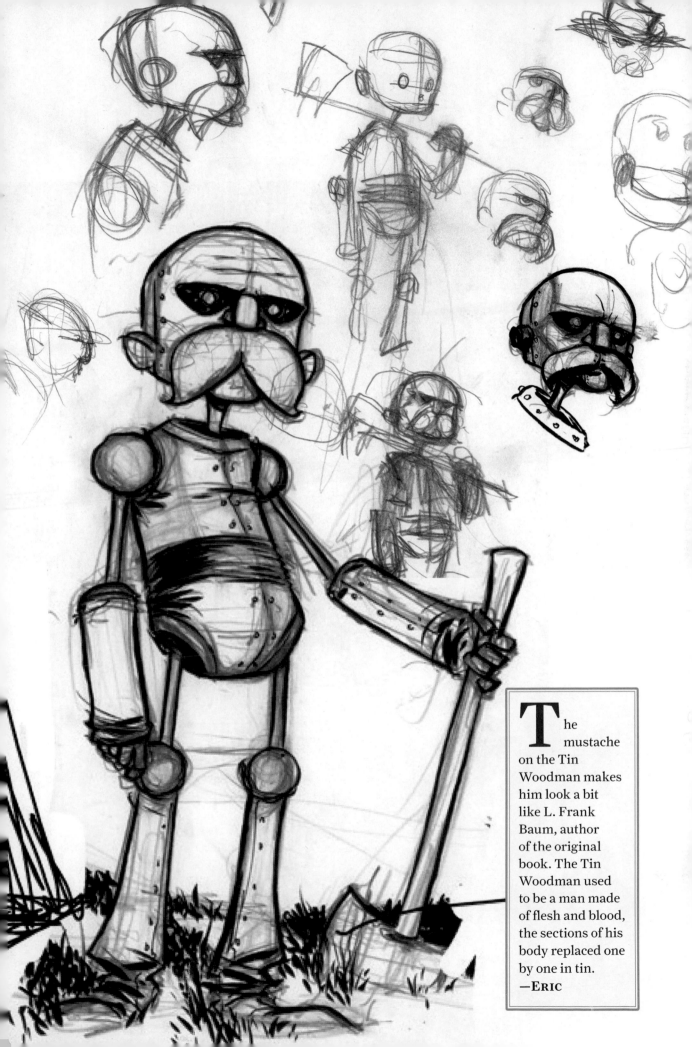

The mustache on the Tin Woodman makes him look a bit like L. Frank Baum, author of the original book. The Tin Woodman used to be a man made of flesh and blood, the sections of his body replaced one by one in tin.
—ERIC

Good Witch of the North

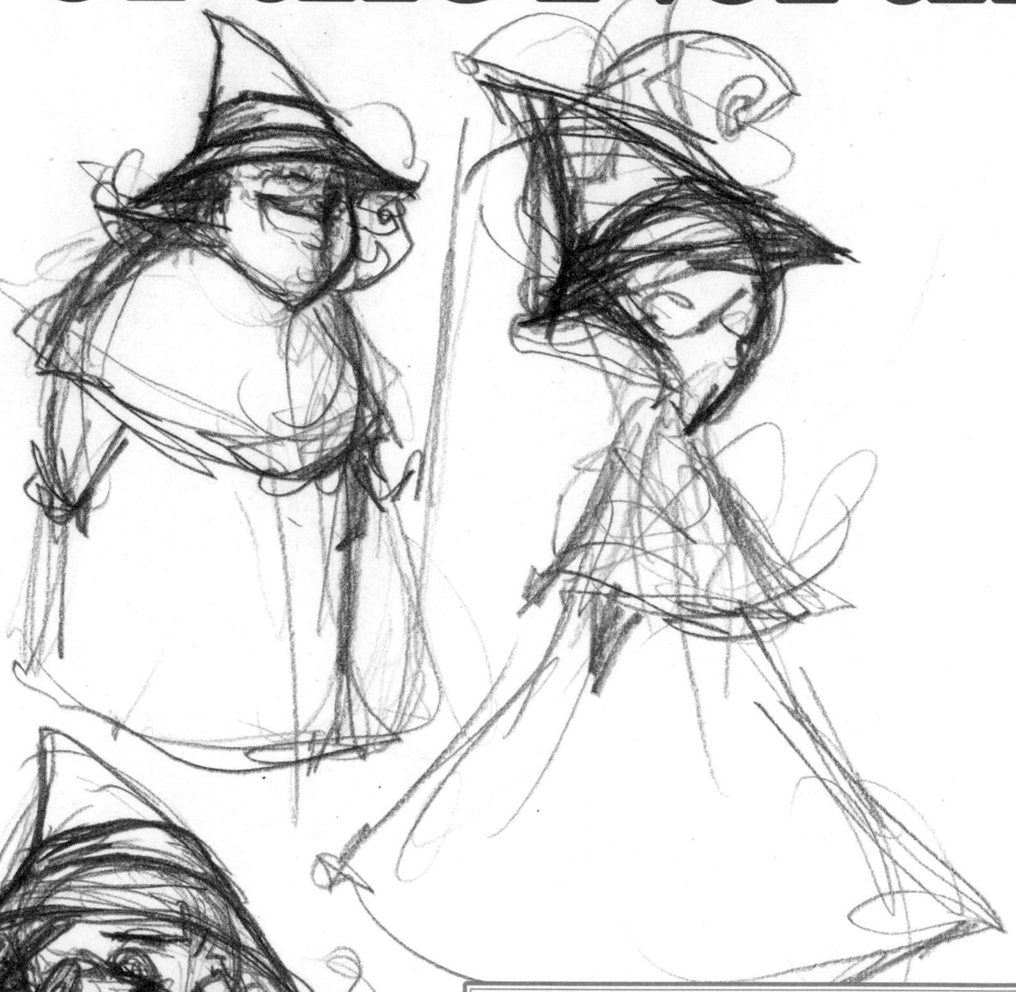

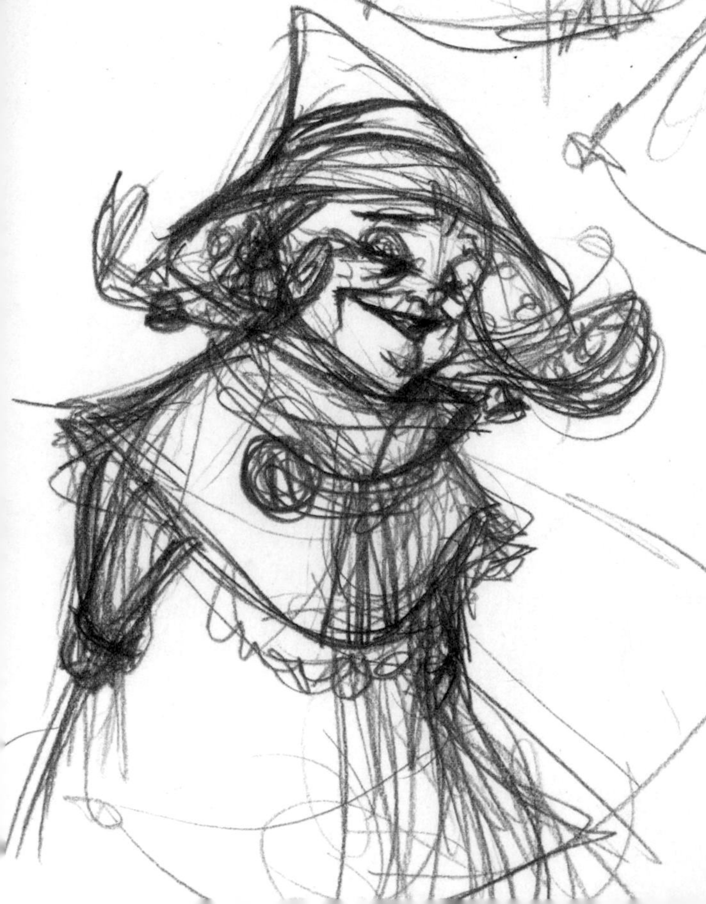

The Good Witch of the North is the first person to welcome Dorothy to the Land of Oz. —**Eric**

I was looking for a soft and calming shape to give to the Good Witch. I wanted her to look like a wonderful grandmother-type figure at first glance without having to say anything. I almost went a little too funny-looking. It's a fine line to walk while cartooning not to make things look silly. There needs to be real emotion behind the fantasy style lines. —**Skottie**

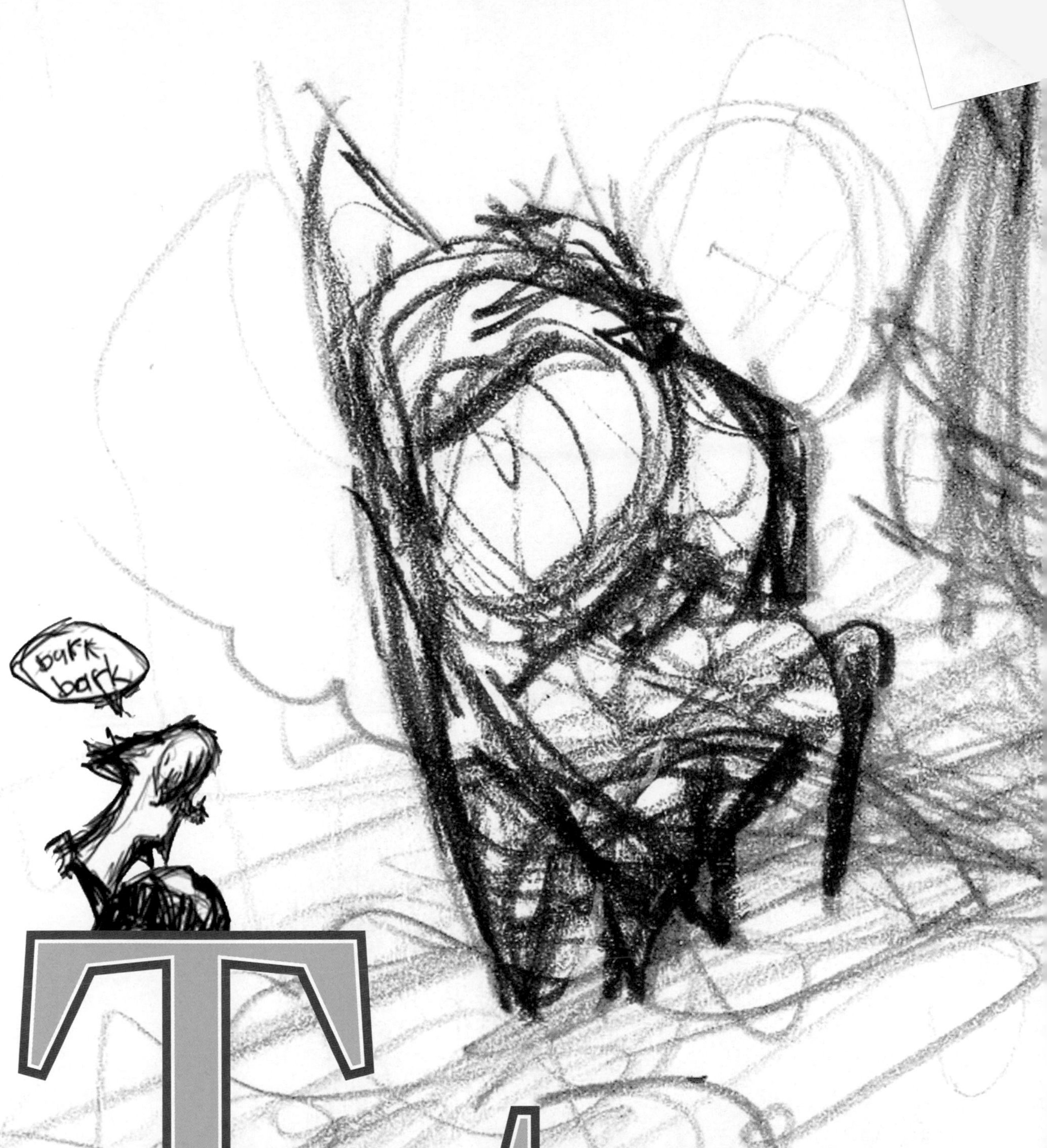
bark bark

Toto

Toto is a smart dog. The truth is that as soon as he arrives in the magical Land of Oz, he gains the power to speak. But he prefers to communicate the way dogs in our world do, so he doesn't let on. —**Eric**

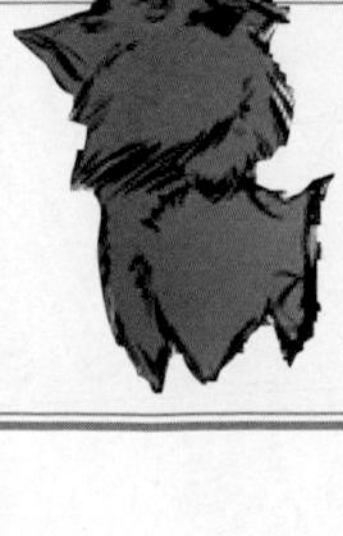

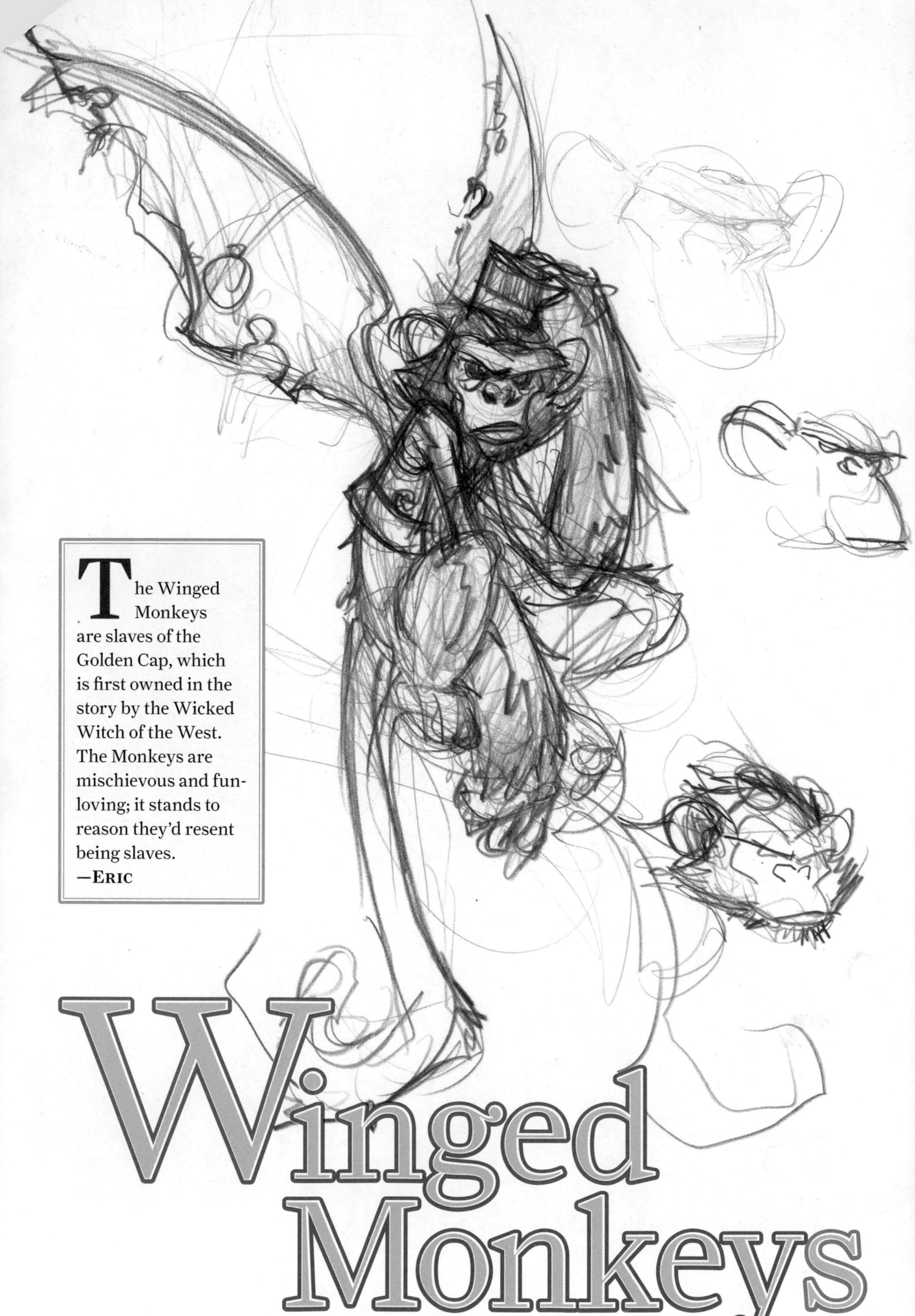

The Winged Monkeys are slaves of the Golden Cap, which is first owned in the story by the Wicked Witch of the West. The Monkeys are mischievous and fun-loving; it stands to reason they'd resent being slaves.
—Eric

Winged Monkeys

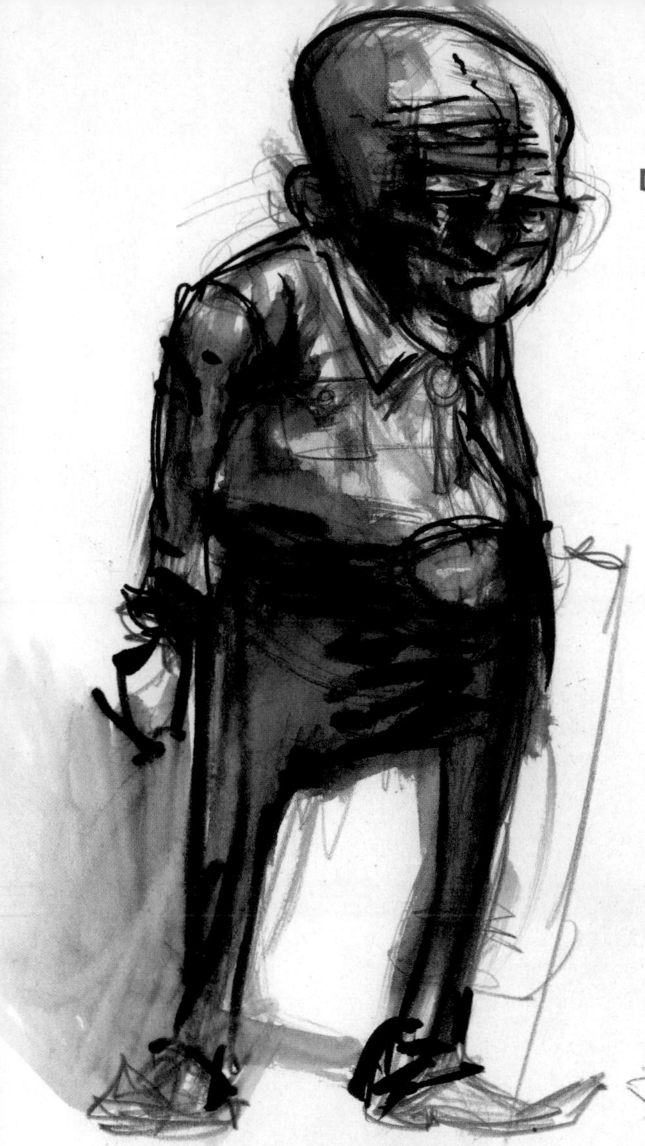

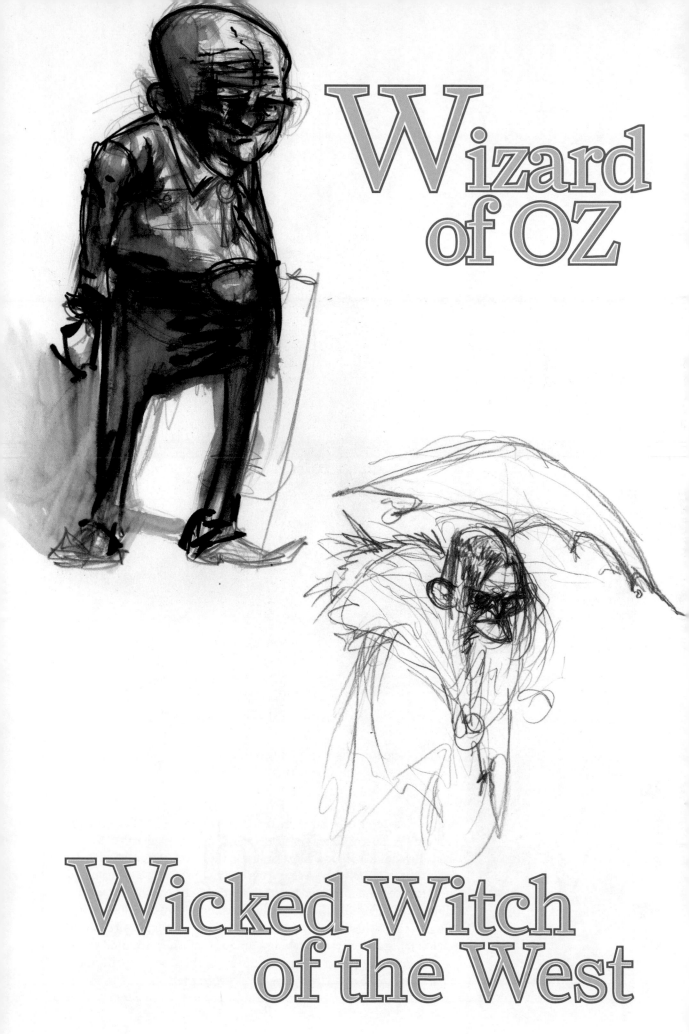

Wizard of OZ

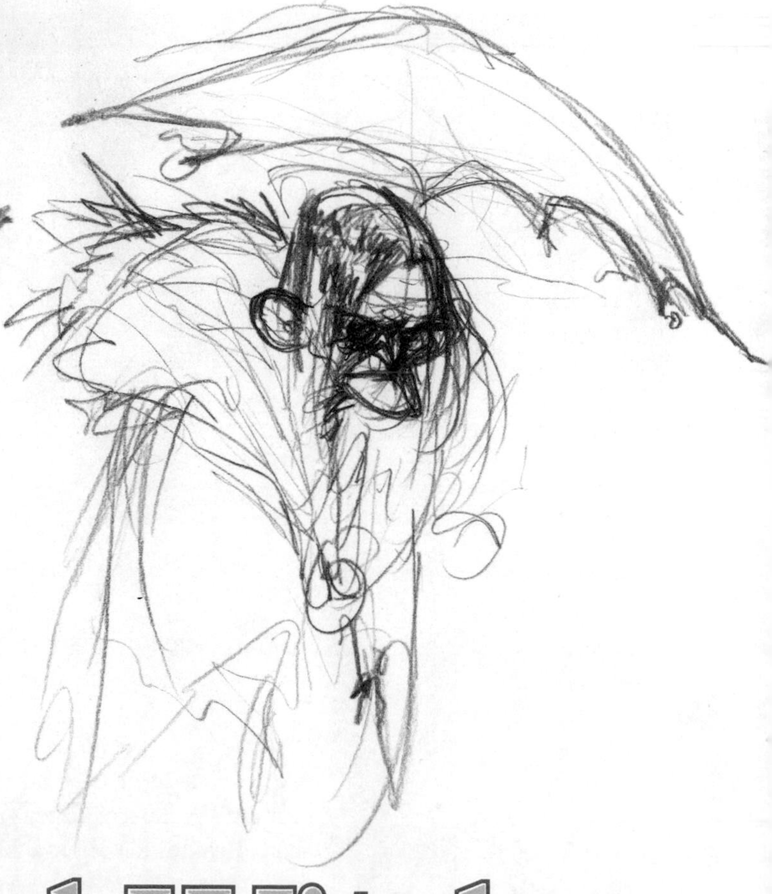

Wicked Witch of the West

Issue #1 Cover

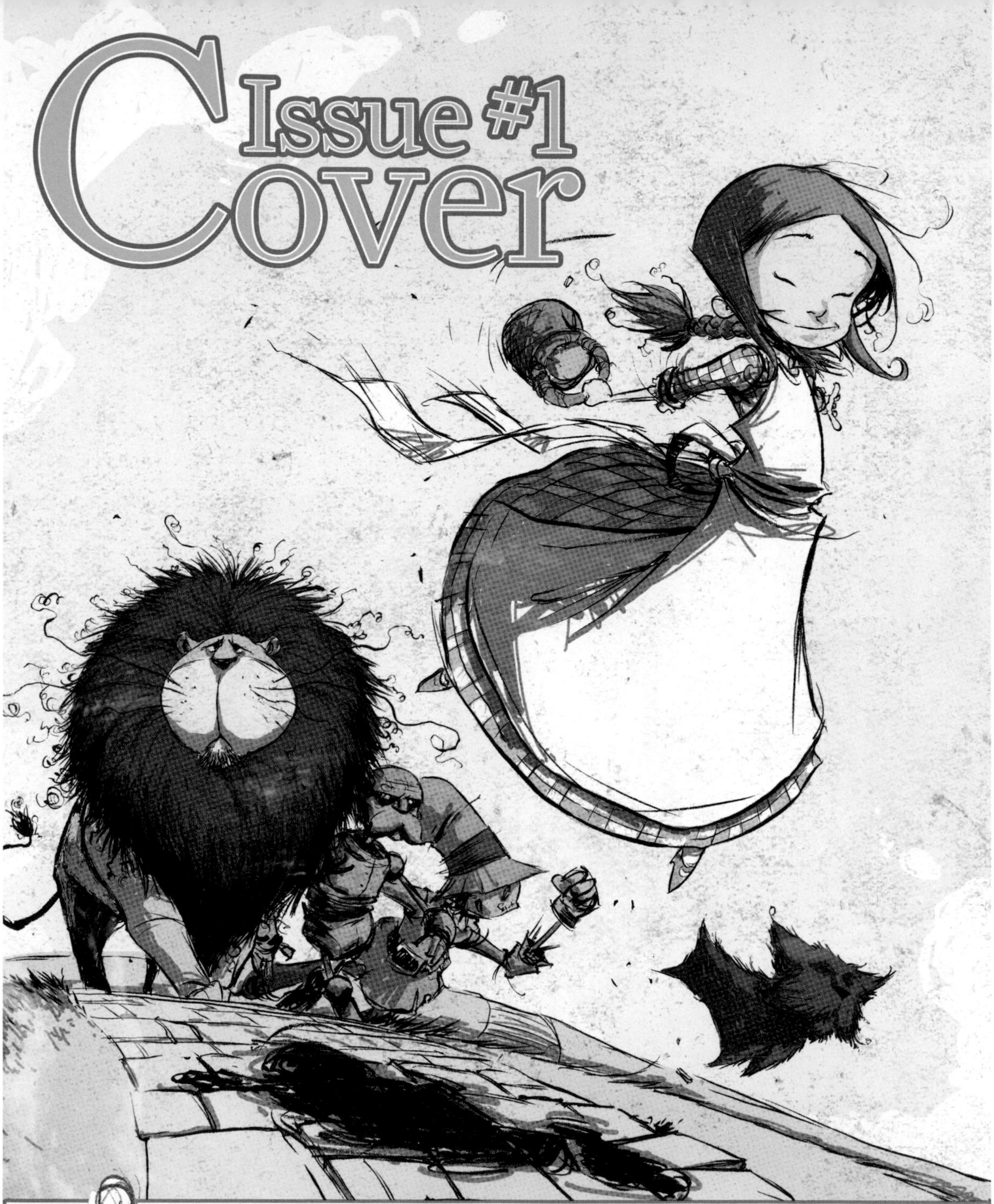

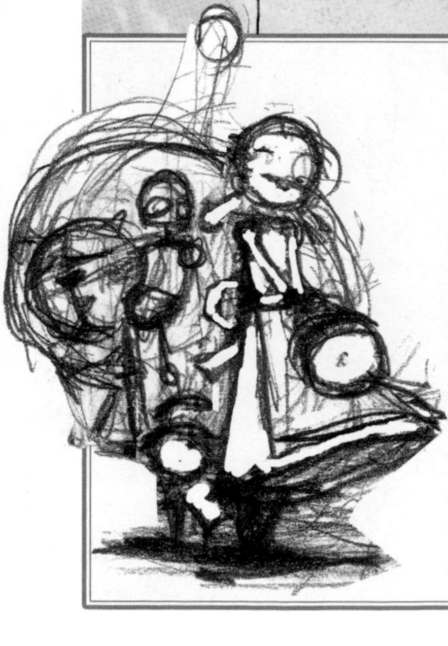

A characteristic grouping. Here the Lion looks more like his roly-poly self. —ERIC

Designing the characters that fill up the pages of The Wonderful Wizard of Oz was probably the biggest challenge I've had. Besides the original illustrations in the novels, there have been countless versions of these characters out in the world. Trying to figure how to give them my visual twist while staying true to the text was a difficult challenge. In the end, it always comes down to shapes. All the bells and whistles will never make up for what shape can do for the character. Each character having a unique shape helps remind you of what kind of person (or not so...um...person) they are. Bringing these characters to life was a true adventure! —SKOTTIE

Issue #2 Cover Process

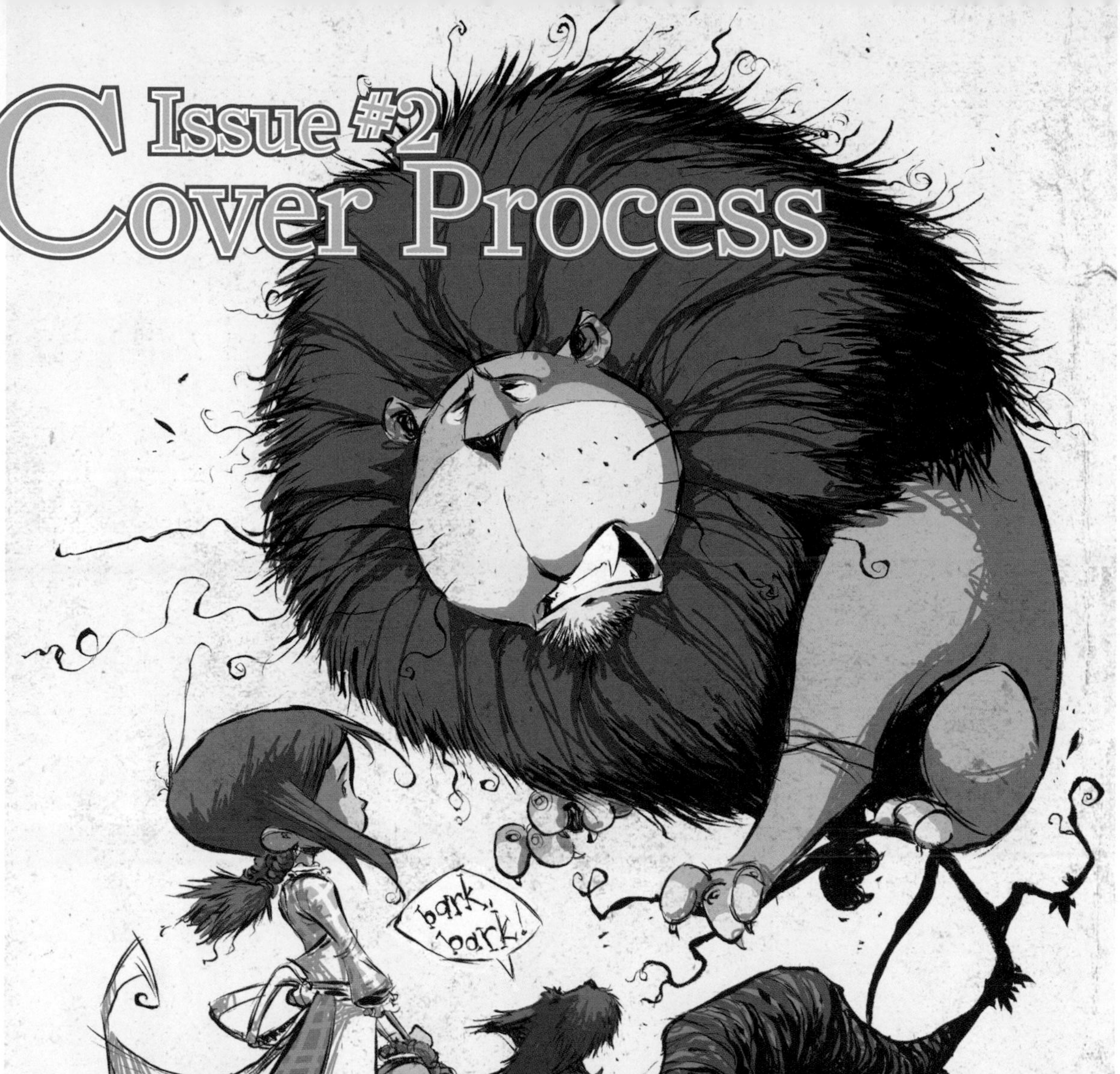
bark, bark!

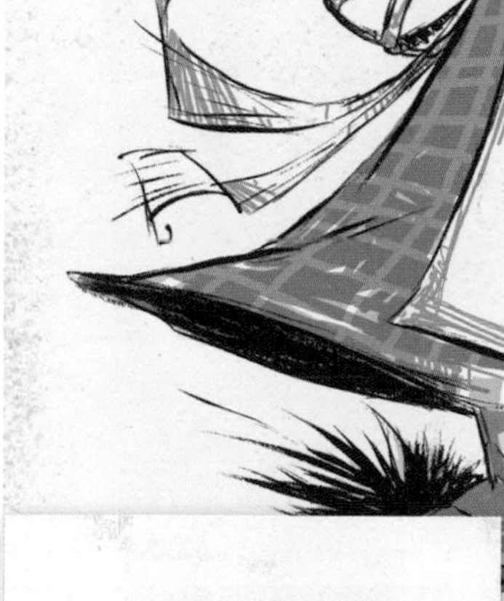

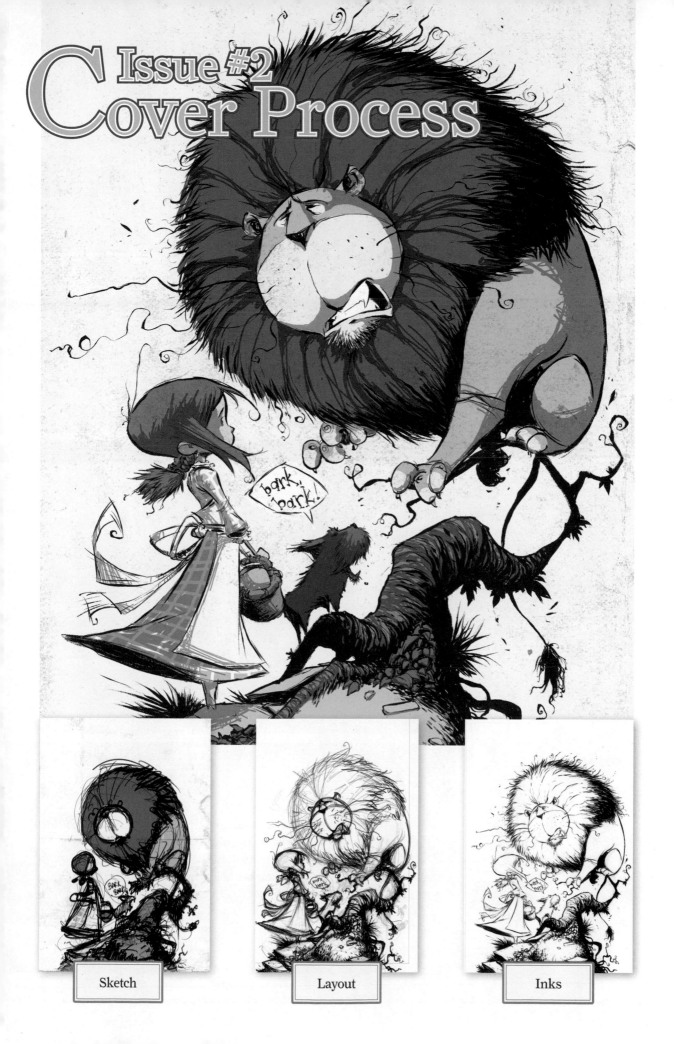

Sketch

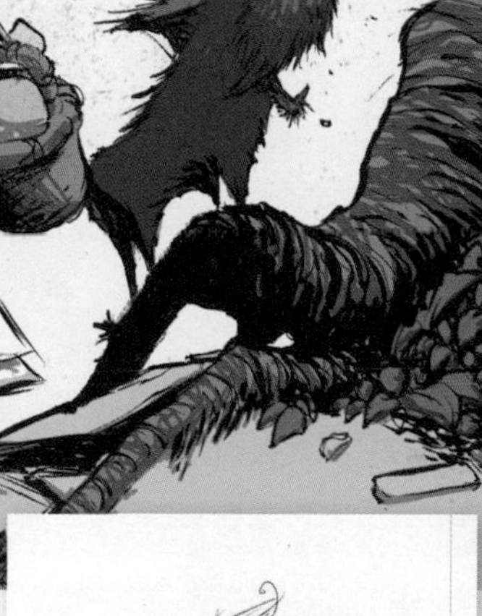

Layout

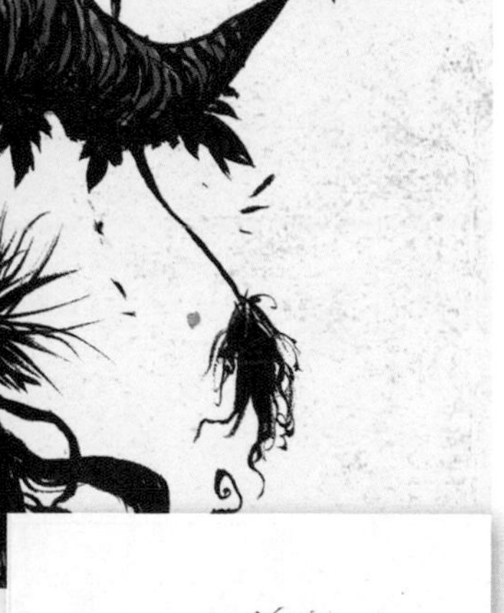

Inks

Issue 5, page 3
Interior page process

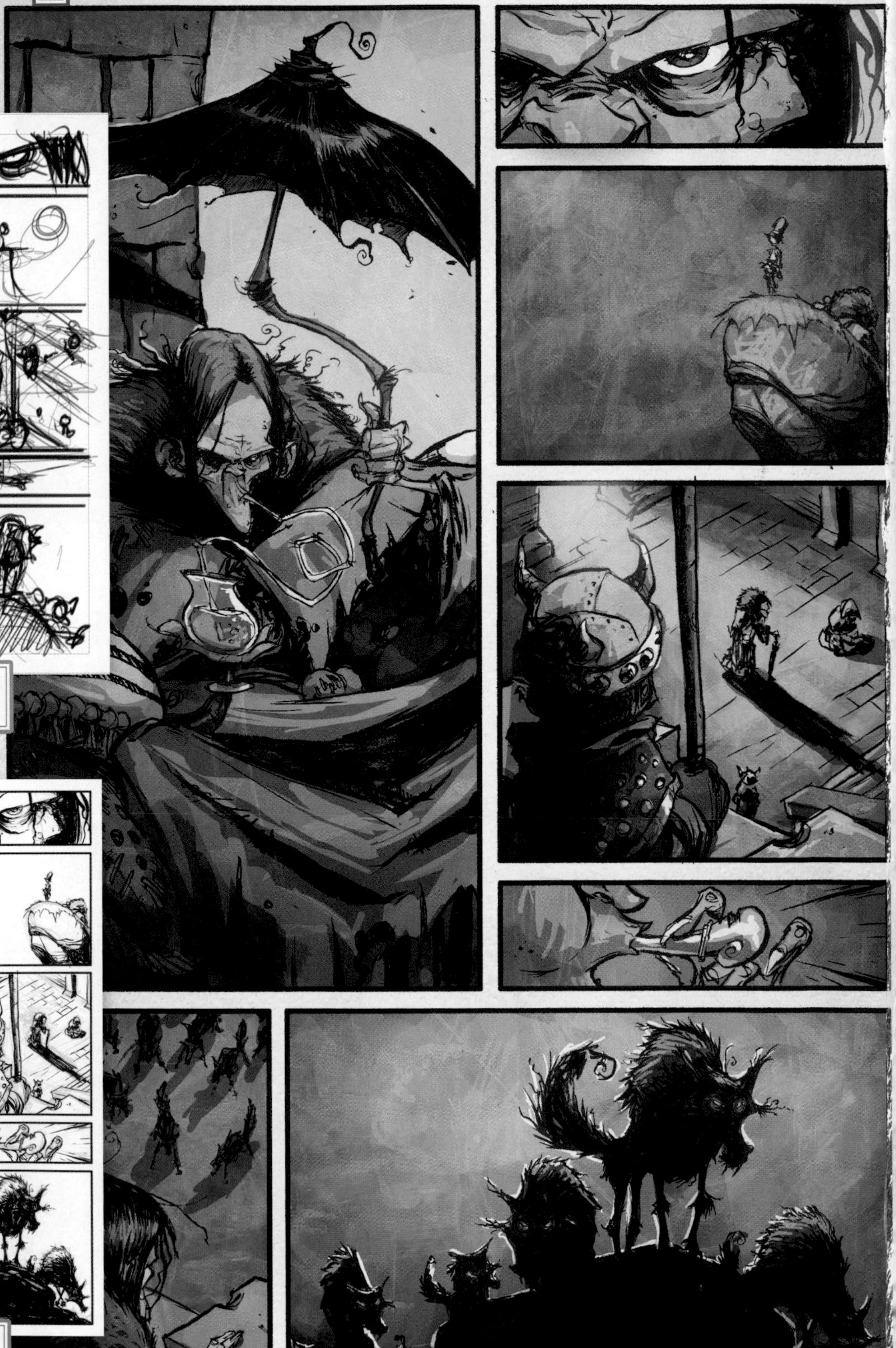

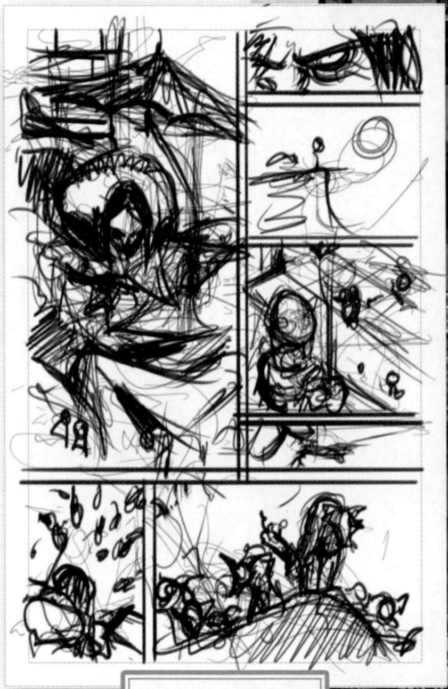

Breakdown

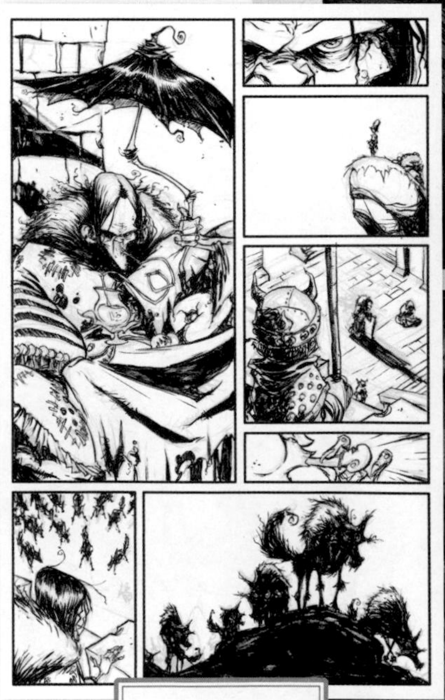

Inks

Peachtree